SERVING VICTORIA

Also by Kate Hubbard

Charlotte Brontë: The Girl who Turned her Life into a Book
Queen Victoria: The Woman who Ruled the World
A Material Girl: Bess of Hardwick 1527–1608
Rubies in the Snow: Diary of Russia's Last Grand Duchess 1911–1918

SERVING VICTORIA

Life in the Royal Household

Chatto & Windus
LONDON

Published by Chatto & Windus 2012

2 4 6 8 10 9 7 5 3 1

First published in Great Britain in 2012 by
Chatto & Windus
Random House, 20 Vauxhall Bridge Road,
London SW1V 2SA

www.vintage-books.co.uk

Addresses for companies within The Random House Group Limited can be found at:
www.randomhouse.co.uk/offices.htm

The Random House Group Limited Reg. No. 954009

A CIP catalogue record for this book
is available from the British Library

ISBN 9780701183684

The Random House Group Limited supports The Forest Stewardship Council
(FSC®), the leading international forest certification organisation. Our books
carrying the FSC label are printed on FSC® certified paper. FSC is the only forest
certification scheme endorsed by the leading environmental organisations, including
Greenpeace. Our paper procurement policy can be found at
www.randomhouse.co.uk/environment

Typeset in Dante MT by Palimpsest Book Production Limited,
Falkirk, Stirlingshire
Printed and bound in Great Britain by
Clays Ltd, St Ives PLC

For my parents

Contents

Illustrations

Illustrations in the text:

All illustrations in the text come from the Reid family archive, unless otherwise stated.

Picture section 1:

All pictures in this section come from The Royal Collection © 2012 Her Majesty Queen Elizabeth II, unless otherwise stated.

Picture section 2:

All pictures in this section come from the Reid family archive, unless otherwise stated.

Acknowledgements

This book could not have been written without the help and generosity of a number of people who made private archives available to me. I owe a great debt of gratitude to Sir Alexander and Lady Michaela Reid, not just for letting me pore over the many albums containing James Reid's letters, diaries and photographs, but for all their kindness and hospitality on several occasions. Michaela Reid's own book on Sir James has been an invaluable resource.

    Similarly, I am extremely grateful to Laura Ponsonby and Catherine and Ian Russell, for allowing me access to the Ponsonby papers at Shulbrede Priory and for their interest and support throughout. I would also like to thank Lord Cobham, for allowing me to read and quote from Sarah Lyttelton's letters at Hagley Hall, and the Earl and Countess of Harewood, for letting me quote from Charlotte Canning's letters and journals at Harewood House. Material from the Royal Archives at Windsor and extracts from letters from Queen Victoria are quoted by gracious permission of Her Majesty Queen Elizabeth II. Many thanks to Pam Clark and her staff at the Royal Archives for all their time and patience, to Sophie Gordon, Curator of Photographs at Windsor, to Lisa Heighway, who showed me many wonderful photographs from the Royal Collection, to Kate Heard, Curator of Prints and Drawings, and to Daniel Bell. Also thanks to the staff at the British Library, the London Library, Lambeth Palace Library and Leeds City Library.

For permission to reproduce photographs and other illustrations I am very grateful to those individuals and institutions credited in the list of illustrations. I would like to thank Michael Hunter, Curator at Osborne House, for answering questions about Osborne and showing me around the Household Wing, Sir Hugh Roberts, for helping me with queries about Windsor Castle and pointing me towards the Windsor inventory, and A. N. Wilson for suggesting the novels of Charlotte M. Yonge as a way of understanding what it meant to be High Church in nineteenth-century England. For help in various ways, thanks to Randal Dunluce, Margaret and Pat Lloyd, Paul Quarrie, Anna Robinson, Desmond Shawe-Taylor and Giles Waterfield. Claudia FitzHerbert read an early draft and Victoria Millar a later one (whilst jiggling her new baby); their comments and suggested revisions have made this a better book. My thanks to them and to all the friends and family who have offered advice, encouragement and good cheer along the way, including Lucy Baring, David and Emma Craigie, Phil Eade, Alexa de Ferranti, Jason Goodwin, Ed and Nicole Hubbard, John and Caryl Hubbard, Flora McDonnell, Rebecca Nicolson, Adam Nicolson, Kate O'Sullivan, John Paul Rathbone, Ben and Harriet Rogers, Sarah Raven, Sweetpea Slight, Denise Stephenson and David and Janie Worthington. Finally, many thanks to my agent Georgia Garrett and to all at Chatto & Windus, most particularly my editors, Jenny Uglow, who provided bolstering at crucial moments and much wise advice, and Juliet Brooke, who guided the book through its final stages so expertly.

INTRODUCTION

When Georgiana Liddell was appointed a maid-of-honour to Queen Victoria in 1841, she received a letter of advice from her mother, Lady Ravensworth. 'You must accustom yourself,' she wrote, 'to sit or stand for hours without any amusement save the resources of your own thoughts.' 'Keep yourself to yourself and whatever spare time you have, employ it well and lay not up your talents in a napkin.' She urged Georgy to be discreet, to 'abhor idle gossip', to shun flirtation and intimacy with the gentlemen of the court, and to spend her salary wisely. And she finished by invoking duty: 'Your first duty is to God; your second to your Sovereign; your third to yourself.'

This letter sets the tone for life at the Victorian court. A sense of duty, discretion, moral rectitude, self-reliance – such were the qualities that would stand you in good stead as a member of the Queen's household, and they were not qualities that there had been much call for hitherto. The morally elastic courts of the Hanoverians and earlier had tolerated, indeed comfortably accommodated, love affairs, adultery and illegitimacy, while a lack of organisation and control had invited abuse: positions were available for favourites, perks were to be enjoyed, and questions weren't asked. Victoria may have been just eighteen when she came to the throne in 1837, but she knew her own mind and she was quite adamant that her court would, above all things, be *respectable*. Abuses would never be entirely eradicated, and scandal did erupt, in a humiliatingly public fashion in 1839, but it was not to be repeated.

In their family life, Victoria and Albert set out to create a model of domestic virtue, and similar standards of behaviour were expected from their court. This did not mean an entirely new personnel, but court appointments were now carefully vetted and those of doubtful reputation firmly excluded. When selecting her ladies and gentlemen the Queen generally looked to the lesser aristocracy, who, it was felt, were morally sounder and more sensible of the honour conferred on them than their wealthier, more fashionable counterparts (the *beau monde* tended to mock when it came to their queen and her consort). Gentlemen were usually ex-army, thus exchanging one form of service for another. Ladies were sometimes grateful for a salary, that, without being lavish, was certainly useful. For those with families, the months 'in waiting' could be hard indeed; for those without, court could offer a refuge of a kind, while maids-of-honour might find themselves a husband (discreet flirting permitted).

The Victorian court, an odd mix of never-ending house party and boarding school, of social ennui and regimentation, was absolutely particular to its time. Edward VII, who enjoyed the *beau monde* as much as Victoria disapproved, presided over a court that had a great deal more in common with those of his Hanoverian forbears than that of his mother, though with George V there was some return to Victorian values. As for today, the notion of service, let alone royal service, is so radically different that comparison seems futile, yet something of the mystery and hush that hung over Victoria's court seems to linger and – royal service tends to run in families – some of the same names that served under Victoria – Adeane, Lascelles, Fitzroy – have cropped up in Elizabeth II's household (the likes of Paul Burrell, though, would have had no place at the Victorian court). Perhaps it's not so very different after all.

I first came across collected letters and diaries, written by Victoria's ladies-in-waiting and maids-of-honour, in the course of writing a short biography of the Queen for children. I found these uneventful records – the stiff evenings, the damp carriage drives, the endless waiting about for 'orders' – curiously fascinating. Their very dullness intrigued. I wondered about these women, how readily they submitted to the dictates and obligations of royal service, whether such service was actually more of a penance than an honour, whether their professed devotion to the Queen was entirely sincere. I wondered about what they didn't say as much as what they did, and I began to read more widely, discovering other members of the royal household. Here, I felt, was a new way of approaching Victoria, through the eyes of those who served her, who knew her as well, arguably a good deal better, than her own family.

I needed, however, courtiers of a particular kind – people who had occupied different positions at court, who might illuminate the Queen in different ways, who were intelligent, capable of putting themselves beyond the hushed, hothouse claustrophobia of court life and, most importantly, not overly cowed by royalty. The Queen, especially in her old age, was a figure of considerable awe. Lord Rosebery (briefly Liberal prime minister) claimed that only two people frightened him – Bismarck and Victoria, and Bismarck himself emerged from his first royal audience wiping sweat from his brow. It was a fear shared by the Queen's children and most of her household. Most, but not all. James Reid, Her Majesty's doctor, and his wife, a former maid-of-honour, privately referred to their royal mistress as 'Bipps'. I wanted to find courtiers who were able to see the 'Bipps' within the Victoria.

And so I came to Sarah Lyttelton, lady of the bedchamber and then superintendent of the royal nursery; Charlotte Canning, lady of the bedchamber; Mary Ponsonby, maid-of-honour; Henry Ponsonby, private secretary; Randall Davidson, domestic chaplain; and James Reid, physician-in-ordinary. Some of them were at court together and became friends; some never met; two of them married each other. For some, royal service became a *raison d'être*, the defining experience of their lives; for others it was a mere interlude, or a prelude to greater things. All six sometimes chafed under the constraints of court life, admitted to frustration, impatience and longing, and indulged in the occasional joke at Her Majesty's expense (open criticism was quite another matter). Between them they served the Queen over the sixty-odd years of her reign, Sarah Lyttelton coming to court in 1838, with Victoria just queen of a year, James Reid supporting her as she lay dying at Osborne in 1901. I came to see Victoria as an increasingly substantial baton, passed on, respectfully, from one to the next.

Serving Victoria tells the stories of six members of the royal household, of their experiences of court and their individual relationships
with the Queen. Victoria was never on terms of intimacy with her
household, but nevertheless their testimonies offer an intimate view
of her, as a woman who gossiped and fussed; who was prone to fits
of giggles, of rage, of weeping; who gobbled her food; who shrank
from confrontation, yet had a compulsion to control; whose own
needs always came before those of her household, yet who took a
genuine and inexhaustible interest in the lives of those who served
her – news of a marriage, a birth, a death (especially a death) brought
an immediate outpouring of congratulation or commiseration. The
Queen, it seems, inspired devotion and exasperation in almost equal
measure.

The royal household, in its entirety, was a vast, many-layered, and
– at least until Albert set to work – hopelessly disorganised operation.
Beneath the ladies and gentlemen came the non-aristocratic doctors,
secretaries, governesses and librarians, and, at the base of the pyramid,
a great army of servants, themselves divided into upper and lower. I
have focused on the ladies and gentlemen of the household: partly as
a matter of record – theirs were better-documented lives – but also
since these were the individuals closest to the Queen (excepting
perhaps her personal servants), who dined with her and played after-
dinner games, who accompanied her on drives and rides and
Continental holidays, who were privy to late-night tête-à-têtes. The
servants, however, in whom the Queen took a lively interest, play
their part, notably Her Majesty's dressers, John Brown, the Munshi
and a variety of alcoholic footmen.

Constructed out of letters and diaries, this is a necessarily partial
and partisan account. The portrait that emerges of life at the Victorian
court, and the Queen herself sitting squarely at its centre, is essentially
domestic. Court was a strangely cloistered existence, removed – quite
literally during the months at Balmoral – and insulated from the 'outer
world', as the household wistfully termed it. The outer world broke
through from time to time – political upheavals, the Crimean and
Boer Wars (Victoria was always more engaged by foreign than home

affairs) – but social concerns or cultural events made scarcely any impact at all.

While inevitably there are gaps in the record – letters missing or destroyed (Charlotte Canning's letters to her husband have vanished, likewise Mary Ponsonby's to Henry, and some of Sarah Lyttelton's letters, including those from the Queen, were dispersed in a sale of family papers) – the primary sources are wonderfully rich. In an age of letter-writing, the Queen herself was an indefatigable correspondent. As were my subjects. The letters, diaries and journals of Charlotte Canning, Sarah Lyttelton, Mary Ponsonby and James Reid are all preserved in family archives. Randall Davidson's diaries – erratically kept, to his chagrin – and his extensive correspondence sit in Lambeth Palace library. The Royal Archives at Windsor contain many hundreds of letters from Henry Ponsonby to his wife, as well as countless letters and memos between the Queen and her household. Some of this material – letters from the Queen to Randall Davidson, much of the correspondence in the Royal Archives, many of Sarah Lyttelton's letters – is published here for the first time. Opening Mary Ponsonby's self-examination diary in Shulbrede Priory (home of Henry and Mary's great-granddaughters), I found, tucked in beside an entry written in 1861, a letter that had lain undisturbed for 150 years.

The fact that the first half of the book, up until the Prince Consort's death in 1861, is dominated by the Queen's ladies and the second by her gentlemen is not entirely accidental. Viewed by Sarah Lyttelton or Charlotte Canning, the young Victoria appears a determined but somewhat indistinct figure, finding her feet, much in thrall to her husband. Her relationships with her ladies, though often affectionate, were essentially remote. For all the devastation of Albert's death, widowhood allowed the Queen to come into her own. It also meant that she needed and sought male sympathy and support, not just practically – in easing her workload – but emotionally. Through the eyes of Henry Ponsonby she comes sharply into focus, both more imperious and more vulnerable, while her relationships with James

Reid and Randall Davidson were infinitely more confidential and less guarded than those with any of her ladies.

Similarly, as the book moves from early to late Victorian, from the artless girl-queen to the glum widow, so the tenor and composition of the court shifts. The household in the early part of Victoria's reign still had something of the laissez-faire, Whiggish, aristocratic court of the Regency, an atmosphere that clung to the Ponsonbys into the 1860s and 70s. But the 1880s ushered in a new, more professional breed of courtier – middle class, alive to the honour and status attendant on a court appointment, dedicated and prodigiously energetic. For all, though, duty was a powerful motivating and sustaining force. Gladstone's 'rule of ought' went hand in hand with royal service.

However, duty did not always seem quite enough. In Trollope's *The Prime Minister*, written in 1876, Plantagenet Palliser expresses amazement when his wife, Lady Glencora, professes an interest in becoming mistress of the robes. How, he wonders, would she submit to 'the swaddling bandages of Court life'? How would she bear 'the intricacies and subserviences . . . the tedium and pomposities'? If you were a Glencora, if you were of an independent turn of mind, or shy and retiring by nature, or simply not a natural courtier, then the 'swaddling bandages' did not come easily. *Serving Victoria* tells how six very different individuals fared.

PART I

'A queen is a very happy woman'

CHAPTER I

Windsor 1838

On 3 October 1838, Lady Sarah Lyttelton sat down at her desk in her Windsor Castle sitting room and began a letter to her daughter Caroline, an account of her first twenty-four hours as lady of the bedchamber to Queen Victoria. The prospect of taking up her new duties had filled her with trepidation, indeed dread – she would always be a reluctant courtier – but on arriving the previous morning she had been met kindly enough by Baroness Lehzen, the Queen's former governess and now a key figure at court, and led up a 'long winding staircase' to her 'apartments'. These were most probably in the Victoria Tower, above Her Majesty's rooms. Ladies-in-waiting, as ladies of the bedchamber were known when on duty, were provided with their own bedrooms and sitting rooms at Windsor. Sarah found 'a large lofty bedroom' and an adjoining corner sitting room, handsomely furnished with a set of rosewood furniture and a piano. The Queen's ladies were free to decorate their rooms with flowers and ornaments (and – just a few years away – photographs) from home, much like pupils starting at boarding school. Sarah may well have brought some such from Hagley Hall, the Lyttelton family home.

She was pleased to note a 'good fire' – the Queen's palaces were notoriously cold – and she revelled in glorious views, through large windows on two sides. Way down beneath her she could see 'a right royal parterre . . . rounded with low battlemented walls and real canons. Large flower beds, statues, vases, and a huge round pool in

the middle with a beautiful bright *jet de'eau.*' Beyond she looked out
to Windsor Great Park and the forested sweep of the Thames Valley.[1]
'The wind is whistling round the old grey walls and the sun is brilliant,
it is all beautiful,' she wrote, ever alive to the romance of the castle,
if not always reconciled to life within its walls.

By October 1838, Victoria had been on the throne for a little over
a year, and a most gratifying year it had been. Weary of the profligacy
and buffoonery of their Hanoverian rulers, the people of England had
taken the 'little Queen' to their hearts. So touching she seemed in her
innocence, her modesty, her dignity, her determination to do her duty
that even the cynics were won over. 'She is at an age at which a girl
can hardly be trusted to choose a bonnet for herself,' wrote Thomas
Carlyle of the nineteen-year-old Queen, 'yet a task is laid upon her
from which an archangel might shrink.'

There had been little in the way of preparation for that task. With
few to advise her, save her mother, the Duchess of Kent, a fond but
foolish woman whom she had reasons to distrust, her governess
Baroness Lehzen, who had plenty of intelligence but no experience
of statecraft, and her uncle Leopold, King of the Belgians, whose
well-meaning, sententious letters were not always welcome, it was
entirely natural that when it came to appointing her household,
Victoria should turn for guidance to the sympathetic and reassuring
figure of her prime minister, Lord Melbourne. Melbourne, leader
since 1835 of an increasingly shaky Whig government, saw to it that
the Queen was surrounded by Whig ladies, a policy he would have
cause to regret. Sarah Lyttelton's Whiggishness could not be faulted
– she both came from and married into the Whig aristocracy.
Furthermore, she was personally known to Melbourne as a cousin of
his former wife, the troubled and troublesome Caroline Ponsonby.
She was almost certainly appointed on his advice.

On that first day at Windsor, Sarah left her room to join her fellow
ladies for two o'clock luncheon. She descended her winding staircase

[1] Sarah's view, of the parterres, pond and cannons, remains much the same today,
though the forests of the Thames Valley have long been swallowed up by urban sprawl.

and walked along the Corridor, the grand and gloomy 550-foot-long gallery, built by Jeffrey Wyattville (originally plain Jeffrey Wyatt) for George IV, which linked the private apartments on the south side of the castle with the public rooms on the north. She hurried under gilded arches, along walls draped in crimson and thickly hung with Canalettos, Zoffany portraits and Gainsboroughs, past marble pedestals bearing bronzes and red porphyry busts, cabinets crowded with china, lamps on carved gilt stands and potted plants. On her right she passed doors to the Queen's private apartments and the guest rooms, to the white, green and red drawing rooms and the state dining room, until, finally, came the household dining room – smallish, octagonal and panelled – in the Brunswick Tower, overlooking the North Terrace.

There, besides Baroness Lehzen, she met Miss Lister and Miss Paget (the maids-of-honour), Miss Davys (the resident woman of the bedchamber and the daughter of Victoria's former tutor, the Rev. George Davys – 'a very nice girl although not at all pretty', according to the Queen, for whom a pretty face amongst her ladies was always a bonus) and the current lord-in-waiting. The latter was the only gentleman who, together with any guests, was permitted to join the Queen's ladies for breakfast and luncheon; the other gentlemen of the household ate in a room adjoining the equerries' room, near the visitors' entrance on the north-west corner of the quadrangle. This segregation of the sexes was continued in the household's sleeping arrangements, the ladies being lodged along the south front of the castle and the gentlemen at a suitably safe distance on the north.

As a lady of the bedchamber, Lady Lyttelton belonged to the part-time members of the royal household. The ladies of the bedchamber, maids-of-honour, women of the bedchamber, lords-in-waiting, grooms-in-waiting, and equerries were drawn from a pool, of eight in each category, and attended the Queen in rotation. For Sarah this meant three month-long waitings a year, with a salary of £500. Only women of the bedchamber were not required to live at court during their waitings (apart from the one resident, a permanent position) and they received a lesser salary of £300. The mistress of the robes – in 1838 the thirty-one-year-old Duchess of Sutherland – was also a non-residential but important post, responsible for negotiating the appointment of new courtiers, drawing up rotas for waitings and attending the Queen on ceremonial occasions. Alongside these rotating, temporary courtiers was the core of the household, the permanent members – master of the household, keeper of the privy purse and private secretary (not an official position until 1866). These formed the household elite. Beneath came a second tier – doctors, governesses, tutors, secretaries and librarians – who were drawn from middle-class rather than aristocratic stock.

Dining arrangements at Windsor reinforced the strictly hierarchical nature of the household. The upper layer, the ladies and gentlemen, breakfasted and lunched in their own separate dining rooms, and came together for dinner, usually with the Queen, while those of lower rank were permitted to join their superiors for breakfast and luncheon, but dined alone, in their rooms. Such divisions extended to the servants: upper servants ate (heartily) in the steward's room, and lower (plainly) in the servants' hall, while a variety of separate meals were served to the military band, to visiting artists, upholsterers and hairdressers, and to whichever of the Queen's dressers was on duty in the wardrobe room.

After lunching, on roast fowls and loin of mutton, Sarah Lyttelton had her first introduction to her royal mistress. There appeared before her a diminutive, girlish figure, much the same age as her own daughters, already showing signs of plumpness and unmistakably Hanoverian about the eyes (pale blue, slightly protruding) and chin (sloping), but with all the charm and bloom of youth and an unexpectedly light and musical voice. Sarah found herself warmly greeted and embraced and invited to join an expedition to Bagshot, to visit the elderly Duchess of Gloucester, the Queen's aunt – ladies-in-waiting were expected to accompany the Queen on her afternoon drives or rides.

Setting off in the carriage, along with the Duchess of Kent and the Duchess's lady-in-waiting, Lady Mary Stopford – 'a nice little red-haired maid' – Sarah found herself with 'sundry things to carry and many nonsenses to do; blundered and boggled as usual'. Since Her Majesty – a firm believer in the benefits of fresh air – insisted on open carriages,

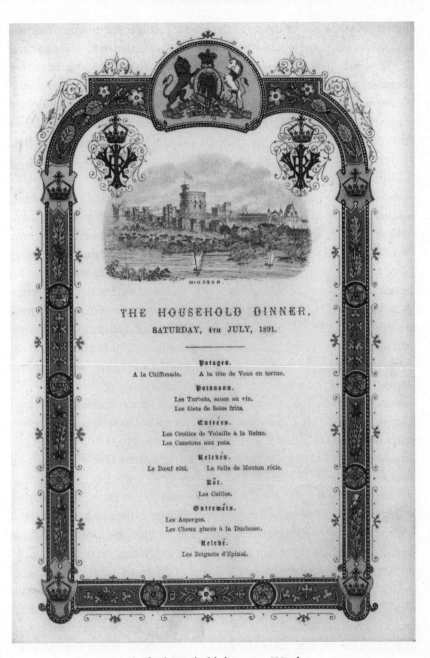

WINDSOR.

THE HOUSEHOLD DINNER.
SATURDAY, 4TH JULY, 1891.

Potages.
A la Chiffonade.   A la tête de Veau en tortue.

Poissons.
Les Turbots, sauce au vin.
Les filets de Soles frits.

Entrées.
Les Croûtes de Volaille à la Reine.
Les Canetons aux pois.

Relevés.
Le Bœuf rôti.   La Selle de Mouton rôtie.

Rôt.
Les Cailles.

Entremêts.
Les Asperges.
Les Choux glacés à la Duchesse.

Relevé.
Les Beignets d'Epinal.

Menu for household dinner at Windsor

her lady-in-waiting had to be on hand with a plentiful supply of shawls and wraps. Acting as a kind of glorified handmaiden was something Sarah would have to get used to. During the drive back to Windsor, the Queen busied herself, to Sarah's mild surprise, with 'a *lesson book*, Sir Robert Walpole's life by Coxe', while the Duchess of Kent dozed.

That evening, after dressing for dinner, Sarah joined the rest of the household, including the gentlemen, wearing the 'Windsor uniform' – knee breeches, stockings, and a dark blue tailcoat with scarlet collar and cuffs, designed by George III – and dinner guests in the Corridor shortly before eight. Here they awaited the Queen before proceeding – gentlemen leading the way, followed by Her Majesty, with the ladies and the Duchess of Kent bringing up the rear – to the dining room. The Queen's dinner that evening was a large affair: Lord Melbourne (who dined three or four times a week and sat, as always, on Her Majesty's left), the Duchess of Kent and Baroness Lehzen (both perma-nent fixtures), the Prince and Princess of Oldenburg (the Queen's current guests) and some of their entourage, Lord Palmerston (foreign secretary), Lord Uxbridge and Lord Torrington (lords-in-waiting), Sir Henry Wheatley (keeper of the privy purse), Lady Mary Stopford, Miss Lister and Miss Paget, Mr Charles Murray (master of the household), Colonel Cavendish (equerry) and Sir Richard Otway (groom-in-waiting). During dinner a military band – the Life Guards or the Grenadiers – played sonorously in the adjoining room, and afterwards the Queen and her ladies withdrew, leaving the gentlemen to their port, but not for long – lingering over port was frowned on in the new era of sobriety.

Evenings were 'the great difficulty in royal society', according to Charles Greville, privy councillor and diarist, a sentiment with which Sarah Lyttelton would come to wholeheartedly agree. Greville did not greatly prize an invitation to Windsor. Though the Queen insisted on personally orchestrating every detail – who was lodged where, who was to ride, or drive, and in what order they were to proceed into dinner – visitors were generally left to their own devices. With little in the way of 'society', or 'amusement' (some considered this a blessing), the billiard room, tucked away on the west front, virtually inaccessible, and the library horribly cold and unfurnished, there was 'nothing but another meal' to reunite them. However, the evenings were the real test. After dinner, back in the drawing room, everyone stood while the Queen walked about saying a few words 'of the most trivial nature, all however very civil and cordial in manner and expression' to each guest (a practice known as 'circling'). Greville, after dining in March 1838, recorded a sample of the royal conversation:

Q. 'Have you been riding today Mr Greville?'
G. 'No, Madam, I have not.'
Q. 'It was a fine day?'
G. 'Yes, Ma'am, a very fine day.'
Q. 'It was rather cold though.'
G. (like Polonius). 'It *was* rather cold, Madam.'
Q. 'Your sister, Ly Francis Egerton, rides I think, does not she?'
G. 'She does ride sometimes, Madam.'
  (A pause, when I took the lead, though adhering to the same topic.)
G. 'Has your Majesty got a nice horse?'
Q. 'Oh, a very nice horse.'
  – gracious smile and inclination of head on part of Queen, profound bow on mine.

Such exchanges concluded, the Queen, and her ladies, sat at a round table, while the Duchess of Kent was set up at her whist table and the gentlemen hovered on the other side of the room. Then, continued Greville, 'two mortal hours' were given over to 'the smallest possible talk'. The only relief came in the shape of nursery games or music – a song or piano piece performed by the Queen or her ladies. This, as Sarah Lyttelton discovered, was the pattern of Windsor evenings.

At eleven, the Queen finally retired, the gentlemen hurried to the billiard room to smoke, and Sarah, who considered palace hours 'not wholesome', fled to the sanctuary and comfort of her room. This, she told Caroline, had 'everything a bedroom can contain' – mahogany canopied bedstead, wardrobe, chest of drawers, dressing table, cheval mirror, wash-stand, chamber pedestal, dressing chair, easy chair, fire screen and bonnet basket – 'all to perfection'. Despite many misgivings and apprehensions, she had survived her first day at court, but adapting to its constraints would not, she feared, come easily: 'The Queen is perfectly kind and civil and good natured. At first however the restraint and peculiar frame of society here was very disagreeable to me, but I have I think got into it and feel settled into a proper stiffness.'

'Stiffness' – a perennial complaint amongst the royal household – had not played much part in Sarah's life hitherto. Born in 1787, into the heart of the Whig aristocracy, she was a child of the eighteenth century and carried with her, during her long life, a certain easy-going worldliness which came to sit quite comfortably with a very nineteenth-century piety. She believed that 'it is a kind of duty to make our letters true and natural, as like ourselves and our talk as possible', and indeed, through her own, with their loose, tumbling syntax, their idiosyncratic idioms – 'throat lumpy', 'boggled' – and sprinkling of Spencer family slang – 'quiz' (child), 'bathing' (melancholy) – her voice comes through quite distinctly: self-deprecating, humorous, immediate, anything but stiff.

The second child and eldest daughter of Lord and Lady Spencer, and a niece of Georgiana, Duchess of Devonshire, Sarah spent her childhood between the Spencer family homes: Althorp, Wimbledon Park and, in London, Spencer House. She could remember, as a small child, the historian Edward Gibbon testing her on her times tables as she played at Althorp. Her mother, Lady Lavinia Spencer, was an acerbic beauty, much painted by Reynolds, fond enough of her children but exacting and not overly maternal – the obligations of beauty perhaps taking precedence over those of motherhood. It was left to Sarah to watch over her younger siblings and to supervise her little brothers' first lessons. 'I know very well I was born to be a school-mistress,' she wrote with prescience. Habits of nurture and duty took root early.

With none of her mother's beauty – her looks, as she said herself, were best described as 'homely' – and little in the way of fortune, Sarah held out no great hopes of marriage until, at twenty-five, she was brought to the notice of William Lyttelton. The Lytteltons, like the Spencers, were Whigs and were known for their commitment to public service, for their High Church faith, and for a strain of eccentricity and melancholia. After a disappointment in love, William confided in Lady Hood, the wife of Admiral Sir Samuel Hood and a great friend of the Spencers, who promptly recommended Sarah, with the pragmatic assertion: 'I know she likes you and I am sure she would do it.' She did and she would. Lord and Lady Spencer warmly approved: William was a second son and not rich, but he stood in line to inherit his half-brother's title, and since his brother was a mentally unstable invalid, that seemed more or less a certainty.

'What happiness is all around me – slippery, dangerous, blinding happiness,' wrote Sarah on her engagement, hardly daring to believe that in handsome, spirited William Lyttelton she had found a husband. As for William, he had secured himself the most affectionate and good-natured of wives, whose placid good sense would balance his own mercurial brilliance. The two were married in March 1813 at Wimbledon Park, where the groom's sister, Mrs Pole-Carew, recorded a charming picture of them sitting side by side on a sofa, 'one munching a hunch of dry bread, the other relishing a piece of hard biscuit . . . looks beaming with love and joy'.

In 1828, on the death of his brother, William became Lord Lyttelton, and he and Sarah, now with five children – Caroline, George, Spencer, Billy and Lavinia – moved into Hagley Hall, the Lyttelton family home in Worcestershire. Hagley is a plain, rather forbidding Palladian house, whose chief attraction resides in its landscaped deer park melting into distant views of the Welsh hills. Nestled close to the house are a church and a cricket pitch, appropriately enough, since religion and cricket were twin Lyttelton passions. Here at Hagley, William abandoned Whig politics for good works and family life, until in 1837, after several years of ill health and shortly before the young Victoria came to the throne, he died, leaving Sarah a widow at fifty.

A few months later, she received a letter from her brother Lord

Spencer, the leader of Melbourne's government in the House of Lords, informing her that the Queen wished to offer her the position of lady of the bedchamber. Sarah was quite thrown by the offer, confessing forlornly that 'the very question and proposal has overpowered me sadly, bringing my loneliness before my mind so'. The prospect of a new life, a court life, merely filled her with longing for that which she had lost. Besides, she considered herself 'eminently disqualified by my disposition and capacity to fit such a place well'.

Despite many sterling virtues, Sarah would always suffer from self-doubt and a chronic lack of confidence (the legacy of a critical mother), remarking on 'the dent at the top of my head where self-esteem ought to stick out'. Now, characteristically, she dithered over the Queen's offer. Writing to her old friend the Countess of Pembroke, she claimed, 'I am beyond anybody gifted with *l'esprit sur l'escalier* – always just too late with a bright thought – never able at the first important moment to decide or even see justly. If I am able (which I dread and tremble to think I may not prove) to conduct myself tolerably well, to keep out of incessant scrapes from indiscreet words and irresolute blunderings, so that I can return from Windsor to my quiet and cross-stitch at Hagley with a tolerably easy conscience, I shall be thankful and surprised.'

Then, aside from her own deficiencies, there were the uncongenial aspects of the courtier's lot – how would she bear all the curtsying, the standing, the driving in open carriages? Would a court position compromise the political ambitions of her son, George? And what would become of her daughters, Caroline and Lavinia, while she was in waiting? On the other hand, a court position might *benefit* those unmarried daughters, money was short and George was bent on marriage, which would mean Sarah making way for a new mistress at Hagley. She declared herself ready to follow her brother's guidance; he was in favour; the offer was accepted. It was arranged that whilst Sarah was in waiting, Caroline and Lavinia would stay with relations, chiefly their brother at Hagley, though they could expect to make short visits to court, as the Queen made a point of occasionally inviting the children and husbands of her ladies, who would otherwise not see their families.

Sarah's first month's waiting both confirmed and allayed her fears. To George she wrote guardedly of 'this new planet and existence . . . I am treated with all kindness by the Queen and with much friendly good nature by all fellow servants and my admiration for Windsor is unbounded . . . the first fright is over, I know my way about and get accustomed to my place – glad I shall be when my month is finally out, certainly, but I am not suffering now'. Windsor itself never failed to delight her – 'the thick walls, glorious breezes and excellent water belonging to this most sublime of dwelling houses'. The court was based here, but decamped to Buckingham Palace, which in 1838 was in a state of some chaos and disrepair, for the London season between May and July, as well as for state occasions, balls, drawing rooms (afternoon receptions, held four times a year, where women were presented to the Queen) and levees (held in the morning, for men). In search of sea air, Her Majesty made occasional visits to the Royal Pavilion in Brighton, the fanciful creation built by John Nash for George IV, while Claremont, the Surrey house belonging to her uncle Leopold, provided a welcome country retreat.

Having been to St George's Chapel twice on her first Sunday at Windsor, Sarah enjoyed the evening walk, on the East Terrace and around the great parterre, with the band playing near the fountain. The Home Park was opened to the public on Sundays and crowds of townspeople and Eton schoolboys clustered around Her Majesty, necessitating an occasional 'tap' from a courtier. 'The scene!' Sarah exclaimed in a letter to Caroline. 'The castle on one side . . . the view on the other; and around us the garden, the jet d'eau, and all under the influence of the very finest military music; and not least pleasing to me Madame Lehzen's pale face . . . with her usual half-anxious, smiling, fixed look following the Queen from one of the castle windows.' She loved too the exhilaration of drives through the Great Park – the Queen's carriage pulled by four white horses 'foaming and gasping after a steady gallop of two and a half hours', encircled by grooms in scarlet uniforms and a posse of gentlemen on horseback.

She marvelled at the below-stairs world, glimpsed whilst accompanying Her Serene Highness of Oldenburg on an inspection of the 'plate', including 'the kitchen with 24 cooks and 17 pieces of meat roasting and the confectionary, a very world of jellies and jams'. Besides the kitchen, with its two great open fires, and a huge steel table with hollow brass legs, steam-heated to keep food warm, there was a green room (for preparing vegetables), a confectionary and a pastry kitchen. The twenty-four cooks included a head chef, three master cooks, two yeomen of the kitchen, two roasting cooks, four apprentices, two larderers and storers, a storekeeper, two green office men, three kitchen maids and two men to supervise the steam apparatus, while the confectionary boasted first and second yeomen confectioners and three female assistants.

As lady-in-waiting, Lady Lyttelton was expected to keep a watchful eye on the maids-of-honour, who tended to find her 'old-fashioned' and thus somewhat 'alarming'. Miss Lister, whose sister had recently died and whose fits of weeping upset the Queen, and Miss Paget, presumably hoping a new arrival would not be entirely au fait with palace rules, lost no time in approaching her 'very coaxy and wheedly': 'Lady L *mayn't* I walk *just for once* by myself on the Slopes? I know it's against the rules, but what harm *can* it do? We *used* to be allowed, but now Lord Melbourne won't let us. I'm sure we never have met anybody there . . . (Says Lady L: "No, no"). Or Lady L, *may* I go out? My feet are so cold, poking up in my room all the morning! I will only go on the Terrace and keep quite in sight. *Pray* let me (Says Lady L: "Yes. Yes").'

Walking on the steep wooded banks falling away from the north and the north-east of the castle, known as the Slopes, was forbidden to unchaperoned maids-of-honour, for fear of assault; the maids-of-honour petitioned tirelessly to have this prohibition overturned. Sarah sympathised, but had little choice but to comply in 'the universal pursuit of keeping them in order. Not that they are disorderly inclined poor little things, but there is a painful recollection of doings in the last reign, which makes everybody *over*-careful now almost.'

Anxiety lest the new reign be besmirched by the 'doings' of the past – the sorry record of the Queen's uncles – remained acute. Under the Hanoverians, maids-of-honour, in the words of Horace Walpole, had been all too 'willing to cease to be so at the first opportunity'. George IV had had no qualms about appointing one of his mistresses, Lady Jersey, as lady-in-waiting to his much-despised wife, Caroline of Brunswick. William IV, in many ways an uxurious husband who presided over a largely respectable court, had nevertheless moved the ten young Fitzclarences, his children by Mrs Jordan, into apartments at Windsor (one, Lady Mary Fox, was housekeeper). Victoria would always treat the Fitzclarences with sensitivity and kindness, but they could not share the same roof. All vestiges of Hanoverian dissipation – the excesses and mistresses and illegitimate children – were now to be removed. Shortly after her accession, Victoria instructed the Duchess of Sutherland to tell the lord chamberlain, Lord Conyngham, how she relied on him to 'preserve the dignity and morality of my Court', as yet unaware that Conyngham had installed his mistress as housekeeper at Buckingham Palace (where the two were found entwined on more than one occasion). The old order could not be swept away overnight, but a process of moral cleansing had begun.

Diffident and retiring by nature, Sarah did not greatly relish her social duties – the entertaining of visiting Royalties and grandees – finding it 'a great gulp . . . to go down to prayers and have to shake hands with numberless kind friends fresh every morning'. Plays were often put on in the Rubens Room on a Thursday – the actors brought to Windsor on a special train – with guests invited to stay until the Saturday. Sarah came to dread this 'weekly shoal of guests who will fill every cranny of the castle, sit down forty to dinner and make the greatest possible hullabaloo and then, Saturday, vanish like smoke'.

Amongst those she encountered, some amused, some alarmed and some bored. She found the Whig minister Lord Clarendon clever and a 'brilliant conversationalist' but disliked his 'bitingly sarcastic and sharp' manner. She struggled to make conversation with Prince

Augustus of Saxe-Coburg (a cousin of the Queen) – 'the man of lead' – until she chanced upon the subject of bear-hunting in Hungary, on which he proved voluble, unbending so far as to confess his distress at the news of the death of his favourite nightingale. She judged the prinked and preening Leopold, King of the Belgians, 'a very majestic personage', winced before the tactlessness of the Queen's uncle, the Duke of Cambridge, with his '"How do you get on here? Rather dull hey?" within two chairs of the Queen at a small table', and spent a self-conscious hour in the middle of the drawing room 'bellowing and being bellowed at' by the hopelessly deaf Duke of Wellington.

As for her colleagues, they were 'all good-natured and some pleasantish', and she greatly liked Baroness Lehzen – 'the only face I ever see that seems to feel what is going on at all' – but her own 'exalted rank' meant she saw all too little of her. She warmed too to the Duchess of Sutherland (mistress of the robes), whom she felt she could talk to 'quite a coeur ouvert about everything chez nous', but the Duchess was only an occasional visitor to court, and in the main, Sarah was beset by feelings of loneliness and isolation – the kind of loneliness induced by an absence of sympathy rather than society. 'Dinner is still barely endurable from stiffness and evenings very heavy . . . and I am sadly by myself and pinnacled up, with only one tight little hand over my head!'

The Queen took immediately to her new lady-in-waiting, finding her a most 'amiable person', happy to indulge her in a game of battledore and shuttlecock in the Corridor. Moreover, Sarah enjoyed the approval of Lord Melbourne, who, apropos of her asking Her Majesty's permission to put on her spectacles, remarked that this 'showed she understood etiquette', because 'formerly nobody was allowed to come to Court in spectacles or use glasses'. Fanny Burney, assistant keeper of the robes to Queen Charlotte, had not been allowed to wear her spectacles at court.

On her part, Sarah Lyttelton looked on her royal mistress with maternal indulgence, as a merry 'zit' (child) – artless, girlish, impulsive, fond of playing ball in the Corridor with visiting children, happy to

jump up from a foot bath and to run with wet feet to fetch a letter
to show her lady-in-waiting, or to appear in Sarah's bedroom in her
dressing gown calling her to come and see a rainbow. She was much
struck too by the Queen's frankness, the 'peculiar sincerity' identified
by Lytton Strachey, who, if sometimes free with the facts, caught the
flavour of Victoria's personality better than anyone. 'There is a trans-
parency in her truth that is very striking,' remarked Sarah. 'Not a
shade of exaggeration in describing her feelings or facts; like very few
other people I ever knew. Many may be as true, but I think it often
goes along with some reserve. She talks it all out, and just as it is, no
more and no less.'

'Everything is new and delightful to her,' wrote Charles Greville,
for once abandoning his usual waspishness. 'She is surrounded with
the most exciting and interesting enjoyments; her occupations, her
pleasures, her business, her Court, all present an unceasing round of
gratifications. With all her prudence and discretion She has great
animal spirits and enters into the magnificent novelties of her position
with the zest and curiousity of a child.' Carried on a wave of public
goodwill, Victoria opened her dispatch boxes and received her ministers
and rode and danced and laughed, loudly and often, showing her
gums. For a girl who had had little enough of society hitherto, it was
heady indeed to find herself feted and admired, to be the object of
such consuming *interest*.

Always susceptible to good looks, she could admire a great beauty
such as the Duchess of Sutherland or enjoy the homage of a handsome
young courtier like Lord Alfred Paget, an equerry who wore Her
Majesty's portrait on a chain round his neck, as did his golden retriever
Mrs Bumps, which naturally endeared both to the Queen. She had
Lord Palmerston, her clever and worldly foreign secretary, on hand to
instruct her in the intricacies of foreign affairs or to advise her on her
chess moves. At Windsor, Palmerston liked to row or swim in the
Thames for two or three hours before breakfast; he also liked corridor-
creeping (not for nothing was he known as 'Cupid'), of which Her
Majesty was as yet ignorant.

And always of course there was Melbourne. Every morning 'Lord M' came to discuss the business of the day; every afternoon he rode out with the Queen through Windsor Great Park; most evenings he sat at her side. So fatherly, so solicitous, and yet so very entertaining, even, occasionally, a trifle *shocking*. For Victoria, scarcely more than a schoolgirl, and an ill-educated one at that, the conversation of a highly sophisticated, witty, informed man such as Melbourne was intoxicating. The story of his wretched marriage to Caroline Ponsonby, as relayed by the Duchess of Sutherland, only added a further layer of fascination, an air of romantic melancholy. At fifty-eight, he was still attractive and still capable of racing a lady-in-waiting down the Corridor at Windsor. Increasing girth, though, was steadily obscuring his good looks; Sarah Lyttelton worried about the effects of his 'very unwholesome diet' – a daily intake of 'consommés, truffles, pears, ices and anchovies'.

But by the autumn of 1838, the sheen of that first happy year was wearing thin, and clouds were looming. The Queen's relations with her mother had become strained – there was the question of the Duchess's debts, as well as the continued presence of Sir John Conroy, the comptroller of her household. The Duchess felt excluded and ill-used, pointedly presenting her daughter, on her nineteenth birthday, with a copy of *King Lear*. Hostilities and tensions between mother and daughter were played out in their households. The Duchess of Kent resented the fact that her lady-in-waiting, Lady Mary Stopford, got on well with the Queen's ladies, while Lady Flora Hastings, another of the Duchess's ladies, went out of her way to make fun of Baroness Lehzen. The Queen herself felt lethargic and oddly out of sorts; she gave way to flashes of ill-temper; she worried about her escalating weight – 8 stone 13lb in December 1838. Walk more, advised Lord M; walking made her tired and sick, retorted the Queen.

CHAPTER 2

A Scandal and a Crisis

Sarah Lyttelton came back into waiting in the spring of 1839 to find the palace in uproar over a scandal that had been simmering since the beginning of the year. 'The whole town has been engrossed for some days with a scandalous story at Court,' wrote Charles Greville on 2 March. 'It was at first whispered about and at last swelled into a report and finally into a charge. With whom it originated is not clear . . . the Court is plunged in shame and mortification at the exposure . . . the palace is full of bickerings and heart-burnings, while the whole proceeding is looked upon by society at large as to the last degree disgusting and disgraceful.'

Sarah, who despite claiming to be 'peculiarly indiscreet' was nothing of the sort, kept firmly aloof from the 'bickerings and heart-burnings'. But she was very much in the minority. Within the confined, airless world of the household – a small group of people, not necessarily sympathetic to each other, lacking in occupation, cut off from family, friends and the 'outer world' – morsels of gossip were pounced on and devoured. And the Flora Hastings affair was gossip of a very high order. Within and without the palace walls people talked of little else during the spring and summer of 1839.

Lady Flora Hastings, a pious, elegant young woman of thirty-two, with a caustic wit and a certain chilly hauteur, had been lady-in-waiting to the Duchess of Kent since 1834. She was heartily disliked by the Queen – 'that odious Lady Flora' – as a friend and ally of Sir John Conroy, and unpopular with the Queen's ladies, with whom she declined to ingratiate herself. These enmities went back to the dreary

days of Kensington Palace, where Victoria had spent a solitary girlhood, bereft of companions, cut off from society and William IV's
court. This isolation – the 'Kensington System' – had been quite
deliberately engineered by the Duchess of Kent, or more accurately
by Sir John Conroy, as a means of ensuring Victoria's dependence and
securing his own and the Duchess's positions if and when the Princess
became Queen.

Conroy was an attractive opportunist who had begun his career as
an equerry to the Duke of Kent, becoming, after his death, comptroller
of the Duchess's household (and embezzling a large part of her fortune
in the process). The Duchess, a warm-hearted but weak-minded
woman – her 'kindness and softness are very delightful in spite of
want of brains', said Sarah Lyttelton charitably – loved her daughter,
but appeared to be on overly familiar terms with her comptroller.
Whether or not they were lovers, as some supposed, she was entirely
in his thrall. Not so Victoria, who, supported by Baroness Lehzen,
vigorously resisted all Conroy's efforts to corral her. Lehzen, steadfast
and loyal, stood as the one fixed point amid the swirling ambitions
around her.

The Queen was a creature of absolutes. Her judgements were
instinctive but categorical. Towards those she loved she was fiercely,
sometimes blindly, loyal, while those who displeased, or worse, were
met with resolute froideur. According to her personal mythology, her
childhood had been a lonely, cheerless affair, with Lehzen her sole
protector in the face of the machinations of Conroy, her enemy. Once
she became Queen, she had the very great satisfaction of asserting
her independence: the Duchess of Kent found herself relegated to
apartments at some distance from her daughter, while Conroy was
trounced – his demands for a pension and a baronetcy were met, but
he was not received at court (he retained though, and this remained
a bone of contention, his position in the Duchess's household). Beneath
the new Queen's much vaunted, and genuine, cordiality, there lurked,
as Sarah noted, a 'vein of iron'.

Lehzen, on the other hand, saw her devotion rewarded. Louise
Lehzen, long-nosed, sharp-eyed, hung about with the faint whiff of

the caraway seeds she chewed obsessively, was the daughter of a Lutheran clergyman from Hanover. She had originally been governess to the Queen's half-sister Feodora, before taking on the five-year-old Victoria. Now, at the new court, she continued to nanny and fuss over the Queen, pursuing her with gossipy notes in occasionally halting English: reporting the indiscretion of a maid-of-honour; warning of the dangers of draughts; urging five drops of tincture of rhubarb to be taken with a little camomile tea; relaying requests to walk in the Slopes 'during Your Majesty's absence, which I have advised not to think of'; describing an equerry demonstrating the new fountain pens by lying on his back and writing 'perpendicularly'.

At her own wish, Lehzen did not hold an official position in the household, but was loosely termed 'lady attendant'. She looked after the Queen's clothes and jewels and acted as a kind of unofficial secretary, with responsibility for Victoria's private expenses – no bill was paid by the Queen until it had first been signed by Lehzen. At Buckingham Palace, a door was knocked through between her bedroom and that of the Queen. Crucially, she had Her Majesty's ear and absolute confidence, and acted as a conduit for information, as the household did well to remember.

In January 1839, on her way back from Scotland, where she had spent Christmas at Loudon Castle with her mother, to Windsor, where she was to resume her waiting, Flora Hastings shared a post-chaise with John Conroy, which gave rise to some prurient speculation at court. Shortly after her return, she became ill with stomach pains and consulted Sir James Clark, physician to the Duchess of Kent and physician-in-ordinary to the Queen. As a young man, Clark had attended Keats in Rome, before becoming physician to King Leopold, who recommended him to the Duchess. Notwithstanding his illustrious patients, his abilities as a doctor were questionable – Lord Clarendon said he wouldn't trust Clark to 'attend a sick cat'. For Flora Hastings he prescribed rhubarb and ipecacuanha pills and a liniment made of camphor and opium. At the same time the Queen's ladies – currently Lady Charlemont (lady-in-waiting), Mrs Campbell (woman of the bedchamber), Miss Spring Rice and Miss Paget (maids-of-honour), along with Baroness Lehzen and Miss Davys – noticed that Lady Flora's abdomen appeared strangely, indeed suspiciously, swollen. And so the whispers began.

When Lady Tavistock, senior lady of the bedchamber, came into waiting at the end of January, she found the Queen's ladies in a lather, begging her to 'protect their purity from this contamination'. It would have been wise at this juncture for Lady Tavistock to have brought in the Duchess of Kent, who was after all responsible for Lady Flora, but the Duchess and the Queen were by now scarcely on speaking terms, and there was little communication between the households. Instead Lady Tavistock, who was known for her mischievous tongue, took it upon herself to inform Lord Melbourne of what was being said. Melbourne, with characteristic insouciance but dubious wisdom, advocated a wait-and-see policy. He then consulted Sir James Clark, who admitted there *were* grounds for suspicion.

On 2 February, the Queen, barely able to contain her excitement, confided in her journal that she and Lehzen believed Lady Flora 'is – to use plain words – *with child*! Clark cannot deny the suspicions; the horrid cause of all this is the Monster and demon Incarnate, whose name I forbear to mention, but is the first word of the second line of this page.' The word was 'John Conroy'. A naïve and suggestible nineteen-year-old, fired up with loathing for Conroy and all associated with him, she was only too ready to believe the worst.

Seemingly sanctioned by Sir James Clark and Melbourne, endlessly debated by the Queen and her ladies, the rumours of pregnancy grew stronger. In mid February, Lady Portman succeeded Lady Tavistock and was duly informed by Sir James of his 'suspicions that Lady Flora was privately married', a suspicion that her refusal to submit to an examination without her stays seemed to confirm. Sir James, with the backing of Lady Portman, went to Lady Flora and told her of what was being said, resorting to the 'privately married' euphemism suggested, apparently, by Lehzen. Lady Flora insisted that thanks to 'walking and porter' she was feeling a little better and the swelling was much reduced – in fact she had had to take in her dresses. 'Well

I don't think so,' replied Clark. 'You seem to me to grow larger every day and so the ladies think.' When he again asked to examine her, Lady Flora again indignantly refused.

Lady Portman then appealed to the Duchess of Kent, assuring her that she was not acting from 'malicious motives', but 'Sir James Clark having expressed his strong suspicion . . . it is impossible that the honour, either of the Court, or of the Lady can admit of the least doubt or delay in clearing up the matter . . . Nothing but the opinion of medical men can possibly be satisfactory . . . it is quite impossible that the Queen should admit the Lady into her presence until her character is cleared.' Lady Flora now had little choice. An examination was carried out by Sir James and Sir Charles Clarke, a doctor known to the Hastings family, specialising in midwifery, in the presence of Lady Flora's weeping maid and Lady Portman, who stood by the window with her face in her hands (not so, said the maid subsequently – she had actually pushed right up to the bed). The verdict was unequivocal – 'there are no grounds for suspicion that pregnancy does exist or ever has existed'.

That evening a tearful Lady Portman came to Lady Flora, as she ate her 'bit of dinner', made a fulsome apology and admitted that 'she had at several times spoken a great deal to the Queen on the subject, especially when she found it was Her Majesty's own idea'. The Queen meanwhile sent a message of regret, followed a week later, when Lady Flora finally felt able to receive her, by a visit. She found her magnanimous – both agreed that for the sake of the Duchess of Kent, all should be forgiven and forgotten.

This was how matters stood when Sarah Lyttelton came back into waiting in March and discovered that, far from being forgotten, the air was still thick with rumour, fuelled by baffling murmurings from the doctors of the possibility of pregnancy despite virginity. Low-level hostility between the two households had by now broken into open warfare. The Queen told Melbourne that her mother's presence was like 'having an enemy in the house'. Lady Tavistock followed Lady Flora about the palace, begging her to shake hands and make up, only to be told that that was out of the question. The Duchess of Kent refused to see Lady Portman or to sit next to Lady Tavistock at the evening whist table. Lady Portman, suffering from strain, begged the Queen to be excused from the drawing room held that April and subsequently suffered a miscarriage.

In an attempt at damage limitation, the Duke of Wellington, always turned to in times of crisis as a wise old uncle, was called in to mollify the feelings of the injured parties – the Hastings family, Conroy, the Duchess of Kent. Too late. When Lady Flora's uncle, Hamilton Fitzgerald, published the extremely frank letter she had written him – 'I blush to send you so revolting a tale' – giving her side of the story, in *The Examiner* (the Tory Hastings family could rely on the support of the Tory press), the affair went public. Lady Flora claimed to be the victim of a 'diabolical conspiracy'. She pointed the finger at Lehzen: 'a certain foreign lady whose hatred to the Duchess is no secret pulled the wires'. Lady Tavistock and Lady Portman had both been 'most active against' her. No blame however was to be attached to the Queen, who had shown her 'regret by her civility'.

Lady Flora's brother and mother now took up arms and swung into action with a flurry of angry letters and talk of duels. Who, they wished to know, was responsible for the original allegation? Baroness Lehzen? Sir James Clark? The Queen's ladies? The Queen herself? Why had Melbourne allowed matters to reach such a point? Why had the Queen, unlike the Duchess of Kent, not instantly dismissed Clark from her service? On 9 March, Lady Hastings, Lady Flora's mother, wrote an eight-page letter to the Queen, simultaneously obsequious and threatening, seeking reparation for the 'atrocious calumnies and unblushing falsehoods against my daughter's reputation' and insisting that 'this is not a matter that can or will be hushed up and it is all important that no time shall be lost in calling the culpable to account'. She wrote a further letter to Melbourne, calling for the dismissal of Sir James Clark. When she found herself ignored – Melbourne's reply was offensively brusque – she published her correspondence with both the Queen and Melbourne in the *Morning Post*. The Queen seethed. Meanwhile Lord Hastings, Lady Flora's brother, railed against 'the polluted atmosphere at court' and wrote to Lord Portman demanding to know whether it was Lehzen who had originally roused Lady Portman's suspicions. Not so, said Lady Portman.

The public could hardly get enough of it all. Sympathies lay firmly with Lady Flora, while the Queen was judged to have behaved harshly and heartlessly. 'Poor, poor Lady Flora,' wrote Elizabeth Barrett Browning. '*Was* it the Queen's doing? Do you think she really *has* no feelings?' Carlyle judged her to have 'behaved like a hapless little fool and indeed looks like one now (very strikingly since last year to my sense)'. By early summer Her Majesty, to her great indignation, was being insulted in public. At Ascot she was pursued by cries of 'Mrs Melbourne' and hissed by two Tory ladies – the Duchess of Montrose and Lady Sarah Ingestre.

Some were more generous. Lady Holland, political hostess and chatelaine of Holland House, thought that the allegations made against Lady Flora spoke of 'more folly than malice, some prudery but no malignity', and that the story had been whipped up by the Tories as a stick to beat the Queen, who had in fact shown sympathy to Lady Flora, insisting that she appear with her at chapel and dine at her table. Like many, Lady Holland thought that James Clark – 'a vain, presumptuous, meddling man, like most modern medicos' – was chiefly to blame. But again like many, she also felt that Lady Flora's letter to her uncle had done her no favours; that it was 'a gross, indelicate disclosure which shocks people. The mischief is to her but the rebound is bad for the Court. The young innocent Queen should never have had her ears polluted by such filthy stories.'

It *was* bad for the court – the Flora Hastings affair was exactly the kind of scandal, harking back to the 'doings' of former reigns, that Victoria had hoped to avoid. But the fact that a malicious rumour had been allowed to blossom into a full-blown scandal, damaging to all parties, was largely attributable to the estrangement between the Queen and her mother – two warring households under one roof created fertile ground for suspicion and allegation. One way out, indeed the only way Victoria could separate herself from her mother, as Melbourne reminded her, was marriage. She herself was perfectly aware that her uncle Leopold was promoting her first cousin, Albert of Saxe-Coburg, as a suitable husband. She had met him once and liked him well enough, despite noting a worrying tendency to sleepiness. But did she wish to marry so soon? Was she ready to give up her independence, her freedom? She would not commit herself; Albert and his brother might make another visit in the autumn, as long as it was understood that there was no engagement; she might 'like him as a friend and as a cousin and as a brother but not more'.

Just when the Queen was feeling particularly vulnerable and beleaguered, a fresh crisis broke. On 7 May, Melbourne informed her that with the government heading for defeat over the Jamaica Bill, which was meant to subdue the Jamaican sugar planters, he felt he had no choice but to resign. The prospect of losing Melbourne, when she had never needed him more, left the Queen distraught: 'All ALL my happiness gone! That peaceful happy life destroyed, that dearest kind Lord Melbourne no more my Minister!' How could she bear the Tories, by whom she had felt so attacked over Lady Flora, let alone their leader, Sir Robert Peel, that 'cold old man'?

Melbourne wrote advising Her Majesty to ask the opposition, under either the Duke of Wellington or Peel, to form a government. She should, he said, be 'vigilant' when it came to the appointment of new ministers, and on the question of her household she should make plain her wish that none be removed apart from those gentlemen who were also in Parliament. When Wellington declined to form a government, the Queen was forced to send for Peel. Try as she might – and she did not try very hard – she could not like him. 'How different, how dreadfully different' appeared Peel beside Melbourne, with his 'frank, open, natural and most kind, warm manner'. With the Queen, 'manner' was everything. She would always warm to the personal approach, to a demonstration of sympathy – not to be confused with familiarity – just as she would always be repelled by excessive formality. Peel was not cold, but he was shy, socially awkward, and, as the son of a Lancashire cotton baron, quite lacking in the urbane ease and aristocratic confidence of such as Melbourne.

They discussed new ministers and touched on the question of the household; Peel felt, quite reasonably, that since he would be heading a minority government, the Queen should demonstrate her confidence in him and his party by making some changes to her exclusively Whig household (the Queen's ladies, Baroness Lehzen, the Queen herself, all were ardent Whigs). There was nothing unconstitutional about this. Though in general only the lords-in-waiting and the mistress of the robes were political appointments, it was still considered tactful, in the event of a change of administration, for the Sovereign to agree to the replacement of at least those ladies of the household married to prominent members of the outgoing government.

Melbourne, to whom the Queen sent frequent bulletins, was sympathetic but firm, urging her to do all she could to facilitate a new government and not to let negotiations founder over the question of her household; in the meantime, he added regretfully, it would not be proper for him to dine at the palace. But in a further letter, on 9 May, the Queen detected a glimmer of hope. 'If Sir Robert Peel presses for the dismissal of those of your Household who are not in Parliament,' wrote Melbourne, 'you may observe that in so doing he is pressing your Majesty more hardly than any Minister ever pressed a Sovereign before.' The Queen saw a way out. Her determination not to have Peel foisted on her could be dressed up as a matter of constitutional policy.

In her next meeting with Peel, she announced that she wished to keep all of her household who were not in Parliament, whereupon Peel, she alleged, '*pretended* that I had the preceding day expressed a wish to keep about me those who *were* in Parliament'. Did she intend, asked Peel, to keep all her ladies? '"All" I said. "The Mistress of the Robes and the Ladies of the Bedchamber?" I replied "All".' When Peel objected that some of these, such as Lady Normanby, were married to Whig ministers, Victoria countered by claiming that her ladies wouldn't interfere, that she never talked politics with them anyway and that besides, many of them were related to Tories.

Peel, nonplussed, withdrew to consult his colleagues; the Queen, exultant, wrote in high tone to Melbourne, claiming that Peel had 'insisted on my giving up my ladies, to which I replied that I never would consent and I never a saw a man so frightened . . . I was calm but very decided . . . the Queen of England will not submit to such trickery. Keep yourself in readiness for you may soon be wanted.' She went on to become quite satirical: 'Was Sir Robert so weak that even the Ladies must be of his opinion?' Would she be deprived of her dressers and housemaids next? Melbourne, whose association with Victoria had been the great happiness and consolation of his declining years, could hardly refuse such an appeal. His Cabinet could not but be moved by such a show of courage and spirit. They rallied behind their little Queen, drafting a letter for her to send to Peel: 'the Queen having considered the proposal made to her yesterday by Sir Robert Peel to remove the Ladies of her Bedchamber cannot consent to adopt a course which she conceives to be contrary to usage and repugnant to her feelings'. Peel declined to form a government; Melbourne returned to office; the Queen had triumphed.

In fact, the scent of victory had quite gone to Victoria's head and she was on very shaky ground indeed. Peel had merely asked for the removal of *some* of her ladies. For 'some' the Queen read 'all', a crucial point picked up on by Charles Greville, who saw her as 'a clever, but rather thoughtless and headstrong girl . . . secretly longing to get back her Old Ministers (if she could by any pretext or expedient), she boldly and stubbornly availed herself of the opening which was presented to her'. Greville put the blame fair and square on Melbourne for surrounding the Queen with Whig ladies in the first place. Many years later, an older, wiser Queen would ascribe the Bedchamber Crisis to youthful folly and inexperience. In 1874, she told her private secretary, Henry Ponsonby, that the ladies should not have been kept, that 'there was mismanagement in ever allowing matters to come to that point', though she chose to point the finger at Melbourne rather than herself.

Meanwhile the Flora Hastings affair rumbled on, with its chief victim, the wretched Lady Flora, now dying in her rooms at Buckingham Palace, as a tearful Duchess of Kent repeatedly warned her sceptical daughter. The Queen did agree to ask Lady Flora's sister to come and stay at the palace – an invitation that was refused – and finally, on 27 June, she visited the patient herself. She was much shocked: 'I found poor Ly. Flora stretched out on a couch looking as thin as anybody can be who is alive; literally a skeleton, but with the body very much swollen like a person who is with child; a searching look in her eyes, rather like a person who is dying; her voice like usual and a good deal of strength in her hands; she was friendly, said she was very comfortable and very grateful for all I had done for her, and that she was glad to see me looking well. I said to her, I hoped to see her again when she was better upon which she grasped my hand as if to say "I shall not see you again". I then instantly went upstairs and returned to Lord Melbourne who said "You remained a very short time".'

On 5 July Lady Flora died; a post-mortem revealed a tumour on the liver. To avoid hostile demonstrations, the cortège left Buckingham Palace at four in the morning; the Queen, against Melbourne's advice, sent a carriage; at Loudon, five thousand people gathered for the funeral.

For Sarah Lyttelton, the event of the summer was neither the death of Lady Flora nor the furore over the Queen's ladies, but the marriage of her son George. George, a passionate lover of classics and cricket, a man of deep High Church faith and powerful if somewhat inarticulate feelings, had, at eighteen, fallen in love with Mary Glynne. In the winter of 1838, Mary and her much-loved and admired elder sister Catherine were travelling in Italy when they met William Gladstone, the future prime minister, who fell in love with Catherine. Back in England, William and Catherine became engaged; three days later, Mary accepted George.

That July the two couples married, in a double wedding at Hawarden, the Glynne family home. Sarah was not present, being confined to Hagley with Caroline and Lavinia, who were suffering from measles. When the newly-weds briefly returned to Hagley before their honeymoon, which was spent in Scotland, along with the new Mr and Mrs Gladstone, Sarah, still in quarantine, kept out of their way, but taking advantage of a momentary absence, she stole into the library 'just like the White Lady', to get some books, and there 'found a small pair of feminine gloves lying about and other little symptoms of a change'. Her days as mistress of Hagley were over.

Back at Windsor in October, a year into her appointment, Sarah was sounding like an old hand: 'Windsor is just as it was, quite single in beauty and magnificence and court is just as it was – court!' Sometimes the month-long waitings seemed very long indeed and she grew quite 'sick of being beautifully dressed and talking French and running up and down stairs and curtseying'. And she felt sadly deprived of books: 'The books you mention I shall be most happy to read,' she wrote disconsolately to George from the Royal Pavilion one dark, wet winter's day. 'I am in a destitute state in that particular just now – nothing but a selection of Goldoni's [Carlo Goldoni, the Venetian playwright] plays to study . . . it pours and patters and the carriages grind the shingly road and the waves keep muttering and moaning and the sky is gloomy gruel and I have finished one Goldoni and am averse to beginning another and I am very stupid.' Still, she had mastered her 'shawling and pinning duties' and felt perfectly 'comfortable' and 'in fewer scrapes'.

But once more she found the court convulsed by the Flora Hastings affair, thanks to a sensational double spread that September in the *Morning Post*, publishing documents that included Lady Flora and Lady Portman's statements and private letters between the various parties. This was a fresh blow for the Queen, whose spirits, with all the elasticity of youth, had just recovered after her embattled summer. Sarah Lyttelton, however, was merely roused, in a letter to George, to leap to Her Majesty's defence: 'What do you mean about the Queen being "found out". Poor little soul there is nothing to find out about her. She has done nothing and said nothing that I know of, to want hiding or discredit her – abt Lady Flora I mean – only no one can know or believe the truth . . . Ly Portman most innocently made a mistake. Sir James Clark rather stupidly made a blunder and these came together like matches or shells upon the mass of combustible intrigue called a court – that is all, but there never will or can be an end of it.' A few days later, after *The Times* had published Clark's account of the affair, defending his own conduct, she continued dismissively, 'I have not seen Sir James Clark's statement – nor do I much care for it. I suppose I may live to the dropping of the subject but I doubt it notwithstanding the greenness of my old age – it grows a dreadful bore.' George's letter, she added, still smelled of the violets he had enclosed with it.

Many years later, in 1885, James Clark's son claimed that Conroy's enmity towards his father was at the root of the Flora Hastings affair. According to Clark junior, Conroy and his puppet the Duchess of Kent had concocted a plot to make Melbourne believe that the young Victoria was 'physically and mentally so backward that she was not fit to reign' and that the Duchess must be regent for at least a year, while 'they intended to have a good time of it'. Sir James got wind of this and went to Melbourne, to assure him that Victoria was 'perfectly fit in every way'; Conroy's plans were scuppered; Flora Hastings provided a means of revenge. This did not, however, explain how Sir James had been so hopelessly mistaken in his original diagnosis.

The press continued to denounce the Queen's 'depraved Court'. While the Queen herself largely escaped censure – if she was guilty, it was of little more than naivety – her household was another matter. James Clark, 'that repulsive toady', was attacked for being a mere tool of the ladies. The ladies themselves, and Lady Portman and Lady Tavistock in particular, were blamed for encouraging malicious rumours and giving their royal mistress lamentably bad advice. Lehzen, that 'foreign woman' – xenophobia fuelling the venom – was vilified for poisoning relations between the Queen and her mother, and for starting the rumours. *The Age* claimed that the court needed to be purged of the 'sinister influence' of this 'vulgar parvenue'. 'Your Majesty would owe it to yourself as well as to those who have been most deeply injured and to your moral People, to banish such a criminal from your Court with merited degradation (if she's guilty),' thundered a 'voice from the grave of Lady Flora Hastings', the anonymous author of a pamphlet entitled *The Dangers of Evil Counsel*.

More generally the court came under fire for fostering nepotism and time-servers. Windsor was dubbed the 'Paget Club House', such was the proliferation of members of the Paget family. Nine were said to hold court positions, including Lady Conyngham (married to the former lord chamberlain), Lady Sandwich (who had replaced Lady Breadalbane as lady-in-waiting, and as a Tory at least ended the exclusively Whig composition of the Queen's ladies), Lord Uxbridge (the new lord chamberlain), his son Lord Alfred Paget (equerry) and daughter Mathilda Paget (maid-of-honour), and Clarence and Constance Paget. The merry, convivial Pagets, who had had the good sense to curry favour with Lehzen as well as the Queen, were portrayed in the press as pleasure-loving and self-seeking, though Sarah Lyttelton, usually a reliable moral barometer, liked them: 'I have a general good opinion of Pagets – in spite of many family failings, there are among them family virtues – honesty and affection to each other and no affectation and some *gros bon sens*.'

Both the Flora Hastings affair and the Bedchamber Crisis exposed the vulnerability of Victoria's court to 'combustible intrigue', the fickle nature of public goodwill, and the Queen's own need of wise counsel and a steadying hand. Conroy finally succumbed to pressure, applied by the Duke of Wellington, and left the Duchess's service in June, but relations between mother and daughter remained cool. And blame could be attached to the Queen, who had at the very least betrayed her inexperience and certainly stood guilty of poor judgement.

Even Sarah Lyttelton confessed to feeling 'regret and compassion and hopelessness and helplessness, which many circumstances of [the Queen's] education and present position and future fate fill one with'. Admiration and affection did not blind her to Victoria's deficiencies, to the fact that in some crucial ways she was ill-equipped for her 'present position'; that a patchy education had been a poor preparation for the business of being Queen and had left an abiding sense of intellectual inadequacy; that her formidable will was allowed too free a rein. Sarah trusted though that a sense of duty and the 'experience of proper serious feelings' would see her through. 'Whatever there may be to find fault with (and there is much less than is supposed in the world) I trust will gradually be amended.'

Key to that process would be someone who could encourage those 'proper serious feelings'.

Just four days after Sir James Clark's statement in *The Times*, the arrival of some guests at court provided the Queen with welcome distraction from the unedifying fallout from the Flora Hastings affair. She had anticipated the visit of her cousins Albert and Ernest Saxe-Coburg with decidedly mixed feelings. However, the sight of Albert ascending the stairs at Windsor on the evening of 10 October, a little dishevelled and sporting a greenish pallor after a terrible crossing from France, but still a vision of beauty, swept away all doubts. 'So excessively handsome, such beautiful eyes, an exquisite nose, and such a pretty mouth with delicate mustachios and slight but very slight whiskers; a beautiful figure broad in the shoulders and a fine waist; my heart is quite going,' she confessed in her journal in a rush of emotion.

CHAPTER 3

'Love rules the court'

While the Queen entertained her cousins, Sarah Lyttelton learned that she was to become a grandmother. Her daughter-in-law Mary was pregnant, as she would be for most of her short life, which led her to refuse an invitation to dine with the Queen. Such invitations were not always received as the prize they were intended; indeed they were dreaded by Mary Lyttelton, though the food and music at Windsor were compensations enough for George. For Sarah, the pleasure of seeing family was quite eclipsed by social strain. Writing to George on 25 October, she insisted that Mary had been quite right to excuse herself: 'the Queen – impertinent little creature – said to me "so sorry not to see your new daughter Ly L but I suppose there are *reasons*". "Oh Madame", I said, "It is such early days! I should not suppose *that*" (no more I did: I knew it, which is quite another thing), "but she is rather delicate and her long journey has knocked her up".' There were reasons too for the Queen to indulge in a little light raillery – she was newly, though not publicly, engaged to Prince Albert.

Once it became public, the engagement met with far from unqualified approval. Awkward questions were asked in Parliament: was Albert a true Protestant? Should he hold higher rank than Victoria's uncles? Wasn't an annuity of £50,000, as had been granted to King Leopold on his marriage to Princess Charlotte, rather exorbitant? The Queen seethed at such treatment of her beloved, especially the reduction of his annuity to £30,000, yet revealed her own intransigence when it came to the matter of the Prince's household. Here it was Albert's turn to encounter the 'vein of iron' running through his future wife.

Not unnaturally, at just twenty years old, faced with the prospect of a new life in an unfamiliar, possibly hostile country, in the awkward role of consort, Albert wished to have some say in the composition of his household, to have some compatriots around him, or at least a few people he knew and trusted. The Queen had other plans: George Anson, hitherto Melbourne's private secretary, would become Albert's, as well as controller of his purse. The Prince was dismayed – this appeared a blatantly partisan appointment, flying in the face of his conviction that the royal household (like the monarchy itself) should be above party, should embrace Tories as well as Whigs. Anson was closely allied to Melbourne, while his uncle, yet another Whig, was being proposed as a groom of the bedchamber. Albert protested that he knew nothing of Anson except that he had seen him dance a quadrille. And dancing prowess was no recommendation in the eyes of the Prince.

'Think of my position, dear Victoria,' he wrote plaintively. 'I am leaving my home with all its old associations, all my bosom friends, and going to a country in which everything is new and strange to me – men, language, customs, modes of life, position. Except yourself I have no one to confide in. And is it not even to be conceded to me that the two or three persons who are to have the charge of my private affairs should be persons who already have my confidence?' The Queen remained obdurate and Albert's objections were brushed aside: 'As to your wishes about your gentlemen, my dear Albert, I must tell you quite honestly that it will not do. You may entirely rely upon me that the people who will be round you will be absolutely pleasant people of high standing and good character.' For Albert's household to 'form a contrast' to Victoria's by containing too many Tories would not do either. The only German allowed to him was his personal secretary, Herr Schenck, whose inferior social status was brought home to him by being barred from dining with the other gentlemen. Not long after Schenck was joined by two German valets, Rudolf Löhlein, rumoured to be a bastard son of Albert's father, and thus his half-brother, and the Swiss-born Isaac Cart, who had been with Albert since boyhood.

On 10 February 1840, Queen Victoria married Prince Albert in the Chapel Royal at St James's Palace. Sarah Lyttelton, being part of the bridal procession, 'saw very little of its effect', while the 'portly forms and finery' of the Duchess of Bedford and Lady Normanby quite obscured a view of the bride, in white satin trimmed with Honiton lace, and her twelve bridesmaids, in simple tulle and white roses, 'like village girls' thought Sarah (Albert's wish to exclude those bridesmaids whose mothers boasted less than spotless reputations had been over-ruled by Victoria). She was not prevented though, from noting the Queen's eyes 'swoln with tears but great happiness in her face; and her look of confidence and comfort in the Prince as they walked away as man and wife was very pretty to see . . . Such a new thing for her to dare to be unguarded in conversation with anybody; and with her frank and fearless nature, the restraints she has hitherto been under from one reason or another must have been most painful.'

Sarah was right: the consuming relationship of Victoria's life had begun. The Queen, writing to her uncle Leopold the day after the wedding, gave way to unrestrained hyperbole: she was 'the happiest happiest Being that ever existed. Really I do not think it possible for anyone in the world to be happier or as happy than I am. He is an Angel and his kindness and affection for me is really touching. To look in those dear eyes and that dear sunny face is enough to make me adore him . . .'

Sarah Lyttelton was very much in the minority amongst the house-hold, and indeed the wider world, in bestowing her warm approval on Albert. There were, admittedly, minor flaws – a shrill, 'sadly disenchanting' voice, a love of coursing for hares – but he was 'hand-some enough to be the hero of a fairy tale and very like one'. More importantly, he was a man of 'candour, truth, prudence and manli-ness', of sensibility as well as sense, as his passionate love of music, and the organ in particular, eloquently proved. One evening while Sarah was sitting in her rooms at Windsor, reading Guizot by candle-light, she heard, from the room beneath her, the melancholy swoop and fall of Albert playing the organ. The mentioning of this at dinner prompted an outburst: 'Oh my organ! A new possession of mine. I am so fond of the organ! It is the first of instruments – the only for expressing one's feelings.' Behind the self-control, the stiff exterior, the hard moral casing, Sarah detected a vein of poetry: 'Nobody but the organ knows what is in him, except indeed by the look of his eyes sometimes.'

Nor, unlike many, did she think him humourless. He would happily pass around caricatures of himself, with a lot of 'boyish' laughter. When the Queen wondered how she was to get through foreign state visits and state functions, Albert advised her to behave 'like an opera-dancer after a pirouette, and always show all her teeth in a fixed smile', and promptly demonstrated a perfect pirouette, ending on one leg, grinning madly all the while.

Of power struggles between the newly-weds – Albert chafed at being 'only the husband and not the master in the house' and longed for greater authority and responsibility – Sarah was apparently oblivious, her romantic heart blinded to all but the romance. Wherever she looked she saw little tokens of love. When she found Albert reading to his wife as she sat 'at cross-stitch, before dressing for dinner', she could but exclaim, 'Oh what a blessing it is that "Love rules the court" as he does! What a mine of blessings there is, all sent thro those potent blue eyes!' While the Queen was sitting for her portrait, Albert came in, fresh from shooting, windswept and flushed, bounded up to her and 'took her hand with the most graceful, smiling bow'. Talking to the Queen one day, Sarah used the expression 'as happy as a Queen' and quickly checked herself, but Her Majesty merely said, 'Don't correct yourself Lady Lyttelton, a queen is a very happy woman.'

And she noted many a 'pretty bit of wifeism'. Was Albert feeling cold, one chilly October evening in the red drawing room at Windsor? Would he like a second fire lit (something Sarah and the rest of the household had been pining for)? He was, and he would. Late one evening, with Victoria yawning and Albert still engrossed in his game of chess, Sarah was asked to '"Tell Lord Alfred [Paget] to let the Prince know that it is eleven o'clock . . . tell him the

Prince should merely be told the hour. The Prince wishes to be told, I know. He does not see the clock." And quite fussy she seemed for fear of a disrespectful message or anything like a command being sent.'

Whatever her reluctance to yield her royal prerogative, Victoria delighted in yielding to the superior intellect of the Prince. 'Her greatest delight,' thought Sarah, was in *obeying* him.' Under Albert's tutelage she learned the names of trees and plants. During a carriage drive one afternoon the Prince came cantering up to point out a swarm of bees and to offer a short discourse on the habits of the queen. His pupil was rapt. And she couldn't conceal her pride in his talents – when the band of the 1st Life Guards played a particularly beautiful piece of choral music during dinner, the Queen turned to Sarah and informed her, with a blush, that it had been composed by the Prince. Sarah noted the 'raised tone of conversation' encouraged by Albert: 'naval matters and scientific subjects' replaced gossip as topics for discussion at dinner, and the royal couple diligently ploughed through Hallam's *Constitutional History of England* together, with a book of Saint-Simon's *Memoirs* for light relief.

The moral shift – part and parcel, with the rise of Evangelicalism, of a national shift – that had begun with Victoria's accession accelerated under Albert. No longer would the court provide the fulcrum around which society danced, as it had during the Regency years. Indeed, with both Victoria and Albert regarding the aristocracy with some suspicion as not in sympathy with the respectable, bourgeois values they espoused, court was now deliberately distanced from society. Albert began to vet court appointments. When Lord Derby, who became prime minister in 1852, sent in a provisional list of household changes, they were rejected by Albert – how, he wondered, could Derby wish to surround the Queen with the 'Dandies and Roués of London and the Turf'?

The Prince's distaste – verging on the hysterical – for sexual impropriety was rooted in his Coburg childhood: his father's mistresses and illegitimate children; his mother's banishment (and subsequent divorce), when Albert was just five years old, for a love affair of her own; his brother Ernest, already emulating his father's amorous career and suffering from syphilis. While remaining fond of his father and brother, Albert was intent on putting a great deal of distance between the scandals of the Coburg court, not to mention the Hanoverian, and the freshly minted Victorian.

The pleasure-loving Pagets, and in particular Lord Uxbridge, who succeeded Lord Conyngham as lord chamberlain in 1839 and installed his mistress as housekeeper at Windsor (as his predecessor had done at Buckingham Palace), did not find favour with Albert, nor did the tribe of Fitzclarences. The Pagets, without being ousted altogether – Lord Alfred remained at court and a favourite with the Queen – found themselves eclipsed. The daily publication of a Court Circular (a practice begun under George III) in *The Times*, where the most mundane doings of the court were solemnly detailed – the state of Her Majesty's cold, her ladies' 'airing in a pony phaeton', the Duchess of Kent's walk on the Slopes, the arrival of a new maid-of-honour – only served to underline its absolute blamelessness.

And buttressing the new regime of probity and correctness was an elaborate system of etiquette, intruding into every aspect of palace life from dress to dining arrangements. The order in which Their Majesties, guests and household proceeded into dinner was subject to complex rules of precedence. Maids-of-honour were not allowed to sit in the presence of the Prince, or speak to him unless he addressed them first. For drawing rooms, held at three in the afternoon, full evening dress had to be worn, with a headdress of three white feathers, lappets (lace streamers) for married women and veils for the unmarried. If anyone wished, for health reasons, to wear a dress with a higher – and thus less draughty – neckline than was usual, special permission had to be obtained from the lord chamberlain. There were rules about how to approach Her Majesty, how to withdraw and how to hold the train of one's dress. Divorced women could not be presented. At levees, gentlemen were required to appear in court dress – a claret-coloured coat, knee breeches, white stockings, buckled shoes and a sword.

The question of walking on the Slopes at Windsor bristled with etiquette. As part of Albert's programme of improvements, the Slopes, hitherto gloomy and dank, were landscaped and planted, and naturally everyone wanted to enjoy one of the new walks, through the rockery, past the waterfall and the grottos, along the trout stream, with the castle walls looming massively above. But the Slopes were forbidden not just to unchaperoned maids-of-honour, but to almost everyone else, for reasons that remained obscure. Sarah Lyttelton tried to use her influence on behalf of her friend Lady Grant, a widow with a house on Castle Hill but no garden, by asking the Prince whether she and her children might walk on the Slopes while the royal family were away, as had always been allowed in the past. The request was considered and refused, thanks to, as Sarah put it, 'those odious things etiquette precedents'. Only as a very great favour were her daughters allowed to enjoy the Slopes; most people, including the Dean of Windsor, who also appealed to Sarah to intercede on his and his family's behalf, were denied.

It wasn't just the moral tone of the court that, in Albert's view, needed stiffening, but the organisation of the entire royal household. On her accession Victoria had inherited a vast, unwieldy and chaotic apparatus, divided into three separate departments, that of the lord chamberlain, the lord steward and the master of the horse. All three of these officers of state changed with the government; none of them lived at court; they enjoyed virtual autonomy; their responsibilities were ill-defined and their duties frequently delegated to incompetent servants. Victoria and Albert were particularly concerned that, in the past, insufficient care had been taken in the appointment of physicians and chaplains.

Under the lord chamberlain came some 445 individuals, including the ladies of the bedchamber, the maids-of-honour, the lords-in-waiting, the grooms-in-waiting, and the medical staff (four physicians to the Person, two sergeant surgeons, a chemist and druggist to the Person, and a physician, a surgeon, an apothecary and a dentist to the household). Also in his remit were the housekeepers to the palaces, the Queen's messengers, the linen room women, a body linen laundress, a chimney sweep, a rat killer, a stove and fire lighter, a poet laureate, a librarian, a principal painter, a surveyor of pictures, an examiner of plays and twenty-four band members.

The lord steward was responsible for the master of the household, the ranger of Windsor Home Park and the domestic servants – the staff of the kitchens and the wine cellar, the housemaids (about forty at Windsor), the night porters, the lamplighters (now only two, as gas lights had replaced oil lamps in much of the castle) and table deckers, while the master of the horse had charge of the equerries, the pages of honour, the footmen, the grooms and the coachmen. To complicate matters further, yet another (notoriously dilatory) department, that of woods and forests, took care of the exteriors of the palaces and repairs. Broadly speaking, everyone above stairs came under the department of the lord chamberlain and everyone below that of the lord steward, but why a housemaid was responsible to the lord steward, and a linen room woman to the lord chamberlain, nobody could explain. Such arbitrary divisions resulted in absurd muddles, chronic inefficiency and waste.

When the Queen asked why the fire in the dining room had not been lit, she was told by a servant in the lord steward's department that 'properly speaking it is not our fault; for the lord steward lays the fire only and the lord chamberlain lights it'. The lord chamberlain's department was responsible for cleaning the inside of the windows and that of woods and forests for the outside – windows remained filthy. If a broken pane of glass in a scullery cupboard needed to be mended, a requisition had to be first prepared and signed by the chief cook, then countersigned by the clerk of the kitchen, then taken to be signed by the master of the household, then passed to the lord chamberlain's office to be authorised, and finally presented to the clerk of works, who was responsible to the department of woods and forests . . . Consequently repairs went undone for months.

The master of the household, Charles Murray, was master but in name, with little authority in his own, the lord steward's, department, and none outside it. So a great many servants were not subject to any real authority at all, and drinking and pilfering were endemic. Endless meals were supplied to those not entitled to them. Carriages were ordered by forging the signatures of ladies-in-waiting. Some of the older ladies were once caught smuggling. Candles were changed every day, regardless of whether they had been used or not, and those unused were pocketed – a traditional staff perquisite. In just one quarter at Windsor, 184 new brushes, brooms and mops were bought, as well as 24 new pairs of housemaid's gloves, 24 chamois leathers and 96 packing mats. Visitors to Windsor had to fend for themselves: guests could roam the castle for hours looking for a drawing room or bedroom. One was forced to spend the night on a sofa in the State Gallery, where a housemaid found him and, thinking him drunk, called the police. François Guizot, the French foreign minister, opened the door to what he hoped was his bedroom only to find the Queen having her hair brushed by a maid.

If the Queen was not always well served by her household, the household did well by the Queen. Positions, if not exactly sinecures, were well worth the having. Out of the £385,000 the Queen received as her civil list, £131,260 went on household salaries, though her personal attendants – initially her dressers, wardrobe maids and hairdresser (these were later transferred to the department of the mistress of the robes, under the lord chamberlain) and later her private secretary and Highland and Indian servants – were paid from the £60,000 allocated to her privy purse. And those salaries were substantial without being lavish, from £2,000 for the lord chamberlain to £400 for both the librarian and the Queen's hairdresser and £320 for the first page of the backstairs. Further down the scale the body linen laundress received £170, the chimney sweep £111, the rat killer £80, a linen room woman £60, and a housemaid between £15 and £40, depending on seniority. And this at a time when a domestic servant in an average middle-class home could expect to earn around £12 a year.

In addition, lower servants received two shillings a day board wages; all enjoyed free medical care, plentiful, meat-heavy meals and, at least for the upper servants, comfortable accommodation. Pensions too were generous – £400 for a retired first page of the backstairs, around £40 for a retired housemaid, £60 for a widow of a page of the back-stairs. Such liberality periodically roused cries of outrage from the radical press, especially during the early 1840s, when a great many of the Queen's subjects were starving, thanks to unemployment, failed harvests and the rising cost of bread. As one William Strange wrote: 'In the present lamentably distressed state of the country . . . there are many salaries paid to the "Ladies and Gentlemen of the Court" for doing absolutely nothing.'

Just how chaotic and unregulated below-stairs palace life had become was brought home by the case of 'the Boy Jones', a seventeen-year-old youth discovered hiding under the Queen's sofa in her Buckingham Palace sitting room in December 1840. It was not his first visit – he had previously sat upon the throne, helped himself to food from the kitchens and heard the newly born Princess Royal 'squall' (after gaining access to the palace a third time, Jones was packed off to sea).

For Albert, the scourge of waste and inefficiency, such incidents merely underlined the need for reform. He set to work, and to help him he called in a fellow Coburger, Baron Stockmar. Trained as a doctor, Christian Stockmar became personal physician, and subsequently general adviser and right-hand man, to Leopold, King of the Belgians, the uncle Victoria and Albert shared. After their marriage, which he had worked to bring about, he shuttled between his family in Coburg and the English court, where his wizened little figure became a familiar sight (Stockmar was permitted to wear long trousers rather than knee breeches to dinner, a rare concession to his poor health and sensitivity to cold). He acted as a trusted counsellor to, and at times intermediary between, the royal couple. He was hypo-chondriacal, serious-minded and conscientious to a fault; he was not perhaps the expert psychologist and authority on the English constitution that he believed himself to be. In September 1841 he produced one of the exhaustive memoranda, of Teutonic thoroughness, in which he specialised; in essence, he declared, the royal household betrayed a fatal 'absence of system'.

Reform did not happen overnight, but in 1846 the Prince finally came up with a scheme whereby the lord chamberlain, the lord steward and the master of the horse were to be maintained with their separate departments, but required to delegate authority in matters of discipline and security to two inspectors, resident in Buckingham Palace and Windsor, who would be directly responsible to the master of the household. The latter now became a figure of real authority – 'considered as the resident representative of the Lord Chamberlain in the Palaces' – with the power to co-ordinate the three different departments. No longer could a lord chamberlain, such as Lord Uxbridge, treat his department as his personal fiefdom, installing mistresses and favourites. War was waged on waste too. At Windsor it was said that the Prince had given instructions that the servants had to provide their own soap, as well as their own mops and brushes, and that they were no longer to be offered tea as an alternative to cocoa, while guests were only allowed two candles in their rooms. Naturally such reforms were unpopular, but they resulted in savings of some £25,000 a year.

With the Queen's pregnancy (far too soon for her liking) Albert's position was transformed, as the Regency Bill named him regent in the event of her death. Victoria began to share the contents of the red dispatch boxes, and from then it was only a matter of time before Albert made himself indispensable. In November 1840, exactly nine months after the royal wedding, the Princess Royal was born. 'I must confess that we regretted much at first that she was not a boy which we had so earnestly wished for,' the Queen wrote to Sarah Lyttelton, 'but we are quite grateful and contented now.'

Sarah had her 'first peep' six months later, and reported 'a fine, fat, firm, royal-looking baby, sitting bolt upright and too absurdly like the Queen; grave, calm and penetrating in her look'. She was dressed in a plain white muslin pelisse and a 'droll little Quaker shaped straw bonnet . . . she laughs, crows and kicks very heartily and the Prince tosses her often'. Sarah thought the Queen like 'all very young mothers, *exigeante*, and never thinks the baby makes progress enough or is good enough, has her constantly with her and thinks incessantly about her'. Nothing, she felt, that wouldn't be put right by a second child.

A year later, Albert Edward ('Bertie'), the Prince of Wales, arrived. This time the pregnancy had been more troublesome and the Queen was left feeling weak and low-spirited, compounded by anxiety that all was not well in the royal nursery. Mrs Southey (sister-in-law of the poet), a widow who had previously run a school for boys, had been engaged at the beginning of 1841 as superintendent of the nursery, on the recommendation of the Archbishop of Canterbury. She did not appear to be taking her duties seriously and, claiming homesickness, spent far too much time visiting friends. The Queen, as she complained to Melbourne, considered her 'totally unfit', while the nurse, Mrs Roberts, and the nursery maids were 'vulgar and from having no real head above them *constantly* quarrelling'. Stockmar, she went on, 'says we must have someone in whom we can place *implicit confidence*. He says a Lady of Rank and Title with a Subgoverness would be *best*, but *where* to find a person so situated, fit for place and if fit one who will be content to shut herself up in the Nursery and entirely from Society, as she must if she is really to superintend the whole.'

Meanwhile the Princess Royal was not thriving, something Sarah simply put down to being 'over-watched and over-doctored; always treated with what is most expensive, cheaper and common food and ways being often wholesomer'. Her diet of 'asses' milk and arrowroot and chicken broth' was measured out 'so carefully for fear of loading her stomach' that Sarah fancied 'she *leaves off hungry*'. In January 1842, when the royal couple returned from Claremont, they found the Princess Royal looking alarmingly white and thin. The Queen and Prince quarrelled violently. A furious note from the Prince to his wife, enclosed in a letter to Baron Stockmar, who had been drafted in as intermediary, read: 'Dr Clark has mismanaged the child and poisoned her with calomel and you have starved her. I shall have nothing more to do with it; take the child away and do as you like and if she dies you will have it on your conscience.'

Believing that keeping 'an influence over the Nursery underlings is one of her great aims', Albert had no doubt who was to blame for

trouble in the nursery: Baroness Lehzen. Lehzen *did* take a proprieto-
rial interest in the children; after the birth of the Prince of Wales, she
asked that the revenues from the Duchy of Cornwall be handed over
to her, for nursery expenses, rather than to the penny-pinching – as
she claimed – George Anson. For Albert this was unacceptable interference. The Queen protested to Stockmar: she was not, as Albert
claimed, 'infatuated' with Lehzen, indeed she hardly saw her any
more; she never discussed the nursery with her; her only wish was
for the Baroness to be given 'a quiet home in my house and see me
sometimes . . . about papers and toilette for which she is the greatest
use to me. A often and often thinks I see her when I don't.'

Opinion was divided over Lehzen. Charles Greville approved of her
as 'a clever agreeable woman', as did Sarah Lyttelton, while Anson
saw her as 'a channel for intrigue and mischief'. Albert, when it came
to Lehzen, quite abandoned his usual self-control and became positively violent: she was frivolous, incompetent and troublemaking, 'a
crazy, stupid intriguer, obsessed with the thirst for power, who regards
herself as a demi-God'.

Lehzen had been at Victoria's side since she was five years old and
had served her faithfully and defended her interests as her own mother,
so Victoria believed, had failed to do. She was deeply devoted to the
Queen and not a little jealous. Before the arrival of Albert, Lehzen,
together with Melbourne, had been the person on whom Victoria
relied absolutely; once she married, it was inevitable that Lehzen
should feel supplanted and Albert threatened. Lehzen's influence over
the Queen *had* greatly diminished, though she still signed all Her
Majesty's bills. But for Albert she was a divisive presence. That was
enough. The Queen was determined to be conciliatory: 'Dearest Angel
Albert, God only knows how I love him. His position is difficult, heaven
knows and we must do everything to make it easier.' And she humbly
acknowledged her own faults: 'the two years and a half when I was
completely my own mistress made it difficult for me to control myself
and to bend to another's will, but I trust I shall be able to conquer
it'. She was ready to submit. Lehzen had to go; the nursery had to
be reformed.

CHAPTER 4

Sarah Lyttelton: Superintendent of the Nursery

What was lacking in the nursery – and this was hardly Lehzen's fault – was good management and a competent successor to Mrs Southey, who, accepting that she had lost Albert's confidence, had written to him asking to be dismissed, confessing plaintively, 'No bird can return to her nest more eagerly than I to my own home.' For advice, Victoria and Albert turned to Stockmar, regarded as something of an oracle in matters of education, and he did not disappoint. In March 1842 he produced a thirty-two-page memorandum, in which he stressed the importance of appointing someone to take charge of the nursery who was 'good and intelligent, experienced in the treatment of children, of kind and refined manners, conciliatory and at the same time firm of purpose'. He already had just such a person in mind and proceeded to sound her out.

If Sarah Lyttelton had hesitated over accepting the position of lady of the bedchamber, this was of a different order altogether, a life-changing and momentous decision. Just when she had settled comfortably into the role of family matriarch, presiding over her children and the grandchildren multiplying at Hagley Hall, she was faced with the prospect of life as a permanent courtier, something from which she instinctively recoiled. Whereas her month-long stints as lady-in-waiting had been mere interruptions to family life, now she would make her home with the Queen. She would no longer live with her daughters and would only rarely, during occasional periods of leave, see the rest of her family. For the first time in her life she would have something like a job, and a demanding one at that. She bought herself a little time by suggesting two other possible candidates for the nursery, and once again consulted her brother, Lord Spencer. If she were to accept the post, she said, it would only be if 'the Queen should heartily concur in it and make the offer her own'.

In April, the Queen, convinced that 'none was so fit as Lady Lyttelton' to be superintendent, but afraid that she would decline the post, recorded in her journal that while out driving, she raised the subject: 'She was very much flattered, much alarmed though at the responsibility, and very diffident as to her own qualities. She however said she would be ready to devote her life to her duties. I said I feared it might be impossible on account of her daughters, but she replied that she would be quite satisfied if her daughters lived in a house near her here [Buckingham Palace] and at Windsor.'

The question of her daughters was the 'chief difficulty' for Sarah. Now, in addition to Caroline (twenty-six) and Lavinia (twenty-one), there was her orphaned niece Kitty Pole-Carew ('Kittich' or 'Kitticle'), whom she had taken into her care and treated as her own. She was anxious that the girls 'should not be considered as belonging in any sense to the society of the court', nor have contact with the royal children, a wish the Queen apparently shared. Their reasons were actually rather similar, though taken from opposing positions: Sarah saw court as a potentially corrupting environment; the Queen was suspicious of unknown members of society, though exactly how the Lyttelton girls could have been a bad influence on the royal children is hard to imagine.

Sarah also understood the importance of defining her role and responsibilities. Anxious not to be a mere underling obeying orders, she stipulated certain conditions: she was to have complete authority in the nursery; while she would naturally obey the royal parents, she reserved the right 'to ask questions, to discuss doubtful points and even to maintain her own opinions by argument, without reserve'; if the Queen and Prince wished to rebuke her, they should do so only in private; on Sundays the nurse should attend the afternoon service while Sarah, having gone to church in the morning, remained in the nursery; she was to be present at any medical examination of the children and have responsibility for their clothes. The prospect of leading a 'retired life' at court, cut off from society, was no hardship, in fact rather the opposite, but she hoped to be able to see her daughters regularly. How regularly was left to her own discretion: she could 'devote as much time to her children as she herself finds conscientiously and practically consistent with the Duties she has undertaken'.

By May, all was settled, and Sarah moved into her new quarters, a bedroom and sitting room in the Victoria Tower, close to the nurseries and above the Queen's private apartments. She was given a carriage for her own use and also to fetch her daughters, and a footman to be shared with the Prince of Wales. She no longer ate with the household, though she occasionally joined the Queen's dinner; luncheons – soup or fish (fried sole perhaps, or cod in oyster sauce), followed by meat (lamb cutlets, roast chicken, grouse, sweetbreads, duck) and a seasonal vegetable (asparagus, sea kale, spinach) – were eaten in her rooms. She read and digested all thirty-two pages of Stockmar's memorandum and assured the Baron that she fully entered 'into the views and principles so clearly explained in it'. As superintendent, she was expected to supervise the nurse, nursery maids and governesses (all prey to squabbling and jealousy), to give the children their first lessons, order their clothes, watch over their health and keep accounts.

Her first introduction to the Princess Royal ('Vicky', or 'Pussy' to the Queen, 'Princessy' to Lady Lyttelton) was not auspicious – she screamed so horribly that Sarah had to leave the room – but she was not discouraged. 'My little Princess is all gracefulness and prettiness, very fat and active, running about and talking a great deal. She is over sensitive and affectionate and rather irritable in temper at present, but it looks a pretty mind, only very unfit for roughing it through a hard life, which hers may be.' Princessy's initial suspicion melted away and she was soon won over by 'Laddle', as she called her new governess, occasionally, in imperious moments, resorting to 'Lyttelton!' First impressions of the Prince of Wales ('Princey') were also favourable:

'to judge by his noble countenance and calm manner', he was, she thought 'very intelligent and looks through his clear blue eyes full at one with a frequent very sweet smile'. Not all would share her estimate of his intelligence.

Under Sarah's wise and tactful management the nursery began to run more smoothly: Mrs Roberts, the head nurse, was replaced by the competent Mrs Sly; relations between nurses and nursery maids became more cordial; the Princess Royal's health improved, and a 'bonne', Mlle Aimée Charrier, was taken on at £125 a year, to teach her French. The Queen allowed herself to feel quite sanguine. 'Ly L. so agreeable and so sensible. She talked of Pussy's remarkable questions and intelligence and the clever way in which she uses her words,' she wrote in her journal after a few months of Lady Lyttelton at the helm.

As Sarah soon realised, the Princess Royal was a child of 'wonderful powers of head and heart', with a quick, retentive mind (something that could not be said of any of her siblings, with the possible exception of Leopold), which she shared with her father, and a sly wit, which she did not. 'Yesterday I was playing with her,' wrote Sarah of the two-year-old Vicky, 'when she suddenly took my old head between her tiny hands and very gently kissed my forehead, before I knew what she was about, and then laughed most slily. It was just as her mother does to her; the very drollest little compliment.' 'My dear Mama,' read Princessy's first (dictated) letter, aged four, 'I wish you very soon to come back and I will give you a very good love. I have been *munching* very well.' (This was not strictly true – she had been refusing to eat pudding or drink milk with her supper.) Her bons mots were passed about court. 'Who is it spits?' she asked, when splashed in the face while sailing in the royal yacht.

When it came to the management of children, Sarah favoured a regime of moderation, order and, most importantly, kindliness, much as her own children had experienced. Tantrums, she felt, were best ignored: 'It is odd that the Princess has exactly the same cry of "Wipe my eyes!" all the time she is roaring.' In principle she was against punishments – 'they wear out so soon and one is never sure they are fully understood by the child as belonging to the naughtiness' – but in the case of Vicky, punishments *were* all too frequently required. After an hour of atrocious behaviour she announced that she wished to speak to Sarah, declaring, '"I am very sorry Laddle but I mean to be just as naughty next time". This was followed by a long imprisonment. We shall see the effect.' On occasion, and this was quite in line with Victorian views on child-rearing, Sarah resorted to 'imprisonment' in a bedroom, or tied hands; even, on the instructions of the Prince, who held rather sterner views on discipline, a whipping for telling lies and 'roaring'.

Aged fifty-five, her own family quite grown up, Sarah now found herself supervising young children, and it was no small task, although nurses and nursery maids took care of the more physical aspects of the job, such as feeding, dressing and washing. Princessy's penchant for climbing meant constant vigilance. The prospect of a carriage drive with just her and the Queen made Sarah distinctly 'stomach-achy': 'a very nice plan for the bit and the Queen if all goes well. But a fearful chance of all going ill: roars, accidents, fatigue, fidget – all manner of dangers. I wish it were all over.' When Princessy was pulled by a footman in a little carriage through Windsor Home Park, Sarah trudged patiently alongside. In December 1842, she found herself sharing the Queen's 'special train' from London to Windsor (Victoria's first railway journey had taken place just months before), 'where nothing but royal live persons and their indispensable attendants are admitted'. With Mrs Sly and Mlle Charrier both ill, no maids-of-honour, all the 'night things, playthings, rusks, shawls etc.' left behind and only the Queen and a nursery maid to assist her, Sarah did her best to control Princey and Princessy, 'who were taken with tearing spirits, and a rage for crawling, climbing, poking into corners, upsetting everything' before becoming 'tired, cross and squally'. With what relief did she finally return to her Windsor rooms, to 'the great luxury of a nice fire, drawn curtains', Mr Sprague (her footman) and her 'reglar fine dinner'.

Finding suitable lodgings for Caroline, Lavinia and Kitty was no easy matter. When the Queen was at Buckingham Palace, the girls could live in the Lyttelton family home at 38 Grosvenor Place, where Sarah could see them and from where they could visit her, in her rooms, in the evenings. At Windsor, Sarah began by renting a house in the Cloisters, opposite St George's Chapel, and later arranged for the girls either to stay as paying guests with her friend Lady Grant, or to lodge in the Home Farm, in the Home Park, with a Mrs Engall, 'a tidy old body', who lived in one half of the house and acted as cook cum housekeeper. 'She sends up the neatest and daintiest luncheons every day to them and the lowest and cleverest bills every week to me,' reported Sarah (one such dainty luncheon comprised fricassee of chicken followed by apple and rice 'covered with a cloak of whipped eggs').

The Home Farm, looking out on to the royal poultry yard, with the royal dairy and the pigeon house close by, was a pretty spot, and once the girls had 'fitted up' their sitting room with books and a piano, Sarah thought it would be a 'comfortable perch' for them, though rather further from the castle than she would have liked. The Queen sometimes invited Caroline and Lavinia to dinner, or a concert or play, supposedly a treat for Sarah, who actually regarded such occasions as a mixed blessing: 'it will be too horrid to be all on the gridiron together – I had so much rather be fried by myself and I wish it all over'. Lodgings for the girls, including servants' wages, came at some cost, and to save money they were frequently sent to stay at Hagley; essentially they were homeless, parcelled about between palaces and family.

Marriage presented an escape from the ignominious existence of court follower, and Lavinia seized upon it, marrying Henry Glynne in October 1843. Henry was the vicar at Hawarden and the younger brother of Mary Lyttelton and Catherine Gladstone, thus further cementing the ties between Hawarden and Hagley. On her engagement, the Queen, as Lavinia told Henry, came up to her one evening to offer congratulations, and then turned to Caroline with, '"It will be a great separation for you", "It will indeed Ma'am", this was all that passed and we felt very much like two maids as usual.' The Prince gave her 'a most gracious bow and said "I beg to wish you joy! It will be a severe separation for Ly Lyttelton". I screwed up courage then and said, "Your Royal Highness has been so kind in allowing Mama to come with us next week"' – Lady Lyttelton had been granted five days' leave, a concession Lavinia considered 'so very nice', but hardly a great one for a daughter's wedding.

Sarah, at least initially, had reservations about Henry Glynne: 'not the man I had dreamt of for her husband, but exemplary in principle and conduct and perfect in temper and highly gentlemanlike and deeply attached to her, his first love, albeit he is 33 years old! If he was a few inches taller and had darker eyes and more firmness in manner and a little more of the kind of talent and strength of mind one wishes to *lean against* in ones journey of life, I believe he would please *me* better, but not her, for she sees no fault and wants no change and though not in love thinks she is and laughs and dances and sparkles and chatters about her happiness, and her Rectory, and her village and schools and curates and old women so that it lights up the room she is in.' Her misgivings were unfounded and it proved a most happy marriage.

Caroline and Kitty remained. Caroline was a bossy and unprepossessing young woman with a defective eye (a childhood accident with scissors) and a crooked shoulder (the legacy of overzealous harp playing). Kitty on the other hand was mild-mannered and self-effacing. Within the family they were affectionately referred to as the 'two dear spinnies' and no one appeared to expect their status to change. Indeed Sarah doubted that marriage could increase the happiness of 'our darling old maids', given that Caroline was a perfectly adequate 'husband' for Kitty. Their lives could not have been easy, though Caroline presented a robust front: 'I have a sort of pride wh. I don't half understand in making the best of my position – besides the duty of it, and I fancy a deal of natural independence and good spirits to help.' Sarah assured Kitty's older sister, Caroline Estcourt, that Kitty 'takes her share in the events and joys and sorrows of Castle and Cloister, with every appearance of resignation'.

When the girls were away, Sarah relied on their letters, partial compensation for 'the perpetual sorrows of separation', but she missed them sadly and worried that they missed her. 'My ladybirds did fly' (not to return for three months), she wrote forlornly one wet day at Windsor, as the children ran up and down the Corridor and she struggled with their Michelmas bills and the Prince of Wales's weaning.

'The children should be brought up as simply, and in as domestic a way as possible; (not interfering with their lessons) they should be as much as possible with their parents and learn to place their greatest confidence in them in all things,' wrote the Queen in a memorandum in 1844. Such precepts were put into practice to a degree. Nursery life was simple, even spartan, in keeping with Her Majesty's views on the benefits of fresh air and bracing temperatures: cold morning baths (unless a child was unwell, in which case warm were permitted), open windows, meagre fires, plenty of exercise in the open air. Food was plain: roast fowl, mutton cutlets, chicken broth and beef tea. Teething babies were given rhubarb and magnesia; sluggish bowels were eased with castor oil. The children saw their parents at least once a day, and often more.

The Prince, as Sarah noted, was an affectionate and involved father: standing on a chair to finish off a house of wooden bricks for Vicky; carefully putting on the Prince of Wales's glove; happy to turn somersaults in the hay or to chase butterflies. The Queen's feelings about motherhood were more ambivalent. She had no great love of babies, and though she became a fond, interested, even proud mother – the kind who would slip a note into a letter from Lady Lyttelton to her daughter-in-law Mary giving 'an account of her children's heights', and begging for 'an answer stating the heights of' hers – she could not help but see her children as an impediment to her greatest delight, her life with Albert. The children were subject to her growing compulsion to control and regulate the lives of those around her, be it family, household, servants or dogs. Sarah was bombarded with notes and memoranda about their health, bowels, diet, reading material, timetables, church attendance and prayers, and in the Queen's absence she was required to send daily bulletins from the nursery.

In August 1842, Sarah found herself left in sole charge of the children for the first time, when the Queen and the Prince made *their* first visit to Scotland. They left at the end of the month, setting sail from Woolwich. Sarah, remaining at Windsor, felt 'as if I ought to dislike the solitary responsibility rather more than I do!' and was reassured by the presence of Stockmar lurking 'in the antipodes of the Castle'. In the absence of the royal parents, she found herself responsible for the security of the children (threatening letters had apparently been received), checking access to their apartments last thing at night, 'the intricate turns and locks and guardrooms and the various intense precautions, suggesting the most hideous dangers, which I fear are not altogether imaginary'.

While Victoria and Albert spent two happy weeks touring Scotland, Sarah reported on the children's activities and the state of their health. The Prince of Wales had taken a shine to his nurse and cut a fifth tooth; Dr Brown (apothecary to the household) had suggested that as an introduction to solids he should be given milk thickened with rusk and a little cream and sugar, and a chicken bone to suck; he had 'quite relished his dinner . . . and grown much more *handy* in eating it', but the next day saw him suffering from some 'derangement of the bowels'. As for the Princess Royal, Sarah found her 'very grave and distant', her smiles sweet but 'rare', and felt that to prevent 'crises nerveuses' she might be better off with the same nursery maid, rather than alternating between two; having been shivery and unwell she had been put to rights by a warm bath and a sleep; her French was improving, thanks to Mlle Charrier, which gave grounds for hope 'that the worst plague of education will be spared Her Royal Highness, I mean the *French lesson*, the very name of which makes one shudder'. Islay and Dandy, the Queen's dogs, were 'quite well and exemplary in conduct', she added as an afterthought.

With Lady Lyttelton in place, Albert had only to dispatch Baroness Lehzen. Ill health was the official explanation for Lehzen's retirement, a fiction both she and the Queen accepted. She was granted a pension of £800 and the gift of a carriage. In preparation for her departure she began to teach Marianne Skerrett, one of the Queen's dressers, some of her duties, such as making copies of Her Majesty's outgoing correspondence in a letter press. This apparently rendered Miss Skerrett 'quite distracted', which is hardly to be wondered at given the contradictory nature of Lehzen's instructions: 'I have advised Miss Skerrett when the paper is not quite damp enough for letter pressing, to leave the letters for four minutes under the press, instead of two. It is always better if the paper is not too wet.'

Towards the end of September, not long after Victoria and Albert returned from Scotland, Lehzen returned various keys to the Queen. On the 28th, Sir James Clark, who had come to say goodbye, found her packing frantically and covered in dust. Early on the morning of the 30th she slipped away, leaving a letter for the Queen rather than saying goodbye in person, thinking it would be less painful. She went to Germany, to live with her sister, who, unhappily for Lehzen, died a few months later. Shortly after her departure, the Queen, who could barely remember a time when Lehzen *hadn't* been hovering at her side, confessed to Sarah, 'it was very painful to me . . . waking this morning, and recollecting she was really quite away. I had been dreaming she had come back to say goodbye to me and it was very uncomfortable at first. I had heard it mentioned before – that odd feeling on waking – but I had no experience of it. It is very unpleasant.'

Marianne Skerrett, who took over some of Lehzen's duties, was quite as much a fixture at court as had been Lehzen herself. Sharp-faced (all nose and chin) and meagre (under five feet, like her royal mistress, and 'thin as a shred of paper'), she was a familiar figure as she scurried about the palace. Amongst the household she was regarded as a 'character', for being opinionated, plain-spoken and 'most eager in her likings and dislikings', while the Queen considered her 'quite a superior person . . . of immense literary knowledge and sound understanding, of the greatest discretion and straightforwardness'. Her father had been a West Indian plantation owner, her uncle had been

Queen Charlotte's sub-treasurer and she herself was highly intelligent, well-read and fluent in French and German.

'Skerrett', as the Queen called her, had served as a dresser since 1837. Dressers – two of whom waited on the Queen, along with two wardrobe maids – were generally of genteel birth and, as upper servants, enjoyed a certain status, with their own bedrooms and sitting rooms in the Augusta Tower, adjoining the Victoria Tower, and a salary of around £120 (this varied slightly according to length of service). Essentially they were glorified ladies' maids, responsible for the Queen's wardrobe and jewels. Their duties included 'scrupulous' checking of Her Majesty's clothes, seeing what needed to be mended or cleaned and that all were 'kept properly and in their places and in proper drawers appointed for them'; thinking 'over *well* everything that is wanted or may be wanted when Her Majesty goes anywhere, likewise when Her Majesty goes to London to hold a Court etc.'; and supervising the wardrobe maids, making sure they carried out *their* duties and attended to their health.

There were none amongst the Queen's servants who had such regular and intimate contact with her as her dressers, and it was thus a highly confidential position. Dressers were explicitly discouraged from forming friendships with other ladies' maids, and both they and the wardrobe maids were usually appointed either on a personal recommendation – Miss Skerrett had been recommended by the Marchioness of Lansdowne, a lady of the bedchamber – or because of some existing court connection. Skerrett, one of whose many duties was to engage wardrobe maids, explained to Charles Andrews, who was known to the Queen as a servant of her uncle Leopold, that his daughter Mary Ann should expect to be in 'continual attendance' on Her Majesty; that her salary would be £80; that 'a good memory, good temper and activity are the things which Her Majesty considers to be indispensable', while cool hands, good health and punctuality were all desirable.

Marianne Skerrett was a kind of supernumerary dresser, as her £200 salary reflected, with duties reaching far beyond the wardrobe, though these were extensive enough: liaising with the mistress of the robes about state 'dress', ordering clothes, negotiating with milliners, shawl makers, hosiers, glovers, shoe makers, hatters, furriers, habit makers, dressing-case makers, jewellers and suppliers of lace, embroidery, tartans and poplins. After Lehzen's departure, she acted as a kind of domestic secretary and general factotum, paying small bills incurred by the dressers and wardrobe maids, writing to tradesmen and corresponding with the lithographers and photographic colourists who endlessly recorded the royal family. It was Skerrett who saw to the 'biting' of the plates when Victoria and Albert took up etching; who arranged for some pigs from one of the Prince's Windsor farms to be sent to a friend of Lehzen's in Germany; who ordered china for Balmoral; who replied to begging letters from the daughter of the Queen's old singing teacher; who organised Christmas presents on behalf of Her Majesty; who ordered 'pockets' and socks for the royal children, although strictly speaking this was Sarah Lyttelton's province.

A great deal of Skerrett's time was taken up in liaising with the artists who painted the royal family and supplied paintings and statues for the palaces. Writing in French, she arranged sittings with the Paris-based Franz Xaver Winterhalter. She asked Edwin Landseer, a favourite of the Queen ever since he had painted her spaniel Dash in 1836, if he could be sure to come to Windsor while the Prince was out shooting, since his portrait of the Princess Royal was to be a surprise Christmas present. She received regular reports from the sculptor John Gibson, who lived in Rome, on works in progress, and enquiries from Thomas Uwins, the surveyor of pictures, about prospective purchases for the royal collection.

Skerrett was something of a rarity at court, not least for the fact that she retained through twenty-five long, overworked years a lively interest in the world beyond court, and the artistic and literary life of London in particular. Landseer was a firm friend and regular correspondent. He lent her books; she commiserated with his gout and complained about packing amid terrible clouds of smoke from the chimneys at Windsor: 'there is no such thing as a *cheerful* glass in this place to look through or into, we are almost blinded and poisoned by smoke, it is not possible to describe the discomfort of *forced* activity among boxes books etc. in a wind and noise one can hardly hear oneself speak and smoke slowly rolling out of chimneys *with fires* and without them! The Queen's and the Pr's rooms are all free I think from these bothers but all the common people of the Palace are miserable with it.'

They discussed Millais and Dickens. Skerrett greatly admired the latter for 'opening the eyes to the miseries and abuses which surround one . . . honour is due to everyone who helps to destroy what is evil and Mr Dickens stands foremost among that honourable sect'. She felt sure that 'change and bettering' would come, though not, in all likelihood, in her lifetime. But on reading *Bleak House* she decided she liked it rather less than the other novels – Dickens, she felt, could not do 'gentlewomen' and she thought the ending 'weak and feckless'. Having seen the great man himself for about five minutes on a rare evening out in London, she reported him 'in good feather'. 'Good bye dear Sir Edwin,' she finished, 'do not say that you cannot read this because it is *real good stuff*.'

Reading Skerrett's letters – barely legible, largely devoid of punctuation, liable to sudden swerves and U-turns – is no easy matter. They give every impression of having been written at speed, on the hoof, in snatched moments of leisure. 'There are things that pass through my head but do not stay long in it,' she confessed. For Skerrett, spinning in perpetual motion, time was a luxury she couldn't afford. Furthermore, as she told the actor-manager Charles Kean, another friend (until she turned against him for allowing fame to go to his head), who frequently urged her to accept a free box to see his latest production, she had a 'great many pin pricks' to contend with.

She devoured, on its publication, Fanny Burney's *Diary and Letters*, explaining to Mrs Barrett, Fanny's niece and the book's editor, that reading it brought up 'a great deal of auld lang syn', as she recognised parallels between Fanny's situation and her own. As second keeper of the robes to Queen Charlotte, Fanny had risen at six, attended the Queen's interminable morning and evening toilettes, been subject to the tyranny of the chief keeper of the robes, 'Mrs' Schwellenberg, and had no more than a couple of hours a day to herself. Like Fanny,

Skerrett felt that hers was a life of some servitude – 'I am not at all mistress of my time and go out little and never see any one here but my sister.'

Sarah Lyttelton had 'pin pricks' of her own. After her first few months as superintendent, she assured her family, in somewhat ambivalent terms, that she was quite reconciled to her new life: 'I am treated with perfect kindness, both positive and negative, by the Queen and the Prince and allowed to be much more free and easy in mind and quiet and uncourtly than I could have hoped to be.' She was managing Princey and Princessy successfully. There was novelty and satisfaction too in actually earning a living and providing for her daughters. 'I sometimes feel glad, as well as thankful, that I am doing what I used to fancy I wished to do, really *working* for my bread.'

But doubts and anxieties persisted, and privately she agonised about the 'questionable step' she'd taken. Was she suited to her position? Could she adequately discharge the responsibilities laid upon her? Was she failing her own children? Holidays, or 'holydays' as Sarah called them, were all too infrequent – a few days when Lavinia got married, and again when she had a baby. When the girls were with her, Sarah worried that their status, attached yet apart from court, was uneasy, even unhealthy; when they were away, she longed for nothing more than to 'dine in long sleeves with dear old Caroline and Kitty'.

At times of crisis or anxiety, Sarah turned to the Rev. Gurdlestone, the vicar of a parish near Hagley Hall, who acted as a kind of confessor and counsellor, and to whom she felt able to voice feelings that otherwise went unexpressed. In the autumn of 1842, she admitted to Gurdlestone that she felt 'sadly insufficient for the task' she had undertaken and requested a prayer 'for the special help of God in doing the awful duties of my office'. She went on to outline 'the dangers to myself from the strange necessity I am under of passing the last years of my life, so domestic and peaceful in its earlier stages, in a court – separated indeed from its gay society in a great degree and most indifferent to its splendours which some years of familiarity reduce to nothing, but still it is a life of luxury tempting one to think much of earthly things – a life too of a good deal of laborious exertion'. She feared both the rigours of the job and the insidiously corrupting effects of palace life.

The prayer was supplied and proved a 'great and daily comfort'. She hoped for more. But two months later she made another appeal to Gurdlestone. Despite being surrounded by 'blessings and comforts' and 'treated with constant kindness and only too much deference and respect', she found herself 'often tried with wretched low spirits, I fear discontent with my place altogether – its toil (no great matter except for an indolent person) and its breaking off almost all inter-course with my family except what I consider as indispensable to my conscience, with my dear daughters who, while I live *ought* to be much with me and are so by the Queen's kind arrangement. These priva-tions and evils I knew of when I accepted my office, but I find them worse to bear than I had believed and yet I *must* bear them . . . Oh could my feelings when I am praying but last when I return to my day's work . . . you are the first and only person to whom I have ever said so much.'

Sarah Lyttelton's High Church faith lay at the core of her exist-ence, and part and parcel of that faith was a sense of duty: duty to her sovereign was simply an extension of duty to God. She struggled to serve both. Writing to her friend Lady Grant, Sarah quoted Gurdlestone, '"Are we on the path of duty? Let us tread it steadily, cheerfully, thankfully. For why? Its end and not far off is Heaven!" But the first question will come across one, at least it does across me and I do not gain the power of answering it.' Duty had prompted her to take up a position for which she had little or no inclination, yet in doing so had she failed in her duty to her family? How could one be sure of having found the 'path of duty', let alone of navigating it with good heart?

Sarah would never quite shake off her feelings of inadequacy, but she was more than equal to the task she had undertaken. The Queen and Prince had found someone of rare good sense, to whom they could entrust their children with perfect confidence; the chil-dren themselves flourished under her wise and kindly rule, benefited from her patient instruction (mistakes made in the education of the Prince of Wales were not of Sarah's making) and grew to love her dearly.

Her distaste for court, rooted in temperament and principle, was another matter. Court would always bring 'its usual trials . . . so strangely mixed of prosperous and adverse, wealth and honours with toil and thraldom, luxury and privation, crowd and loneliness all jumbled together!' Lack of books, indeed the general intellectual poverty of Victoria's court, was a perpetual source of frustration. After George and Mary Lyttelton had lent her a volume of Macaulay, she wrote: 'having been for a few days able to read, with a sort of delight difficult to describe, it feels like rain upon dry ground – though of no real use, all dries up again and is wholly forgotten in a few hours, but still it must be better for one than *only* casting up accounts and keeping peace among nurses or even teaching the multiplication tables'. She never became reconciled to her life as a courtier – that 'ugly word, though the thing *ought not* to be by any means at least in this court' – and often suffered from loneliness (exacerbated by the separation of the nursery from the rest of the household, not that she saw this as a deprivation) and always from the absence of her children. Material comfort and social status meant little or nothing to Sarah; what sustained her was the belief that 'in accepting my awful office I did that which I was bound to do'.

CHAPTER 5

Charlotte Canning: Lady of the Bedchamber

With no country residence of their own, and eager, especially in the summer months, to escape the foul air of London, as well as the formality of Windsor, the Queen and Prince liked to visit Claremont, the eighteenth-century Palladian house in Surrey belonging to Victoria's uncle Leopold. The Queen was much attached to Claremont, partly because of its link to her uncle and partly because it was small (relatively), pretty and private – a house not a palace. Sarah Lyttelton was rather less enthusiastic. Though allowing Claremont to be 'a very handsome private chateau' and the gardens beautiful, she deplored the 'stiff dinners, ditch water and cold bedrooms'.

However, in July 1842, Claremont provided two attractions. First was the presence of Archdeacon Wilberforce, chaplain to Albert. The silver-tongued Samuel Wilberforce, known as 'Soapy Sam', was a High Churchman – though careful to distance himself from the Oxford Movement – and thus a man after Sarah's own heart. His Sunday sermon at Claremont did not disappoint: 'It was in manner and language the highest in eloquence and his voice and earnest simplicity . . . leave one with no wish except that one could remember every word and oh, practise every precept. I was so pleased, sitting close behind Prince Albert, to observe him nodding his head in warm approbation repeatedly and then turning round gently to see if the Queen was equally impressed. Everybody says he will be a bishop' (Wilberforce became Bishop of Oxford).

With the Archdeacon 'to listen to and Lady Canning to admire', Sarah admitted her breakfast was a good deal more enjoyable than usual. This was the second attraction – Lady Charlotte Canning, the Queen's new lady-in-waiting. 'A very pleasant talk with Lady Canning in the afternoon,' wrote Sarah, 'she is exceedingly agreeable and admirable in every way I think – so simple and unselfish.' She also noted, with approval, the wreath of dahlias (dahlia wreaths, symbolic of dignity and elegance, were commonly worn by the Queen's ladies) in Charlotte's hair. This was the occasion of Charlotte Canning's first court waiting.

In May 1842, on the resignation of Lady Dalhousie, a vacancy had arisen in the royal household, and the Queen had written to Charlotte, reminding her that they'd known each other since childhood – they'd met holidaying in Ramsgate – and inviting her to become her new lady of the bedchamber. It was a position she had been close to offering her the previous year.

The question of to what extent the Queen's ladies were considered political appointments was a somewhat murky area, as Victoria had recognised and shamelessly exploited to her advantage in the Bedchamber Crisis of 1839. In the summer of 1841, with a general election looming and the Whigs clearly heading for defeat, nobody wanted a repetition of the debacle of 1839. The Queen, coached by the Prince, had in fact mellowed towards both the Tories and Robert Peel himself. And with Albert by her side she could contemplate the loss of Melbourne with relative equanimity.

A memorandum drawn up in May 1841 stated: 'The Queen considers it her right (and is aware that her Predecessors were particularly tenacious of this right) to appoint her Household. She, however, gives up the great offices of State and those of her Lords-in-Waiting, Equerries and Grooms-in-Waiting, who are in Parliament, to the appointment of the Prime Minister, subject to her approval.' She went on to add, 'the Queen has always appointed her Ladies of the Bedchamber herself, but has generally mentioned their names to the Prime Minister before appointing them'; if there were grounds for objection, 'the Queen would probably not appoint the lady'. However, women of the bedchamber and maids-of-honour were appointed by her alone without consultation. This was a significant change of position from 1839, when she had flatly refused Peel's request to give up any of her ladies of the bedchamber; now she was willing to consult, even to make concessions.

Meanwhile, the Prince, aided and abetted by George Anson, was working behind the scenes to ensure that Peel's path into office should be a smooth one. Anson was sent to Peel, without the Queen's knowledge, to discuss the question of the ladies, and in particular those – the Duchess of Sutherland, Lady Normanby and the Duchess of Bedford (formerly Lady Tavistock) – married to prominent Whigs. Peel insisted that there was to be no question of *forcing* the Queen – indeed, he would find that 'repulsive' to his feelings; rather he hoped that she herself would announce the resignation of the three ladies in question; it should come from *her* not him.

In July, the Tories swept into power. Peel showed perfect tact and the Queen showed herself perfectly amenable, agreeing to the resignation of the Duchess of Sutherland, Lady Normanby and the Duchess of Bedford, though the departure of the latter brought a temporary reversal, as Anson recorded: 'The Queen said the Tories would say if she submitted to this that she had been vanquished and lowered before the world. The Prince said I fear the Ladies' gossip is again setting about you. The Queen on that burst into tears which could not be stopped for some time.'

But her tears subsided and she accepted the new Tory regime and the consequent changes at court with good grace. Lord Liverpool became lord steward, Lord De La Warr lord chamberlain and Lord Jersey master of the horse (all three suggested by Peel, in consultation with the Queen), while Lady Dunmore and Lady Jocelyn were appointed as the new ladies of the bedchamber. Lady Jocelyn, formerly Frances Cowper, had been one of the Queen's bridesmaids. Her mother, Lady Cowper, Lord Melbourne's sister, had recently married her long-standing love, Lord Palmerston, a development of which Her Majesty could not quite approve, finding remarriage, especially amongst the middle-aged, distasteful. Frances was also newly married, and Sarah Lyttelton could not help feeling that she should not be separated from her husband – 'it does not suit my views of honey year habits at all' – but the Queen saw the presence of the beautiful Fanny 'as a nice sugar-plum for herself'.

Sarah lamented the loss of the Duchess of Sutherland, to whom she'd grown attached, and dreaded the arrival of 'some odious new Duchess', but she was soon 'quite at ease and becalmed by' the new mistress of the robes, the Duchess of Buccleuch. Meeting Peel one evening at Windsor, she was 'struck with the quickness and watchful, cautious, characteristic sagacity' which he applied to learning 'a new round game', and noted that the Queen 'was excessively and pointedly civil to him'.

From 1841, *only* the mistress of the robes, amongst the Queen's ladies, was considered a political appointment, changing with the government, and when it came to selecting those ladies, Her Majesty, as she explained to Melbourne, tried to 'choose moderate people who would not have scruples to resign in case another Administration should come in, as changing was disagreeable to her'. In 1841 she had decided against asking Charlotte Canning to join her household precisely because her husband was a member of Peel's new government. A year later, she changed her mind.

If a template had existed for the ideal lady of the bedchamber, then it would have been hard to find one more fitting than Charlotte Canning: irreproachable of character (a prerequisite at the Victorian court), discreet (we might wish she had been less so), intelligent (an attribute not always to be found amongst the Queen's ladies) and beautiful (like many not blessed with good looks, Victoria was highly susceptible to those of others). If the Queen wished to fault her, it could only have been for her High Church leanings, which she personally regretted but was prepared to overlook. As the daughter of an ambassador and the wife of a clever young politician, Charlotte was well-travelled, well-connected and socially adept: court held no particular terrors. Furthermore, she was a proficient maker of wreaths – as noted by Sarah Lyttelton – a talented artist and fluent in French, all useful accomplishments when in royal service.

As to whether it was a position that Charlotte welcomed, we can only guess. There were financial considerations to be taken into account: the Cannings, while not rich, had a London house, nine servants, a carriage and a yacht (standard aristocratic trappings) to maintain – her £500 salary could only have been welcome. And personal considerations too: Charlotte's seven-year marriage had brought her neither great happiness, nor children. While separation from their families, for a month at a time, was a very real hardship for some of the Queen's ladies (Sarah Lyttelton noticed Lady Dunmore writing a letter to her husband with tears in her eyes as she gazed at photographs of him and her children), such was not quite the case for Charlotte. However, the question of clothes gave her pause for thought: the necessity of stretching her wardrobe to accommodate all manner of occasions, from drawing rooms to nautical expeditions, not to mention the frequent court mournings. But this was a minor cavil. Charlotte didn't need long to consider the Queen's offer, replying the next day with expressions of 'heartfelt thanks' and assurances that to serve 'Your Majesty's Royal Person' could only be a 'source of pride and gratification'.

The duties of a lady of the bedchamber had changed considerably since the reign of Elizabeth I, when, as the most senior of the Queen's ladies, she would have helped with Her Majesty's dressing and toilette (now the province of the dressers and wardrobe maids), a position of intimacy allowing unique access and thus opportunity for advancement. Elizabeth I's ladies were divided into four tiers: ladies of the bedchamber, ladies of the privy chamber, ladies-in-waiting, and, finally, maids-of-honour. By the nineteenth century, ladies of the bedchamber and ladies-in-waiting had become synonymous, ladies of the privy chamber had disappeared altogether, none performed any kind of menial or bodily services and relations were altogether more formal. Elizabeth's ladies also waited on a rota system, but, unlike Victoria's, who had to obtain special permission if they wished, for example, to go to London for the day, they were free to come and go from court as they pleased. Charlotte's duties, tending to the irksome rather than the arduous, were essentially companionable and social: accompanying the Queen on her daily rides or drives, attending state occasions and drawing rooms, keeping the maids-of-honour in order and entertaining visiting Royalties. She was expected to dine with the Queen, unless the royal couple were dining tête-à-tête, and to show enthusiasm for after-dinner card games, dancing and music.

Victoria's ladies were, in the main, drawn from the minor aristocracy, the wives, widows and daughters of peers, who, if not exactly in need, were certainly not averse to a modest boost to their incomes. The less exalted position of woman of the bedchamber was frequently offered to well-born women in slightly distressed circumstances, someone, for instance, who lived alone above a shop in Sloane Street on £400 a year. Connections were all-important, with court appointments frequently passed both across families and through generations. In 1842, Charlotte's cousin Caroline Cocks was already a maid-of-honour, and a few years later the Queen would invite her sister Louisa to join her as lady of the bedchamber.

What sort of young woman was this new recruit? That she was viewed as a person of distinction is suggested by her invitation in February 1842 to an elaborate luncheon held by Baron Bunsen, the scholarly Prussian ambassador, in honour of King Frederick William IV of Prussia. Apart from the Baroness, who thought her 'most amiable and conversible . . . a thoroughly harmonious person', Charlotte found herself the only female guest 'among eighty savants', an odd assortment including Quakers, clergymen, artists, politicians, Thomas Carlyle and Dr Arnold. She was placed next to the King. If she could hold her own at the Bunsens' lunch, she could certainly do so at court. And indeed she did. Government ministers like Lord Palmerston and Lord Granville did their best to arrange their visits so as to coincide with Lady Canning and benefit from some intelligent conversation; maids-of-honour regarded tea in her rooms (ladies-in-waiting, since the birth of the royal children, were lodged in the Augusta or York Towers at Windsor) as the greatest of treats, and were invariably grateful for her presence – calm, sensible and amused.

Charlotte was born in 1817, in Paris, where her father, Lord Stuart de Rothesay, was ambassador. Lord Stuart was the grandson of the

3rd Earl of Bute, while his wife, Lady Elizabeth, was a daughter of the Earl of Hardwicke. The 'short and stumpy' Stuarts were generally agreed to be a remarkably plain pair, yet by some genetic quirk they produced, in Charlotte and her younger sister Louisa, two remarkably beautiful daughters. Charlotte's looks were too emphatic for prettiness; rather, with her mass of dark hair, broad cheekbones, strongly marked brows and heavy-lidded dark blue eyes, she was strikingly handsome. A portrait by Winterhalter, commissioned by the Queen in 1849, shows her in profile (just a hint of matronliness creeping in) with her hair plaited and coiled at the nape of her neck; so long was Charlotte's hair that while being brushed and dressed it would constantly get under the feet of her maid. Her features speak of strength; her expression of serene self-possession. Louisa, on the other hand, was a softer, more soulful beauty, much admired by the Pre-Raphaelites. When Charlotte and Louisa visited William Holman Hunt in his Cheyne Walk studio in 1853, to view *The Light of the World*, Hunt confessed to being quite overwhelmed by the sight of the 'beautiful sisters' ascending his staircase.

Charlotte spent her early childhood in Paris, where she acquired the perfect French that would later stand her in good stead at court. When Lord Granville succeeded Lord Stuart at the Paris embassy in 1831, the Stuarts returned to London and took up residence in their newly built house in Carlton House Terrace. Three years later, shortly after Charlotte came out, she caught the eye of the handsome Hon. Charles Canning, son of George (the former prime minister), recently come down from Oxford with a first, and on course for a political career. He proposed. Charlotte, who had fallen in love, wished to accept him. Her father, however, thanks to a long-standing political feud with George Canning, refused to countenance the match. Charlotte was apparently reduced to keeping watch from the terrace of the Stuarts' house for a glimpse of her beloved as he rode along the Mall. But under family pressure, Lord Stuart relented, and on 5 September 1835, at St Martin-in-the-Fields, the two were married.

Charles Canning, or 'Carlo', as Charlotte called him, was elected to Parliament in 1836, shuttling across to the House of Lords a year later, on inheriting his title. When Peel came to power in 1841, he became under-secretary for foreign affairs. Outwardly Canning possessed all the attributes of a model husband: good looks, good name, good prospects. His deficiencies were more personal in nature: a chilly remoteness and reserve and, later, quite flagrant infidelity. For Charlotte, marriage brought no small measure of humiliation and disappointment, without the consolation of children. While sustained, or at least supported, by the twin pillars of faith and duty, her dignity and strength of character would be much tested.

At twenty-five years old, the new lady of the bedchamber was just two years older than her royal mistress, though some way ahead in terms of sophistication and maturity. Charlotte had settled into the lines of her character. The Queen, on the other hand, was still in many ways unformed: the force of her personality was clear enough; what direction that force would take was not. Physically they could hardly have been more different – the stately beauty beside the dumpy hausfrau – but there were differences of manner, of disposition too. Where the Queen, at least in private, was passionate, impulsive and frank, a high-spirited young woman who would run into Charlotte's room to show off a baby, or to gossip, Charlotte was self-disciplined, circumspect and proud (excessively so, thought some), a noble figure in the eyes of her friends, and one increasingly hung about with sadness.

They shared, however, these two young women, immense natural dignity and a keen sense of duty. Both were strong characters, yet prepared to bow to the better-trained intellects of their handsome husbands, with whom they were much in love. While they did not become friends – the Queen, as Charlotte rightly observed, did not make friends of her ladies – a good deal of mutual respect and affection grew between them.

In November 1842, Charlotte busied herself with 'preparations for the trousseau' which her long waiting would require. At the beginning of December, a letter from Sarah Lyttelton summoned her to Walmer Castle, on the Kent coast, which the Duke of Wellington had put at the Queen's disposal to escape the 'fevers' at large in London, and where the household huddled against the icy draughts that whistled about the castle ('needless to go out for air', commented Sarah) and succumbed to heavy colds. Lehzen had left a few months earlier, and with 'no Baroness to carry messages', Charlotte found that she saw a good deal more of the Queen. Two weeks later, the royal party returned to Windsor, where Charlotte was to celebrate her first royal Christmas – Charles had been invited to join her – and where she would remain until after the New Year.

Christmas presented the royal family at its most domestic and virtuous, a novel enough spectacle: 'you can't think how simple and happy all the Royalty looked, just like any other family of the most united and domestic tastes', wrote Eleanor Stanley, who became a maid-of-honour in 1841. This very ordinariness was of course a crucial factor in Their Majesties' appeal. On Christmas Eve, Sarah Lyttelton took Charlotte and the maids-of-honour, Georgiana Liddell (Georgy became a favourite with Charlotte, who thought her 'cleverer and more solid' than her many sisters – one of whom, Lady Normanby, was a former lady of the bedchamber – but with 'all their good temper') and Harriet Lister (dismissed as 'very babyish but perfectly harmless'), to visit the royal children in the nursery. The Princess Royal, dressed in dark blue velvet, white shoes and yellow kid mittens, was extremely loquacious and did her best to persuade Georgy Liddell to try on a frock she had just been given by her grandmother, the Duchess of Kent. Charlotte regretted not seeing more of the children – with none of her own, she enjoyed those of others – or of Sarah, who was much taken up by her charges.

Present-giving took place, German-style, that evening. Before dinner, the household were called to the oak room, the Queen's dining room, near her private rooms in the Victoria Tower. There they found the Queen and the Prince standing by a large table covered in a white cloth and bearing a Christmas tree decorated with sugar plums, gilt walnuts and candles. Around the tree were piled presents, which the Queen, who had carefully written the labels herself, proceeded to hand out. Charlotte received a bracelet hung with a tiny reproduction of

Winterhalter's portrait of Her Majesty, together with a paisley shawl, while the maids-of-honour had enamel brooches with two rubies and a diamond in the shape of a bow, an almanac and some gingerbread. The Queen's gifts followed a tried and tested formula: for the ladies a piece of jewellery, a mildly improving book, a pocket book, sometimes a print of the royal children; and for the gentlemen, riding whips, pencil cases, pins, studs or rings.

It was then the turn of the household to witness the royal present-opening, in the Queen's sitting room. Here individual trees, for the Queen, the Prince, the Duchess of Kent and the children, were set up on tables, surrounded by presents, which were dutifully admired and exclaimed over. On Christmas Day the Cannings attended a service in the private chapel (one of Albert's innovations, formerly the room used by the band) and joined in a 'great deal of feasting' on 'enormous meats and pies'. Sarah Lyttelton, having attended, along with Caroline, the Queen's dinner on Christmas Eve, passed the day quietly, taking luncheon (smelts, turkey, pork and cauliflower) in her rooms and spending the evening with her girls.

In later years, the Windsor Christmases palled for Charlotte and the present-giving in particular became 'a *very* disagreeable cere-mony', though the presents themselves gave satisfaction. When she was entrusted with the task of buying books, to be included in the governesses' Christmas boxes, she passed on the commission to her mother: 'a French book and an English book are wanted to be added to some Christmas presents for the governesses and poor Skerrett is quite in despair how to get them . . . any book if nicely bound wd do . . . an illustrated Sévigné or any modern book with or without prints – or annuals, but not too trashy . . . Please send the parcels with "for the Queen" written outside and let the shops know that what are not taken will be sent back.' On reflection, Charlotte advised against Martin Tupper's *Proverbial Philosophy* – too trashy perhaps – but thought the more high-minded Ruskin's *Stones of Venice* or Mrs Jameson's *Paintings, Sacred and Legendary Art* might be suitable.

The New Year was celebrated quietly, as the Queen was five months pregnant, and only one guest, the Duke of Wellington, joined the royal dinner. On New Year's Day, Charlotte was presented with an annual by the Queen, who was apparently more than satisfied with her, recording in her journal: 'After luncheon walked out with Lady Canning who is a remarkably nice person, so quiet, unaffected and gentle and so ready to do anything.' Charlotte wrote to her mother, diplomatically: 'I have liked this quiet waiting very much but of course am happy to go home again.' Home was the Cannings' house in Grosvenor Square, where she returned on 3 January.

To expect trenchant views from Charlotte is to be disappointed. The particular cast of her personality dovetailed with her circumstances, as a conventional, aristocratic young woman in the mid nineteenth century, to make her no more likely to complain of the selfishness or caprices of the Queen than of the infidelity of her husband. For a woman like Charlotte, self-pity, blame or resentment simply had no currency. It seems more useful to regard her as admirably disciplined rather than frustratingly proper, though proper she certainly could be. In 1846, the Duke of Atholl described his amazement at receiving a note from Lady Canning inviting him to dinner, which had been left *open* (an open letter could be read by anyone, thus proclaiming the blamelessness of its contents), which merely confirmed his view of her as 'the most proper person I ever met . . . a model of correctness'.

The very qualities that commended Charlotte to the Queen make her an opaque commentator and correspondent. Her letters, written to her mother and her sister, in her neat, regular hand, faithfully record her court waitings, her travels with her husband, matters of dress, small domestic dramas, the marital prospects and health of relatives and acquaintances (all preoccupations shared by the Queen), but rarely judge, applaud or complain. We know that she had considerable natural intelligence, that she held strong opinions; we sense that in the main she chose to withhold them. All her letters to her husband, where Charlotte might have been franker and less guarded – though knowing something of her marriage, perhaps not – have disappeared.

There are, however, hints: small darts aimed at the Prince; the occasional groan of boredom; a flash of impatience.

In person, Charlotte was apparently more forthright, even irreverent. Mary Ponsonby, who, as a maid-of-honour in the 1850s, came to know her well, and was one of the few Charlotte counted as a real friend, remembered how she delighted in the Windsor library, in Mary's 'audacities' (humour was not one of Charlotte's salient characteristics – something else she shared with the Queen – but Mary made her laugh) and in 'talking over the absurdities of the place': the solemn nodding at mealtimes, for example, which greeted the Prince's pronouncement that eating was a waste of time.

When not in waiting, Charlotte led the life of many an aristocratic wife, one of enervating idleness: country house visits, shooting parties (Charles Canning was a keen shot), expeditions on the Cannings' yacht, the *Fair Rosamond*. Highcliffe Castle, the Stuart family home, featured largely. Lord Stuart de Rothesay, a fan of the Gothic revival that swept England during the 1840s (the 'de Rothesay' was a romantic embellishment) had re-created Highcliffe, in Gothic style, from the ruins of the original house built by his grandfather, Lord Bute, on a spectacular, if precarious, site overlooking Christchurch Bay in Hampshire. There, in November 1845, Lord Stuart died, and thereafter Charlotte spent much of her time managing the house and working on the garden.

The greatest possible treat for Charlotte – though all too infrequent – was a visit to Curraghmore, the Irish estate belonging to the Marquis of Waterford, husband of her sister Louisa. Like Charlotte, Louisa was childless, profoundly religious and a fine artist – Dante Gabriel Rossetti thought she 'would have been really great, if not born such a swell and such a stunner', and much the same could have been said of Charlotte. Louisa's marriage to the Marquis of Waterford was greeted with general surprise. Waterford, commonly known as the 'mad Marquis', was a figure straight from the pages of *Tom Jones*, a lover of hunting, women and high-jinks, such as jumping his horse over a laid dining-room table for a bet. To Charlotte and Lady Stuart, who lamented his 'rough manners', he seemed a most unlikely choice for the gentle and saintly Louisa.

Theirs, however, was an immensely happy marriage. Under Louisa's civilising influence Waterford became a reformed character, a reforming landlord and a model of uxoriousness. The Waterfords, unlike the Cannings, enjoyed perfect contentment: Lou described to Charlotte how after a 'temperate meal of tea, chicken and roast potatoes', she would spend the evening reading aloud to her husband. Only in exceptional circumstances could Waterford contemplate separation from his wife, so when, in 1851, the Queen, who liked to keep household appointments within families, broached the possibility of Louisa replacing Lady Portman and joining Charlotte as a lady of the bedchamber, the violence of the reaction from Ireland was predictable. It was left to Charlotte, no doubt aware that for the retiring Louisa, the prospect of a court appointment was equally unwelcome, to relay Waterford's objections to the Queen. Her Majesty regretted that 'your sister's duties as a wife' prevented her from becoming one of her ladies, but could only allow the excellence of her reasons.

'Everything else changes, but the life here never does and is always exactly the same from day to day and year to year,' wrote Georgy Liddell. Life at Windsor proceeded with gentle monotony. Charlotte's mornings, after prayers in the chapel and nine o'clock breakfast with the other ladies (a substantial protein-rich meal, of fowl, tongue, mutton cutlets and omelette), were taken up with correspondence, her own and the Queen's. After luncheon she would wait in her rooms for 'orders', a note perhaps announcing that Her Majesty wished Charlotte, so long as she did 'not object to an open carriage' (objection of course was not an option), to accompany her on a drive, or a walk, or to ride out. The Queen busied herself with the minutiae of such arrangements; if riding, an equerry would receive *his* orders as to who was accompanying her, which horses they were to ride and when they were to be ready. Charlotte, to her relief, found that she was rarely required to ride – she preferred to walk – since there was usually a maid-of-honour 'ready enough to think it an immense treat'.

Alternatively Charlotte might find herself watching the royal couple go through their paces in the new riding school, or joining them for a game of skittles, or walking through the Home Park, which Albert was in the process of transforming, and where he was keen to show off his projects. In addition to the riding school, he had built new stables, a dairy, an aviary, a mushroom house and kennels (complete with a dog hospital and a sitting room for the Queen's use), where a Highland woman looked after rare breeds such as Cashmere or Chinese dogs. At the Home Farm, where the Lyttelton girls lodged, one of two model farms, there were cows, pigs, poultry, pigeons and guinea pigs to be inspected. On Albert's orders old roads were diverted and new built. Sarah Lyttelton declared herself delighted by a new carriage drive 'up a steep hill round which we wound, to a tower called the clock tower which overlooks an ocean of fir trees, clothing a magnificent foreground and then Virginia Water and an immense blue distance – all quite a new part of the Great Park lately opened to carriages'.

As lady-in-waiting, it fell to Charlotte to enforce the rules and regulations with which the maids-of-honour, only a few years younger than herself, were hedged about. In 1846, a 'horrid' set of new rules appeared 'framed and glazed' in the lady-in-waitings' room: maids were forbidden to leave the castle before lunch, and only afterwards if there were no orders from the Queen. If alone, they could go no further than the parapet on the East Terrace. This made Windsor 'really feel like a prison', wrote Eleanor Stanley, who hoped the new rules might be relaxed since both Charlotte and Sarah Lyttelton thought them absurd.

The presence of Albert did not make for livelier evenings; indeed, rather the opposite. The Prince, according to Lord Melbourne, had quickly grown bored of gossip and chess, and wanted 'to bring literary and scientific people about the Court, vary the society and infuse a more useful tendency into it'. However, he met resistance from the Queen, who 'had no fancy to encourage such people', since she felt her education had 'not fitted her to take part' in intellectual conversation. Sarah Lyttelton may have detected a loftier tone of conversation around the dinner table, but Charlotte greatly regretted that potentially controversial and interesting subjects – politics, for example – were shunned in favour of safe platitudes. 'One could never hear anything' at court, she grumbled, 'as those who could tell one were all on their good behaviour and nobody liked to talk politics.'

After dinner, in the drawing room (the white or green drawing room when the party was a large one), Charlotte generally joined the Queen's table, or made up a whist four with the Duchess of Kent. Otherwise she sat with the maids-of-honour, busying herself with some needlework, or playing rounds of patience or solemnly watching the royal card game, or Albert at his four-handed chess. Cards – commerce, vingt-et-un or bagatelle – and dancing – quadrilles or country dances – at least provided some relief from desultory conversation. Nain Jaune (Pope Joan), a round game introduced in 1841, played for small sums (any coins given to the royal couple had to be either new, or first washed with soap lest they sully the 'royal hands'), became particularly popular. Speculation, played at the royal table in 1843, left everyone 'in fits' of hilarity. Sunday evenings were given over to less frivolous spelling games.

The household may have yawned their way through Windsor evenings; not so the Queen, who as a young woman was easily, and frequently, amused. What could be more delightful than puzzles or spillikins, or singing duets, or merely sitting and gossiping with her ladies? Georgy Liddell described an unusually 'gay' evening when Her Majesty, an enthusiastic dancer, had a polka lesson and the Prince began spinning counters, 'so I took to spinning rings which you know I am adept at doing and the Queen was delighted. It always entertains me to see the little things that amuse Her Majesty and the Prince, instead of their looking bored as people so often do in English society.'

Parties and state visits meant dinner in the Waterloo Gallery, occasions of extra formality and stiffness, generally dreaded by the Queen's ladies. Recitals were laid on – both Victoria and Albert were extremely fond of music – and Charles Kean and his wife regularly brought Shakespeare productions to Windsor. There were visits to the theatre too, by no means an unmixed pleasure for the lady-in-waiting, who had to juggle Her Majesty's many different wraps, her bouquet and bag and opera glasses, without being provided with the comfort of a seat. In June 1850, Charlotte stood for four and a half hours behind the Queen's chair at a command performance of *As You Like It*, with Charles Macready as Jacques, at Drury Lane. A few years later, Charlotte and Eleanor Stanley accompanied the Queen and Prince to the Haymarket Theatre to see *The Bee and Orange*, a play apparently every bit as silly as its title, and pronounced by Eleanor and Charlotte to be 'awfully stupid', though the royal couple thought otherwise. 'It is certainly a nice thing about them that they are so easily amused,' observed Eleanor, ingenuously.

Whatever trials her waitings brought, there was a value for Charlotte in submitting to the obligations of service. As Lady Jocelyn, her fellow lady of the bedchamber, wrote: 'I have no husband or children from the day I come into waiting to the last of the month. I forget what they are like; the sound of the clock in the quadrangle fills me with a sense of duty, of bore and of worth.' At court, free will and autonomy were, of necessity, suspended. The demands of royal service, while not exactly comparable to those of marriage, required similar reserves of patience, self-discipline and forbearance. Mary Ponsonby, who revered Charlotte as a model of rectitude and self-denial, wrote how she 'stands before me after so many years, a clear, distinct and noble outline . . . she told me what wonderful training it had been to give up, for two or three months in the year, all authority, to give no orders and to realise one was just a number and didn't count'. In many respects, life at court provided an object lesson in the subjugation of self, a lesson that could be usefully applied to life beyond.

CHAPTER 6

'Gone Afloat'

The early 1840s, years of economic depression and religious tension for the country at large, were almost cloudless for Victoria and Albert and their growing family. Harmony reigned in the nursery and beyond. The children flourished. Victoria and her mother, thanks to Albert's efforts, were quite reconciled. The Queen had entirely overcome her aversion to Sir Robert Peel; indeed, she felt increasingly attached to him, largely thanks to the mutual regard and respect that had grown up between her prime minister and her husband. Peel was a man after Albert's own heart, one who brought his virtues – moderation, common sense, integrity – to his politics, who put principle above party. And Peel took pains to include the Prince in the business of government, to send him papers that *he* then read to his wife. The royal couple had negotiated the terms of their marriage to the satisfaction of both, with Victoria content to sit back and look on, admiringly, as Albert took the reins.

Sarah Lyttelton delighted in noting charming vignettes of family life: Albert driving his children in a sleigh; birthdays, with new clothes, and cowslip balls and the children reciting verses and music, all 'very bowery and flowery, nothing but sweet smells and book-muslin and brilliant presents and happy faces'. On 24 May 1843, at Claremont, where the Queen celebrated her birthdays (until the acquisition of Osborne), Sarah looked on indulgently as Albert, looking 'very rayonnant', came into the nursery in his dressing gown to fetch the children: Princessy dressed in a muslin frock, embroidered with lilies of the valley and rosebuds, and a green silk apron to match, and Princey 'beautiful too in his sky-blue velvet'. Albert had arranged the Queen's presents on a table under a bower of flowers in the breakfast room; the main present was a sketch by Landseer of the sleeping one-month-old Princess Alice, watched over by Dandy the terrier.

By August, the Queen had recovered from Alice's birth and was in the mood for some 'merriment'. Such was promised by an expedition to France, where Victoria and Albert had been invited by Louis Philippe, King of the French. It would be the Queen's first trip abroad and the first time an English monarch had set foot on French soil since Henry VIII had met Francis I at the Field of the Cloth of Gold in 1520, but, as the Queen was keen to stress, this was to be a strictly private visit, an informal stay at Louis Philippe's Normandy home, the Chateau d'Eu. Her ministers remained circumspect: Louis Philippe was suspected of nursing hopes of placing a son on the Spanish throne, something the British government strenuously opposed. Foreseeing possible embarrassment, Louis Philippe's daughter Louise, Queen of the Belgians, advised her mother to prevent the King at all costs from talking politics with his guests.

Still the auspices were good. Louis Philippe was determined to delight his guests – stocks of English beer and cheese had been laid in – and the Queen was determined to be delighted. Hearing that she was to be included in the royal party (such expeditions were arranged separately from regular court waitings) came as happy news for Charlotte Canning too. She puzzled as to how to 'fit up clothing that will suit court and sea combined', but her spirits, like the Queen's, were high – France promised to be a good deal more 'amusing' than Windsor, and besides, she always relished 'a glimpse of abroad'. She decided that rather than writing letters, she would keep a journal for the benefit of her mother and sister, and laid in a good stock of paper in preparation.

A royal expedition brought, as Miss Skerrett put it, a 'general accelaration', requiring a great deal of planning and work on the part of the household and servants: travel arrangements – carriages, horses, trains – were undertaken by the equerries and packing by the dressers, one of whom travelled ahead with the luggage. Departure times were subject to frequent last-minute changes. 'Oh the orders and counter-orders on these royal journeys!' sighed Eleanor Stanley.

On 26 August, the Prince's birthday, the Queen presented her husband with a languorous portrait of herself by Winterhalter, with her hair loose and trailing across a bare shoulder, and laid on a 'fete' at Virginia Water, with dinner and fireworks and 'illuminated ships' sailing about. The next morning Charlotte was woken at 4.30 by her maid, Sarah Norris, and, having finished her packing, joined the rest of the suite in the Corridor, where the Queen kissed her children goodbye and commended them to the care of Lady Lyttelton, who was 'sad and dispirited' at the prospect of being left behind 'in something like a responsible position'. 'My head is full of packing cases,' she wrote to Caroline, 'and my legs ache with running up and down all day and my eyes are heavy with having been up at half past 5 to see the Queen off.'

Charlotte and the maid-of-honour Georgy Liddell shared a carriage from Windsor with the Queen, who, recorded Charlotte 'was in the greatest spirits, making projects and conjectures about her voyage', and the Prince, who 'talked of all the farms and properties he ought to buy to improve his shooting' (an acid note creeping in). Also of the party were Lord Liverpool (the lord steward), Lord Aberdeen (Peel's foreign secretary), Sir James Clark and George Anson.

At Farnborough everyone boarded the train, 'fitted up for the occa-sion' with a crown on top, to Southampton. The royal couple worked their way through three red dispatch boxes, and cheering crowds gathered at every station. A special lamp, 'an invention by which a lamp was thrust into the top of the carriage instead of an embroidered crown as if by magic when we got into the tunnels was amusing'. It failed to work though in the final and longest tunnel, which did not in the least discomfort the Queen, a tunnel virgin.

In Southampton, as the rain fell steadily, and laden with cloaks, dispatch boxes and bouquets of flowers from the ladies of Southampton, the royal party were rowed in a barge to the brand-new royal steam yacht, the *Victoria and Albert*. This was captained by Lord Adolphus Fitzclarence, one of William IV's children by Mrs Jordan, and had been 'luxuriously fitted up' according to Charles Greville, but with an eye to the comfort of Their Majesties rather than anyone else. Charlotte agreed: the Queen's cabins were 'delightfully cool and sweet', while the berths for the household, though roomy and comfortable enough, were boiling hot and stank of 'bilge and oil'. The officers fared even less well, with berths so cramped – 'wretched dog-holes', said Greville – that they were driven to sleeping on deck.

Before sailing for France, the royal party took a short cruise around the Isle of Wight and along the south coast. First stop was Ryde, then East Cowes, where the Queen wished to visit Norris Castle, where she had stayed as a child. She insisted on entering all the bedrooms and was only deterred by coming face to face with a half-dressed man peering out from behind a door. Back on the yacht, everyone apart from Charlotte, who was an experienced sailor, having made many expeditions on the Cannings' own yacht, gradually succumbed to seasickness and retired to their cabins (Albert was much put out to read reports in the English newspapers claiming he had suffered severely but the Queen not at all). Only Charlotte and Lord Adolphus were left to proceed 'proudly to luncheon' together. Meals on board were bad: a ship's cow provided fresh milk, but as the shops seemed to be shut wherever they moored, there was little in the way of fresh food, while a sheep given to the Queen at Portland could not be killed because she had 'taken an affection for it'. They were reduced to monotonous dinners of macaroni.

The *Victoria and Albert* steamed on, along the Dorset and Devon coasts, as the sun beat down, browning the complexions of the ladies. Charlotte and Georgy Liddell managed to find a cool spot on deck, near the cow shed, where they were joined by the Queen, who sat on a camp stool placidly plaiting paper to be turned into bonnets. It transpired that she had positioned her considerable weight over the hatch to the grog tub: 'Please my Lord, the grog tub's jammed,' Lord Adolphus was told. Once informed, she moved most graciously, on the condition that she was allowed to sample a glass: 'It would be very good if it were stronger' was the verdict.

The Queen asked Charlotte to make sketches of Sidmouth, where her father had died, and Torquay. On reaching Plymouth, they moored and were taken ashore on the new royal barge, made of mahogany. Driving through the streets of Plymouth – Charlotte in an open landau with the Queen and Prince – the heat, crowds and noise of cheering were overpowering. That evening the household, including Lord Adolphus, dined at the Queen's table before watching the fireworks. Charlotte went to bed with her ears ringing. Travelling with Royalties was not, she felt, for the faint-hearted. 'I should like to see many of my friends accept the post of lady-in-waiting – to get in and out of carriages and boats with rarely, if ever, anyone to hand you . . . Then for those who mind a shot, perpetual firing; then for those who are frightened in a carriage, mobs, scrambling, kicking horses, receiving the utmost provocation.'

On 1 September they arrived at Falmouth to chaotic scenes of welcome. The Queen was rowed in her barge around the bay, pursued by 'cutters, luggers, barges, lighters, jolly boats, a steamer, gigs, all loaded with people', and the air was filled with 'the sounds of crunching and smashing of boats'. Back on the yacht, the Queen received addresses from the mayors of Falmouth and Penryn and apologies from the mayor of Truro, who in the excitement had fallen, in full regalia, with his address, into the water. After dinner, Charlotte and Georgy Liddell stood on deck and watched porpoises diving through the wake, gleaming palely in the dusk.

Ship life brings claustrophobia. Charlotte grew increasingly irritated by Lord Liverpool, an old friend to the Queen and the Duchess of Kent, but in her view an opinionated, garrulous bore: 'the most provoking of men . . . He interferes with everything, hollers out all sorts of directions in the barge; stands up to wave his hat to people to get out of the way, and makes the most undignified noise, when there are people whose duty it is to do all this quietly and properly. I think him odious . . .' When Lord Liverpool locked himself in his cabin, it looked for one glorious moment as though he would have to be extracted through a porthole; there was universal 'regret that this was not done'.

Albert also came in for criticism, so given to sententious pronouncements, so convinced of his rightness and yet, in Charlotte's view – and as she loved to point out – so often wrong. His geography, for example, was shaky: he mistook the New Forest shore for the Isle of Wight and the Hitchin river for Southampton Water. When the royal party was taken to inspect a man-of-war in Plymouth, Charlotte commented tartly, 'The Prince knows nothing at all about a ship – he ought to study the subject a little before he goes upon this kind of expedition.' She did not share Sarah Lyttelton's admiration for Albert. Rather, like most of her class, she liked to regard the Prince as a dry-as-dust pedant with all the self-satisfaction of the autodidact. There was something embarrassing and fatally un-English about his appetite for knowledge, let alone his enthusiasm for imparting it.

As the *Victoria and Albert* neared Le Tréport, the Prince de Joinville, one of Louis Philippe's sons, came on board to greet the Queen, followed by the King himself. Louis Philippe cut a curious figure, physically unprepossessing – stout, florid, extravagantly whiskered, a 'toupet' resting on his disproportionately large head – and distinctly lacking in majesty. The eldest son of Philippe Egalité, the Duke of Orléans, he had fought in the revolutionary army before being restored to the throne, as King of the French, in 1830. He liked to promote his bourgeois credentials and kept a kind of open house at the Palais-Royal: all were welcome to wander in and shake the hand of the 'Citizen King'.

He received the Queen warmly, kissing her on both cheeks and escorting her in his barge to the shore, where Queen Marie Amélie and the ladies of the court waited under a tent. At the quay stood a large and splendid carriage – 'a mixture between one from Louis XIV's time and a marketing cart from Hampton Court' – with three rows of seats, lavish gilding and drapes and curtains of flowered chintz, drawn by twelve 'Wouwerman-like fat, jumping horses, very much caparisoned'. Into this piled the royal families, French and English, while Charlotte and the rest of the party followed in another carriage, 'less like Louis XIV and more like Hampton Court'. They galloped the three miles inland to the Chateau d'Eu at alarming speed, through clouds of dust.

The chateau, originally built by Henry of Guise in 1578, had been enlarged by Mademoiselle de Montpensier in the seventeenth century and restored by Louis Philippe. Charlotte was pleased with her quarters, a good bedroom and sitting room on the top floor, with Georgy Liddell next door. That night about fifty people sat down to a 'very handsomely done' dinner in a long downstairs gallery. Charlotte was seated between Monsieur Guizot, the French foreign minister, and the Prince de Joinville, and found herself bemused by French dining habits – the pile of bread and rusks beside the King's plate, the table covered in crumbs and debris which no one bothered to clear. The Queen, she noted, seemed nonplussed by her 'great French loaf'.

The next morning was a Sunday, and there being no available Protestant church, Charlotte, Georgy Liddell and their maids read the service together in their rooms, before going to the Queen's drawing room. Here the French royal family arrived en masse to escort the Queen to breakfast. The latter was another bewildering and elaborate meal: 'soup, and hot meat of all kinds and wine; then came eggs; the sweet things and then tea, coffee and chocolate and bread and butter. All the meals of the day in one.' Afterwards they were given a tour of the chateau and the pictures, a mixture of 'good originals' and 'bad copies' according to Charlotte, who considered herself a good judge of art and made unsuccessful attempts to persuade the Queen of the merits of the Pre-Raphaelites. Finally they set out on a bone-shaking drive in badly sprung charabancs, bouncing over deeply rutted roads and narrowly avoiding overturning.

The visit, like the weather, looked set fair, with English and French Royalties vying to outdo each other in expressions of mutual regard. The Queen was happy to find herself at ease 'in a family circle of persons of my own rank, with whom I could be on terms of equality and familiarity'. She told Charlotte that she felt like one of the family and Charlotte noted that she was 'as amused as a child could be'. Indeed, for Victoria, who looked on 'abroad' with naïve wonderment, everything about France was novel and fascinating – baguettes, crucifixes by the side of the road, French matrons in their white caps.

The Prince too was happy, swimming in the sea and reporting to Baron Stockmar that 'the old King was in the third heaven of rapture, and the whole family received us with a heartiness, I might say affection, which was quite touching'. Louis Philippe repeatedly assured Victoria that he was 'enchanted', while Queen Marie Amélie, with whom she was 'very merry and laughed a good deal', was all that was civil and amiable. Politics were not discussed, but Louis Philippe privately (and fallaciously) assured the Queen, the Prince and Lord Aberdeen that he had no dynastic ambitions towards the Spanish throne.

Regular reports arrived from the Royal Pavilion, in Brighton, where Sarah Lyttelton was ensconced with the children, including baby Alice. As in France, the weather was extremely hot, but the nursery remained cool and airy. There were drives out along the East Cliff. Sarah visited a toyshop, to 'lay in a stock of playthings'. Vicky had been well behaved, 'except a fit of unaccountable rage' the previous evening. Princey's cold was no worse; he was sitting, with some reluctance, for Winterhalter; and his 'worst crime' was 'a tendency to throw his cows and his soldiers out of the window'. As for intellectual progress, Sarah was cautiously optimistic: he was taking note of everything he saw during his drives and talking 'incessantly', 'but I fear it is not quite intelligible enough to bear a comparison with the Princess's language . . . just as forward as the generality of children, and no more – but with every *promise* I think as to disposition and intellect'.

After the stiffness of Windsor, Charlotte was struck by the relative informality of the French court – 'little form . . . compared to what we are used to'. She was surprised by the dowdiness of the French ladies, with the exception of the pretty, young and clearly 'dreadfully bored' Princess de Joinville, a daughter of Pedro I of Brazil. Victoria's clothes, too, left much to be desired. On the first, stiflingly hot, night at the Chateau d'Eu, Charlotte was 'very much distressed' to see her in a 'scarlet china crape', lavishly trimmed with lace and not flattering to her distinctly rosy complexion.

The Queen, whose total absence of chic would always be the subject of much comment abroad, displayed a robust disregard for sartorial niceties, favouring the cheerfully clashing ensembles of the bourgeois matron, sometimes bought from Caley's, the drapers in Windsor High Street. An outfit worn for a visit to Cambridge in 1843, of a blue satin gown, a pink crepe bonnet trimmed with lilies of the valley and a black and gold Indian shawl, was entirely typical. Viewing the Queen's gowns, hung around the walls of her room on the royal yacht, Charlotte thought them 'decidedly badly chosen and quite unlike what she ought to have', which sentiments Her Majesty's dresser apparently shared, since she 'never ceased sighing and lifting up her hands . . . and lamenting how little she cared about her dress'.

Charlotte was much occupied at the Chateau d'Eu in working up sketches for the Queen, and did her best to get out with her water-colours after breakfast. She was a highly competent amateur artist. Ruskin, a friend and self-appointed tutor to her sister Louisa, was generally sparing in his praise – his letters to Louisa are full of exhortations to try harder, do better and shed the 'habit of dashing and blotting' – but he felt that Charlotte 'gets finer things in pure colour than you do – as far as she goes she is perfect in her style of work and could, if she would, paint divinely'. She had studied with the Scottish watercolourist William Leitch, who began his career as a scene-painter and snuff-box decorator in Glasgow, going on to spend several years in Italy, where he taught and established contacts with various aristocratic families passing through Rome, probably including the Cannings. Charlotte introduced Leitch to the Queen, who subsequently engaged him to instruct her and the children. He apparently developed a 'great relish for society' and was as much in demand for his lively company as his painterly skills. The Queen took full advantage of Charlotte's skills, deliberately arranging her waitings so she could accompany the royal couple on their travels, and commandeering many of her watercolours for the souvenir albums which Victoria and Albert had begun to compile as a pictorial record and celebration of their life together.

Every morning at the Chateau d'Eu, one of the French maids would enquire as to the colours of the ladies' evening gowns, pass on the appropriate orders to the gardener and construct dahlia wreaths in time for dinner (so expert was she that Charlotte dispatched her own maid Norris for instruction). Dinner was served early, at seven, and tended to be lengthy, hot and something of an ordeal, especially if you were unlucky in your neighbours. Charlotte judged Prince

Augustus of Coburg (the same 'man of lead' whom Lady Lyttelton had once had the misfortune to sit next to at Windsor) as 'without exception the dullest man I ever met – I think Lord Crewe [a byword for dullness] might appear to great advantage compared with him'.

After dinner, Louis Philippe laid on concerts: one night Beethoven and Gluck performed by the Musique du Roi, on another solos by a violoncello, a pianoforte and a French horn. The latter was played by a man who could sound 'two or three notes at once', with the unfortunate effect, wrote Charlotte, of 'making everybody laugh. The Duke of Montpensier had the giggles and it caught from one person to another till all were in tears and the poor performer's sounds became stranger and stranger. I kept grave very long indeed but my lips shook and some very deep notes vanquished me at last. I was very sorry for the poor man, but his back was partly turned and I hope he did not find out and between each spasm every good natured person called out *"c'est etonnant! merveilleux!"*.

But the principal entertainments during the five days at Eu were the grand open-air luncheons of which Louis Philippe was fond and took much pleasure in organising. Guests were transported to the Fôret d'Eu in the hideously uncomfortable charabancs. For the first of these picnics Charlotte shuddered and bumped on a bench seat for over two and a half hours, to the accompaniment of Lord Liverpool's 'incessant talking in disagreeable French'. They arrived to find a long, open tent, decorated with gilt minarets and lined with buff-coloured merino cloth, over a table set for seventy-two.

According to the *Illustrated London News*, 'Forty decanters of wine, alternated with carafes of water were set on the table in English style; whilst down the middle were placed the collation, comprised of meats, pâtés, confectionery of the most *recherché* description, in fact everything that the most exquisite taste could suggest and wealth provide.' The royal party sat on mahogany chairs, with camp stools for everyone else, and a band played throughout. After lunch, the Queen and Louis Philippe walked about sedately, arm in arm. The Duchess of Orléans, the subject of much melancholy interest and curiosity on the part of the English party – her husband, Louis Philippe's popular eldest son, had been tragically killed in a carriage accident the previous summer – appeared, still in deep mourning, and ate in public for the first time.

Charlotte did not share the Queen's enthusiasm for life at the Chateau d'Eu. Indeed, the word 'tiresome' regularly creeps into her journal. The hours spent waiting about in the gallery after breakfast were 'rather tiresome', as were the ladies of the court, with their inane civilities, not to mention being crammed into charabancs with the same companions day after day. One 'dullish' evening was spent dawdling in the downstairs gallery, while 'the Queens and Princesses sat round a table and Louis Philippe walked about. We had albums and sat behind them in a double row.' Of course all this – the waiting about, the long evenings – was familiar enough to Charlotte, but she had hoped for more. At least she felt able to criticise the French court more freely.

On 7 September, after successfully procuring an English-style breakfast of tea, egg and bread and butter, rather than 'soup and large strong sausages', Charlotte helped the Queen with her clothes – her dressers having already left – before everyone piled back into the same great carriages that had brought them from Le Tréport. Charlotte received a 'most beautiful' bracelet from Queen Marie Amélie, a 'good, amiable woman . . . so kind and sincere', as a souvenir of her visit, while Victoria was presented with a box of Sèvres china and two pieces of Gobelin tapestry (back at Windsor, the tapestry was installed in the oak dining room, but, being too wide, was turned back at each side in order to fit the wall – 'the Prince after that flatters himself he is a man of taste and talks of encouraging the fine arts!' sniffed Eleanor Stanley). On her part, the Queen left a generous £1,000, as well as presents, to be distributed amongst the French servants. As the *Victoria and Albert* steamed away across a glassy sea, Louis Philippe stood in his barge calling out, 'Adieu, adieu.'

Back on English soil, the royal party installed itself in the Pavilion at Brighton, where they found Sarah Lyttelton and the children. Charlotte thought the Pavilion like being on the set of a ballet – 'it is the oddest sensation to be actually living amongst all these dragons and nodding mandarins' – while the Queen was 'quite unhappy . . . to have to live in a house again; she says it feels like a prison and she longs to be at sea'. She did not have long to wait, for on 12 September the *Victoria and Albert* set sail once more, this time bound for Ostend, and Victoria's uncle Leopold.

A 'cockling sea' made for a stormy crossing. The maid-of-honour, this time the Hon. Clementina Hamilton, took to her bed wearing her boots and was dosed with quinine. Albert, scoffed Charlotte, 'flattered himself he was getting used to the sea', claiming 'it does not lift me off my legs so', a confidence that proved short-lived. The Queen breakfasted 'stoutly' in her pavilion and made Charlotte sit with her for three hours on deck, remaining in high spirits apart from 'five minutes under the influence of an over powering smell of roast goose – even then a little O de Cologne set her right and she laughed heartily at the sight first of PA dreadfully overcome, then Ld Liverpool and then Ld Aberdeen, all vanishing in haste'.

The Queen, generally a good sailor, would always relish 'the sailor-gypsy life' at sea. According to Adolphus Fitzclarence, 'nothing could be more agreeable and amiable than the Queen on the royal yacht'. She and the Prince happily dined on deck surrounded by sailors, encouraged them to dance and chatted to the boatswain. Her Majesty's only fault was impatience, an insistence on landing, for example, at the earliest opportunity, regardless of official procedure – 'in sea phrase, she always wants to go ahead'.

Whatever trials the French visit had brought paled in comparison to those of Belgium – 'Eu was 20 times better fun for me,' wrote Charlotte, wearily, in her journal. She dismissed Ostend, where they were billeted amongst various houses belonging to King Leopold, as 'an ugly little town with shabby small houses', several of which the King kept for taking the sea air. Charlotte and Miss Hamilton were lodged in one of these, the royal couple and the gentlemen in others. Leopold was a great stickler for etiquette, and the Belgian court, unlike the French, was excessively formal. After dinner, where all too often Charlotte found herself next to the ubiquitous Lord Liverpool, everyone stood in a circle – chairs placed behind them, against the wall – while the two queens, Victoria and Louise, talked to each other or slowly perambulated around the circle for as much as an hour. Only when they finally sat were Charlotte and the other ladies permitted to sit themselves. The men remained standing, backs to the wall.

Charlotte found she had 'much more Ladies' Maid work to do for the Queen than ever before'. She suffered from lack of sleep, thanks to the noise from the street and the heat, for the weather continued 'broiling', ruining her six bonnets and making the full programme of sightseeing – Bruges, Ghent, Brussels, Antwerp – all the more enervating. Only Brussels won Charlotte's approval – 'one of the prettiest towns I ever saw'. Here she shopped for neckcloths and music and sat through a long and 'tiresome' concert in the park. Charlotte Brontë, then living in Brussels, caught sight of the Queen, a 'little, stout, vivacious lady, very plainly dressed', driving through the town, laughing merrily.

As in France, Victoria continued to be 'exceedingly amused with the foreign look of everything'. Charlotte judged her enthusiasm to be more general than particular, her interest pricked, as it always would be, by the quotidian details of ordinary lives. She paid slightly grudging tribute to Prince Albert's better-trained critical faculties: he 'naturally enough being used to all this pays more attention to what he is shown and as to the merits of pictures and statues he can judge well'.

As the week drew to an end, melancholy farewells were said between Their Majesties, and the Queen boarded the *Victoria and Albert* on 21 September with red eyes. She had 'showered snuff boxes and rings and pins on all the gentlemen who have had to do anything for her and £500 to the servants', while Charlotte came away with another bracelet, from Queen Louise. She discovered that even the ship's officers were full of talk of how badly dressed Victoria had been (at Ghent, her bonnets would have done 'for an old woman of 70 and her pink petticoat was longer than her muslin gown'). They were back at Windsor, looking 'very grand and gloomy', by lunchtime. 'The Queen gave her orders that the yacht would not be wanted any more this year with a heavy sigh.' Indeed, they were 'all very sorry to leave her'. Charlotte looked forward, though, to chapel and a good walk.

CHAPTER 7

Osborne

The Queen's 'glimpse of abroad' left her feeling 'pent up' and restless. 'During our morning walk,' she wrote in her journal, 'Albert and I talked of buying a place of our own, which would be so nice.' They had been longing for a country home for some time, away from the foul air of London and the formality of Windsor. The Pavilion at Brighton was not to the Queen's taste – 'a strange, odd Chinese looking thing' – and besides she didn't like the townspeople peering at her under her bonnet. Claremont, while pretty and pleasing, did not provide real seclusion and anyway belonged to the King of the Belgians. They wanted a Claremont of their own.

It was Robert Peel who heard of a suitable-sounding property on the Isle of Wight. In December 1843, negotiations began for the purchase of Osborne House from Lady Isabella Blatchford. Lady Isabella drove a hard bargain, but Osborne, together with a 1,000-acre (later increased to 2,000) estate was eventually bought for £26,000, paid from the privy purse, thanks to Albert's economies. The Queen had fond memories of the Isle of Wight, having stayed in Norris Castle. Osborne promised privacy, pretty country, sea air and, above all, the opportunity to create a family home. 'It sounds so snug and nice to have a place of *one's own*, quiet and retired and free from all Woods and Forests, and other charming Departments who really are the plague of one's life,' the Queen wrote happily to her uncle Leopold.

The New Year saw Charlotte back in waiting at Windsor. The royal children, she reported, were 'quite darlings': Princess Alice 'like

a fat cottage child', the Prince of Wales sunny-natured and charming
in a Russian moujik's shirt and the three-year-old Princess Royal
remembering Charlotte's name – to her surprise – after a four-month
absence. She found harp-playing and reel-dancing all the rage
(Eleanor Stanley reported that attempts to teach the Queen reels
were hampered by her refusal – a matter of dignity – to 'hop'). Her
Majesty had also taken a fancy for duets 'a 8 mains', an alarming
prospect for Charlotte, who was not particularly musical and practised frantically in her room: 'I have now my piano strewed with
music books for playing duets on 2 pianos for four people at once.
They say the effect is beautiful but it requires excellent time and I
shall be in a great fright when the time comes.' Watching Her Majesty
throwing herself into English country dances one evening, Charlotte
felt sure she couldn't be pregnant again. She was wrong: Prince
Alfred was born in August.

Duets and dancing came to an abrupt end on 29 January with
the death of Albert's father, the thoroughly disagreeable and unlov-
able Duke of Saxe-Coburg. According to Sarah Lyttelton, the Prince,
whose memories of his Coburg childhood were swaddled in a warm
nostalgia that enveloped his unsatisfactory father, wept copiously,
while every time the Queen looked at him, her eyes filled 'afresh'.
'Here we sit together, poor Mama, Victoria and myself and weep,
with a great cold public around us, insensible as stone,' wrote Albert
to Baron Stockmar, pathetically. The Queen, who had barely known
her father-in-law and had frequently been embarrassed by his
requests for money, made the Prince's grief her own and expressed
it with what would become characteristic and disproportionate
extravagance: 'we feel crushed, over-whelmed, bowed down by the
loss of one who was so deservedly loved, I may say adored, by his
children and family; I loved him and looked on him as my own
father; his like we shall *not see again*.' Death had rendered the Duke
a paragon.

Charlotte was sympathetic. 'It has been a great grief to the Prince
and the Queen has been quite cast down by it too,' she wrote, 'the
poor Dss of Kent has felt her brother's death most severely and

there never was such a gloom as it cast over them all.' However, the mourning requirements were a more pressing cause for concern: 'the mourning is Private and will last a year, so we shall wear black gloves in waiting for 8 months, but at home we are to keep to the Court mourning of 6 weeks'.

European Royalties, not to mention Victoria's numerous relations – usually one and the same – died with relentless regularity; in 1851, the Queen told Eleanor Stanley that she'd been in mourning for nine months of every year for the past four years. Mourning, whether court (worn as a mark of respect for sovereigns, and generally short) or private (for family, and of longer duration), was thus an occupational hazard for the Queen's ladies. It meant donning black morning, walking and dinner gowns (made of silk or, for everyday purposes, merino or bombazine – wool, or a silk and wool combination, free of disrespectful shine) liberally trimmed with crape (a lightweight silk fabric, crimped to look dull), black capes, 'coal-scuttle bonnets' also festooned with crape, black-trimmed petticoats, and black accessories, including gloves, shoes, stockings and fans, jet jewellery and black embroidered handkerchiefs. For drawing rooms, 'black crape and silk, black gloves, flowers, feathers, lappets and fans' were required. To complicate matters further, full mourning could be abruptly and temporarily alleviated, in honour of a birthday or a marriage, to half-mourning, when shades of lilac and purple, grey, black and white or grey and black were all permissible, with the adapting of every item of clothing to follow suit.

'Great events make me quiet and calm,' declared the Queen proudly, 'and little trifles fidget me and irritate my nerves.' The latter was certainly true – when it came to the minutiae of daily life, the Queen *fussed*. 'Great care about little trifles' was something Charlotte noticed with increasing frequency. She thought this an unfortunate tendency in a man, but 'in a Queen no one much minds', and if the patience of the household was sometimes tried, there were always plenty of visitors at court happy to indulge Her Majesty, to acquiesce 'in all the little things wanted to be got or done – openings and shuttings of doors and windows and getting cushions, shawls etc. and detailed orders on dress'. Detailed orders on mourning dress were a case in point.

The many and various permutations of mourning gave rise to many and various orders from the Queen, at once precise and arbitrary. With the ladies in mourning (six months of black silk and crape for the Prince of Leiningen, Victoria's half-brother), they were suddenly ordered – 'fancy our horror' – into white or grey for the Princess Royal's birthday. Eleanor Stanley had no choice but to wear her white muslin, this in November, but was comforted by the assurance of the lady-in-waiting that she could 'perfectly go out this afternoon in my black merino, putting on a white bonnet'. When the birthday of the Princess of Leiningen fell during a court mourning, 'we were told that we might if we liked make our mourning a little slighter in consequence'. Unsure what that meant, Eleanor appealed to Miss Skerrett, who asked the Queen and reported back: 'We have just got the order, which is to wear white gloves, white or lilac flowers, coloured jewellery and black silk or lace. Really these niceties are too plaguy!'

To accommodate such 'niceties' required ingenuity and expense, and Charlotte frequently resorted to a 'cheap contrivance'. In 1851, with the court in mourning for the Queen of the Belgians, she worried that she was 'going too much like a bride to Court tomorrow, but the Queen orders us all into white. Luckily I was provided with a complete silk worn last year and still perfectly clean, so this time I go for the cost of new ribbons.' When she couldn't make do, she could turn to one of the mourning warehouses that opened in London during the 1840s, like Jay's Mourning Warehouse in Regent Street. Mourning clothes, a means of proclaiming status as much as respect, had become big business, and entire stores were given over to their supply. At Peter Robinson's Court and General Mourning House, one headed for the 'Mitigated Affliction Department' to buy half-mourning.

In March 1844, the Prince left England for a three-week visit to Coburg. This was the Queen's first separation from her husband, and in Sarah

Lyttelton's eyes, she behaved 'like a pattern wife . . . so feeling and so wretched and yet so unselfish and encouraging him to go and putting the best face upon it to the last moment'. Sarah admitted, though, that she would be 'thankful when the trial is over . . . we all feel sadly wicked and unnatural in his absence'. On his return, Albert threw himself into plans for Osborne.

Since the existing house was far too small to accommodate the royal family and household, he designed a new one, Italianate in style – the view from the house reminded him of the Bay of Naples – in collaboration with the master builder Thomas Cubitt. Here was a project after Albert's own heart, requiring vision, energy and artistry, a showcase for his many talents, or so at least believed the Queen. 'It does my heart good,' she declared, 'to see how my beloved Albert enjoys it all and is so full of admiration for the place and of all the plans and improvements he means to carry out.' On 23 June 1845, the foundation stone for the new house was laid.

Osborne House

That August, while Charlotte Canning accompanied the Queen and the Prince on a visit to Germany – Victoria's first sighting of Albert's homeland – Sarah Lyttelton remained at Osborne, in the old house, with the children. In a journal kept for the Queen's benefit, she recorded nursery events: the children had slept till seven despite the noise of hammering from the new building; Princess Alice was being tormented by gnat bites; the Prince of Wales had been 'very passionate on the beach'; Prince Alfred was not talking yet, but had 'a very good manly temper'. The Princess Royal's behaviour, both precocious and challenging, ran true to form. When Sarah announced that there would be a 'holyday' for Prince Albert's birthday, Princessy 'began the day by saying that as tomorrow was a great festival, she thought of being naughty all day today, as prelude I suppose, and for the first hour or two, was disposed to keep her word. But luckily some forcible arguments on the subject have taken effect.' Gazing towards the English coast, through the rain, 'looking as it does in such weather very near and dark', she observed, 'I think England has swum up close to us!'

Charlotte was finding the German tour 'by no means of unmixed pleasure', with a great deal of 'pomp and ceremony', gruelling evenings of dinners, concerts and performances of Schiller, frequent requests from Her Majesty for drawings, and constant rain. By 26 August, Albert's birthday, the royal party were in Coburg, at the Rosenau, the Prince's boyhood home, and Charlotte awoke to a birthday serenade 'of Hymns and Valses'. The Queen presented her husband with a painting by Thomas Uwins, *Cupid and Psyche*, a walking stick and a snuff box, and that evening, after dinner, there was a concert with music composed by Albert and his brother. 'Perhaps you will think me a courtier when I say the Prince's was very pretty,' wrote Charlotte.

At Osborne, Sarah and the children had a celebration of their own in honour of the birthday. There were presents: doll's house furniture, a tea set and a box with a lock for Princessy, a drum and fife for Princey, a white dog for Alice, and a windmill for Alfred; Miss Skerrett made wreaths for the princesses; portraits of the Queen and Prince were crowned with garlands; and a band played on the lawn. 'The

evening of a festival is almost always disastrous,' wrote Sarah with
the wisdom of experience, and sure enough, all the excitement proved
too much for the Princess Royal, who 'fell into a transport of rage
on perceiving that the day was nearly over, and shrieked and roared
in the open carriage'.

By the following summer the new house was nearing completion.
Sarah described the scene: 'Patches of children, each attended by their
scarlet footman, shining in the distance – Mr Anson escorting Lady
Jocelyn across the park with her two babies. The Prince very busy
with the builders. The equerries charging about – all looked rather
interesting and royal.' She felt greatly relieved to be away from London
and Buckingham Palace, which was still undergoing a programme of
renovations: 'the horrid dirt and misery of the last days of London
. . . what with the smells of the overflowed drains, and the darkness
of every staircase and passage from the tarpaulin over what were the
skylights and the haggard looks of the wretched overworked mopping
maids and the dreadful bustle of the final packing up and departure
of the two courts and among it all the dazzling dullness of the Ball
and the thing I most felt and remember there Miss Dawson's pale face
and serious expression meeting my eye at every turn and raising so
many sad thoughts and fears and then having in the hurry missed
poor dear Caroline and not said goodbye to her on our long parting,
altogether made a heavy load of small evils'. Osborne, on the other
hand, was 'wonderfully green' and pretty, its peace marred only by
'the constant noise of the new building'.

Caroline Dawson was a maid-of-honour with whom Sarah's son
Spencer had fallen in love and whom he hoped to marry. Spencer,
handsome, wayward, impecunious and overly fond of gambling, was
not the son-in-law Caroline's parents had in mind. Sarah, as ever
anxious to smooth the path of true love, did her best for her son,
making appeals to her brother and the Queen. In a letter to the latter
she admitted that though Spencer was by no means 'free from levity
and extravagance', she felt that this was nothing a 'virtuous marriage'
would not put right; since lack of money was the principal obstacle
to marrying Miss Dawson, could Her Majesty help in finding him a

place? Could she perhaps recommend him to Sir Robert Peel? A minor place at court *was* found for Spencer, and his uncle settled some money on him, but Sarah's romantic hopes were dashed: Caroline's family refused consent and Spencer married elsewhere. Such an unhappy episode did Sarah feel this to be, and so sensitive Miss Dawson's feelings, that some years later, in 1850, when Caroline came to visit her in her rooms at Windsor, she made her sit with her back to Spencer's portrait lest the sight of it prove too painful.

While at the beach with the children in June 1846, Sarah saw Peel departing on the new royal steamer, the *Fairy*, and judging from the look on the Queen's face – 'as if *something* had happened' – suspected that he must have resigned. She was right. By 1846, after the horribly wet summer of the previous year and another failed harvest, and with famine worsening in Ireland, Peel had come to believe (along with Victoria and Albert) that circumstances demanded the repeal of the Corn Laws, which imposed a tariff on imported grain, thus keeping the price of domestic grain – and bread – artificially high. However, repeal came at some cost, fatally splitting the Tories and forcing Peel out of office, when the protectionists in his own party took their revenge and helped defeat the Irish Coercion Bill. The Queen had no choice but to ask Lord John Russell, leader of the Whigs, to form a government. But she mourned Peel and her old friends Lords Aberdeen and Liverpool, claiming 'we felt so safe with them'. The new government, she feared, brought 'much less high and pure feeling'. Particularly unwelcome was the new foreign secretary Lord Palmerston, who was most definitely neither 'safe' nor 'pure'. At least as far as the new lord chamberlain, lord steward and lords-in-waiting went, she and Albert had 'contrived to get a very respectable Court'. Osborne, she hoped, would lift her spirits after the 'sad leave-takings'.

When Charlotte Canning arrived at Osborne, she found herself pressed into service as drawing master to Her Majesty, until Edward Lear, who had been engaged to give the Queen some lessons in landscape watercolour painting, came to take over. Victoria, who drew well, was an attentive pupil, asking meekly: 'What shall I do now? Do you think I should add some green? Is that blue enough?'

and then doing 'exactly as she was bid'. There was talk too of a royal visit from Osborne to Highcliffe, the Stuart family home on the Hampshire coast, and Charlotte wrote to her mother to warn her. The Queen's intentions could only be guessed at – royal plans constantly changed – but she might, it seemed, appear at any moment on the *Fairy*.

This naturally threw Lady Stuart into a state of alarm, not allayed, one imagines, by a stream of notes from Charlotte detailing the Queen's requirements and advising the removal of loose covers, the putting down of carpets and the provision of fresh flowers, seltzer water and tea. If luncheon was required, then Lady Stuart should 'remember cold beef, that is always in favour. *No mutton.* Chickens, prawns and sand eels. No *onions*. I think a gateau napolitain wd be good as it keeps, but with all this I doubt the necessity of *any* luncheon. Seltzer water is the great necessity under all circumstances. Some hot water and milk in a bedroom for washing off dust perhaps may be wanted.' She did not feel that her mother should ask Canning to be present – 'his hair wd stand on end at the bare idea'. In the event, guests, bad weather and other distractions at Osborne meant the visit was never made.

'Last evening a household dinner,' wrote Sarah Lyttelton in September, 'Colonel Grey [an equerry who became private secretary to Albert in 1849] and Lady Canning. Such an influx of brains and brilliancy. I never spent a more *intellectual* and pleasant evening.' On the 15th, the royal family moved into the new house, known as the Pavilion, with Lady Lyttelton and Lady Canning in attendance and the maid-of-honour, Lucy Kerr, throwing an old shoe – a Scottish custom – after the Queen as she passed through the door. Sarah described their first evening: 'nobody caught cold or smelt paint and it was a most amusing event the coming here. Everything in the house is quite new and the dining-room looked very handsome. The windows, lighted by the brilliant lamps in the room, must have been seen far out at sea.'

After dinner came a kind of house-warming ceremony: all stood to toast the royal couple's health, while the Prince, with obvious emotion, quoted the first lines of a German hymn, by Luther, to 'bless our going out and coming in'. Sarah thought this entirely appropriate – 'truly entering a new house, a new palace, is a solemn thing to do' – and she found the house 'airy, spacious, clean and substantial'. She was also 'quite agreeably satisfied by the real comfort of my little room', actually a good-sized bedroom and sitting room next to the children's nursery on the top floor of the Pavilion, with ravishing views out across parkland to the Solent sparkling in the distance, and her maid conveniently lodged above her in one of the towers.

For Albert, who had thrown himself into the building of Osborne and the creation of a family home, the move was indeed a solemn thing. He had worked closely with Cubitt on the plans and layout; he had discussed materials – iron girders, cement stucco, plate glass, sea shells as insulation; he had commissioned painted ceilings and frescoes (a sensual *Omphale and Hercules* by Anton von Gegenbauer opposite his bath); he had designed a billiard table, light fittings and an ingenious device that allowed the royal couple to lock their bedroom door without leaving their bed. The resulting house, which, despite its Italianate features – a flat roof, two campaniles, a loggia, terracotta stucco – still has the look of a substantial suburban villa, is more functional than beautiful; 'airy' and light-filled on a bright summer's day, bleak and institutional under grey skies. But inside it was set out so as to allow Victoria and Albert to live on an intimate, domestic scale. Their interconnecting private rooms in the Pavilion were smallish and homely. As the Queen dressed for dinner – her dressing room led directly off her sitting room, where Their Majesties' desks nestled snugly side by side – she could hear the Prince playing the harmonium in *his* dressing room and the children rampaging in the nursery upstairs. Servants were close by too – bedrooms for a wardrobe maid, valet and page just a step away, dressers and nursery staff on the floor above. This was hardly the hurly-burly of family life in a terraced house, but, to use one of the Queen's favourite expressions, it was *gemütlich*.

The ladies' drawing room, Osborne

A couple of days after the moving-in ceremony, Albert insisted on
Lady Lyttelton and Lady Canning each planting a tree in their honour;
Charlotte chose an oak and Sarah a deodar cedar, and each held their
tree as Albert shovelled in soil. For the time being the household
remained in the old house, which was subsequently demolished to
make way for a new Household Wing, with an equerries' room, offices
for the master of the household and private secretary, a communal
sitting room, a dining room, a billiard room, bedrooms, and a separate
smoking room for the gentlemen close by. When this was completed
in 1848, Charlotte and Eleanor Stanley had barely moved into their
new rooms – a sunny corner room, crowded with chintz and mahogany
furniture, on the first floor for Charlotte, with Eleanor next door –
before they received a visit from the Prince, eager to see how they
were settling in. He proceeded to spend several hours arranging the

furniture, heaving the piano and choosing pictures. Since the new
wing was too small to accommodate the entire household, Barton
Manor, just a mile away, was bought as lodging for the equerries, and
a few years later, in 1851, the Main Wing was added, housing the
council room and rooms for the royal children and some of the
gentlemen.

The furnishing and embellishing of Osborne's interiors continued,
to elaborate and highly coloured effect. Albert, aided by his adviser
Ludwig Gruner, bought and commissioned a mass of furniture, arte-
facts, paintings and sculpture. The early Renaissance paintings (a
Mantegna, a Fra Angelico, a Duccio triptych) that he loved were hung
in his dressing room and family portraits by Winterhalter in the dining
room; antler furniture was bought for the Horn Room; cut-glass
pedestal chandeliers commissioned for the drawing room and a set
of Minton porcelain for the Queen's dressing table. The Queen's more
sentimental tastes were allowed some expression too: throughout the
house children, dogs and favoured courtiers and servants were celebrated and immortalised in portraits, busts and photographs.

To adorn the stairwell Albert commissioned a fresco of *Neptune
resigning the Empire of the Seas to Britannia* from William Dyce, who
was also responsible for the frescoes in the new Palace of Westminster.
Dyce's fresco did not meet with unqualified approval amongst the
household. The abundance of naked flesh at eye level was rather too
much for the nursery maids and Mlle Charrier (the fresco was at the
top of the stairs, on the children's floor), and shocked Eleanor Stanley:
Britannia was mercifully clothed in a yellow gown, 'but all the others
are in the Royal Africa minus the boots'. Sarah Lyttelton, called out
to the staircase by the Prince to watch Mr Dyce at work, found him
'one of the least agreeable and most dry and half-sneering mannered
men I have ever met', but couldn't help feeling 'a sort of fellowship'
with him on account of his friendship with William Gladstone.

In the Grand Corridor, with its floor of Minton tiles, that linked
the Household Wing to the Main Wing and the Pavilion, and acted
as a – predominantly classical – sculpture gallery, stood several sculptures commissioned from John Gibson, who had lived in Rome since

1817 and studied with Canova. Over the winter of 1846 the Cannings spent eight months in Italy, five of them in Rome. The Queen had charged Charlotte with two commissions – to acquire a pug dog and to visit John Gibson, who was working on a statue of Her Majesty. Having been to Gibson's studio, Charlotte reported the statue a success, her only qualification being that Gibson's technique of colouring the marble worked well when it came to tinting the border of the robe in red and blue, but rather less so in the case of the sandals, tassels and tiara, tinted in pale yellow. When the statue arrived in England in July, the Queen judged it 'very fine but we cannot quite approve the face'. The quest for the pug, however, had not yielded results: there were no pugs to be found in Rome, but Charlotte had enlisted the help of a Mme Potemkin, the same who had procured a pug for her fellow lady of the bedchamber, Lady Gainsborough. Mme Potemkin had recommended Bologna as a good source.

The Queen replied from Claremont: 'The account of my Statue has *delighted* the Prince and pray say everything kind and complimentary to Gibson (who is such a good and amiable Man) about it, from us.' She continued, ingenuously, 'I have made such great progress in my Drawing since I saw you, and I am sure you wd be surprised and say as Leitch does "I can hardly believe YM has done these".' Enclosed in her letter was a sketch of Osborne, 'which I have had done after one of Mr Lear's Drawings and wh I beg you to give him and to tell him of my perseverance in drawing'. Lear was also living in Rome.

Sarah Lyttelton liked Osborne and did not wonder at the Queen's 'passionate fondness' for it: 'I have always thought the life of a country gentleman and his family which Your Majesty and His Royal Highness have condescended to imitate is about the richest in materials for happiness.' Sitting in her rooms, looking out at a glorious sunset, listening to the strains of Albert's harmonium floating through her open window, she felt perfectly content. Her only, but considerable, sorrow was the absence of her daughters – a convenient 'perch' for Caroline and Kitty proved hard to find at Osborne, and Sarah frequently found herself 'reduced to a pen and ink diet'. Leaving Osborne always brought 'a mixture of regret – the mornings are so pleasant and healthful . . . not interrupted by 50 notes and tradespeople and jobs that they overbalance the woeful dullness of the evenings – they do not improve'.

She was not alone in lamenting the dullness of the evenings, which, with few guests, little in the way of entertainment and no possibility of escape, surpassed even those at Windsor. In general the household were much less enamoured of Osborne than was Sarah. Miss Skerrett found it 'uncommonly dull', missed her London acquaintance and felt 'cut off from everything but sea and air'. Charlotte Canning's enthusiasm was muted – the house was dismissed as 'rather on a Londony plan', which was hardly surprising given that Cubitt had built most of Belgravia, though she approved its comforts (plumbed baths for Victoria and Albert – a rarity in the 1840s – water closets for all and a heating system) and fine views. She likened it to the Trianon, but, 'Whatever it is, it perfectly enchants the Queen and Prince and you never saw anything so happy as they are, planting their trees with their 5 babes playing around them.' Having supervised the gardens at Highcliffe, Charlotte had views on the subject, and Albert's landscaping came in for some criticism: 'They have made really a beautiful garden of terraces with quantities of alcoves and statues but the landscape and rather large formal things are in want of a little setting to rights and I longed to doctor some lines of walk.'

The Queen firmly believed in the benefits of bracing temperatures, and in her palaces thermometers, set into ivory obelisks, sat on every mantelpiece to ensure the rooms remained healthily cool. Osborne, with its great plate-glass windows, kept open, naturally, was a notoriously cold house, despite its new-fangled central heating. After dinner, in the drawing room, jauntily upholstered in canary yellow and frequently no more than 40° Fahrenheit, the shoulders of the ladies turned quite blue. Princess Beatrice, the Queen's youngest child, when asked one day at Osborne by her German governess what windows were made for, replied 'to let in wind'. Ministers complained about the distance to the Isle of Wight, and rough crossings on the *Fairy* were dreaded by all, even, occasionally, by the Queen – 'rather amusing', thought Eleanor Stanley, 'when one contrasts it with the complete indifference with which *our* coming in any weather is regarded'.

For the household as well as the royal family, Osborne at least brought relative freedom. They drove about the island in charabancs (modelled on those at the Chateau d'Eu), they walked and rode and, later, bicycled and played golf. The maids-of-honour were allowed the rare privilege of 'tête-à-tête walks, a thing that would make everybody's hair stand on end at Windsor'. There were summer fetes for the estate workers, with country dancing, ale-drinking, sack races and hornpipe dances performed by the crew from the royal yacht – 'noisy, merry and intensely boring', sighed Sarah Lyttelton. In summer, the royal family and household lived an outdoors kind of existence far removed from stultifying Windsor: the Queen liked to breakfast outside, and dinner was often eaten on the terrace. At such times it was a beguiling place: Albert directing landscaping operations; the Queen looking on and sketching; 'detachments of royal children' in brown Holland frocks and straw hats running through the arbours, or shelling peas and washing potatoes. Each child had his or her own plot for growing vegetables, which they were encouraged to cook in the Swiss Cottage, a prefab structure imported from Switzerland in 1854, like a very grand Wendy house, complete with a miniature working kitchen range. There was a fort for the boys and, as at Windsor a model farm, managed by Albert.

But beneath the idyll lurked something rather darker and less innocent: rampant alcoholism amongst Osborne's tenants. The Queen, who thoroughly disapproved of excessive drinking on the part of her own class, showed remarkable tolerance towards that of her servants. On learning that a man who worked in the cellar at Windsor was to be dismissed for drinking, she immediately took his part, writing to the master of the household: 'poor R. Albertanson – he must clearly leave the Cellar and she wished him long ago to be moved from a place which led him into temptation, but she thinks he ought *not* to be *entirely* dismissed . . . Barker the Gentleman Porter was removed from the Cellar for similar offences and has been perfectly steady ever since. R. Albertanson has a v nice wife and for the sake of her and his family the Queen would wish some small place to be found for him.' A place *was* found, in the silver pantry. The point was not Albertanson's alcoholism, but the fact that he had been unfairly exposed to temptation.

When Canon Prothero, the rector of Whippingham church, took it upon himself to draw Her Majesty's attention to the 'intemperance' of the Osborne tenants, especially Land, the former keeper, a 'most habitual drunkard', the Queen was indignant and defensive. She claimed that she had seen no evidence of 'this supposed evil' at Osborne and that Prothero 'must have been misinformed respecting Land as HM has taken much trouble to ascertain the truth and has found no corroboration of the accusations made against him. The Q cannot give up her opinion of the character of one who has served her so well and faithfully.' Faithful service excused all manner of sins. Prothero was put firmly in his place by being told not to impose himself on the Queen's tenants – visiting the sick for example – unless explicitly requested to do so. Turning a blind eye to drunken servants was one thing; meddling clerics quite another.

CHAPTER 8

In the Highlands

Osborne's many charms could not quite dispel Victoria and Albert's yearning for Scotland. The seeds of their love affair with the Highlands had been sown during their first visit in 1842, but really took root on their next, in September 1844, when Lord Glenlyon lent them Blair Atholl, his Perthshire house, for three weeks. Charlotte Canning, also a lover of Scotland (she frequently accompanied her husband on shooting parties), was more than delighted to be included in the party and, with half-mourning for the Duke of Saxe-Coburg finally over, to put aside her black gloves, ribbons and fan and set sail once again on the *Victoria and Albert*. They embarked from Woolwich, with, in addition to Charlotte, Lords Aberdeen and Liverpool (as yet still in office), Sir James Clark, George Anson, Car Cocks and Mlle Charrier, who had charge of the Princess Royal, in attendance. Sarah Lyttelton, personally much relieved not to be 'gone afloat', remained at Osborne with the Prince of Wales, Princess Alice and Prince Alfred. 'Little cheeks are blooming and spirits very good,' she reported.

The *Victoria and Albert* had supposedly been improved by a new ventilation apparatus, the work of Dr David Reid, the heating engineer who had designed the elaborate and problematic ventilation system for Charles Barry's new Palace of Westminster. That of the royal yacht proved equally troublesome, not so much expelling fumes as redirecting them. At any rate, it did not prevent a heavy swell from taking its toll, and all, save Charlotte, gradually disappeared from view. Mlle Charrier, who had been dreading the voyage, was reduced to a 'state of immobility', as were the Queen's dressers. It was left to

Charlotte to wait on Her Majesty, who was prostrated in her cabin, and, once again, to sit down for dinner *à deux* with Lord Aldolphus. With calm seas the sick recovered, the Princess Royal ran about crying 'I don't know what to do I am so merry', and they anchored in the Tay without mishap.

Charlotte thought Blair 'the oddest house there ever was' in terms of configuration. She and the other members of the household were lodged on the first floor, with the Queen and the Prince on the second, where, in the interests of greater comfort, a good deal of room changing and furniture shifting proved necessary. The Glenlyons had in fact gone to considerable expense in preparation for their royal visitors, in the way of new furniture, new carpets and a new bridge. They themselves had moved into the factor's house.

Any inconvenience presented by their accommodation was quickly forgotten. In his precise, oddly stilted way, Albert wrote to his step-mother: 'We are all very well and live a somewhat primitive yet romantic mountain life, that acts as a tonic to the nerves and gladdens the heart of a lover, like myself, of field sports and of Nature.' And what delighted Albert delighted Victoria, who remained in the highest spirits throughout her stay at Blair. The landscape, the air, riding, sketching, walking (having given birth to Prince Alfred just five weeks earlier, she resorted to a 'wheeling chair' for any great distances), watching dearest Albert shooting, living at close quarters – all were immensely enjoyable. After dinner she would come and sit, 'full of jokes and fun', in Charlotte's bedroom.

Both Victoria and Albert felt instantly and surprisingly at home in Scotland. For Albert this was largely a matter of the landscape, which reminded him of the hills and forests of Gotha, while for Victoria it was the Highlanders themselves – she warmed to their lack of preten-sion and pretence, even their religion. While at Blair, she attended a service at the Presbyterian kirk, accompanied by Charlotte, much against Charlotte's own inclinations. She thought, wrongly, that the Queen did not enjoy the service, though 'the Prince said it was very like what he was used to in Germany, by which I suppose he meant he liked it'. For High Church Charlotte, sitting during the Psalms was 'quite unaccountable'. She and Car went to the more congenial, if spartan, 'Episcopal Chapel', with its floor of bare earth and a board to kneel on, but a service 'very well done'.

At Blair, Albert pursued his love of 'field sports' with rather more determination than skill. Lord Glenlyon had laid on grouse shooting and stalking and made every effort to put stags in the Prince's way, but nothing could disguise the fact that he was a poor shot. Charlotte faithfully recorded (with a certain relish) the stags missed or wounded, the hind shot by mistake. But besides lacking proficiency, Albert, to English eyes, was guilty of the more serious crime of bad sportsmanship. Sometimes he shot stags from Blair's windows, which left the Queen, who insisted on watching, shaken and the Princess Royal 'dreadfully distressed'. The following year, during a visit to Gotha, a *battue* was laid on – deer were rounded up into an enclosure and shot at close range, leaving fifty-five bodies and causing outrage in the English press. The *battue*, wrote Charlotte, was 'a piteous sight, much the worse from the bad shooting'. Even the Queen could not help feeling that it was 'hardly real sport'.

Charlotte generally passed the morning at Blair writing letters. Later, if there were no orders from the Queen, she seized the opportunity to steal away, taking a pony and her sketching materials. The Queen had requested a number of 'views', but was also making efforts of her own, beginning with drawing from a window, then informing Charlotte that she had 'a great longing to draw some dirty children'. Charlotte was to find these, rather as Lord Glenlyon procured stags for Albert, and make a start, then the Queen would 'come quietly and look on and draw them when not observed'. She was kept busy too making heather wreaths for the ladies, since hers were considered superior to those of Monsieur Isidore Marchand, the Queen's hairdresser, which made Isidore jealous.

Charlotte enjoyed Blair, though she clashed regularly with Lord Glenlyon, finding him irascible and tyrannical and feeling that the expeditions he'd organised for the Queen were too much for her. He must, she thought, consider her 'a complete spoilsport and the incarnation of fuss'. And since it was Lord Glenlyon who, a few years

Queen Victoria and Prince Albert in 1854

The only known photograph of Lady Sarah Lyttelton, taken in 1860, when she was seventy-three and had long retired as superintendent of the nursery

A rare photograph of the Queen with her ladies, at Osborne in August 1854. Lady Jane Ely, lady-in-waiting, is on the right, and Flora Macdonald, maid-of-honour, holds a royal dachshund

Also at Osborne that August, Mary Bulteel *(standing)*, maid-of-honour, with Lady Ely, who Mary scorned as a fawning courtier. Both wear court mourning

Lady Charlotte Canning, lady-in-waiting, with Mary Bulteel at Balmoral in 1853, shortly after Mary's appointment. The two became firm friends during their waitings

Charlotte Canning's watercolour of the Queen's arrival at the Chateau d'Eu, Normandy, in a char-à-banc. 'The body was like an enormous coach with a good deal of gilding & coats of arms & containing 2 or 3 rows of seats. The top was flat & supported with little pillars with draperies & curtains of flowery chintz', wrote Charlotte. Her picture was commandeered for one of the Queen's souvenir albums

(*Above left*) Sir James Clark, the Queen's incompetent physician-in-ordinary.
(*Above right*) Marianne Skerrett, dresser to the Queen for twenty-five years. 'Quite a superior person', said Her Majesty. (*Below left*) Lily Wellesley, wife of the Dean of Windsor and object of one of Mary Bulteel's *engougements*.(*Below right*) Eleanor Stanley, maid-of-honour for twenty years and author of lively letters about court life

In January 1861, the Queen wrote of a 'household marriage, which was settled the day before yesterday...Mary Bulteel to Colonel Ponsonby!...I shall be very sorry to lose Mary but am very glad of the marriage as I feel she will still be in the Household.' Henry Ponsonby was one of Albert's equerries

A melancholy Charlotte Canning, shortly before she left court in 1855 to accompany her husband to India

Charlotte in Calcutta, 1861. Six years in India have taken their toll and she looks older than her forty-four years

later, as the Duke of Atholl, exclaimed at her 'correctness', she was probably right. On the other hand, she liked Lady Glenlyon very much, though when, in 1852, she was mooted as mistress of the robes, Charlotte judged her 'clever and nice but too inclined to giggle'. Charlotte was not a giggler.

Towards the end of their stay, Lord Aberdeen heard news of an otter, and everyone took themselves to the banks of the Garry to see him hunted – a wretched spectacle, with the otter 'very stiff after living four days in a box' and no match for the hounds. The sight of the keeper holding the dead otter over the heads of the dogs put Charlotte in mind of Landseer: 'there was plenty to draw in every style and *Punch* and the *London News* may make the most of it – all our friends in their kilts wading abt, Isidore wading across for a good sight and all the reporters skulking about and the Queen on her pony with an umbrella and mackintosh'. Charles Landseer, Edwin's lesser-known and less charming brother, had come to Blair to sketch for the Queen, but, according to Charlotte, had proved recalcitrant and unhappy with his subject – a group of figures in front of the house. Charlotte's own protégé, on the other hand, William Leitch, who had also been summoned to Blair, declared himself 'delighted with his orders' and behaved impeccably.

As the visit drew to an end, the Queen dispensed presents and Albert gave Charlotte and the rest of the suite 'a little souvenir of himself', in somewhat dubious taste – 'the teeth of a stag set like acorns with green enamel leaves'. To commemorate Blair, the Prince designed and commissioned 'The Atholl Inkstand', a startling construction of silver, silver gilt, granite, marble, quartz and stag teeth, which he presented to the Queen for Christmas the following year. On 1 October, a fine, still morning, the royal party left for Windsor.

Victoria and Albert made a further Scottish visit in 1847. Taking the two eldest children with them under the supervision of their new governess, Miss Hildyard, who had brushed up on her botany in preparation, they sailed around the Western Isles in the *Victoria and Albert*. Albert then climbed Ben Nevis and they ended up at Ardverikie, a hunting and fishing lodge on Loch Laggan lent them by Lord Abercorn, which, despite being permanently enveloped in mist and rain, only confirmed their admiration for the Highlands and their desire for a Scottish retreat of their own. Scotland offered real seclusion – as Osborne did not – as well as bracing air, the benefits of which were loudly extolled by Sir James Clark, who had published a thesis on the effects of climate on health. According to Clark, East Scotland was drier than West. The following year, Victoria and Albert bought from Lord Aberdeen the lease on Balmoral, a small turreted castle of whitewashed granite near the river Dee.

The Year of Revolutions, 1848, began at Windsor with little in the way of gaiety – a week's mourning had been ordered for the death of a distant royal relative – but peacefully enough. The Queen, who was seven months pregnant, distributed gifts in the riding school to Windsor tenants and staff. The royal children drove about in a little barouche – a Christmas present from the Queen Dowager – pulled by a Shetland pony. There were flaming raisins for Twelfth Night and much talk of a new novel, *Jane Eyre*: 'some like it, some abuse it', said Eleanor Stanley, 'but all say it is very clever and wonder who wrote it'.

Over the previous year, however, unrest, fuelled by nationalism and economic depression, had been building through Europe – in Austria, Hungary, Germany, France, Italy, Spain, Portugal and Greece. In Britain, Chartism – a working-class movement calling for electoral reform – was gaining ground, while Ireland, in the grip of the terrible potato famine, remained a running sore. By 1848, Curraghmore, the Irish estate of Charlotte Canning's brother-in-law, Lord Waterford, was under siege, despite his best efforts to help his tenants. In March, Charlotte sent Louisa £25 to help the local people. Three months later, Waterford's fears for his wife's safety exceeded even his loathing at being parted from her, and he insisted that she go to England.

The first revolution of 1848 erupted unexpectedly in France, in February, when Louis Philippe found himself forced to abdicate and to flee with his family to England, where they threw themselves on the Queen's hospitality. Sarah Lyttelton reported the arrival of the 'refugees', without clothes, money or jewels, at Buckingham Palace. The French royal children were appallingly behaved and 'very high-born looking but puny and *very* small', hardly surprising she thought, considering that the night they arrived they consumed 'an immense supper of white soup, beef, chickens and loads of raspberry jam tarts and then were *immediately* put to bed without any washing!' The Queen, though full of sympathy for Louis Philippe, could not help thinking that he had partly brought about his own downfall by 'those unlucky Spanish marriages' (despite all assurances to the contrary during the happy visit to the Chateau d'Eu, he *had* married one of his sons, the Duke of Montpensier, to the Spanish Infanta). Metternich, the Austrian Chancellor, was toppled in March. In Italy, Lombardy and Venice rose up against the Austrian invaders, with further revolts against local rulers in Naples, Sicily, Tuscany and Rome.

Against this background of insurrection and uncertainty, the news of an impending Chartist meeting sent the British government into a spin of alarm. The Chartists intended to march to the House of Commons to present a 'monster petition' (the third such); 150,000 people, it was rumoured, were expected to gather on Kennington Common on 10 April. Such a crisis called for the reassuring and crowd-pleasing figure of the Duke of Wellington, who was drafted in to organise London's defences – the British Museum was barricaded, the Bank of England fortified, bridges were manned, troops placed at strategic points and some 85,000 special constables enrolled. On 8 April, at the urging of the prime minister, Lord John Russell, the royal family, now including Princess Louise, a 'right royal baby', and just a few weeks old, were bundled off, in pouring rain, to Osborne. On the evening of the 9th, Charles Phipps, an equerry, walked the streets of London in an attempt to gauge the public mood – was the Queen censured for her flight? It seemed she was not.

At Osborne, however, Charlotte Canning and Eleanor Stanley both considered it 'very cowardly'. And, in the event, wholly unnecessary, since the Chartist meeting proved a damp squib, a small orderly affair involving no more than 20,000 people. The petition was taken to the House of Commons in three cabs; many signatures were found to be false. George Lyttelton, Sarah's son, who had volunteered as a special constable, described to his mother how he'd paraded up and down Pall Mall with his 'blue stick and Crown badge' only to discover that 'there were rather more special constables than any other persons'. Reaching the portico in front of Hanover Chapel, which they had been instructed to clear, they found just fourteen women and two boys: 'the policemen however waged truculent war against the boys and abolished them from the portico and we marched back again covered in glory. The day might be called the triumph of failure on the part of the Chartists.'

Victoria's Britain was left untouched by the revolutions that swept across Europe during 1848, though one of John Gibson's sculptures – Her Majesty, this time in classical costume – nearly became a casualty. In Rome that November, Pope Pius IX's prime minister was assassinated, with a republic declared the following February. French troops, arriving to restore the Pope, met stiff resistance led by Garibaldi, and Gibson found himself caught up in the turmoil. Writing to Miss Skerrett in May 1849, he explained that delivery of the statue – a surprise birthday present for the Prince – would be delayed, because although it was finished and had been handed over to the polisher, the latter had fled Rome, 'leaving the work incomplete', along with his son, who was a priest – three priests had been shot and none were to be seen in the streets. Gibson himself, like most of the English in Rome, had decamped to Leghorn, where he intended to remain until 'the heat is over'. On his return in November he made a few finishing touches to the statue and finally dispatched it to England, a little late for the Prince's birthday. It was placed in the Grand Corridor at Osborne, where it stands today.

For Victoria and Albert, any anxiety about their own positions was swept aside by the excitement of taking possession of Balmoral. Their first visit was in September 1848, with Charlotte Canning in attendance. They sailed from Woolwich to Aberdeen and from there proceeded by carriage (when the railway network was extended as far as Perth, and eventually, in 1867, to Ballater, stormy voyages on the

Victoria and Albert became a thing of the past, much to everyone's relief). The castle was small, pretty and cosy, as the Queen described in her journal: 'There is a nice little hall with a billiard room; next to it is the dining room. Upstairs (ascending by a good broad staircase) immediately to the right and above the dining room is our sitting room, a fine large room – next to which is our bedroom, opening into it a little dressing-room which is Albert's. Opposite, down a few steps are the children's and Miss Hildyard's three rooms. The ladies live below and the gentlemen upstairs.'

Writing to her mother, Charlotte emphasised the smallness. 'It is a very small house and wd be comfortable for a few people and a due proportion, but now with eight at dinner every day besides the three children and their governess, there are sixty servants. What these do and who they are I have no guess for the proportions are unlike any other establishment. Housemaids were altogether forgotten and two had to be improvised who had never played the part before.' Charlotte's maid, Rain, claimed that 'she was better lodged as far as space and what she called convenience' in the Cannings' yacht than at Balmoral, and Charlotte agreed that the Queen knew nothing of 'common ways and capabilities of homes and small establishments' and did 'not care a bit how one's maid is put about'. Though Victoria prided herself on her consideration for servants, and always took the greatest interest in the personal lives of her own, in actuality she gave no more thought to their comfort and convenience than to those of her ladies and gentlemen.

Living cheek by jowl meant the putting aside of formalities and the opportunity of seeing the royal family in an 'easy unceremonious way'. Luncheons, wrote Charlotte, were 'quite in a new style', with the Queen, the Prince, the children, the household and Miss Hildyard all eating together; and she delighted in the sound of the Prince of Wales and Prince Alfred, whose rooms were beneath hers, merrily singing away. Charles Greville, visiting Balmoral, approved the unstuffiness of the royal couple, finding 'the Queen in very good humour and talkative; the Prince even more so, and talking very well; no form, and everybody seemed at their ease'. 'They live,' he added, 'not merely like private gentlefolks, but like very small gentlefolks, small house, small rooms, small establishment.' The only guard for the royal family was a single policeman.

The weather, true to Scotland, was bitterly cold, to which the Queen, who insisted on windows being left ajar to let in plenty of health-giving Scottish air, remained impervious, though as a sop to her less hardy household, fires were permitted all day, 'a comfort' Charlotte 'never expected'. Both castle and royals were swathed in tartan, the Queen's in satin and Albert in a kilt of Royal Stuart, for which, as Eleanor Stanley noted, he was rather 'too fat and substantial'. After dinner, during which Albert regaled the company with minutiae of the day's kill (a few years later Charlotte remarked that 'the Prince's shooting improves – I mean his gillies' not his skills'), the dining room was cleared for reeling, with a Scottish dancing master. Charlotte received regular letters from her sister, who had returned to Ireland that September. Curraghmore was still in a state of siege, with twenty-five soldiers billeted in the house and Lou forbidden to go out of sight of the windows, for fear of kidnapping. The Queen read Louisa's letters 'with the greatest interest'.

Both the Queen and Prince were enchanted with Balmoral. Victoria sketched, loyally accompanied Albert deer-stalking – something the household suspected he would rather she didn't – and made informal, impromptu visits to local crofters in their cottages, bearing presents of petticoats and dresses. Amongst the plain-speaking, rough-mannered Highlanders, she felt entirely comfortable. One in particular would figure largely: sitting on the box, behind the coachman, on a carriage drive at Balmoral in 1854, Eleanor Stanley noticed a 'most fascinating and good-looking young Highlander, Johnny Brown'.

Charlotte also found life at Balmoral congenial. Admittedly she did not relish compulsory activities like the Highland Games at Braemar, or the much-dreaded annual gillies' ball. The latter took place in the 'new iron house', an early prefab construction of corrugated iron on a timber frame, decorated with heather and broom. The household – the gentlemen were encouraged to appear in Highland dress – reeled dutifully, and the royal children enthusiastically, with the gillies and servants, who quickly reached levels of extreme drunkenness. But Charlotte, like the Queen, loved the 'views', the riding and the walking – she was said to walk 'like a goat', though the four-hour ascent of Loch-na-Gar, with Her Majesty on a pony led by a gillie, left her stiff. These, for Charlotte, were ample compensations for the hours of waiting in chilly rooms to hear whether her company was required on the Queen's afternoon drive or whether she might have leave to order a carriage for herself. There were cranberries to be picked and the local shop at Crathie, run by Mrs Symons and a good source of blue and white ticking petticoats, to be patronised.

Charlotte was kept busy sketching for the Queen at Balmoral, and Landseer too came to paint. Attractive and famously good company, Landseer was nevertheless a prickly character who required delicate handling, as the Queen appreciated, remaining patient and good-humoured in the face of his chronic dilatoriness with royal commissions.[2] His Scottish visits were arranged by Miss Skerrett, who sometimes accompanied him on jaunts – 'feats', as she called them – for which he had a rather greater appetite than she. In his absence, she wrote proudly describing a 'feat' undertaken on her own initiative. She had set off for Loch Muich, which the Queen wanted her to see, in the dog cart, walked the length of it, crossed two waterfalls, endured storms of hail and wind, seen 'the best rainbow ever made', arrived back at 2.30, changed into dry clothes, 'was with the Queen while she made a sketch of a picturesque child' and finally 'sat down to write a few lines' to her old friend.

Charlotte Canning was back in waiting in December, this time at Osborne, where she awaited, with sinking heart, the arrival of the Duke and Duchess of Nemours (son and daughter-in-law of King Louis Philippe), a lethally dull pair whom it was Charlotte's unenviable task to entertain. After their arrival in February, the French royals had been installed at Claremont – temporarily it was hoped, though they

---

[2] Always prone to hypochondria and depression, Landseer took to the bottle in later life and was certified as a lunatic in 1872.

showed no sign of leaving – where they became mysteriously ill. By November, the Dukes of Nemours and Joinville and Queen Marie Amélie were very ill indeed, and it was finally discovered that they were suffering from lead poisoning, from the water in a new cistern. At Osborne Charlotte thought the Duke of Nemours looked 'quite like death . . . quite blackened and blue and yellow'. The Nemours' company indeed proved wearisome – they were not 'much improved but rather the reverse for they are both so very dull. She is very pretty and nice to look at but beside having a tiresome voice she has nothing to say and everybody's mouth is shut by the number of topics we are all scrupulous of broaching in their presence.' The Queen, however, was devoted to Victoire Nemours: she was family (a first cousin), she was beautiful and she was virtuous; the possibility of dullness, in itself a kind of virtue in the eyes of Her Majesty, was simply not recognised.

Along with the Nemours came Charlotte's cousin Car Cocks, having endured an appallingly rough crossing to the Isle of Wight, 'thro' storm of wind and rain'. Car had become the subject of sentimental interest amongst the household: after eleven years as a maid-of-honour, she had fallen in love with the Rev. Charles Leslie Courtenay, Canon of Windsor and domestic chaplain to the Queen. Mr Courtenay had breeding – he was a son of the Earl of Devon – but no fortune; Car's parents, Lord and Lady Somers, were refusing consent. The Queen, however, like Charlotte, was very much in favour; as a happy young wife, she delighted in a court romance.

January 1849 saw both Charlotte and Car out of waiting and the Queen avid for information about the progress of the courtship. Charlotte provided what she could, writing 'a little gossip to Ly Lyttelton to stay the poor Queen's stomach'. Back came the reply: 'Lady Lyttelton writes me that the Queen is very impatient to know more and Mr Courtenay was looking his part well, very pale and interesting and preaching good sermons.' By February, Courtenay's finances were found to be sufficient, all was settled and the Queen could write to Charlotte to say how glad she was 'to hear that the difficulties are overcome, and that Lord and Lady Somers have consented to dear Car's marriage'. They were married in June in the palace chapel.

That summer the Queen and the Prince returned to Balmoral, together with their four eldest children. In pursuit of further seclusion, a couple of shiels (stone huts used by the gillies) at Allt-na-Guibhsaich, some five miles away from the castle, had been turned into a retreat. This was now ready, and Victoria and Albert were able to make their first visit, taking just a maid-of-honour, Caroline Dawson, Caroline's and the Queen's maids, Albert's valet, Löhlein, a footman, Shackle, and Macdonald, the head keeper, in addition to the couple who looked after the house. As the Queen described: 'To the one in which we live a wooden addition has been made. We have a charming little dining-room, sitting-room, bed-room and dressing room, all en suite.' There was also a little room for the maid-of-honour, another for the maids and a small pantry. With walls and ceilings prettily papered it all felt deliciously cosy. The second shiel, linked by a corridor, contained a kitchen, store room and loft where the male servants slept. Here was true romantic isolation – the possibility of living a kind of comfort-able camping existence with the minimum of attendants, beyond the reach of dispatch boxes and telegrams. What could be more delightful than to row around Loch Muich as dusk fell, fishing for trout, before returning to an early dinner and an evening of whist? However, the charms of Allt-na-Guibhsaich were quite lost on the household, who referred to it, disdainfully, as the 'Hut'; Charlotte thought it ugly but comfortable.

Charlotte was also summering in Scotland. The Cannings sailed around the Western Isles in the *Fair Rosamond* for seven weeks before moving on to stay with Lord and Lady Ashburton at their hunting lodge, Glen Truine House, at Kinguise. Also of the party was Thomas Carlyle, who took a dim view of the accommodation, dismissing the 'rather foolish-looking turretted diminutive pretentious grey granite house' as a 'wretched establishment', where they were 'crammed like herrings in a barrel', with inadequate supplies of hot water. But he was no more enthusiastic about his fellow guests: the 'two Lords' – a 'fat' Lord Sydney and a 'small leanish' Lord Canning – could talk of nothing but shooting, while their wives were dismissed as 'polite, elegant-looking women but hardly beyond the Belcher range' (Lady Belcher being a society lady of the 'twaddling', sketching variety with whom Carlyle had no patience).

On further acquaintance Carlyle somewhat revised his opinion of Charlotte, commending her knowledge of wild flowers and declaring her a 'good creature', though he took a sardonic view of her passion for sketching: 'Our ladies "sketch" sitting on blocks of granite and looking out for "effects" upon the distant mountains.' He marvelled too at how Charlotte could stand her husband's incessant snoring, which rendered Carlyle, in the adjoining bedroom and notoriously sensitive to noise, quite sleepless. Charlotte also complained about the size of the house and the lack of comforts – 'the worst is that there are no tubs – this with millionaires for one's host' – but apparently did not consider Carlyle's presence worthy of mention. From the Ashburtons she went to Balmoral, to resume her waiting, and found the Queen 'very happy – delighted with that simple wholesome life and going about amongst the people and knowing them all, not only their names but their histories'.

Balmoral was only held on a lease and was anyway too small to comfortably accommodate Royalties and household. In 1852, John Camden Nield, a wealthy and eccentric bachelor, who lived, like a fairy-tale miser, in a substantial Cheyne Walk house with little but a tallow candle, a bed made of boards and a cat, left the Queen over £250,000. News of this windfall was received, according to Charlotte, with equanimity: 'The great fortune did not seem to make much effect. The Queen only said – "how very odd".' She added, complacently, that Nield must have known that she wouldn't waste his legacy. And indeed she did not: part of the money (£30,000) was used to buy the freehold of Balmoral – the castle and the 17,400-acre estate – and to build a new, larger house, designed by Albert in collaboration with the architect William Smith. In 1853, the first stone was laid; two years later it was habitable.

CHAPTER 9

'The object of Education'

Sarah Lyttelton would always congratulate herself on being excused the royal migrations north. 'The Queen has returned in her usual devoted, passionate admiration for the Highlands. Leaving them is always a cause of actual *red eyes*,' she told Catherine Gladstone incredulously after Victoria and Albert's first visit to Balmoral. Fortunately for Sarah, there was always a new baby in the nursery who required her care. Princess Louise, born in 1848, was the latest addition, joining the Princess Royal, the Prince of Wales, Prince Alfred, Princess Alice and Princess Helena. Prince Arthur would be born in 1850, and, after Sarah had left court, Prince Leopold in 1853 and Princess Beatrice in 1857.

The education of this growing brood required, so Albert believed – and in this as in all things he had the full support and approval of his wife – a *system*. In devising such, he turned to Baron Stockmar, who set out his recommendations at some length. 'The object of Education,' he wrote, 'is to develop and strengthen the good and subdue or diminish the evil dispositions of our Nature.' The sons of George III, whose tutors had been 'incapable of engrafting on their minds during their youth the principles of truth and morality', demonstrated all too clearly the perils of the wrong kind of education. It was most important that Victoria and Albert's children should not only 'be brought up to be moral characters but also fitted to discharge successfully the arduous duties which may eventually devolve upon them'. The message was loud and clear: the importance of education as a force for moral good was paramount.

For their first lessons – reading, writing, arithmetic and religious instruction – the children were entrusted to Lady Lyttelton. When it came to teaching, Sarah advocated a regime of patience, flexibility and good humour. She did not see the point of conflict: 'the moment I suspect a dawn of obstinacy, arising about a letter or a word, I always say it myself, we never shd get another lesson done if once there was a battle'. And she believed that 'a lesson given in a hurry, and within strict limits as to time, is more irritating and fatiguing than one taken easily, with time to spare for interruptions'.

But by 1846 it had become apparent that the six-year-old Princess Royal was altogether too much for her. For all, or perhaps because of, Vicky's remarkable abilities and winning ways, she was a handful. Like all precociously intelligent children, she was easily bored and fond of testing the adults around her. Sarah had to contend with biting, tantrums and fibs. Saying goodbye to her governess as the Queen and Prince embarked on a cruise in the summer of 1846, together with their two eldest children, the Princess 'was most tender and touching in her regrets at leaving me . . . and if at the last minute she had not quarrelled with her bonnet and tried to bite my hand in her rage, I should take it all for steady affection'. She was much given to 'falsehoods' (bare-faced lies), insisting to Sarah 'that I had desired she should walk out after supper *in her pink bonnet* which I had not done, nor even mentioned the subject. She was imprisoned with tied hands, and very severely admonished.' Mlle Aimée Charrier was grandly informed that Sarah 'had enjoined her to call her "Charrier" without the "Mamselle"' and 'it required all the weight of my years and decent character and scarcely was it enough to get my denial fully believed'.

Vicky needed to be stretched in ways that were beyond Sarah's capacities. In 1846, Sarah Anne Hildyard, known as 'Tilla', the daughter of a clergyman, took over the education of the Princess Royal at a salary of £200. 'Our new governess,' the Queen told her uncle Leopold, 'is a sensible quiet person, who seems well accustomed to teach children and able to keep up her authority wh unfortunately poor dear Ly Lyttelton is quite incapable of doing; really latterly Vicky set her

quite at defiance and was extremely naughty with her.' For Sarah, the arrival of Miss Hildyard, a 'rare blessing', came as a relief, allowing her to concentrate on the younger children and her other duties.

'I have been overwhelmed with my usual sentimental and intellectual occupations, revising inventories, casting up and copying out quarterly bills, ordering winter clothing and starting my team of governesses smooth and even in Windsor ways,' wrote Sarah wearily in 1847. A great deal of her time was spent not so much on teaching as on managing the stream of nurses, nursery maids and governesses who came and went with varying degrees of satisfactoriness and unfailingly succumbed to petty rivalries and grievances. Mrs Sly, the head nurse, was succeeded by Mrs Thurston, who, after a somewhat shaky start, showed herself to be extremely good with the children and remained in her post for more than twenty years. Mlle Aimé Charrier, who, Sarah felt, was not all she could be, was eventual replaced by Mlle Hollande. She looked, initially, as though she mi entertain airs and graces, but turned out well: 'I perceive no lor any symptoms of fancying herself above her work or in any re dissatisfied – she has a French levity of manner but it is con with steady good intention and I think she will prove valuable Hollande proved in fact a 'perfect treasure'. Sarah judged the (governess, Mlle Grüner, 'amiable' with a 'studious turn of r

Just a year younger than the Princess Royal – but sev behind intellectually – the Prince of Wales seemed fated stand in the shadow of his brilliant sister. Physically sm speak, reluctant to learn, he could not but be outshon were all the royal children. Virtually from babyhood, ' marked down by his parents as a problem – a hopele child, lacking in self-control, self-discipline and applica fact in all his father's virtues.

Sarah took a rather different view. At three years o the Prince 'very intelligent and generous and good few passions and *stampings* occasionally; most exen and manner, bows and offers his hand beautifull *la militaire* – all unbidden'. For all the rages an

could not be faulted for good manners and sweetness of nature. A sparrow with a missing tail that came to the schoolroom window for crumbs caused much distress: 'after many expressions of pity he said "perhaps his wife has died and he has pulled out his feathers by way of mourning"'. This made Sarah laugh.

Far from resenting his more able older sister, he was much devoted to her, paying her 'many attentions'. When, as often, she was in disgrace, he would stand outside the locked door of her room relaying 'kind messages' or 'a morsel of pleasant news'. And Sarah commended his honesty – 'such truth! He inherits all his mother's.' Stockmar was not alone in thinking the Prince 'an exaggerated copy of his mother', with the implication that this was *not* a good thing; their very similarities – wilfulness, emotionalism, quick temper – perhaps go some way to explaining the Queen's impatience with, even antipathy to, her eldest son. She saw in him the very faults she regretted in herself. Sarah, however, pounced on signs of improvement: after a cruise in the *Victoria and Albert* in 1846, she felt convinced that he was 'more forward' and had developed a taste for views and scenery; a Scottish tour a year later left him 'much improved in size and manliness . . . and continues most promising for kindness and nobility of mind'.

Admittedly, Princey was not a natural scholar. Despite 'great quickness and power of learning', Sarah reported to the Queen, he 'is uncommonly averse to it and requires much patience from wilful inattention and incessant interruptions, getting under the table, upsetting the book and sundry other *anti-studious* practices'. He could be 'passionate and determined enough for an autocrat', and he was certainly boisterous, with 'spirits and boyish eagerness' that required rather a large space to work them off in', but, after all, such behaviour was hardly unusual from an energetic small boy. The solution, Sarah believed, to his fondness for 'violent exercise and enjoyment of life' was simply to keep him occupied.

After the challenges presented by the Princess Royal and the Prince of Wales, the other children offered little difficulty, but fewer rewards. lessons with Alice and Alfred were 'as soothing as they used to be trying with *les aines*'. Alice read well and produced 'creditable

dictées' but she was 'neither studious, nor, certainly, so clever as the Princess Royal'. Alfred was happy enough to sit on Sarah's lap and listen to 'History of England stories'; though rather naughty and less affectionate than the others, she judged him 'a virtuous, sturdy, genuine boy . . . but he will require a good education' (whether nature or nurture were at fault, 'Affie' grew up strikingly deficient in charm and intellect). Neither child was 'much given to wit'.

For Sarah, 'prosperity' consisted 'in uninterrupted lessons – adversity in Mme Rollande [Mlle Hollande's replacement] being unpunctual, Mlle Grüner ill, Miss Hildyard oppressed, or the children being called away on treats'. All too frequently lessons were interrupted: a visit from a haberdasher bearing silks and ribbons; jaunts to the zoo, the circus or the theatre; rehearsals for the plays and tableaux regularly performed by the children (in 1854, Eleanor Stanley reported the Queen as shocked by Prince Arthur's 'scanty' costume, and though his nurse assured her that he was wearing 'flesh-coloured decencies', he was still sent away to be properly dressed). Then too there were the frequent absences for sittings, for portraits of the royal children. In the spring of 1849, Winterhalter was at Windsor 'painting numberless portraits for surprises – upsetting lessons, puzzling hours and driving one quite wild with bewilderment and interruptions'.

Treats aside, Victoria, and especially Albert, gave considerable thought and care to the education of their children. This was particularly so in the case of the Prince of Wales, not merely because of the position he would one day occupy, but because of the perceived faultiness of the raw material: to counter those 'anti-studious practices' and delinquent tendencies, a 'Plan' was required. In 1846 they once again called in Stockmar.

Stockmar, naturally, had a good deal to say. He felt the five-year-old Prince to be 'essentially a nervous and excitable child with little power of endurance or sustained action in any direction and that the utmost care and judgement will be required in his physical and mental training to improve his stamina and develop his faculties to their full extent'. An understanding of the physiology of the brain would be useful, indeed essential, in dealing with such a child – 'to promote the further development therefore of the intellectual and moral organs of the brain *the only effectual way is to exercise the corresponding faculties regularly and systematically*'. 'Dry bracing air' was recommended to 'impart tone' to the nervous system.

On Stockmar's recommendation, Dr George Combe, the renowned Scottish phrenologist (and educationalist) was consulted. His report was not encouraging: 'the brain of the Prince of Wales appears to me to be abnormal in *condition* and in *form* . . . deficient in the region of the intellectual organs . . . the feeble quality of the brain will render the Prince of Wales highly excitable'. 'The one thing needful above all others with the Prince of Wales at present,' pronounced Stockmar, 'is as far as possible to promote the uniform, equable and sustained action of his feelings, affections, moral sentiments and intellectual powers. To do this requires a very favourable combination of good sense, kindliness, firmness, readiness and activity of mind, great tact, thorough control of temper and unwearied patience.' Clearly the moral and intellectual education of the Prince was to be no easy task, requiring a quite exceptional individual.

Stockmar followed up his diagnosis with a further, highly prescriptive, memorandum, suggesting prospective timetables for both the five-year-old Prince of Wales and the six-year-old Princess Royal. The children were to have lessons in French, German, writing, reading, arithmetic, geography and scripture. They should get plenty of health-giving fresh air – two hours in the morning and an hour in the afternoon – and have tea at six with either Her Majesty or Miss Hildyard. Even Princess Alice, at just three, was to have daily lessons in English, French and German. Stockmar went on to recommend suitable books – *New Cobwebs to Catch Flies, Rhymes for the Nursery by the author of Original Poems, Hymns for Infant Minds, Little Robert and the Owl, Danish Fairy Tales* – and advised that the children 'should not be made to look upon Sunday as a gloomy day' (the Queen herself greatly disliked a 'Sunday face'), and that, as well as attending church, they should be encouraged to amuse themselves. He subsequently wrote to the Queen, apologising for the fact that his paper was not quite as comprehensive as it might have been.

A few months later, in January 1847, the Queen and the Prince produced a memorandum of their own, based on Stockmar's recommendations. The children, they decreed, were to be divided into classes according to age. In the nursery class, up until the age of five or six, they were to be taught English, French, German and counting, but the emphasis was to be on physical development. Aged four they would begin religious instruction. The second class was to be taught by Miss Hildyard, under the supervision of Lady Lyttelton; there were to be no lessons on Sunday, and the children were to kneel to say their prayers in the presence of Miss Hildyard. The Prince was to remain in class two until the age of six or seven, before entering a third class with a tutor, and then, at twelve or thirteen, a fourth class. The Princess Royal was to stay with Miss Hildyard until she was nine or ten and then go into a third class with a 'Lady Governess'.

Timetables were drawn up. In 1848 the Princess Royal began her day, at 8.20, with arithmetic, punctuation or writing, before going out at 9. At 11.15 came scripture, writing or reading, followed by German at 12 and half an hour of music at 1. After luncheon and another hour outside, she continued with French at 4, dancing at 5 twice a week, otherwise chronology as far as Edward VI, history or poetry, and finally, story-book reading at 6. All lessons, apart from French and German, were given by Miss Hildyard. The Prince of Wales followed a similar schedule.

These instructions were reinforced by memos from the Queen to Lady Lyttelton: it was most important that the timetables 'be strictly adhered to'. The Prince of Wales and the Princess Royal were to breakfast with Miss Hildyard, and Princess Alice with Lady Lyttelton, while Prince Alfred was now to come down in the morning to the Queen instead of Princess Alice. The two older children were to take their exercise with Miss Hildyard; the Queen was to give the Princess Royal religious instruction, while Lady Lyttelton undertook that of the Prince of Wales; Lady Lyttelton was also to be responsible for Princess Alice's English lessons. Having consulted Stockmar, the Queen informed Sarah that the Princess Royal was to attend an afternoon service on Sundays when a private chapel was to hand, as at Windsor or Buckingham Palace, and provided there was no sermon; the Prince of Wales, however, was still 'much too childish' to attend any service for at least a year.

It was no accident that the Princess Royal did not receive her religious instruction from Sarah. The Queen enjoyed perfect confidence in her superintendent of the nursery, save in the matter of religion: 'It quite grieved Her Majesty that Ly L. should have so many opinions (good perhaps in themselves but very peculiar on some points) from which she entirely differed. She could not help it in some degree shaking her confidence in her . . .' By 'peculiar' opinions she meant Sarah's supposed 'Puseyite' views. The Queen's religious position was self-determined and idiosyncratic. She had been brought up by a Lutheran governess and was married to a Lutheran husband; she found excessive displays of faith deeply suspect; her sympathies were firmly Broad Church. In the 1840s, a time of acute religious anxiety, the faintest whiff of Puseyism sent Victoria into a spin of alarm.

Edward Pusey, Oxford Professor of Hebrew, was a leading light of the Oxford Movement, which had originated in 1833 with a sermon preached by John Keble – also an Oxford professor – on the subject of national apostasy, calling on the government not to attempt to limit the powers of the Church by reducing the number of Protestant bishoprics in Ireland. This was followed by the publication of tracts (theological papers) written by Oxford academics like John Henry Newman and Pusey (known as Tractarians), defending High Church doctrines and seeking to reinvigorate and purify the Anglican Church by returning it to its pre-Reformation Catholic nature – that is, Anglo-Catholic not Roman (a crucial distinction, though one many failed to make). The movement culminated in 1841 with the publication by Newman of Tract No. 90, which argued that the Thirty-Nine Articles, to which members of the Church of England had to subscribe, *were* compatible with Catholicism. This provoked howls of outrage the length and breadth of England.

The immense alarm and anxiety occasioned by the Oxford Movement – though it seems an arcane and esoteric furore today – was entirely due to the spectre of 'Popery' hovering behind it. For many, including the Queen, Tractarians were simply putative Roman Catholics, a suspicion only confirmed when some Tractarians *did* convert (Newman himself in 1845). In fact the Queen firmly believed in religious toleration; her indignation was directed at Tractarians, or 'Puseyites', rather than Roman Catholics, because they seemed to her disingenuous, Catholics *masquerading* as Anglicans – 'R Catholics at *heart* and *very insincere* as to their professions of attachment to the Church'. For someone of Victoria's transparent nature, insincerity was a grave failing.

Sarah Lyttelton had first-hand experience of the shame of losing a family member to 'Romanism'. Her brother, George Spencer, an Anglican priest, converted and was ordained into the Catholic Church in 1830 (he began a prayer campaign for the conversion of England and later became a Passionist monk, known as Father Ignatius). On George's conversion his mother, Lady Spencer, went into mourning, while for Sarah it was 'so deep an affliction . . . that it weighs us all down'. She did not however sever relations with George and indeed was occasionally grateful to him for stiffening letters, which 'had a really marvellous effect on me – as if I had been trailing on the ground and he had just picked me up and tied me to an oaken post . . . What I mean about George's letter strengthening me is as to my place. I feel quite a fresh comfort in his view of it, and have repeatedly since caught myself quoting his words to myself *"called to it"*, with much pleasure.' But she couldn't help feeling relieved when he visited her in his priest's robes at her London home in Grosvenor Place, rather than at Buckingham Palace.

High Church in Sarah's case (and in Charlotte Canning's) did not mean Anglo-Catholic, let alone Anglo-Roman, but simply an enthusiasm for worship, and prayer in particular, and a punctiliousness about its forms. Amongst the fervently High Church Lytteltons, Sarah looked moderate (she assured her heavily pregnant daughter Lavinia that it would be perfectly acceptable to sit in church during the psalms and hymns). There was a good deal of romance about the Oxford Movement, inherent in the concept of the continuation of medieval

Catholicism, and Sarah was a romantic. She was drawn to the idea of a revitalised Anglican faith, to High Church practices such as fasting and confession. But this was a long way from embracing Catholicism, and like many, including the Queen, she was much alarmed at the number of converts to 'Romanism' in the mid 1840s – 'it begins to frighten me . . . as long as the Bishops are all steady, I do trust we shall only loose the good riddances'.

According to Lady Holland, Sarah, though 'very strict in religion has not given in to any of the extremes which divide society so much'. The Queen, with her horror of religious extremes, was not so sure. Was it really necessary for Sarah to receive the sacrament 'on every opportunity' – three times in just five days over Easter? Did the children have to kneel to say their prayers when they could just sit up in bed? (They continued to kneel.) And what if some of Sarah's Puseyite ideas should feed into the Princess Royal's fertile imagination? 'I dread the *extreme* and I must say *besotted* notions of religion now so prevalent . . . as I dread it being attempted to instil these Doctrines into our daughter's mind.' This was the crux of it: Lady Lyttelton's religious views were a matter for her own conscience, but Victoria did not want them instilled into her daughter.

To avoid such an eventuality, the Queen took on the Princess Royal's religious instruction herself, while Sarah oversaw that of the Prince of Wales, presumably considered a blunter instrument. Sarah, worried that Vicky's religious education was not all it should be, was greatly relieved when Gerald Wellesley, the resident chaplain at Windsor (later Dean of Windsor) stepped in. Twice a week the cadaverous Mr Wellesley, 'very thin and black and ascetic looking . . . a little Wellingtonish', taught the Princess her catechism, 'making her fully understand it with a Bible to refer to – she is to write an account of each conversation in her own language . . . she asks questions and takes great interest in it thank God! I believe her religious education will now indeed be as good as one could wish.'

There was some talk of Samuel Wilberforce, the High Church Bishop of Oxford, being appointed tutor to the Prince of Wales, who, by

1849, according to the 'Plan', was due to move on from Miss Hildyard. Much though Sarah admired Wilberforce's sermons, she could not quite approve of him as tutor to the Prince. He betrayed, she felt, a want of seriousness, a certain levity, playing chess with Albert on a Sunday for example – 'it is of course harmless, but, but – I want something to set against the constant compliance and increasing charm, which continues quite irresistible, but is hardly what I should like to look up to in my Princey's tutor'.

In the end Henry Birch, recommended by Sir James Clark, was appointed tutor to the Prince of Wales at £800 per year. The handsome thirty-three-year-old Birch had been a master at Eton, and appeared eminently qualified to take on the Prince, though his ecclesiastical ambitions and suspected Puseyism presented, as with Lady Lyttelton, a small cloud of anxiety for the royal parents. Birch, who had been primed as to the problematic nature of his pupil, steeled himself for the task ahead: 'He must obey – I must command – His temper must yield – His affection must be won. How one and the same hand is to effect this, I know not. I must see Baron Stockmar', reads a note to himself.

Under Mr Birch, the Prince of Wales's day began at 7.15. After breakfast he had religion or calculating from 8.15 till 9, a quarter of an hour downstairs with his parents, English between 9.15 and 10, then exercise outside until 12 o'clock luncheon, followed by writing and sums at 12.30, German or French at 1, and dinner at 2. After half an hour of play, lessons were resumed at 3.30 with drawing (taught by Mr Leitch) dancing or music (with Mr Anderson), then, at 4, history, geography or natural history. Supper, during which Mr Birch might read him 'some amusing book', was at 5. He saw his mother at 7 and went to bed at 8. Followed six days a week, this was a relentless and demanding regime for an eight-year-old boy.

As with the Princess Royal, there were some differences when it came to religious instruction. When Birch was told to avoid any mention of the catechism in his teaching, he threatened to resign. The prohibition was withdrawn. To clarify matters Albert read Mr Birch a memorandum in December 1849. The Prince of Wales was to be taught the catechism and to attend a Sunday evening service when there was a private chapel on hand; Mr Birch himself was at liberty to attend a Sunday service (at Balmoral this meant the local Presbyterian church, to his dismay); playmates for the Prince were no longer to be invited on Sundays, to avoid offending those who were not asked (Birch thought this a mistake; and that the Prince would benefit from the company of other boys); lastly, 'whatever relaxation can be procured for Mr Birch to diminish the tension his daily duties expose him to will be tried to obtain' (sic). Nobody, it seemed, saw Birch's position as a sinecure.

Initially Mr Birch struggled. He found Bertie 'extremely disobedient, impertinent to his masters, and unwilling to submit to discipline'; he was late for lessons, unkind to his brothers and sisters, and 'thoroughly rebellious'. But after a year he was able to report to Stockmar that although there had been times when he 'almost despaired of being able to instruct or manage him', now he seemed 'to have found the key to his heart'. Master and pupil had grown fond of one another. In October 1850, Birch told Albert that he felt much of the Prince's bad behaviour could be explained by the fact that 'he was undergoing a sort of transformation from the child to the boy and was determined to see how far he could go in resisting and opposing authority of all sorts . . . such expressions as "when I get this property I will shoot that pheasant" are childish yet significant symptoms of what may be going on internally', and showed, Birch thought, an awareness of his position. Birch himself displayed an awareness of the psychological changes at work within a small boy. 'The regulation of the temper and conduct of the Prince of Wales,' he continued, 'must be a work of patient care and watchfulness, of mixed kindness and severity not for months but years,' but he felt there had been progress. So too did George Combe, the phrenologist, who detected some improvement: the intellectual organs, though still only moderately developed, were larger than three years earlier, but unfortunately 'the organs of Combativeness, Destructiveness, Self-Esteem, Concentrativeness and Firmness' were all large too, resulting in a self-willed, obstinate child.

Sarah Lyttelton approved of Mr Birch. He was, she told her son,

George, 'quite *en train* and hitherto all goes well – Princey is heard
singing to himself very loud and jumping about in his beautiful new
rooms'. She relayed to Mary Lyttelton a story told her by Mr Birch:
while out walking, he and the Prince had passed a carpenter's shop,
where, seeing a man at work, Princey had begged to have a go himself.
'Mr Birch consented and actually staid with him above an hour (how
much better than any lesson!) learning and teaching him and talking
to the man and helping (but not much) till the Prince had made a
monstrous bungling foot stool with his own hands' which he carried
home 'triumphantly' on his shoulders. 'How I do hope and wish the
man may stay on,' Sarah added.

Sadly for Bertie, Mr Birch resigned in 1852. Albert felt his son was
not making sufficient progress: the 'Plan' was failing; he needed to be
driven harder. Birch's intention of taking Holy Orders also caused
concern (on leaving court he accepted a lucrative living from Lord
Wilton). There was much regret on both sides. Mr Birch 'poured out
his sorrows' to Eleanor Stanley. Charlotte Canning noted that his
leaving was 'a terrible sorrow to the Prince of Wales, who has done
no end of touching things since he heard that he was to lose him
three weeks ago. His little notes and presents which Mr Birch used
to find on his pillow were really too moving.' In Birch's place came
Mr Gibbs, from a dissenting, middle-class background, and thus, in
the eyes of the Queen and the Prince, much more reassuring than
suspect High Church aristocracy. Prior to his appointment Gibbs
submitted to an examination by George Combe, to assess his suitability.
The results were deemed favourable: 'a brain of sufficient size to give
him force of character, animal, moral and intellectual . . . has the
elements of selfishness and ambition strongly developed, also those
which, in certain circumstances, might produce hardness and severity
of temper . . . has the love of children and benevolence'. References
to 'hardness' and 'severity of temper' might have given pause for
thought.

Mr Gibbs, a dry martinet of a man, did indeed prove severe, and
though remaining in his post until 1858, he never won the affection
of either the Prince of Wales or Prince Alfred, who was also in his

charge. On his arrival, the day after Mr Birch's departure, he went for a walk with the two princes. Apologising for their silence, the Prince of Wales explained, 'You cannot wonder if we are somewhat dull today. We are sorry Mr Birch has gone. It is very natural is it not?' Gibbs stepped up the Prince's regime, to little effect other than to induce violent rages – hurling, stamping and screaming. Dr Becker, the Windsor librarian, who taught the princes German, wrote to Albert warning him that Bertie's rages were the result of being over-worked. His letter was ignored.

Whether it was thanks to being stretched intellectually – under Miss Hildyard the Princess Royal perfected her French and German, studied Latin and read widely, including Gibbon's *Decline and Fall of the Roman Empire*, George Eliot, Dickens, the Brontës, and Shakespeare – or simply the result of growing up, Sarah saw decided signs of improvement in Vicky's behaviour as the years passed. She was shaping up, Sarah believed, to be a really 'fine character'. When the royal family returned from their summer visit to Balmoral in 1849, Sarah considered all the children to have greatly benefited from their Scottish sojourn, but the Princess Royal in particular: 'so enormously improved in manner, in temper, and conduct altogether as really to give a bright promise of all good . . . Her talent and brilliancy naturally have lost no ground. She may turn out something remarkable. At my window just now she began with much foreign gesture, quite naturally though, lamenting over leaving Scotland. "Oh, where are the mountains! I look all around for the dear mountains! And the river! It was like a silver ribbon binding all together, so beautiful!" She repeats number-less long German verses by heart and seems to have got on much in her lessons.'

But Vicky had lost none of her originality and wit. While out riding, Miss Hildyard suggested that Madame Rollande, the new French governess, should use a broken whip, which she herself always used when riding with the children, whereupon, wrote Sarah, Vicky 'said in the sharpest, sly way, "Oh no! that whip won't do at all for her. She is much too grand to use what you use. You are only Miss Hildyard;

she is Madame Rollande de la Sange!" just as fully entering into the finery as she will do at twenty, and formidably satirical her turn is – no ridicule or foible escapes her. Luckily Miss H is on her guard, with plenty of cold water for such jokes.' Listening to Sarah playing chords on the piano, Vicky observed, 'I like chords, one can *read* them. They make one sometimes gay, sometimes sad. It used to be too much for me to like formerly.'

However, occasional tantrums still erupted, as on one fine summer's day at Claremont: 'I have just had to sit by a dreadful roar of Princessy on this hot morning, without the smallest perceptible reason – it lasted half an hour, through every variety of noise and convulsion and despair. How very odd it is – one can't guess what it can be about – real tears and wretchedness all the time at nothing. Such high summer and lovely place and agreeable society and constant kindness and interesting nursery events and all well got through in spite of my cough, good health too – what would I have? I know very well but still think myself rather beastly for feeling any regrets.' Whatever satisfactions her position had brought – knowing that she had answered the call of duty and shown herself competent, knowing that she was needed and appreciated – Sarah could never quite banish her regrets.

CHAPTER 10

Departures

Sarah Lyttelton spent the summer of 1849 on the Isle of Wight, with the younger children. As southern England sweltered under cloudless skies, she felt immensely grateful for the sea breezes of Osborne, where building works on the new house continued, with a first-floor loggia (later glassed in) connecting the Pavilion to the Household Wing. She wrote to the Queen of the 'extraordinary beauty of the open Gallery', which 'afforded' her 'real happiness in many an hour of lovely sunset and moonlight during this unequalled summer'. There had been the usual celebrations for Albert's birthday, with the children arranging nosegays around a statue of the Prince and finding, at its feet, presents for themselves. What with 'the excitement of this cere-mony and the fine frocks and the sailor's dress and the little *air de fête* we tried to get up in honour of this happy day', Princess Helena had succumbed to 'her first fit of rage' since Her Majesty's departure, requiring a spell in 'custody'.

By October, Victoria and Albert had arrived back at Osborne, with the Queen, as ever, extolling the glories of Scotland, insisting that 'Scotch air, Scotch people, Scotch hills, Scotch rivers, Scotch woods, are all far preferable to those of any other nation in or out of this world; that deer stalking is the most charming of amusements etc.'. Sarah remained sceptical: 'The chief support to my spirits is that I shall never see, hear or witness these various charms. This soothing thought helps me to smile on happily.' Rain and gales arrived too, the children raced up and down the new gallery, and Sarah was once more deep in 'accounts, tradesmen's letters, maids' quarrels, bad fitting of frocks, desirability of rhubarb and magnesia and by way of intellectual pursuits, false French genders and elements of the multiplication table'.

Then came shocking news: George Anson, Albert's former secretary and, since 1847, keeper of the privy purse, had suddenly dropped dead at his wife's feet. This was not entirely unexpected, since Anson had been suffering from bad headaches and poor health for some time, but he was only thirty-seven and his wife, having suffered several miscarriages, was seven months pregnant. All were greatly shocked. Despite the Prince's initial misgivings, Anson had become a true friend, and his death came as a very great blow. 'No words can express what a loss he is to all here,' wrote Sarah to Catherine Gladstone, 'the Prince was quite overcome and still looks very ill and as if he never could smile again' and the Queen too was 'much afflicted'. The real, and irreplaceable, loss, she felt, was not so much of an 'efficient and able' servant as of 'so warm and faithful a private friend'.

Charlotte Canning, arriving at Osborne in order to attend the Queen on her journey back to Windsor, agreed that Anson had been the Prince's 'only intimate friend in England'. She found the Prince 'so cut up, he looks quite altered and low', while the Queen, having 'sobbed and cried all afternoon', came to Charlotte's room to talk it all over. For three days the royal couple dined alone and were scarcely seen. Anson's death meant a shake-up in the household: Colonel Charles Phipps, Albert's secretary since 1847, now became keeper of the privy purse and General Charles Grey took his place.

An outbreak of cholera at Windsor – an epidemic that killed 53,000 people in England and Wales – meant that the Queen and Prince delayed their departure from Osborne, leaving everyone 'lopsided'. When they felt it was safe enough to return, they decided that Lady Lyttelton and the children should be left behind. Sarah waited anxiously for the all-clear from Windsor: 'this doubt and chance and the heavy gale whistling and rattling and moaning around and through us and the gloomy sky and falling leaves, mingling but too naturally with a sadness I cannot shake off about Mr Anson's death and his widow's state made me feel very cheerless'. Gloom prevailed. At Windsor,

Eleanor Stanley reported, 'the dullness of our evenings is a thing impossible to describe'; even cards seemed to have been given up.

By the end of October Sarah was back at Windsor, in time to accompany the Princess Royal and the Prince of Wales to the opening of the new Coal Exchange. The Queen, suffering from chickenpox, had had to bow out and was most 'wretched at being prevented from going to see the children received on their first state occasion'. Albert took her place, with Sarah and Mr Birch in attendance. They sailed in the royal yacht, accompanied by barges – one bearing the Queen's swans – from Whitehall to London Bridge, a magnificent spectacle as Sarah described: the weather was 'Italian'; figures could be seen sitting on the dome of St Paul's; 'every inch of ground, every bridge, roof, window and as many vessels of all sorts as could lie on the river . . . were covered, close packed with people', cheering lustily. At the Exchange, the Prince of Wales and the Princess Royal had their own luncheon upstairs and were given some wine by a man who was so overcome that he 'actually shed tears' and had to leave the room. To Sarah's relief the children acquitted themselves well, while she herself made no 'blunders', except once addressing the Lord Mayor as 'sir' instead of 'my lord'. She felt proud and emotional and was able to 'enjoy the sight and sound of all London's loyalty which was really sublime and touching'. Subsequently the Princess Royal told her dresser that 'it was very nice being the only great Lady' and being fussed over, but she had been greatly disappointed not to get any pudding.

The glorious summer of 1849 was followed by a bitterly cold winter. 'Snow and gloom and candles at breakfast' (the private rooms at Windsor were still candlelit), wrote Sarah, from Windsor, in the grip of a black frost. When she asked Albert if he would look over the quarterly accounts, he replied, 'yes, certainly, if *you* will consent to my doing reel steps all the time to warm myself', and proceeded to hop gently from foot to foot. Christmas Eve found her awaiting Caroline and Kitty for dinner. 'Here I am established once more at my old writing table and with my harness shaking on very smoothly so far.'

'Harness' was not a word she used lightly. By 1850, after eight years as superintendent of the nursery, she was feeling increasingly restive, lamenting her 'most solitary life – visions of fellow-creatures all about but not one I feel much interest or connection with except the babies', and confessing to feeling 'dissatisfied with my own lot . . . till I remember how wrong and thankless such a feeling is'. Her loneliness and the pain of missing her children had not diminished, indeed, rather the opposite. At sixty-three, she simply felt too old for the job, and her responsibilities weighed heavily – 'my prospect is fast closing in and growing limited to court and work and little frets and worrits of my strange life. It is one of my chief and bright supports to think in any moments of leisure and loneliness of all the happy spots in the free and out-of-door world where my dear ones are settled . . . a kiss to the dear babykin from his mysterious live Granny,' she wrote to Lavinia. Duty no longer seemed quite enough to keep her 'slipping and swerving and floundering . . . along the narrow way'. She longed to return to the 'free and out-of-door world'.

In March 1850, she caught a chill and was dosed with henbane, which brought on an 'attack', a kind of paralysis, wrongly identified by Sir James Clark – that master of misdiagnosis – as a stroke. Sarah recovered, but her family felt that the time had come for her to retire, and Lord Spencer wrote to the Prince to tell him so. However, neither the Prince nor the Queen could quite bear the prospect of losing Lady Lyttelton. Instead it was agreed that her duties should be lightened; henceforth she would do no teaching, and would occupy a merely supervisory role.

Then tragedy intervened. In October, Sarah heard that Lavinia was dangerously ill after giving birth to her fourth child. She hurried to Hawarden, but, by the time she arrived, Lavinia was dead, leaving Henry Glynne a widower with four small daughters. On Sarah's return to Windsor, one of her first visitors was Charlotte Canning, come to condole – 'she does feel with us so nicely and seems to have thought so deeply and piously about our loss', Sarah told Mary Lyttelton. Lavinia's death determined her to act on her desire to leave court. Her duty now, she felt, lay with her family, and she knew too that her daughter Caroline would wish to be of help at Hawarden: 'I could not remain tied by duties, away from all my family, now that I and much more Caroline, may be sometimes called upon and shall always be most anxious to be of use if possible to the poor children at Hawarden. I have besides a longing to be with my remaining children after the awful break in their circle, which I feel no reason for resisting.' She told Baron Stockmar that she wished to resign. The Queen took it well, accepting Sarah's reasons as 'unanswerably strong' and agreeing that she could leave in the New Year – 'she said it with all the feeling and kindness of which I have received such constant and unvarying proof through the whole long 12 years during which I have served her'. Sarah wrote too to the Rev. Gurdlestone, her spiritual touchstone, anxious that he should approve her 'step'.

Meanwhile she waited to hear what kind of pension she might be granted: 'the Queen and I have our usual interminable talks about anything or nothing and I have had one long visit from the Prince but not a word has been dropped about it'. By Christmas all was settled: she was to have a generous £800 a year. 'How rich and envied it would make many a clergyman with 10 children!' It made her quite 'ashamed'. Her greatest dread was the royal children 'being grieved' at her loss, but at least she approved of her successor, Lady Caroline Barrington, hitherto a woman of the bedchamber, as kindly and fond of children and, which was almost equally important, 'both intimate with the Queen and thoroughly acquainted with Court'. Now it was just a question of waiting for the uncomfortable 'interval of sitting out' to be over.

The final parting came in January, an emotional ordeal for Sarah. 'The last day was unpleasant enough throughout – nothing but good-bying. Then in the evening I was sent for to my last audience in the Queen's own room and I quite broke down, and could hardly speak or hear. I remember the Prince's face ("pale as ashes") and a few words of praise and thanks from them both; but it is all misty and I had to stop on the private staircase and have my cry out before I could go up again.' 'Poor Lady Lyttelton,' wrote the Queen, 'was very much overcome.' Then Sarah 'made all' her presents 'with very full success', and in turn received, from the children, a bracelet hung with their miniatures. 'The darlings all came up in succession and a bad spot of road it was to get through. I dare neither look back nor look forward. Upward, in trembling and fear and humiliation I can look, with something but not enough, of hope and trust for them for whom I undertook so much and have done so little – them, whose sins and final doom I have in some sort to answer for, and *how*? They all cried and were most touching. The Prince of Wales, who has seen so little of me lately, cried and seemed to feel the most. The Princess Royal said many striking and feeling and clever things.' She was greatly touched, a few months later, to receive a pair of bantams from Bertie.

For Caroline and Kitty there was regret too. There had been little 'luxurious or gay' about their lives as court satellites, but the change would be a great one and both felt 'much on leaving Windsor for good'. As Sarah's train steamed towards London and the castle, that 'piece of sublimity', shrank to a silhouette against the darkening January sky, she finally allowed something like relief to steal over her. 'It was not till after a *long* nap in the railroad that I felt my job was done, and woke with a pleasant *subsided* feeling, and as if the worst was over, and the beginning of rest came into my mind.'

Court waitings for Charlotte Canning had come to offer some respite and distraction from the humiliations and disappointments of her marriage, which, by the late 1840s, was much shadowed by her husband's infidelity. Lord Elgin, who had been at school and Oxford with Charles Canning, thought it 'one of the saddest instances he had ever known of a true love marriage turning out unhappily'. In November 1849, while Charlotte was in waiting, Charles was invited to Windsor to shoot. Sarah Lyttelton, who was present, described how, as General Grey and the Prince of Wales went to pick up a dead pheasant, Canning fired, grazing Grey's temple and promptly falling to the ground himself. Charlotte, seeing her husband laid out, 'then raised by two men like a corpse', gave a shriek and ran to him, assuming, as she told Sarah, that he was dead. In fact Canning had merely fainted – something he was prone to at moments of high emotion – thinking that he'd shot the Prince of Wales. Gossip had it otherwise: his collapse was put down to a recent 'stormy interview' with his mistress and his anxiety lest it come to the ears of the Queen. Charlotte was 'said not to be in the least disturbed about this lady'. And certainly no hint of blame or unhappiness enters her letters. But to allude to Canning's faithlessness would have been unthinkable, an act of gross disloyalty, a dereliction of duty. Hers was not a nature to allow for admissions of unhappiness. Sadness, though, could be read in her face.

'What a week of horrid events we have had,' Charlotte wrote on 1 July 1850. While in her carriage, returning from a visit to the dying Duke of Cambridge at Cambridge House, the Queen (newly recovered from the birth of Prince Arthur in May) had been struck a smart blow above the eye with a brass-topped cane by Robert Pate, a retired lieutenant of the 10th Hussars. This was the fifth attack on Her Majesty by deranged young men. The force of the blow was deflected by the brim of her bonnet, but she was still left, briefly, unconscious, and badly bruised. Three of her children and her lady-in-waiting Lady Jocelyn were in the carriage with her, and Charlotte arrived moments later to see Pate being marched off by a policeman. He was, she reported 'quite a gentleman', and a familiar face to many, used to seeing him taking his daily walks in the park, but 'certainly mad'. That evening the Queen attended the opera and was loudly cheered. When the Cannings dined at Windsor a week later, the bump on her forehead was still plain to see.

Then a couple of days after Pate's assault, Sir Robert Peel attended a meeting of the Exhibition Commissioners to discuss the Great Exhibition, a project conceived and driven by Prince Albert and warmly supported by Peel. As Sir Robert returned home, he was thrown from his horse on Constitution Hill, and on 5 July, after three days of agonising pain, he died. This, thought Charlotte, was a 'dreadful blow to the country', and she noted how terribly cast down were the Queen and Prince. Peel was widely mourned, and by none more than Albert, who had kept in close touch with him since he had left office in 1846 and had come to regard him, the Queen felt, as a 'second father'.

Almost a year later, on 1 May 1851, the Great Exhibition opened to wild acclaim, a personal triumph for Albert. Visitors marvelled as much at Joseph Paxton's great, glittering greenhouse (dubbed 'Crystal Palace'), an elegant, light-filled structure of glass and iron, its soaring transept enclosing three of Hyde Park's great elms, as at the variety, inventiveness and sheer oddity of its contents – 14,000 exhibits from around the world. Sarah Lyttelton attended the opening ceremony, and afterwards wrote to the Queen to congratulate her on 'so noble, so daring and so benevolent a plan', a fitting testament, she thought, to the Prince. The Queen replied, full of warmth and gratitude. It had indeed been 'the proudest and happiest day of as you truly call it my "happy life". . . To see this great conception of my beloved husband's great and good mind which is always labouring for the good of others, to see this *great* thought and work crowned with triumphant success in spite of difficulties and opposition of every imaginable kind and sort – and of every effort which jealousy and calumny could resort to – to cause its failure, has been an immense happiness to us both.'

Since leaving court, Sarah Lyttelton had set up home in London, in Stratton Street, with Caroline and Kitty, while making frequent visits to the rectory at Hawarden, and to Hagley, where as 'General Granny' she dodged cricket balls and taught her grandchildren French. To Caroline, she was rather more frank on the subject of the Exhibition, admitting that she had 'no enthusiasm for the trade and industry part of it and think that passage in Prince Albert's speech a piece of mere German philosophy, worthless at best', but overall it seemed to her an entirely worthwhile enterprise, benefiting those who deserved it and a splendid vindication of all the Prince believed in and had worked so hard for in the face of much doom-mongering and mockery. She couldn't help but share the Queen's pleasure 'on witnessing the full and unexpectable success of her husband's great undertaking, which must redound to his honour (everywhere except in London) and shew what he is made of, as to talent at least . . . I believe it is universally sneered at and abominated by the *beau monde* and will only increase the contempt for the Prince among all fine folk. But so would anything he does.'

More than six million people (a third of the entire population of

Britain) visited the Exhibition. Many, like Her Majesty, went more than once. Charlotte Canning accompanied the royal family on several visits as it drew to a close in October. On the 15th, she was with the Queen as Her Majesty made some last-minute sketches. The next day she attended the closing ceremony, where the Prince read a report and expressed thanks, the Bishop of London offered a few prayers, and 'so the Exhibition ended'.

The Great Exhibition proclaimed peace, prosperity and Britain's status as a champion of free trade and an industrial and imperial power. It stood too as a monument to Albert's vision and determination. Three years later, Britain was at war in Europe for the first time in forty years, and Albert was dubbed a traitor. Religion, nationalism and imperialism all played their part in the Crimean War. In the Holy Lands, long-standing disputes centred on Latin monks (supported by France) and Orthodox (backed by Russia) jostling for control of key shrines, while through the early 1850s hostilities rumbled between Russia and Turkey over the question of the protection of the vast numbers of Greek Orthodox Christians within the Ottoman Empire. In June 1853, Russia occupied the Turkish principalities of Wallachia and Moldavia, on the pretext of protecting the rights of their Christian subjects. In October, Turkey declared war on Russia, and a month later the Russian fleet destroyed the Turkish navy at Sinope. This – a perfectly legitimate act of war – was reported in the British press as a 'massacre', and provoked national outrage and a great surge of Russophobia. The prime minister, the peace-loving Lord Aberdeen, had no desire to be drawn into war as Turkey's ally, but the pro-war party, lead by the ever-bellicose Lord Palmerston and bolstered by mass public support, argued that the Russian threat must be resisted, that propping up the weak and crumbling Ottoman Empire was crucial as a bulwark against Russian expansionism, especially as that might interfere with Britain's trade interests and access to India.

The wave of xenophobia that swept Britain engulfed the Prince, to his, and the Queen's, great dismay. All popularity garnered by the Great Exhibition was quite forgotten. Now Albert was accused of being pro-Russian and anti-Palmerston, of corresponding with foreign courts, of unduly influencing the Queen and leaning on ministers, of interfering with the army, of simply being too *foreign*. So insistent became the attacks that in January 1854, the government took the step of declaring, in Parliament, their absolute confidence in the Prince's loyalty. The Queen was somewhat mollified.

'All our gentlemen are boiling over with martial ardour,' wrote Eleanor Stanley in February. Enthusiasm for war now ran high at court. Victoria and Albert, who initially, like Aberdeen, had not wished to fight for Turkey (remembering the Tsar's amiability on his visit to Windsor in 1844, the Queen had been reluctant to think the worst), had come to believe that 'the power and encroachments of Russia must be resisted'. In March 1854, Britain joined France and declared war on Russia.

Country and court became gripped by war news (the Crimean War was the first to be properly reported and photographed). That autumn at Balmoral, the household waited impatiently for 'telegraphic messages' and newspapers, especially *The Times*, with William Russell Howard's reports, and pored over a map showing where the British troops had landed and the objective of their campaign – the fortress and port of Sevastopol. The victory at Alma brought much excitement, tempered by news of heavy losses. Preparations began for a great bonfire to celebrate the supposed fall of Sevastopol, and were then abandoned when it proved a rumour. But increasingly reports were dominated by the appalling conditions in the Crimea – the lack of supplies, of medical facilities, of nurses, the dreadful state of the military hospitals at Scutari, the sufferings of the troops: two thirds of the casualties of the Crimea were due to disease – cholera, dysentery, scurvy – rather than combat.

In October, Charlotte Canning wrote to her mother, 'the Government sends out a band of nurses to Scutari and Miss Nightingale is to head them. Her family have consented and there can be no one so well fitted as she is to do such work. She has such nerves and skill and is so gentle and wise and quiet, even now she is in no bustle or hurry tho' so much is in her hands.' Charlotte had some first-hand knowledge of Florence Nightingale, since the year before, in her capacity as chairman of the committee for the Institution for the Care of Sick Gentlewomen in Distressed Circumstances, she had engaged her as superintendent, to reorganise their new hospital in Harley Street. She found Nightingale 'tall and thin, with dark hair and a good clear complexion . . . not handsome, nor very attractive in manner, very quiet and businesslike, but wonderfully clever, full of information on all subjects, a good classical scholar, knowing Greek and Hebrew and those sort of things, and having besides, most useful of all, the knack of getting round people and bringing them to think as she does . . . with her quiet, rather stern manner, she has an immense deal of fun about her and sees things in an amusing light'. Now Charlotte found herself responsible for interviewing nurses for Scutari and doing her best to weed out the likes of 'Lady Scripture Readers', since 'there are so many such volunteers and only *really* useful people are taken'.

At Windsor for Christmas, Charlotte found that 'everybody knits'. The Queen was insistent that her ladies busy themselves knitting woollen comforters and socks for the troops, while she herself worked on a comforter for her cousin George, Duke of Cambridge, the youngest of the commanders in the Crimea.

In June 1855, Charlotte wrote to Louisa, 'What did you think of the news Mama told you?' With Lord Dalhousie retiring as governor general of India, Charles Canning was being mooted as a possible successor. 'I cannot yet tell you what answer is to be given,' continued Charlotte, 'but there are really no reasons, but one's own feelings and dislikes against it and I think it will be that we go, but I don't know and will not take part in the decision but only be ready to follow like a dog. If it was only for one year I wd delight in it, but 5 is terribly long.' Canning decided to accept the governorship. Some claimed, later, that the appointment was engineered by Lord Lansdowne, a family friend, as a means of breaking off his love affair.

Something of Charlotte's feelings about the posting comes across in a letter to Catherine Gladstone, a close friend since girlhood (Charlotte was godmother to her daughter). She longed to talk it all over with Catherine, but had to make do with writing: 'It is an immense change to one's existence, but I felt it wd have been most wrong to try and sway C, to refuse for 100 reasons he might have had cause to regret it and I really believe he will do his duty well and it is not right to shrink from undertaking such a duty for mere reasons touching one's comfort . . . the very bad side is the long time and leaving so many one loves far behind, but with no children, no duties in a property in England, no bad health or even doubts about health, one really cd have had not one excuse to give – you see that I prob- ably am better pleased to go than nearly any one you could think of, but the pain of leaving home for so very long . . . you know I care little for "society" and am very fond of new places and seeing all that is to be seen, the further the better, so as to the journey and the life in India I hope to do very well and I am sure there will be no want of duties and interests . . . I am very sure you know better what I feel about it all than I can put it in words. Your affectionate feeling towards me I thank you for, from my heart, and you are one of those I shall count upon finding 6 years hence exactly the same as now.'

'The pain of leaving home for so very long', a small gasp of anguish, is virtually extinguished by the crushing weight of 'duty'. Having dutifully served the Queen, Charlotte would now dutifully follow her husband to a place far removed from everything and everyone she held dear, knowing it would be six long years before she returned. Before she left, Catherine sent her a prayer book and requested a lock of Charlotte's hair.

Charlotte's last waiting took place in September, at Windsor, where she found 'the Princess Royal and Prince of Prussia going on very happily'. That summer, at Balmoral, Vicky had become privately engaged to the Crown Prince Frederick William ('Fritz') of Prussia, though since she was just fourteen, the marriage was not to take place for another three years. 'After our breakfast we took leave of the dear Cannings with great regret,' wrote the Queen in her journal on 22 November, 'they start on the 26th.' Charles and Charlotte, together with Charlotte's maids Rain and West, travelled to Marseilles, where they boarded a ship bound for Egypt, then India, reaching Calcutta in February.

CHAPTER II

Mary Ponsonby: Maid-of-Honour

Before leaving for India, Charlotte Canning had made a point of seeking out and saying goodbye to a young friend she had recently made at court – Mary Bulteel. Mary had become a maid-of-honour in 1853, and despite a fifteen-year age gap, she and Charlotte had forged a warm friendship during the months when their waitings coincided, founded on shared intelligence and religious sympathy. 'I have very few friends,' Charlotte told Mary, 'and I never take *engougements*, so you may believe me very fully when I say I always think of you as one of the best and most cared for of my friends.' Both subscribed to a deeply held High Church faith, and both maintained a certain critical detachment from court life, but where Charlotte was controlled and discreet, Mary was ardent and outspoken, giving voice to much that Charlotte left unsaid.

It was Mary's proud claim that she owed her court appointment to her acting ability – the Duchess of Sutherland had seen her act and, knowing she could also ride, walk and play the piano, all desirable attributes in a maid-of-honour, had recommended her to the Queen – as well as to the fact that she was not a typical courtier. This says rather more about Mary herself than about Victoria. She may have been right about the acting: she was a brilliant mimic and an entertaining after-dinner guest. That the Queen regarded her lack of courtly credentials as a recommendation is crediting Her Majesty with rather more imagination than she possessed: members of the royal household were chosen for their suitability, not the opposite. Despite Mary's insistence that her family, the Greys, were not courtiers, she almost certainly owed her appointment to those very family connections: her uncle, General Charles Grey, was Albert's private secretary (and later the Queen's), while her aunt, Lady Caroline Barrington, had taken over from Sarah Lyttelton as superintendent of the royal nursery.

However, it was certainly true that the Hon. Mary Bulteel (the 'Hon.' was a courtesy title given to untitled maids-of-honour) was cast in a very different mould to such born-to-be, vocational courtiers as Lady Jane Ely, or Lady Augusta Bruce, or the Hon. Harriet Phipps – pliable, discreet creatures who accorded Royalties all proper reverence and regarded royal service as a 'sacred duty'. Mary was altogether too independent-minded, too individual, too arrogant perhaps for institutional existence – and Victoria's court *was* a kind of institution. She took a dim view of Royalties in general, and there were few things she despised more than royalty worship, or 'royal culte' as she called it.

Maids-of-honour tended to come from aristocratic families of moderate means – such as the Bulteels – for whom the £300 annual stipend was a useful supplement. A letter recommending a prospective maid-of-honour (Fanny Drummond) to the Queen gives some idea of the kind of qualities looked for: Miss Drummond was 'neither too shy nor too much the reverse'; she 'never moons or is in the clouds, but has always all her wits about her and plenty of courage and spirit. But with this she is gentle, obedient and very amenable, to any little reproof'; although 'lively' she was 'not wildly fond of balls and going out'; she was 'well principled and steady', never 'dull' and had 'her own resources in music and drawing'; without 'much depth of character', she had no 'guile', enjoyed a joke and held 'no strong views on church matters'.

Mary, on the other hand, was not always 'amenable' to reproof, adored balls and going out, and held very 'strong views on church matters', but she was certainly not 'shy', or 'dull', or lacking in courage and spirit and she had resources aplenty. At any rate, she was deemed suitable and the appointment was made. As maid-of-honour, she would spend three one-month periods a year at court under the supervision of a lady-in-waiting. She would be expected to speak French and German, to ride and to play the piano (the ability to sight-read being a great advantage). On alternate days she would present Her Majesty with her bouquet before dinner. She might be asked to keep the Queen company while she sat for a portrait, or to ride or walk with her, or to play skittles. She might be called upon to entertain the royal children – playing hoops, or skipping perhaps, in the Corridor at Windsor – and an aptitude for cards, dancing, needlework, sketching and amateur dramatics would stand her in good stead.

Mary Bulteel was born into the Whig aristocracy. Her maternal grandfather, the Liberal prime minister Lord Grey, passed the Reform Bill in the same year as her birth – 1832. Both her liberal politics and her sense of position, of social status, would always be of the greatest importance to Mary, notwithstanding an element of contradiction of which she herself was well aware. Her early childhood was spent at Flete, the Devon house inherited by her father John Crocker Bulteel. When John Bulteel died in 1843, leaving substantial debts (a legacy of the lavish programme of improvements carried out at Flete), his wife Elizabeth took Mary, her brother and two sisters to London, to live in a modest house in Eaton Place.

There was something of George Eliot's Dorothea Brooke about the young Mary – a moral earnestness, a yearning for self-improvement, a vivid spiritual life. After an encounter when she was fifteen with Samuel Wilberforce, the Bishop of Oxford (so admired by Sarah Lyttelton), Mary embraced the Oxford Movement and became fervently, earnestly religious. Aged twenty, she began to keep a 'self-examination diary', subjecting her conduct to rigorous daily scrutiny. 'This book is intended to contain a solemn confession of sin in thought, word or deed (please burn after death),' she wrote, a request that was ignored. Sins were duly recorded: reproving siblings too harshly; failing to say grace either before or after breakfast; wanting 'to be thought good by people at church'; being 'greedy at luncheon'; 'arguing and disputing when asked to do something by Mama'. With time, and with the discovery of the work of John Stuart Mill and George Eliot, as well as writers in what she called 'the scientific school', doubt crept in and Mary's High Church fervour diminished. Her emotional intensity, leavened by a humorous cynicism, did not; later it would be channelled into quasi-romantic attachments to other women.

In appearance Mary was small and neatly made, with an ascetic face composed of clean lines and planes, heavy-lidded grey-blue eyes and a disconcertingly cool, appraising gaze. She had a taste for practical, masculine pursuits: carpentry, silver-work, pool and book-binding. She was fastidious and exacting, of herself and others. Ethel Smyth (the composer and one of Mary's younger women friends who fell in love with her) rightly identified 'an intense seriousness' in Mary, which 'underlay the rather cynical 18th century views it pleased her to air in argument'.

On her appointment, in March 1853, Mary was summoned to Buckingham Palace 'to kiss hands' (a prescribed ritual for a new maid-of-honour). Grabbing a straw bonnet and a cloak, she drove to the palace, with just the merest flutter of nerves as her carriage passed through the gates, and there met her aunt, Lady Barrington, who presented her with her maid-of-honour's badge, a picture of Victoria, surrounded by diamonds, hung on a red bow. Lady Barrington escorted her to the Queen's sitting room, where she duly curtsied, kissed Her Majesty's hand and was kissed in return. The Queen was all sweetness and affability ('such a warm heart, such talents and cleverness and most agreeable', she wrote of Mary), enquiring after her family and expressing a desire to hear her sing – she should be sure to bring her music to Osborne. With the interview over, Mary 'made a low curtsey, backed out of the room, restrained my shrieks, cut nine pirouettes and remained in a state of indescribable collapse outside the door'.

She would always be partial to the 'luxe' of palace life (not to be confused with good taste – just as frequently noted were the 'atrocities' of the furnishings), and her quarters at Buckingham Palace did not disappoint. Her bed was 'the very essence of comfort', with sheets 'like floss silk', not to mention 'heaps of hot water and tubs', while the sitting room (a luxury not provided at Osborne or Balmoral) that she shared with her fellow maid-of-honour, Lucy Kerr, was furnished with two red morocco writing tables, two armchairs and footstools, two pairs of silver candlesticks, a sofa, two cabinets for books and

workboxes and a pianoforte. There was even a balcony. Her Windsor
quarters were equally satisfactory, while at Osborne, drawing the
curtains in her room, lighting the candles, 'poking' the fire and finally
ringing for tea seemed the very 'height of comfort'.

At Osborne Mary experienced her first royal dinner, a potentially
nerve-racking occasion, but one she took in her stride. The 'orders'
came in the afternoon, via the lady-in-waiting Lady Mount Edgcumbe,
who, having been a neighbour of the Bulteels in Devon, was familiar
to Mary: there was to be one dinner, Royalties and household
combined. Waiting for orders – was Mary required to drive with Her
Majesty? Or to ride? Or to dine? – would become a familiar feature
of court life. Such orders were all too often countermanded by further
orders. Eleanor Stanley reported that the Queen 'ordered us to walk
with her at four, but soon afterwards there came another message
that "Her Majesty had changed her mind", which horrified Lady
Charlemont [a lady of the bedchamber] as she said it was disrespectful
to suppose the Queen could change her mind, as if she was capri-
cious'. Mary learned to keep an open mind and to ask no questions,
since one never knew 'from dining to going to the end of the world
ten minutes beforehand what is expected of one . . . I go or don't go,
exactly like a bundle and as I am told.'

In anticipation of dinner, she changed into a white silk dress,
arranged blue and silver cornflowers in her hair and pinned on her
maid-of-honour's badge. By eight she was ready and 'like a ginger
beer bottle fizzing with impatience', but was made to wait while Lady
Mount Edgcumbe fussed over gloves and shawls until they could finally
proceed to the dining room. Mary sat between Baron Stockmar, who
was making one of his regular visits to court, 'green, wizened' and
'turned inside out by heartburn', and an equerry, Colonel Wilde. When
the latter attempted to speak to Mary's uncle, General Grey, who was
also present, Mary remarked to Stockmar, 'that will never do, they
are both as deaf as posts'. The Queen, whose own ears were extremely
sharp, called out across the table, 'Yes, both!'

Afterwards, in the drawing room, Mary, somewhat to her alarm,
found herself called up for a tête-à-tête with Her Majesty, who had

seated herself on an ottoman, while the household stood around her in a semicircle, looking on. Fortunately the subject of Mary's mother's bad knee came up, and since the Queen took a lively interest in matters of health, it proved a rich conversational topic. At a subsequent dinner, Mary, who was a competent pianist and sang well, described the ordeal of having to sing, alone, to her own accompaniment, while various Royalties sat silently playing whist and Uncle Charles and Prince Albert pocked billiard balls. She got through 'Hélas dans ma prison' without mishap, and then accompanied the Queen as she sang 'Marie Stuart'. Musical ability was a very great boon for a maid-of-honour, since she might well be called upon to join the Queen and the Prince for some pre-dinner practice or a post-dinner performance, accompanying – often 'at sight' – the royal couple, or a visiting royalty, as they sang, German choruses perhaps, or a Mozart requiem.

Whatever amusement was offered by the novelty of court life quickly palled for the new maid-of-honour. As a spirited twenty-one-year-old, she had to submit to the petty rules and regulations with which a maid-of-honour was expected to conform. She was not allowed to receive visitors, including family, in her rooms, but only in the downstairs waiting room. She was not supposed to keep a diary. She could only leave the palace, for a drive, or just a walk on the Slopes, if chaperoned, and then she could not pass the windows of rooms occupied by Her Majesty. Such was the anxiety lest the virtue of the maids be compromised that the Queen was most unhappy at the idea of Eleanor Stanley sharing a carriage for the few miles between Balmoral and Abergeldie (the Duchess of Kent's Scottish home) with Mary's uncle, the elderly, married General Grey. It was permitted but only on the proviso, repeatedly insisted upon by the Queen, that 'it was not to be drawn into a precedent'.

For a young woman who relished sophisticated company and lively debate, and in the grand Whiggish circles she'd moved in – with weekends at Woburn and Ampthill, Mary had enjoyed plenty of both – innocuous pleasantries over dinner followed by a game of spinning tables (a form of ouija board much enjoyed by Victoria and Albert) were hardly likely to satisfy. To Mary, with her aristocratic confidence and intellectual turn of mind, the Victorian court appeared ludicrously bourgeois and 'exceedingly dull'. She considered herself 'rather superior' to most of her colleagues, advising them to read Carlyle and Ruskin. However she was 'forgiven her earnestness' thanks to her 'turn for mimicry'; she was excellent company and a most welcome addition to the household.

The Victoria and Albert whom Mary encountered in 1853 were both, though only in their thirties, suffering to some degree from the strains of mid-life. Overwork – and especially the labour of the Great Exhibition – had prematurely aged Albert. The delicate-featured youth who had set the Queen's heart racing (as he always would) was now pallid and paunchy, with the air of a man burdened and oppressed by responsibility and duty. And the Queen was feeling the effects of eight babies in thirteen years. She had recently given birth to her fourth son, Prince Leopold (for the first time with the aid of chloroform), and had been left feeling 'nervous' and easily upset – a form of postnatal depression – which led to painful scenes with Albert. These were usually sparked by a 'trifle', such as the Prince complaining about her turning the wrong pages of a book 'from inattention', escalating, on the Queen's part, into a hysterical outpouring of tears and recriminations. Albert would withdraw and sit down to compose a careful 'Dear Child' letter, admonishing, somewhat disappointed, unfailingly reasonable and patient. 'If you are violent I have no other choice but to leave you to recover yourself, then you follow me to renew the dispute and to have it *all out*.' He sincerely pitied her for her sufferings, her 'fidgety nature', her insistence on controlling and regulating others, especially her children. 'If only,' he wrote, 'you were rather less occupied with yourself and your feelings . . . and took more interest in the outside world, you would find that the greatest help of all . . .' Whether such letters had the intended emollient effect is questionable, but the Queen never doubted the Prince's superior judgement, his essential *rightness*; the fault lay in her; she berated herself for her lack of self-control and made valiant attempts to do better.

If Mary heard gossip about such scenes, and she most probably did, she left no record. Sadly, given her intelligence, her forthrightness, her absence of 'royal culte', we know little of her first-hand impressions of Victoria and her court, since only a handful of her letters, together with a brief memoir, survive. In the latter, looking back at her early days at court, she acknowledged that her initial views of the Queen and the Prince were coloured by her own 'very ardent high church theories'. The opinions of the Prince (a good Lutheran) in particular – 'for he had opinions which the Queen at that time cd not be said to have – used to rouse up the most fierce antagonism in my mind being in opposition as they were to all my favourite ecclesiastical doctrines'. Inevitably both Victoria and Albert failed to come 'in any way up to my conception of what they should be in loftiness of aims of self denial, of strength of purpose in character'. Later such judgements appeared 'arrogant and absurd'.

However, she did not soften towards Albert. Mary described to her mother how she had taken it upon herself to de-stiffen her room at Osborne, by rearranging the furniture. She pulled the pianoforte away from the wall, put the sofa 'crooked . . . instead of stiffly in the middle of the room', and placed an armchair 'crookedly and comfortably' near the fire. 'If Prince Albert says anything about the pianoforte I shall stop his mouth with a little bit of scientific theory about the properties stone walls have of absorbing sound.' Mary, like Charlotte Canning and many of the Queen's ladies, couldn't resist little digs at Albert (Georgy Liddell noted that whilst playing Nain Jaune, the Prince was 'charmed whenever any one fails to claim the forfeits or prizes'). They subscribed to the prevailing view amongst the English aristocracy, of Albert as a faintly ludicrous figure; as Mary rightly said, the *beau monde* patronised him as a kind of 'foreign professor', hopelessly lacking in *savoir faire*. In the build-up to the Crimean War, the derision of the aristocracy spread into downright hostility amongst the middle classes.

Mary's verdict on the Prince was particularly ungenerous, and betrayed many of her own snobberies and prejudices. While acknowledging his many virtues (kindness, reliability, selflessness), noting (as had Sarah Lyttelton) 'a strong vein of poetical feeling unexpressed even to himself' but shown in his love of music, and admiring his good sense and sound judgement, 'his quiet, strong, convinced, just way of looking at a question . . . a calm, philosophical way, intensely German, of weighing the pros and cons', she could not really like him. That 'intensely German' said it all; Albert was the victim of much anti-German prejudice. His handshake, his voice, the way he sat on his horse, his clothes (dressed for hunting in thigh-length red leather boots, white breeches, an open-necked shirt and a black velvet jacket, he may have appeared irresistible to his wife, but to those who knew about such things he was just plain *wrong*) all marked him as hopelessly, irredeemably un-English. Then, too, he lacked humour (a fatal flaw in Mary's eyes), unless you counted a penchant for practical jokes, which produced 'immoderate fits of laughter' (Lord Granville told Mary that there was no point in telling your best stories to Royalties 'when pretending to pinch one's finger in the door would answer better'). He was 'without a spark of spontaneity'; he had none of the Queen's 'frankness' and 'instinct'; he could not share her absorbing 'interest in everyone's remotest concerns'; his intellectual ability was only 'on the level with a very intellectual German on the second line'. Mary believed him unpopular amongst the household, barely deigning to talk to, let alone flirt with, the ladies, who generally bored him, and with no friends among the men.

Up to a point she was right: Albert operated according to strictly rational tenets; shyness and reserve came across as stiffness and formality; his refusal to flirt did not endear him to the ladies; his humour, such as it was, tended to the ponderous, while irony, that quintessential spice of English conversation, was a closed book to him (as it was to the Queen). But such objections were largely questions of personal taste. Mary underestimated the Prince's intellectual abilities and failed to acknowledge his astounding energy, his high-mindedness, his culture, his affection for his wife and children, the breadth and range of his enthusiasms – for design, music, architecture and self-improvement. Those – significantly, all men – who came to work with and know Albert well, both politicians (Sir Robert Peel, Lords

Clarendon, Granville and Palmerston) and household officials (Charles Phipps, Charles Grey, later Henry Ponsonby himself), greatly admired and respected him.

The Queen, however, largely escaped censure. Both Mary and Victoria combined diminutive stature with immense natural dignity. There any obvious resemblance ended. Intellectually, spiritually, politically, they stood poles apart. Mary made no secret of her liberal views, contributing regularly to W. T. Stead's Liberal *Pall Mall Gazette*, while the Queen, after her early support for Melbourne's Whigs, became more of a Tory with every passing year. Mary supported women's rights, for which the Queen had no time at all, and sat on the committee that founded Girton, Cambridge's first college for women. She studied Rousseau and John Stuart Mill, and came to know and greatly admire George Eliot. The Queen bravely tackled *Adam Bede*, but her tastes were firmly middlebrow, inclining to 'pretty, simple stories full of truth and feeling', and there was no question of Eliot, openly cohabiting with the married George Lewes, being received at court.

A. C. Benson (son of the Archbishop, brother of the author E. F., and, later, editor of Victoria's letters) became a great friend of Mary's, describing her as 'a woman who was not merely dawdling passively along the highway of life'. He thought too that while 'not in the least like Queen Victoria yet somehow she reminded me of her'. He was right. Neither Mary nor Victoria were passive dawdlers; both felt keenly and strongly and did not shy from making those feelings known. For all their differences, it was perhaps a certain similarity that, as Benson said, led Mary to understand 'the character and temperament of the Queen, which in spite of her apparent simplicity was really a very complex, impassioned and emphatic character, better than anyone'.

Mary believed, probably correctly, that Victoria found 'clever' women alarming; she certainly regarded her maid-of-honour with some wariness, her politics in particular. But she was prepared to tolerate any waywardness in Mary because she recognised in her, and respected, an honesty, a rare enough quality amongst her ladies. On her part Mary, while accepting that she could never expect any kind of intimacy with the Queen, and despite being occasionally treated 'like a charwoman', came to feel a 'deep affection' for her, which was returned in kind. It was a tribute to them both.

For the maids-of-honour, court operated quite effectively as a deeply respectable marriage market (as it always had done, though not always so respectably; Elizabeth I, who bossed, bullied and occasionally slapped her maids, and insisted they obtain royal consent to marry, had Bess Throckmorton put in the Tower after becoming pregnant by Sir Walter Raleigh). Whereas in earlier reigns young women came to court in the hope of ensnaring a well-connected, ideally royal, lover, now girls of good backgrounds but moderate means hoped to acquire husbands of solid if not scintillating prospects. Several did so: Caroline Cocks and the Rev. Charles Courtenay; Mary Seymour and Colonel Thomas Biddulph (master of the household); Mary herself. In the event of her marriage, a maid-of-honour could expect a £1,000 dowry from the Queen, though there was a tacit understanding that she would not engage herself too swiftly.

In 1854, however, just a year into her appointment, Mary accepted a proposal from William Harcourt, a rising star of the Liberal Party. Harcourt was clever and a good talker, and Mary above all things loved to talk, but her engagement brought on immediate agonising. 'Engaged to be married to William Harcourt,' she wrote in her diary. 'More earnestness and devotion required for fear of being led away – uncertain in my own mind whether this act is to bring a curse or a blessing on us both, worn out by anxiety and doubts.' These were hardly the happy effusions of a bride-to-be. The following year she broke off the engagement and thus avoided incurring any royal displeasure. But she was left wondering whether she was suited to marriage at all – might she not be better employed serving God?

A maid-of-honour naturally hoped to be in waiting with sympathetic colleagues, who made the long evenings of stilted conversation, nursery games and standing in icy drawing rooms counting the minutes until the Royalties retired more tolerable. Her fellow maids

(maids-of-honour waited in pairs) did not greatly interest Mary, but she much admired Lady Jocelyn and Lady Macdonald, both ladies of the bedchamber, as well of course as Charlotte Canning. It was Charlotte who became her confidante when she considered entering a convent. Writing from India, Charlotte did her best to try and dissuade her, urging patience and caution, reminding Mary how young she was, how much good she could do in the world: 'I think the time for usefulness *will* come if you look for it without going far out of your way. While you earnestly try and do your appointed duties and neglect no opportunity of widening and deepening them.' She confessed too to being greatly relieved to discover that Mary did not, as she had feared, have 'an inclination towards the Roman Church'. Of her own life in India Charlotte was dismissive – 'dilettante is far too good a name for my line, "Drone" would be truer much'.

Mary decided against joining a religious community, but the exigencies of court waitings were not so different in kind, albeit without the spiritual rewards. One thing she valued about royal service was 'the absolute necessity of forgetting self in the service of others; the discipline of an almost religious rule in everyday life'. The suppression of self in the interests of a higher good – such was a positive of court life for Mary, just as it had been for Charlotte. But 'self' had a way of intruding. When it came to Mary's daily reckoning with her diary, court provided rich pickings, a wealth of opportunity for vanity, gossiping, idleness and attention-seeking. During one of her first waitings: 'talked too much of self in the carriage. Not watchful in conversation. Provoked with Queen for not talking to me more. Too anxious to hear what Baron Stockmar was saying to the Queen.' Later she confessed to 'yielding too much to the fascination of manner and look in Lady Jocelyn'; to 'talking for effect and exaggerating to Lady Canning'; to 'allowing myself to be put out of spirits by Lady C's going away'; to not being 'careful enough to avoid talking over peculiarities and little absurdities in the Queen and other people, vain of my singing and unkind in telling Lady Churchill about want of truth in Lucy Kerr'. She fell short in her church attendance and commitment to prayer, was prone to indiscretion, argued too violently 'with those that don't agree with my opinion', cared too much about being liked and took too much pleasure in being thought clever.

It was salutary then to remember another piece of advice from Charlotte: 'You will be delighted with your waiting at Balmoral or Osborne. You will see the Queen intimately, riding, dancing, playing, dining. You will think she cannot get on without you. And then you will come back one day to Windsor and somebody else will have taken your place and you will have become a number on a list.' Mary should never make the mistake of believing herself irreplaceable.

CHAPTER 12

Glimpses of Abroad

In February 1855, after mounting anger at the sufferings of British troops in the Crimea over the winter and mismanagement of the war in general had brought the resignation of Lord Aberdeen, the Queen reluctantly bowed to public pressure and asked Lord Palmerston to form a government. None followed the war more closely, nor felt more keenly for her soldiers, than Her Majesty, but she saw Aberdeen go with regret. To exchange 'my dear kind, excellent friend Ld Aberdeen . . . for Ld Palmerston is somewhat of a trial', she confided in her journal. Both she and the Prince had found Palmerston impossibly high-handed as foreign secretary. However, seventy-year-old 'Pam', who, crucially, understood the power of public opinion and the press, was wildly popular (in fact he proved a disappointment as a war leader, though the royal couple found him a much less troublesome prime minister than foreign secretary).

It was with Palmerston's encouragement that Emperor Napoleon III and his Empress Eugénie were invited to Windsor in April. The Emperor had announced his intention of going to the Crimea to personally take charge of the siege of Sevastopol, a proposal the British government and Victoria and Albert regarded with alarm; it was hoped that he could be dissuaded from such a course during his stay. Following the abdication of Louis Philippe in 1848 and a *coup d'état* in 1851, Louis Napoleon Bonaparte had declared himself first president, and then emperor, of the French. This was an uncomfortable development for Victoria – she was after all sheltering the Orléans family who were still ensconced at Claremont – and there was a sad irony in the fact

that the Emperor would be sleeping in the very same bed once occupied by 'poor King Louis Philippe'. The impending visit was anticipated
with some nervousness on her part and a lavish programme of redeco-
rating at Windsor.

In the event it was a resounding success; all distrust melted away
and the Queen was entirely charmed by the imperial couple. She
thought Napoleon odd-looking, extremely short with a disproportionately large head and a comedy moustache, but he was exactly the
kind of character – unknowable, enigmatic, a touch outré, everything
in fact that she was not – designed to fascinate her. She was pleased
to note that he seemed more German than French; she found his
belief in omens and his 'Star' romantic; she approved of the respectful
manner in which he referred to the unlucky Orléans family; and she
appreciated his interest in and kindness towards her children. There
was much talk of the Crimea and the siege of Sevastopol in particular,
and eventually Napoleon abandoned all plans of going to the Crimea
himself. Really, felt the Queen, it was quite 'incredible' that she, 'the
grand-daughter of George III, should dance with the Emperor
Napoleon, nephew to our great enemy, now my nearest and most
intimate ally, in the Waterloo Room too'.

As for the Empress, the Queen's admiration for her beauty and
grace (on which even Albert, normally impervious to female charms,
remarked) was merely confirmed. So taken indeed had she been by
Eugénie's chic that the previous year orders had been given for the
ladies to appear at dinner 'coiffées à l'Imperatrice', which involved turning
one's hair into ringlets and pulling it back from the face. Eleanor
Stanley reported how she and her fellow maid-of-honour Beatrice
Byng, together with the lady-in-waiting Lady Ely (Lady Canning
succeeded in excusing herself), appeared 'duly Imperatriced', whereupon the gentlemen, with the exception of the Prince, laughed 'unmer-
cifully'. The Queen, Imperatriced herself, made no comment at all,
which her ladies considered 'hardly gracious'.

The return visit – eight days in Paris, to coincide with the Paris
Exhibition – took place in August, with Mary Bulteel, to her pleasure,
in attendance. Anxious to hold her own beside Eugénie, the Queen

became uncharacteristically preoccupied with 'questions of toilettes and other arrangements' and her dressers had several days of frantic packing before the royal party set sail, from Osborne, on 18 August, in the new *Victoria and Albert*, which Mary found 'most glorious . . . fitted up in brass and mahogany like a huge toy'. Frieda Arnold, the Queen's dresser, who travelled with her, along with a wardrobe maid (Sophie Weiss, the second dresser, had been sent ahead with the luggage), was equally impressed. The new yacht, she reported, had three decks, a lower for servants and sailors, a second, half below water level, where Frieda had a tiny cabin with a sofa bed, table and chair, and an upper, which housed the Queen's generous, splendidly furnished suite of rooms. All the furniture was 'fixed down', the tables had 'little iron railings round them to prevent things falling off' and 'little hidden passages' allowed the servants to move about the ship unseen.

Also of the party were the Prince of Wales, and the Princess Royal, whom Mary was instructed to keep amused during the voyage (and who became a lifelong friend), Mary's uncle General Grey (secretary to the Prince), Colonel Biddulph (master of the household), Lord Alfred Paget (clerk marshal), Colonel Phipps (keeper of the privy purse), Lord Abercorn (groom-in-waiting) Lord Clarendon (foreign secretary), Lord Breadalbane (lord chamberlain), Sir James Clark, Miss Hildyard, Mr Gibbs, Lady Churchill and Lady Ely.

Lady Churchill, a tall, elegant figure of some distinction, had become a lady of the bedchamber in 1854 and Lady Ely in 1851. Jane Ely was a widow, pretty, sweet-natured and timorous (some years earlier Charlotte Canning reported her as reduced to tears when their carriage passed through a tunnel), much loved, and much bullied by the Queen, but rather despised by Mary, who regarded her as the epitome of the supine, fawning courtier, 'foolishly cringing to all the little miseries of etiquette'. Mary did not suffer fools gladly and Lady Ely was certainly foolish; she was also guilty of being '*banale*' (Mary liked to pepper her conversation with French phrases, the legacy of a French governess), another lamentable failing.

From Boulogne, where they were met by the Emperor, the Queen and her suite took a train to Paris. 'It is impossible for imagination to conceive anything so gorgeously magnificent as the entry into Paris,' wrote Mary, dazzled by the brilliantly lit station swathed in crimson velvet fringed with gold, the 'magnificently dressed' crowds and the troops in their 'gorgeous uniforms' lining the streets. This was Mary's first sight of France and she found much to delight her. Paris, under the Emperor, had been transformed by Baron Haussmann's building programme, with the Rue de Rivoli, the completion of the Louvre and the Palais de Justice, the restoration of the Tuileries and the landscaping of the Bois de Boulogne.

The royal party were based at the palace of St Cloud, to the south-west of Paris. Charlotte Canning, visiting the previous year, had been struck by the 'quantity of rooms and good furniture and good flowers' which quite 'beat our English Palace'. The Emperor's court was all about showmanship and effect, and beside its glamour and opulence that of Victoria looked exceedingly bourgeois and drab. On arrival the ladies found their luggage missing and nothing but full ball gowns to wear, which put Lady Ely, naturally, 'in a terrible fuss', but left Mary and Lady Churchill, whom Mary considered 'quite brilliant' alongside Lady Ely, merely relieved to be excused from dinner. For Mary, the stay at St Cloud had plenty of farcical moments, as she reported with relish. She had been assigned a 'voluble' footman, who had been primed as to the English obsession with regular baths, but who proceeded to persecute her, refusing to leave her alone, insisting on being present at her *toilette à la Pompadour* and bursting into her room whenever she tried to bathe. Mary managed 'to battle him during the bathing moments, but at all other times he made good his entrance, despite her shrieks and remonstrances'. During dinners at St Cloud there were frequent scuffles behind Mary's chair and cries of 'Imbecile!' while large white-gloved hands reached on to the table to gather up crumbs. Lady Churchill was quite horrified to find three wine glasses by her plate at breakfast.

Mary found the sun-baked August days long and distinctly gruelling – a three-and-a-half-hour tour of the Exhibition, followed by driving about 'in a melting sun and glare', then an hour of waiting for orders, a 'disputatious visit' from a milliner, a lengthy dinner, an hour of standing, a two-hour play, and, to round it off, an interminable drawing room and levee. So tired was she by the end of the day that her prayers were 'hurried and often wandering' and self-examination fell quite by the wayside. The Queen's dressers were equally exhausted. Frieda Arnold ran up and down stairs endlessly preparing Her Majesty's toilettes, rarely got to bed before two or three a.m., and felt immensely grateful for the occasional glass of champagne which flowed 'like water in the Emperor's household'.

The Queen, however, remained tireless and entranced by Paris – the boulevards, the clear, bright, smokeless air, the 'quantity of gilding', the general 'brilliancy of effect'. 'I am delighted, enchanted, amused and interested and think I never saw anything more beautiful and gay than Paris, or more splendid than all the Palaces,' she told her uncle Leopold. 'No royal person ever known in history comes up to her indefatigability,' declared Lord Clarendon, on his knees having escorted Her Majesty on a lengthy and oppressively hot tour of the Tuileries and the Louvre.

Mary accompanied the royal couple on an incognito shopping trip (she and the Queen in 'common bonnets', with a black veil for the Queen), during which Her Majesty was much put out by a woman failing to recognise her: 'the Queen bridled as she always had a penchant for being recognised when she was incognito. When she said "they do not seem to know who I *am*", it was a sure sign that she was beginning to be bored.' Mary also noted how, as was often the case, it was the glimpses of ordinary lives that intrigued Her Majesty – people eating outside cafés, or a cutler's shop with the knives and scissors arranged in a circle in the window, which prompted the Queen to declare 'but this should be done in England'. Mary 'tried to explain that it was done, only that she didn't see it'. Lady Ely continued in a 'terrible fuss' over the milliners, lace makers and other tradesmen who descended on the royal party.

The Queen's wardrobe, to which she had given so much thought, was subject to the usual comment and mockery, in particular a startling ensemble for her arrival in Paris, involving a large white silk bonnet with streamers and a tuft of marabou feathers, a green mantle and parasol which failed to match her dress, and a 'voluminous object' on her arm which revealed itself as a white satin bag embroidered with a giant gold poodle. Mary noted the out-of-date gowns and an unfortunate predilection for something Her Majesty termed a 'lilac cravat', while the Empress Eugénie, dressed by Worth, managed to look exquisite at all times, despite her pregnancy. Nevertheless, the Queen, with her 'genius of movement' and her 'wonderful dignity, her manner of bowing to the crowd and her want of all preoccupation', was the more impressive figure, while the Empress, for all her elegance, 'could not help always worrying over trifles'. At the opera, sitting after the national anthem, Eugénie instinctively looked behind her, to make sure of a waiting chair, while Victoria, confident that there would always be a chair, did not. True queenliness could not be dimmed by any number of unfortunate handbags and lilac cravats.

To mark the end of the visit, the Emperor laid on a dazzling ball at Versailles, in La Galerie des Glaces, where ranks of mirrors reflected the banked and garlanded flowers, the uniforms of the gentlemen and the white gowns of the ladies, the Nubian servants, and the shimmer of chandeliers, torches and diamonds. An astonishing display of fireworks culminated, to the Queen's gratification, in a tableau of Windsor Castle outlined against the night sky. Mary 'became quite reckless' and gave herself 'up to dancing', while noticing the 'imperturbable' Emperor out of the corner of her eye.

The Queen's burgeoning friendship with the Emperor (sealed by his having one of the royal dogs shipped to France) was much 'puzzled' over by her ministers. Mary overheard Lord Clarendon murmuring, 'What is she hatching? And looking amused and satirical.' 'Isn't it odd,' the Queen remarked innocently to her foreign secretary, 'the Emperor remembers every frock he has ever seen me in!' She found their confidential tête-à-têtes immensely flattering; she felt that she 'should not fear saying anything to him'. Clarendon understood it perfectly: Napoleon's flirtatiousness, as he told Charles Greville, 'was of a character to flatter her vanity without alarming her virtue and modesty'.

*   *   *

As Mary danced at Versailles and sharpened her wit on Jane Ely, Charlotte Canning struggled to come to terms with her new life in Calcutta: the swamping heat and humidity (books, gloves, shoes all 'furry with mildew in a day'); the swarms of insects (cockroaches the size of mice, bats, red ants); the strangely oppressive presence of the servants padding silently about. She wrote faithfully to the Queen every six weeks, as had been requested, and Her Majesty became much fascinated by her accounts – 'if it was not for the heat and the *insects* how much I should like to see India' – and wrote regularly herself, enclosing photographs of the children, including the latest addition, baby Beatrice. There was much that Charlotte came to love about India as a country, but life in Government House brought a formality and monotony beyond anything she had experienced at court. 'It is really a very proper place,' she told her mother, 'its greatest sin is its intense dullness, with some frivolity of a dull kind too . . . People, you say, tell you that I have done good and have influence. I am not in the slightest degree aware of it, and not conscious that I have done anything but lead a more idle and selfish life than I ever did before in all my days.'

In 1857 dullness evaporated amid the horror and anxiety of the Mutiny. This was largely confined to sepoys in the East India Company's Bengal Army (the East India Company, with its own army, navy and taxation system, ruled about two thirds of India). Myriad discontents had been simmering amongst the sepoys – housing, pay, uniforms, poor relations with officers, the British annexation of Oudh in 1856, fears about interference with religion and caste – but the trigger for mutiny came with the rumour that cartridges for the new Enfield rifles, which the sepoys were required to bite, had been greased with cow and pig fat, thus offending both Hindus and Muslims. In April Charlotte told the Queen that the cartridges had been withdrawn, 'but the notion that their caste was to be broken and that they must become Christian spread widely'. There was an outbreak in the 19th Regiment, which had to be disbanded at Barrackpore (the Governor General's country home outside Calcutta) on Charlotte's birthday, but the Mutiny proper began in May, when the entire native garrison at Meerut rebelled. The Cannings went ahead with the traditional ball at Government House to celebrate the Queen's birthday on the 24 May, but trouble spread to Delhi and beyond.

The Mutiny only involved a relatively small section of the Bengal Army, but its horrors and heroisms loomed large, especially in the imaginations of the British public, as news filtered back of the massacre at Cawnpore (125 British women and children butchered and thrown down a well), the siege of Lucknow (capital of Oudh), and the deaths of Generals Anson, Barnard, Wheeler, Havelock and Sir Henry Lawrence. Wild rumours of atrocities committed by native troops were rife. At court it was reported 'that a lady has arrived "minus" nose and ears' and that a certain Colonel and Mrs Farquarson had been 'sawn asunder'. The Queen, recognising that atrocities were the 'inevitable accompaniments' of war, and hoping they were exaggerated, made anxious enquiries of Lady Canning. Information was hard to come by, wrote Charlotte, but Cawnpore was 'the worst' she knew of: 'Poor little scraps of journal, one by a child, and a letter from a lady to her mother with verses of "Farewell" were picked up in that house where they were murdered. The sight of those rooms makes strong men faint . . .'

India and its people aroused all the Queen's finer instincts – her lack of prejudice, her tolerance, her humanity. While Canning was widely condemned for the moderation and restraint of his response to the Mutiny ('clemency' was not intended as a term of approbation), Victoria's support was unwavering. 'We have great confidence in Lord Canning,' she assured Charlotte, 'and trust to hear soon of the fall of Delhi. Still I fear that there is a dangerous spirit amongst the Native Troops and that a fear of their religion being tampered with is at the bottom of it. I think that the greatest care ought to be taken not to interfere with their religion . . .' She felt profound sympathy and concern for India, and the Cannings: 'my heart *bleeds* for the horrors that have been committed by people once so gentle . . . I feel for you and Lord Canning most deeply! . . . I cannot say how sad I am to think of all this *blood shed* in a country which seemed

so prosperous – so *improving* and for which, as well as for its inhabit-
ants, I felt so great an interest.'

For Charlotte, the strain of the Mutiny, not to mention the hostility
and criticism levelled at her husband, was immense. To her sister Louisa
she admitted that she'd never wanted Canning to be made governor
general, that she'd hated leaving England, but now she wanted 'to see
all straight here again'. By December things were looking straighter
– Delhi had fallen and Lucknow had been relieved. This, wrote the
Queen, was 'cheering' news, though she herself was much preoccupied
by the impending departure of the Princess Royal, who was to marry
in the New Year: 'Our poor Victoria is wretchedly low at taking leave
of *all* she loves and cares for – and of every fete and anniversary being
the *last* she shall spend here as a happy innocent Child! She feels that
she leaves a *very very* happy Home and I am sure she will feel very
sad and lonely at first – tho' she is excessively attached to Prince
Frederic [*sic*] and he to her.' Charlotte, who had been commissioned
to send a box of Indian muslin for Vicky's trousseau, replied sympa-
thetically and sent a piece of embroidery as a present of her own.

Another letter, sadder and more heartfelt, had to be written. This
to Catherine Gladstone, whose much-loved sister Mary, married to
Sarah Lyttelton's son George, had died at Hagley in August 1857, her
heart quite worn out after her twelfth baby. For Sarah, who with the
rest of the family gathered at Mary's bedside for the last few days of
her life, the tragedy of Mary's death, at forty-four, leaving twelve
children, seemed to be outweighed by the fact that she died so *well*:
'so fine a death, so peaceful and pleasant to think over there never
was . . . She sat up, supported by pillows – white and thin, grave and
altered indeed; but looking grand and gentle too, and like a Christian
Matron soon to leave us . . . Her appearance and expression were
most striking, full of a calm holy dignity – as if her mind were raised
above this world . . . She said to me "Now don't fash yourself about
the children; you are too old for that. Your province is to look after
him [George], to comfort him".' Charlotte, knowing what Mary had
meant to Catherine, knowing too what her own sister meant to *her*,
wrote: 'I used so often to think there were hardly any two sisters who

were to each other all that you two were excepting my sister and myself and I shudder to think what such a loss must be.'

After the Mutiny, the government of India was transferred from the East India Company to the Crown, and Charles Canning became viceroy. The loneliness of Charlotte's position as viceroy's wife was much exacerbated by that of her marriage, which had benefited little from Canning's separation from his mistress. Those around her noted her sadness: 'By the side of Canning we see the gentle and tragic figure of his accomplished wife, her youth and beauty ebbing away under the appalling strain, her happiness, though not her devotion, shadowed by a cloud, the blame for which has been exclusively his,' wrote the future viceroy, Lord Curzon. Johnny Stanley, a young ADC to Canning, and a little in love with Charlotte, was frequently angered by Canning's treatment of his wife: one night at dinner he 'snubbed her dreadfully for nothing and her poor face looked so pained, she tried to laugh it off but it was a very agonised laugh . . . She is so constantly thinking only of him and how to please him and he is as sulky as possible.'

Coolly aloof in her muslin gowns, barricaded by unhappiness, Charlotte felt little sympathy for Raj society, which in turn found her proud and cold. Stanley, whom she likened to a 'merry page', was one of the few she warmed to. When her cousin Colonel Stuart was appointed as military secretary, he wrote, 'Poor thing! There is much to gratify her in her husband's grandeur of character and success, but her lines have not fallen in pleasant places here.' Stuart's wife Minny became a friend of a sort, or at least a self-appointed friend (Johnny Stanley thought Minny a tiresome 'prosing Christian'), but none was any kind of substitute for her sister Louisa.

It was then immensely distressing to receive a 'telegraph' in May 1859 announcing the death of Lord Waterford in a hunting accident. Charlotte, stunned and disbelieving, immediately wrote to her mother – could it be true? Had Louisa been with Waterford when he died? (She had.) 'I cannot imagine what Lou will do or how she can bear such a dreadful sorrow, he is the very last person I expected never to see again, he was so strong and full of life. What a dreary future for

Lou, a long life of quiet, patient sorrow.' She remembered the warmth and affection with which Waterford had always treated her. A letter arrived from the Queen, overflowing with sympathy for both sisters: 'I have been so shocked and my thoughts constantly turn to that lonely, beautiful Widow, who has seen all she loved best in this world – *carried home* at night a lifeless corse! Dearest Lady Canning we *do* feel so much for *her*, so much for you – who will learn these woeful tidings so far away – and cannot be a comfort to her in her *deep* grief!' More than anything Charlotte longed to be with her sister. Johnny Stanley, to whom she had grown into the habit of talking about Lou, provided a measure of comfort.

With Charlotte Canning in India, another, younger woman came to dominate Mary Bulteel's life at court: Lily Wellesley, the fair, pretty wife of Gerald Wellesley, Dean of Windsor. During the late 1850s Mary became a regular visitor to the Deanery, which adjoined St George's Chapel, and where she found something of a refuge and, in Lily, a source of solace and support: 'she helped me to bear my burden, the quiet and peace of the Deanery, the quiet routine of services and duties, the patient sympathetic presence made me as happy as I could be then. She was my first very great friend and I had unlimited faith in her . . . certainly Lady Canning was on a still higher pedestal but she was older and the personal sympathy was not as strong.' Lily was the first of several crushes, or *engougements*, to use Mary's term, which were to figure largely in her emotional landscape.

A shared and deeply held faith drew Mary to Lily, but, as she recognised, and deplored, 'personal sympathy', rather than religious, lay at the heart of her attachment. 'Too much engrossed in Lily's society – the feeling carrying me too far in making me forgetful of everything else,' she confessed in her diary in 1859. Just as with Charlotte Canning, Mary was drawn to Lily's air of noble, sad self-sacrifice, to her 'devotion to duty', an ideal she aspired to yet felt she fell short of. But disillusionment set in as less admirable qualities revealed themselves, 'the love of small power, the love of admiration, the proneness to gossip', and Mary came to 'scarcely believe the person I know now and the image on a pedestal I almost worshipped then can be one and the same'. Lily was toppled and the friendship cooled, though visits to the Deanery continued.

In the autumn of 1860, Mary accompanied Victoria and Albert (created Prince Consort by the Queen in 1857) to Coburg, where they were to visit Baron Stockmar, who had recently retired, and Vicky, now the Crown Princess of Prussia. They were also to meet Vicky's first child – the future Kaiser – as well as her new baby, a daughter. The royal party reached Coburg on 25 September to discover that the Dowager Duchess of Saxe-Coburg and Gotha, Albert's stepmother, had died the day before, an event that cast a pall over the visit, instantly plunging everyone into 'the deepest German mourning'. Mary had to send immediately 'for every kind of funeral garb', including – at the insistence of the Queen, with her usual enthusiasm for the niceties of mourning – 'crepe weepers' (long bands or streamers, very rarely seen by 1860) to be worn in her hair instead of 'frivolous black flowers'. Further misfortune followed. On 1 October, while driving back from Coburg, Albert had an accident – his horses bolted and he just managed to jump free of his carriage before it crashed into a wagon waiting at a level crossing. Though suffering only minor cuts and bruises, he was left disproportionately shaken, confessing to Vicky that at the moment of the accident he thought the end had come, and welcomed it. Ten days later, walking with his brother Ernest outside Gotha, and pausing to contemplate a beautiful view, he suddenly started weeping, claiming he was standing before it for the last time.

Despite the beauty of the landscape, Mary found the palace at Coburg uncomfortable and cheerless, as she did Albert's beloved boyhood home, the Rosenau. The evenings were especially dreary, reaching new levels of stiffness German-style, with the chairs arranged around the walls of the room. The Crown Princess complained to her about her prison-like existence in Berlin and begged her to come and visit, and Mary later made several trips to Prussia, where Vicky's life became increasingly wretched, especially after the death of Frederick William. In search of some light relief, Mary 'slipped out and explored the town with Uncle Charles and Colonel Ponsonby and foraged to buy soap!' This is the first mention of Henry Ponsonby in Mary's letters, though it would not have been their first encounter – Henry had been an equerry to the Prince since 1857.

On 26 January 1861, the Queen wrote to Vicky of a 'household marriage, which was settled the day before yesterday . . . Mary Bulteel to Colonel Ponsonby!' She went on to enter into the particulars: 'For the last fortnight I saw (what many had seen before) a great and marked attention on his part towards Mary which was quite different to ordinary flirtation. But Mary gave him no encouragement; however on Thursday, the day she went out of waiting, she went to the Deanery and he followed her in the cloisters – and proposed. She gave no answer and was in a state of great distress etc. for she had turned her face against all marriage – said she "had put her foot in it" and in short was quite upset.' It was Lily Wellesley, continued the Queen, who urged her not to refuse 'so amiable and good and nice a person', though, she added, 'a little bit of a flirt'. Henry was accepted that evening, after the play, in the Waterloo Room. The Queen was philosophical about losing her maid-of-honour: 'I shall be very sorry to lose Mary but am very glad of the marriage as I feel she will still be in the Household.' Shrewdly, she hinted at some ambivalence on Mary's part, believing 'she would not have accepted him if her friends had not advised her to do so'. In her diary, the newly engaged Mary wrote, 'bewildered and don't quite know what to make of my own feelings'.

There *was* ambivalence: emotional; possibly sexual. Mary, at twenty-nine, looked to have turned away from marriage. She had contemplated entering a convent. Her failed engagement to William Harcourt had left her bruised. Since then she had formed close emotional attachments to other women, and would continue to do so (she also enjoyed the companionship of younger, homosexual men, such as her nephew Maurice Baring and Arthur Benson, both members of Henry James's coterie). She liked and admired Henry Ponsonby without necessarily loving him. She did not perhaps wish for a husband at all, let alone one who was a member of the royal household, with all that that would entail – a life tied to court, to a Queen whose demands would always take precedence over those of wife and children.

Nevertheless, the wedding took place in April. In addition to the £1,000 dowry, the Queen gave Mary a locket and a shawl of Irish lace. After honeymooning in France and Italy, Mary Ponsonby considered herself 'happy but misgivings at having chosen the world instead of His service'. 'I can truly and I do truly look up to my husband,' she continued, 'because he is far better than I am in his absolute truth, fearlessness, honesty and unselfishness, but I know now that the devotional in religious as well as the imaginative in other matters must be kept to myself.' She admitted though that she had 'got to care more than I ever thought possible about my husband's love', and set about settling into her new home at Windsor, 6 The Cloisters, opposite St George's Chapel.

If, for Mary at least, this was a match founded on pragmatism rather than passion, it grew into a most affectionate and companionable marriage, with both parties bringing an amused, ironical eye to the absurdities of the world and of the Victorian court in particular. The Ponsonby family, like many of their class, affected a certain satirical 'tone' – a generous measure of intellectual snobbery mixed with a dash of xenophobia – towards the royal family, privately referring to their august sovereign and her consort as 'Eliza' and 'Joseph' (the nineteenth-century equivalents of Charlene and Wayne). Mary considered both Victoria and Albert on 'more natural terms with the servants' than with members of their household, with the result that 'their standard of taste ran the risk of being vulgarised' – this was unfair to the Prince, while it was precisely the Queen's bourgeois qualities that endeared her to so many of her subjects. Arthur Ponsonby, Henry and Mary's son, went rather further – the royal family actually resembled servants in matters of taste and style: 'They use old-fashioned rather ungrammatical language and have the same love of funerals and diseases and are touching and fussy.' He went on to declare, 'we regarded them as a very ordinary rather second rate family . . . except for the Queen who had real distinction and was the Queen essentially and absolutely', sentiments echoed by Mary; the Queen was not to be tarred with the same brush as common-or-garden Royalties.

After a year of marriage, Mary could write, 'less thought of self from having H with me – the absence of vanity and selfishness in him doing more to disgust me of my faults than all else'. She regretted that in religious matters they were not 'more together', and she continued to be preoccupied with Lily Wellesley, but she regarded Henry as a finer character, and as such a spur to self-improvement, a corrective to her own failings. Mary had not married for love, but, as she confessed to Ethel Smyth, love came later.

CHAPTER 13

Three Deaths

In January 1861, Dr William Baly, recently appointed physician extraordinary, and the intended successor to the now elderly Sir James Clark, died in a freak railway accident at Wimbledon – the floor of his carriage gave way beneath him and he was run over. Albert, who had become attached to his new doctor, was greatly upset. He seemed, as the Queen told Vicky, 'completely overwhelmed by everything'. Dr Baly's death was just the first in a succession of blows that, over the year, lowered him further.

On 15 March, the Queen and the Prince Consort, summoned by Sir James Clark, hurried to Frogmore, where the seventy-five-year-old Duchess of Kent was dying. She had suffered several attacks of erysipelas (a streptococcal infection of the skin), and she now had a painfully infected arm. That night the Duchess's lady-in-waiting, Lady Augusta Bruce, sat up with her mistress, occasionally lying down on the floor to rest. Three times she saw the Queen, in her white dressing gown, accompanied by her dresser, Sophie Weiss, steal into the room to gaze at her mother, who had sunk into unconsciousness. The following morning the Duchess died. The Queen wept bitterly and the Prince, much overcome himself, was, thought Augusta, most 'tender' towards her.

Victoria plunged into an ecstasy of grief. For all her frequent mournings, this was her first direct experience of death, the first loss that had truly touched her. Going through her mother's papers brought home just how greatly loved she had been, and guilt, for their period of estrangement when she had first come to the throne, compounded grief. For the already overworked Prince Consort, who had been appointed sole executor, the Duchess's death brought a further burden.

In her misery the Queen turned to Augusta Bruce, the sister of General Robert Bruce, governor to the Prince of Wales, who had become lady-in-waiting to the Duchess of Kent in 1846, a position to which she brought an almost religious devotion. Though humorous, intelligent and sophisticated (she had grown up amongst the salon society of Paris), Augusta accorded Royalties the kind of reverence of which Mary Ponsonby, who found her 'a little affected', though 'clever and agreeable', was quite incapable. Having loved and served Victoria's mother so faithfully, Augusta now became the Queen's own prop and mainstay.

A few weeks after the Duchess's death, the Queen made Augusta an official as well as an emotional prop, by inviting her to become her resident bedchamber woman, 'the thought of having you, who dearest Mama loved as a Child, near me in future, is an indescribable comfort for my poor bleeding heart and I trust that you will love the Child of that dear blessed One who is at rest and peace now!' Taking up her new post, Augusta moved into her quarters in the Edward III Tower – a bedroom looking on to the Round Tower and a tiny sitting room with a view of the Long Walk. In London she was given her own apartment in St James's Palace as a *'pied à terre'*. But the Queen wanted to bind her still further; Miss Skerrett had intimated that she wished to retire and the Queen hoped that Augusta would be prepared 'to be at the head of the personal Department and to write and do many things she does'. Aware of the demands that this 'considerable bondage' would entail, Augusta hoped to secure good holidays, 'necessary for one's mind and spirit', to have the use of her own carriage, and, like the superintendent of the nursery, Lady Caroline Barrington, to attend the Queen's dinner on an occasional basis, rather than as a matter of course. She was unsure about her salary – in addition to her £300 from the lord chamberlain, as resident bedchamber woman she thought she might get an extra £100 from the privy purse.

At Osborne, where the royal family went in April, Augusta spent her days closeted with her new mistress – 'the Blessed One' – writing letters and lists of things the Queen wished to give as souvenirs of her mother, work she loved 'because it is still with the Queen and for our beloved one'. To her relief, she was not required to join the rest of the household for dinner (Their Majesties were dining alone).

To Augusta, the Queen's bouts of weeping and obsessive need to talk over the past seemed no more than soft-heartedness and the natural feelings of the bereaved daughter. To others, her grief seemed excessive, indulgent, even unbalanced. Excessive and indulgent it certainly was. Victoria cleaved as closely to those she loved in death (though in the case of the Duchess of Kent it was perhaps the idea of her mother as much as the reality) as she did in life; grief became a *raison d'être*, and since she was quite incapable of emotional restraint, it was expressed extravagantly, repeatedly and at inordinate length. The Queen herself admitted to Vicky, 'I do not want to feel better. I love to dwell on her . . . and not to be roused out of my grief.' She visited the vault at Frogmore, where the Duchess was buried, every morning and evening, as if, wrote Lord Clarendon, 'it was a satisfaction to feed her grief'. He hoped 'this state of things won't last or she may fall into a morbid melancholy to which her mind has often tended and which is a constant source of anxiety to Prince Albert'. Rumours started circulating that she had actually gone mad.

In August, the Queen wrote to Charlotte Canning – in reply to her letter of condolence – a twenty-one-page torrent of emotion. Five months had seemingly done nothing to diminish her grief: 'to lose a *Mother* and *such* a Mother, from whom except for a *very* few months I had *never* been parted . . . My *health* has never really suffered at all, but my nerves (never of the strongest) were *very* much shattered . . . I lived as in a dream for some weeks and only after a time did I feel the shock it had given me. I remained very quiet and *weak*, I could have remained entirely in the country – but *duty* required a return to Town . . . but London is a dreadful place with a *sore* heart! I held two Drawing rooms and saw *few* (very few people) to dinner, but otherwise of course, remained quite in private. But it is very hard in my position to be *obliged* to do anything of that kind when one's *heart* longs for seclusion. *All* Anniversaries are *dreadful*! All birthdays *most painful* . . .

Then *again* returning here in July – *when* dearest Mama always came here and spent some days before we went to Scotland – I felt *so* wretched! The *blank* seems only to increase as time goes on – and you keep *hoping* and believing *against* your *reason* that the dear *One must* return! . . . I have so *much* to thank God for! *Such* a Husband – such affectionate Children, that I will not murmur at *what* I have lost – but *such* a loss *cannot* be replaced . . .'

Writing to her sister-in-law, Charlotte described the Queen's letter as 'simple and true as a child's', continuing that she'd always felt that the Queen 'has had credit for qualities not hers and that nobody knew what real softness and feeling she has in some ways . . . Just as every body would say she was never sea sick so it was always thought nothing shook or "upset" her'; in fact, far from having 'the hard head and strong sense people fancied', she actually suffered from 'very weak nerves'. This, in Charlotte's view, was at the root of the 'prevailing idea about her mind going awry'. However, the particular symptoms of Victoria's grief – the fragile nerves, the longing for seclusion, the exquisite poignancy of anniversaries – would become all too familiar to her household.

A couple of months before the Queen's outpouring, Charlotte had been surprised to receive another letter, from George Lyttelton, a widower for the past four years. Might Charlotte's sister Lady Waterford, wondered George, consider him as a husband – his means were 'inadequate', where she was rich, he had a troop of charming children, where she had none. The fact that he scarcely knew her, indeed hadn't seen her for twenty years apart from glimpsing her 'for a few minutes, not to speak to, some days ago', a sighting that had presumably prompted his unconventional proposal, did not deter him in the least. Charlotte's reply does not survive, but was apparently most kind and tactful.

Climate, unhappiness and the strain of the Mutiny had all taken their toll on Charlotte. A photograph taken in 1861 shows her at forty-four, still handsome, but thin and worn, her dark hair threaded with silver. More than anything she yearned to be reunited with her mother and Lou, so it was to her immense joy that the date for the Cannings' departure from India, twice postponed, was finally fixed for January 1862. After six and a half long years, she was going home. There was just time to make an expedition to Darjeeling, a place she had always longed to see. Not having felt 'so strong of late', she rather dreaded the rigours of the journey, but determined to set off, taking with her a couple of army captains and her maid, at the beginning of October.

The journey, by palanquin and pony, proved gruelling indeed, but once there, all was forgotten beside the magnificence of the mountains – forested, verdant and strewn with orchids. Charlotte wrote cheerful, affectionate letters to 'darling Carlo' (some thought their marriage had grown a little happier in recent years), her spirits undampened by constant rain and chronic insomnia. But spectacular scenery took second place to bubbling excitement at the prospect of going home. The Queen had offered Canning the rangership of Greenwich Park, a position that came with a largish red-brick villa on the edge of Blackheath, for which Charlotte had many plans. They would, she thought, need to put in a couple of sash windows to bring in more light; there was plenty of space for a garden, even a poultry yard and dairy; they should probably keep the barouche; overall the house would 'answer so well to store away things and one can have charming dinners of friends and fresh whitebait for them'. At the beginning of November she embarked on the return journey to Calcutta, loaded with plants for Blackheath. Those dinners with friends and whitebait were only a matter of months away.

Charlotte's return was eagerly awaited by Mary Ponsonby. 'Mary Ponsonby is here – looking very thin and in bad looks – the usual happy fate of poor brides!' the Queen wrote cheerfully in October (for all her own marital happiness, she liked to view young brides as lambs to the slaughter). In early December, Mary opened a newspaper to read that Charlotte Canning had died in Calcutta, of 'jungle fever'. 'I have been very wretched these last few hours,' she wrote in her diary, somewhat incoherent from shock, 'and I do not think I can ever take the same interest in anything again, all somehow almost unconsciously had the background of her return to help me on, so I cannot believe she is really dead, dead. I have never seen anyone like her. The only friend I ever had that in every thing she said and thought consistently brought me without effort into a holier, pure, more lofty tone about every subject and I feel so lonely for I have never swerved for a moment during her absence in putting her first and admiring beyond all the true, simple, humble spirit that made her all unconscious of her gifts and her influence. I have loved her so and she is dead.'

Alongside this entry she tucked the newspaper cutting announcing Charlotte's death and a letter from Lily Wellesley: 'Mamie darling – I left you alone this eve not because I thought you did not care to have me near you, but because I knew what kind of grief it was that had come upon you. I know that no human being can ever fill the void that such a loss must leave in your heart. Therefore darling, after the first burst of sorrow had lulled I knew that He who had seen fit to inflict the blow would in His own way give or send the healing that you need and I left you to Him, as I knew while I prayed for you in our room you were doing the same in the next. Darling, for some time we must not speak of it again, for we both thank God understand each other and there is no use in dwelling on it in conversation, unless it were a relief to you which I doubt. All I write this for is that you may feel there is one human heart very near to you, who will be ever ready, while God gives her life, to serve you day and night if need be and although I can never replace her to you . . . yet she never loved you more truly than I do.' Mary may have grown disillusioned with Lily, but it was Lily she turned to in her grief.

On 5 December, the Queen told the Prince Consort of Charlotte's death. The Prince, whose health had been steadily deteriorating over the past year, was by now extremely unwell himself – feverish, irritable and restless. He lay on a sofa in his dressing gown, or wandered from room to room at Windsor, unable to eat or sleep. A few weeks earlier he had been much depressed by the news that the King of Portugal, a cousin, of whom he'd been very fond, had died of typhoid fever at only twenty-five. His spirits were lowered further by anxieties about the Prince of Wales.

Bertie, as far as his parents could see, was interested in virtually nothing but clothes (the Queen habitually accompanied references to her eldest son with lamentations – 'Oh Bertie alas! Alas! That is too sad a subject to enter on'). Marriage, it was hoped, might steady him, though Bertie himself was unenthusiastic about the most promising candidate, the beautiful Princess Alexandra of Denmark. Then, while at the Curragh camp near Dublin, where he had been sent to gain some experience of army life, he began a liaison with an actress, Nellie Clifden. This was not in itself especially shocking, but to his father, in his lowered state and with his particular horror of sexual impropriety, it was a body blow. He felt Bertie had 'sunk into vice and debauchery'. On 22 November, already suffering from insomnia and rheumatic pains, Albert went to Sandhurst to inspect some new buildings, and caught cold. A few days later he insisted on travelling to Madingley, near Cambridge, where Bertie was studying, to talk to his errant son and impress upon him his disgrace. After a long walk with the contrite Bertie in the damp fenland chill, he returned to Windsor 'at very low ebb'.

He roused himself, though, to intervene in the *Trent* affair. Civil war had begun in America the previous April, with the British government favouring the Southern states. In November a British mail steamer, the *Trent*, carrying two envoys from the Confederacy, bound for Europe, was intercepted by a North American warship and the envoys were removed. This, in the eyes of Palmerston and his Cabinet, was a flagrant and unacceptable breach of international law; a belligerent dispatch was written, demanding reparation. On 1 December, at seven in the morning, Albert dragged himself to his desk and read this dispatch with alarm. It carried with it, he felt, a high risk of war. Though scarcely able to hold his pen, he composed an altogether more conciliatory memorandum, suggesting that the warship must have acted without the knowledge of President Lincoln. His amendments were approved and the dispatch was redrafted before being sent to Washington. The envoys were released. War between Britain and America was averted. It was Albert's last act for his country.

It seemed that the Prince's doctors, Sir James Clark and William

Jenner (Dr Baly's replacement, and supposedly an expert on typhoid), could do nothing for him, though they assured the Queen that there was no great cause for alarm. Lord Palmerston, who received regular bulletins on the Prince's condition from Charles Phipps, and who had no faith whatsoever in Clark, urged that another doctor be called in, but Phipps felt that to do so would only alarm the Queen, and it was crucial to keep her calm. The Queen herself stubbornly refused to doubt the competence of either Clark or Jenner. On 6 December the Prince seemed better, but the next day a rash appeared on his stomach, a telltale sign of typhoid fever, as Jenner explained to Her Majesty, though he remained optimistic: people survived typhoid, and the Prince was still a fairly young man.

Albert asked to be moved into the Blue Room, where William IV and George IV had both died, and had his bed placed near the window. He asked for music, and Princess Alice (newly engaged to Prince Louis of Hesse-Darmstadt), who was nursing him devotedly, played his favourite Lutheran hymn on the piano in the next-door room. The Queen sat by his bedside and read Walter Scott aloud. Two additional doctors were now finally summoned to Windsor, Sir Henry Holland and Dr Watson. Watson in particular felt the Prince's case to be very serious indeed. But on 10 and 11 December he seemed to improve slightly. On the 12th, Henry Ponsonby came back into waiting. News of the Prince, as reported at household dinner, did not suggest he was in any great danger, and Henry wrote to his mother that though he was 'low and weak . . . none of the doctors think badly of him'. His mind wandered rather – he kept his gaze fixed on the Raphael Madonna on the wall of his room, murmuring about her beautiful expression – but the Queen was 'only a little fussed'. Henry himself was preoccupied by rumours that, with tensions between Britain and America running high, his regiment, the Grenadier Guards, might be sent to Canada.

Augusta Bruce, as ever a stalwart support during these anxious days, wrote bulletins on the Prince's condition for the Queen and walked or drove most afternoons with her and the Duchess of Atholl, the current lady-in-waiting, and chatelaine of Blair Castle, where the Queen had made a happy visit with Albert back in 1844. Despite the diagnosis of 'gastric fever' (a euphemism for typhoid), Augusta thought appearances 'favourable', though she worried about the Prince's low spirits. Then, on the 13th, while the Queen was out walking, Jenner told her that he thought Albert was 'sinking' – he was breathing with difficulty and semi-delirious. Pneumonia had set in. Sir James Clark, who was running between the Prince and his own dangerously ill wife, felt Her Majesty must be prepared, and Augusta was deputed to break the news. The Queen cried repeatedly, 'the country; oh the country. I could perhaps bear my own misery, but the poor country', as Augusta and Miss Hildyard did their best to comfort her. A grim urgency settled over the castle; a telegraph was sent to the Prince of Wales; Colonel Biddulph, General Bruce and General Grey moved the Prince's bed to the centre of the room.

That night Augusta slept on a sofa in the Victoria Tower. The next morning the Prince seemed 'quite calm', only 'wandered' a little, and showed his wife 'every mark of love and tenderness' (the Queen, leaning over him, asked for, and was given, 'ein Kuss'). This led her to think him better, though by evening the doctors had become 'more and more desponding'. The Prince of Wales, who had hurried to Windsor, was allowed into the room, followed one by one by the other children; their father smiled at them but could not speak. Albert asked for Charles Phipps, who came and kissed his hand, as did Thomas Biddulph and Charles Grey, who both broke down. The Queen sat quite calmly by his bed as sips of brandy were given in a vain attempt to raise his pulse.

Outside in the Corridor members of the household gathered, scanning the doctors' faces as they came and went. At half past ten a white-faced Dean of Windsor hurried past and into the Blue Room. Towards eleven o'clock, Princess Alice whispered to Augusta, as they sat at the bedside, 'that is the death rattle', and hurried to fetch her mother. In the near darkness the Queen and Princess Alice knelt on either side of the bed, the Prince of Wales and Princess Helena at the foot, and around them the Prince and Princess of Leiningen, who happened to be visiting, Charles Phipps, Charles Grey, Thomas

Biddulph, General Bruce, Gerald Wellesley, the Duchess of Atholl, Miss Hildyard, the doctors, Albert's valet Löhlein and Augusta. All watched silently as the Prince drew his last breath and the Queen let out a piteous cry – 'Oh yes, this is death. I know it. I have seen this before' – and fell upon his body.

She was carried by the gentlemen into the red drawing room, where she lay on a sofa and called the children to her, clasping 'them to her heart' and assuring 'them she would endeavour, if she lived, to live for them and her duty'. Then she thanked the doctors and appealed to each gentleman: 'You will not leave or desert me now.' Augusta helped the dressers put her to bed. She herself slept on a sofa outside the room, until the Queen called her in at five and 'wept and talked' for two hours. The next day the order went out from the lord chamberlain's office: ladies were 'to wear black woollen stuffs, trimmed with crape, plain linen, black shoes and gloves and crape fans'; gentlemen 'to wear black cloth, plain linen, crape hatbands and black sword and buckles'.

Charles Phipps wrote to Palmerston, 'The Queen though in an agony of grief, is perfectly collected, and shows a self-control that is quite extraordinary. Alas! She has not realised her loss – and when the full consciousness comes upon her – I tremble – but only for the depth of her grief. What will happen – where can She look for that support and assistance upon which She has leaned in the greatest and the least questions of her life?' This was the crux of it: character and circumstance had combined to make the Queen peculiarly dependent on Albert. As she herself admitted, 'I did nothing, moved not a finger, arranged not a print or a photograph, didn't put on a gown or a bonnet if he didn't approve it.' Now, at just forty-two, she found herself alone.

Partly from lack of information, partly because of false hopes encouraged by the doctors, the death of the Prince Consort took most by surprise. The household were hardly less stunned than the Queen, incapable of little more than gazing at each other aghast and murmuring, 'the poor Queen!' 'It is really a most terrible event,' wrote Henry Ponsonby on the 16th, 'and the quick way it has come upon all of us who a week ago scarcely thought the illness anything is awful.' The Prince of Wales, he reported, had thrown himself into his mother's arms crying, '"indeed Mama I will be all I can to you" and she kissed him very much as she said "I'm sure my dear boy you will"'. Henry was 'very glad of this as it will be a good thing for both to think of in future' (in fact the Queen's relations with her son would be blighted for some time thanks to her conviction that Bertie's 'Fall' had been instrumental in his father's death). Her Majesty, wrote Henry, was calm, having been given opiates the night before, and was to go to Osborne. Mary Ponsonby wrote to her mother of the Queen's 'utter desolation' and 'the utter consternation of everyone – the standstill everything has come to – the spring and centre of each being gone . . . I cannot conceive what she will do, for if her will were ever so strong, she cannot have the power or capacity to do his work; and for her grief my very heart aches.'

There was no question of the Queen attending Albert's funeral. This was not unusual – women in nineteenth century England rarely went to the funerals of close family members, as the emotional rigours were thought to be too much for them. Instead Her Majesty was persuaded, by her doctors, to leave Windsor, setting out reluctantly for Osborne on 19 December. 'It was a terrible moment,' recalled Augusta Bruce, who accompanied her. 'She felt on leaving that all that could be taken from her, of him, had been.' The night before, Miss Skerrett wrote to Eleanor Stanley, her usual convoluted jumble of news, philosophy and non sequiturs, and using ordinary paper rather than black-bordered mourning paper, for reasons she explained. 'Yesterday evening everything was packing, vans loading, and almost everything got downstairs, when at seven o'clock an order came to stop as the Queen had resolved not to go till the next day; that is the reason why I am writing to you on improper paper – if in real misfortunes there can be really a choice! But all my proper paper was packed up yesterday and I have used every bit; I must mention this because there is an affectation, you know, in neglecting what is conventional as well as clinging to it.' She believed the Queen's best hope lay in keeping busy: 'there is nothing for a case like hers but to be really and truly employed, not in all the small kind of things on which so much time is spent, but I am afraid she will try to combine the two. There is nothing so incomprehensible to a human mind as another human mind, the impossibility of forming a just judgement of what is in it and what it really feels and how it considers itself and aggravates its loss; like the man in the play I can only say, 'Verstand steht stille!' the world and what is in it are all made to go on, and they will one way or the other, but the idea of entering into another human mind is the vainest of all things.'

News spread fast. Sarah Lyttelton, waiting anxiously at Hagley (she'd had a reasonably optimistic report, written by Augusta Bruce on the Queen's behalf, on the 10th), received a letter from Catherine Gladstone, on the 17th, in which Catherine quoted a letter *she* had received from Lily Wellesley. 'We are all so overcome we can scarcely write – the Queen strives with all her heart to resign herself to the will of God . . . The country does not know the extent of the misfortune wh has just overwhelmed it. Let us pray it never may. And let us thank God that she is supported by a higher hand in this fearful time. Thanks to Him our Queen's first thought was the Prince of Wales. We all here pray that everyone who has access or ever will have access to Her will keep that – in every way – it is her only hope and still more the country's. This is a wild letter but you will forgive.' The Gladstones had gone to Chester to buy mourning and had been 'struck by the unusual feeling shown – the appearance of people speaks of our common sorrow'. William was 'holding himself ready' for the funeral. Would Sarah let Catherine know of any details she had?

For Catherine, though, the news of Charlotte Canning's death had been a more personal sorrow: 'In the midst of this one's heart melts at the silence from India, another 9 days must elapse and we have only those awful words "Lady Canning died of jungle fever and is buried at Barrackpore". How shocking how desolating it feels and that poor mother and sister must wait knowing nothing – life going on and life ending as one gigantic event after another sweeps away friend after friend till one stops to ask where are they? And what shall we do?'

Louisa indeed knew nothing beyond the stark announcement of Charlotte's death. She had immediately hurried to her mother at Highcliffe, from where she wrote to a cousin, 'You can scarcely imagine the weary, weary days of waiting in suspense, without hope, to know what dreadful cause ended so fatally. I feel as if my light has darkened . . .' Details of the 'dreadful cause' slowly filtered back to England. The journey from Darjeeling back to Calcutta, 'palanquin-travelling day and night', had left Charlotte much 'knocked up'. Fatally it had also taken her through malaria-ridden swamps. By the time she had arrived home, on 8 November, she was weak and feverish; by the 12th she couldn't leave her bed. When the doctor told Canning that her case was hopeless, he fainted away, and for the next four days and nights he never left her side. On the 18th, less than two months before she was due to leave India, she died, unconscious, in her husband's arms. That night her coffin was taken to Barrackpore, a place Charlotte had loved, and at dawn, as the fading moon gave way to a fiery Indian sun, she was buried in the garden, beneath a banyan tree. Afterwards Canning locked himself in his room, and during the days that followed he could be seen, every morning and evening, standing alone at the graveside.

He sent the Queen a restrained account of his wife's last days: 'there never was any pain, probably at last no consciousness, but the same gentle, patient, unrepining look which from the beginning had never left her face for an instant'. The Queen replied, from Osborne, at the beginning of January, in rather less restrained terms. His loss, chiming as it did with hers, had a particular poignancy: 'Lord Canning little thought when he wrote his kind and touching letter of the 22nd November that it would only reach the Queen when *she* was *smitten* and *bowed* down to earth by an event similar to the one which he describes . . . To lose one's partner in life is, as Lord Canning knows, like loosing *half* of one's *body* and *soul*, torn forcibly away – and dear Lady Canning was such a dear, worthy, devoted wife! But to the Queen – to a poor helpless woman – it is not that only . . . To the Queen it is like *death* in life! Great and small – *nothing* was done without his loving advice and help – and she feels *alone* in the wide world, with

many helpless children (except the Princess Royal) to look to her – and
the whole nation to look to her – *now* when she can barely struggle
with her wretched existence!. . . Though ill the Queen was able to
tell her precious angel of Lord Canning's bereavement, and he was
deeply grieved, recurring to it several times and saying "What a loss!
She was such a distinguished person!" May God comfort and support
Lord Canning and may he think in his sorrow of his widowed and
broken-hearted Sovereign – bowed to the earth with the greatest of
human sufferings and misfortunes.'

The Bishop of Calcutta, wishing to offer comfort, visited Canning
'in his dreary little sitting room at Government House'. Attempting
to speak of his wife, Canning broke down, sobbing. 'Considering that
his manner was chiefly marked by a cold and stern dignity,' remarked
the Bishop, 'I never saw before a stronger instance of the heart asserting
its supremacy'; talking about the Queen and her letters at least seemed
to afford him 'some relief from his own grief'. Flagrantly unfaithful
to Charlotte in life, Canning was quite broken by her death, transformed into an old man overnight, unable to walk without a stick,
beset by languor, depression and insomnia. After returning to England,
he went to see Charlotte's cousin Colonel Stuart, at Highcliffe. 'The
grand, pale, sad face came here,' wrote Lady Stuart, 'with evident
suffering but wondrous self-restraint.' The Queen, she felt, could at
least cry, but Canning's 'reserve' made him 'shut his sorrow into his
heart'. Just seven months after Charlotte's death, Canning died himself,
from liver disease (anguish, said some). On hearing this, Charlotte's
mother threw up her hands, tears streaming down her face, and cried,
'This *is* judgement!' The Queen, who had not been aware of the
circumstances of the Cannings' marriage, saw it rather differently,
writing to Canning's sister Lady Clanricarde, 'he is again with *her* after
only 7 months separation! Oh for him now blessed! How enviable to
follow so soon – the partner of your life! How I pray it may be God's
will to let me follow him soon too!'

In January, Victoria sent Sarah Lyttelton, who, as the Queen knew,
had admired and appreciated Albert, and who had borne witness to
Her Majesty's happiness, a brooch, containing a photograph of the

Prince, accompanied by a letter. 'Dearest Lady Lyttelton!' she wrote. 'You knew and saw far more than others could or did! . . . I feel as if my real life and existence had ended with that dreadful day when he left me.' The Prince, she added, had been resigned to death – 'he said that he was sure if he had a dangerous illness, he should make no struggle'. Now she only looked to her own.

PART 2

'My heart is utterly and completely broken'

CHAPTER 14

'Someone to lean on'

Sarah Lyttelton thought that she had never known a wife 'more in constant want, in constant habit of consulting and leaning upon her prop' than the Queen. After the death of the Prince Consort, the 'prop' on whom Victoria had relied absolutely, her need for others to lean on became acute. 'Baby' Beatrice was some comfort, but otherwise the children were of no great recourse, being too preoccupied with their own lives (especially once married, as Alice in 1862, Bertie a year later and Helena in 1866) to provide the kind of sympathy and support – absolute and unquestioning – that she required. For this she looked to her household.

Osborne, where the Queen remained closeted for the first few months of 1862, seemed to Augusta Bruce 'like Pompeii, the life suddenly extinguished'. A visitor was struck by the change: 'You are all so thin, there are such lines of care on every face, I could not but look around at Luncheon and marvel at even that outward change.' Miss Skerrett, who never relished being immured at Osborne, wrote to Landseer, saying that she thought it unlikely that the Queen would come to London at all that year, but she herself hoped to be sent 'on business', and so perhaps to see Sir Edwin and tell him something of her 'liberation'. After twenty-five years at court, she now longed for nothing more than to return to the world beyond. 'This year I shall I do hope and trust be able to say and do to a certain extent what I have so long been wanting to do and in fact if I do not I may as well finish my life in this kind of life.' She *was* liberated, and, with a pension of £70, went to live with her sister in Marylebone, though she continued to visit court.[3]

In February, Augusta Bruce reported that the Queen slept reasonably, wept a great deal and dined alone, although her half-sister Feodora, who was visiting, Princess Alice or Augusta herself occasionally joined her. 'The Ladies might be angry,' wrote Augusta somewhat disingenuously, 'for the Queen sends for me so often, makes me walk or drive when none of the children can, and dine sometimes tête-à-tête, but they are all so kind about it.' They were not quite so kind behind her back. 'We are under the gentle rule of King Charles [Phipps] and Queen Augusta [Bruce],' wrote Lady Caroline Barrington, with a hint of asperity. In the airless bell-jar of court, jealousies and rivalries flourished like weeds. 'Dear Augusta', so selfless and devoted, had made herself indispensable, enjoying apparently exclusive access to and influence with the Queen, while the other ladies scarcely even saw her. Lady Barrington told Lord Clarendon that she'd only seen Her Majesty 'once by accident' since the Prince Consort's death three months earlier.

Just as Augusta, former lady-in-waiting to Victoria's mother, stood as a link to and reminder of a happier past, so Charles Phipps, keeper of the privy purse, had once been a loyal and trusted private secretary to Albert. It helped too that Phipps, with the demeanour and temperament of a kindly sheep – amongst the household he was known as 'Lord Paramount' and regarded as a well-meaning ditherer – showed himself endlessly acquiescent before the royal will. The same need that made the Queen cling to those with links to the dead lay behind the preservation of the Prince's rooms – the jug of hot water placed daily on the washstand, the clothes laid out, the fresh flowers strewn on the bed, the watch kept wound, the blotting book on the desk left open, a pen at the ready – not to mention the ever-multiplying memorials and punctiliously commemorated 'melancholy anniversaries'. Grief, for Victoria, was

---

[3] Miss Skerrett died in 1887, aged ninety-four; she left the Queen a Hogarth portrait of a colonial family, the Popples, one of whom was her grandmother.

to be fed and nurtured. As she told Vicky, 'my very misery is now a necessity and I could not exist without it'.

By March, back at Windsor, Augusta thought the Queen better and calmer, comforted by seeing the progress of Albert's mausoleum and 'determined to walk in the path of duty'. The tête-à-tête dinners with Her Majesty continued. Vicky, according to Lord Clarendon, attributed Augusta's influence simply to the fact that she said '"Yes Ma'am" to everything and if she said "No Ma'am" a few times the Q wd cease to think her the paragon of cleverness she now does'. Clarendon also noted that the Queen had become 'embarrassed about the waitings of her Ladies' and couldn't bear the thought of Lady Churchill because she had 'never known grief'.

In September 1863, the Queen, about to leave for Balmoral, complained of her 'utter loneliness with no lady even – except Augusta – who is of any real recourse, for Lady Churchill good and excellent as she is, is not that'. Jane Churchill generally enjoyed the absolute confidence of the Queen, and frequently recommended ladies (she made a point of commenting on their looks, or lack of; a prospective maid-of-honour was not pretty, 'but it's a face that grows on one'). Her husband, however, was very much alive and well. Augusta had not known grief either, but at least she was not, as yet, enjoying the blessings of a happy marriage. Besides, her stocks of sympathy seemed inexhaustible, and sympathy was a quality, a qualification almost, the Queen increasingly looked for in her ladies.

Widowhood now became a recommendation in itself, with fellow widows, such as Lady Ely, or Lady Barrington, much in favour. The Queen enjoyed a consoling visit from Mrs Lilly, once her monthly nurse, whose own husband had died shortly after Albert. In 1864 she wrote to her newly appointed lady of the bedchamber, Lady Waterpark, who had lost her husband, a lord-in-waiting, the previous year: 'I think that we understand one another and feel that *life* is ended for us, except in the sense of duty.' Lady Waterpark was reminded that 'all those in waiting on me wear the sable garb which I think suits best our sad sisterhood'. Only members of the 'sad sisterhood' could fully enter into and comprehend Her Majesty's suffering, the extent of her loss.

Aside from the Queen's personal devastation, there were practical considerations in the wake of the Prince Consort's death. What was to become of his staff? It was decided that they should simply be absorbed into Her Majesty's household. Henry Ponsonby, along with the Prince's other three equerries, was appointed extra equerry to the Queen with a reduction in salary from £500 to £300, and the expectation that he would in time be made a full equerry. Charles Grey, the Prince's secretary, became private secretary to the Queen (this was not made official until 1866). Carl Ruland, his German librarian, became her German secretary and Rudolf Löhlein, his valet, an 'Extra Personal Attendant'.

These German attendants, men who had been close to Albert, comforted the Queen but were greatly resented by the rest of the household, who regarded their promotion as unwarranted and unsuitable. 'I have all your feelings about Lohlein and Ruland, and see as little as you do what is to be done,' wrote Charles Grey to Charles Phipps, 'these are in fact the men who have the Queen's confidence on all subjects, and who see her at all times, and who carry her orders. I confess I was somewhat shocked at receiving through Lohlein, a verbal message as to the purport of a letter I was to write to the Prime Minister, on the subject of a difference with another of her ministers.' This was largely household xenophobia. The court became *less* German after Albert's death, and even more so after Stockmar's in 1863, when Carl Ruland returned to Germany (amongst rumours that he had become too familiar with Princess Helena). Herr Sahl became the Queen's new German secretary and librarian, and signally failed to maintain Albert's carefully devised system for cataloguing correspondence.

One of the very few whom the Queen wished to see in her grief was Sarah Lyttelton, who was invited to Windsor in 1863. Twelve years had passed since Sarah had last beheld the castle walls looming up before her carriage, years of loss and change: the Queen a widow; the Princess Royal living in Berlin as Crown Princess of Prussia; Princess Alice in Darmstadt with her husband Prince Louis of

Hesse-Darmstadt; the Prince of Wales recently married to Princess Alexandra; her own son George a widower; her brood of twelve motherless grandchildren.

Windsor, now a palace of mourning and memorials, felt both familiar and strange. Shown into Miss Hildyard's room, she found Miss Hildyard herself, looking aged and thin, and Mrs Thurston, the children's nurse, who would finally retire, tearfully, in 1868, mollified by a pension of £150 and a furnished apartment in Cumberland Lodge. Princesses Helena and Louise appeared, both in pale grey, 'their poor plain faces . . . much the same colour as their gowns', and then a page announced that the Queen was ready to receive her. She found Her Majesty in her white widow's cap – like Sarah's own – and deep mourning. 'Her face is very peculiar,' Sarah told her daughter Caroline, 'so very fat – large cheeks and very small sharp chiselled features, quite unlike anybody else – but her complexion I thought unaltered, pink all over and not clear.'

Having kissed Sarah, the Queen sat and talked for over an hour, smiling once or twice but otherwise 'extremely grave'. The children were mentioned briefly – the Prince of Wales still disappointingly 'childish' and 'not like what his father was at his age' – but in the main 'she dwelt on the various *symptoms* (one may call them) of her grief – saying she still felt very ill (I believe this is quite a delusion poor thing) – knocked up by every day's toil . . . "I must work so hard all day long and no one to help or advise me – no one *above me*! People talk to me of time, time doing me good – how can it? Every moment a fresh wretchedness comes on – a fresh need of the support I used to find always ready and near . . . I am ashamed of myself – I do feel less happy than I ought when I see people happy – so odd and wrong! I *can't bear* to look at a man and his wife walking together".' After exchanging a few words with Augusta Bruce, Sarah trudged all the way round the castle walls in search of her carriage and just made her train home.

The Lyttelton connection to court was not quite at an end. Shortly after her visit to Windsor, Sarah received a letter – might her grand-daughter Lucy consider an appointment as a maid-of-honour? Sarah gave Lucy cautious encouragement: 'It is a peculiarity of court life that it does admit of real kindness, or the want of it . . . and to a thoughtful mind with a dash of poetry in it, such as yours dear child, I am sure it is an improving life, if taken rightly for a short time . . . the evenings though . . .' and she trailed off. She added that Lord Clarendon had told George Lyttelton that the Queen 'is very much better, though she does not admit it'. She certainly was *not* admitting it, insisting to Vicky, in the same month, that 'my constant, hard and unassisted work irritates, excites and exhausts my poor, shaken nerves – and it is only by great quiet and great sympathy that I can find repose and relief'.

Lucy, having taken up her appointment, felt initially forlorn at court. Household dinner (the Queen was still dining alone) was 'sepulchral' and there was little to enliven her days beyond a game of whist with elderly courtiers, or an expedition with Lady Ely to see the kennels and dairy at Windsor, or the still unfinished mausoleum at Frogmore. When she did eventually dine with the Queen, she found her 'talking and laughing cheerfully', though looking sad. The greatest jolt to the fervently High Church Lucy (more so than any of the Lytteltons – she had been greatly disgusted by Matthew Arnold's failure to kneel in church, for want of a hassock, when staying at Hagley) was the paucity of the Sunday observances. It was really most 'startling to one's feelings to go to a Sunday service in a chapel bonnetless, as the household have to here', not to mention 'no chanting' and 'inferior hymns'. But Lucy's time at court was brief. In less than a year she had become engaged to Lord Frederick Cavendish, second son of the Duke of Devonshire (in 1882 Lord Frederick was assassinated by Fenians in Phoenix Park, Dublin). The Queen, who had not had time to become attached to Lucy and who recognised that it was a great match for her, took this with fairly good grace: 'I must congratulate you but I must scold you a little too!'

Unsurprisingly, given that the Queen was unable to rejoice in the sight of a happy couple, the news that 'dear Augusta', so devoted and sympathetic, was to be married to Dr Arthur Stanley came as a severe blow. 'Dear Lady Augusta at 41, without a previous long attachment, has most unnecessarily decided to marry!! It has been my *greatest sorrow* and trial since my misfortune! I thought she would *never* leave *me!*' she wailed to Prince Leopold. The childlike, other-worldly Dr Stanley, author of a popular biography of Dr Arnold, his headmaster at Rugby, was Professor of Ecclesiastical History at Oxford, and soon to be Dean of Westminster. He had accompanied the Prince of Wales on a tour of the Holy Land in 1862, along with the Prince's governor, Augusta's brother General Robert Bruce, who had succumbed to fever during the trip and died soon after. The Queen thoroughly approved of Stanley, as a cleric and a Broad Churchman, finding him 'charming . . . the most unclerical and yet religious clergyman I ever talked to. Such a large tender refined mind.' As a husband was quite another matter.

Stanley and Augusta had originally met in Paris, in the rooms of Madame Mohl, long-forgotten but once a leading light of salon society, who had gathered together everyone from Chateaubriand to George Eliot. But their marriage was encouraged, indeed engineered – both parties being hesitant and shy – by Stanley's sister and by Augusta's sister-in-law Katherine Bruce (after Robert's death, Katherine had become an extra woman of the bedchamber, replacing Augusta when the latter went on leave). In the autumn of 1863, Katherine wrote to Miss Stanley that since rumours were rife amongst the household and she was being persecuted with questions, she thought Augusta and Stanley should be brought to the point and had decided to ask them to lunch – 'He wd call upon me and wd talk of his travels during the repast and I wd then slip out (whispering "On Stanley, on!") and they then really ought to arrange everything in five minutes.' Given the Queen's dislike of courting couples, she thought nothing should be said to her 'till the event is settled and the day named'. 'They suit each other perfectly, know each other thoroughly and being both of mature years, shd lose no more time,' concluded Katherine briskly. They were married in December.

Soon afterwards the Queen told Vicky that 'Dear Augusta (Stanley – I can't bear to call her so) spent some hours with us on Monday, quite herself and not at all like a married woman.' Having at first 'so wondered that Augusta should like to give up her independence' – an 'amusingly Royal idea', thought one of the Queen's ladies – she reluctantly reconciled herself to her loss. In fact she did not lose her entirely, since Augusta occasionally came to court as an extra woman of the bedchamber. Stanley, however, was henceforth demoted to the 'little Dean'. 'Augusta and the little Dean were here on Monday – looking as unsuited as possible. He runs after her like a little boy and looks at her whenever he speaks!!' wrote the Queen incredulously.

In June 1862, shortly after Mary Ponsonby had given birth to her first child, a daughter, named Alberta Victoria 'by the Queen's wish', Henry was told that his regiment was to be posted to Canada. The Ponsonbys set sail for Montreal in July, with Mary leaving her six-week-old baby in the care of her mother. They remained in Canada for just over a year, returning in September 1863 to be reunited with their daughter and to once again take up residence in the Cloisters at Windsor. For the next seven years Henry's time was divided between his duties as colonel with the Grenadier Guards and those as equerry (he had been promoted to full equerry). The latter duties were hardly arduous, amounting to little more than laying on horses and carriages, organising travel arrangements and providing companionship, over three months a year. Henry soon established himself as a popular and amusing member of the household, rather too much so in the view of the Queen, who, hearing roars of laughter emanating from the equerries' room, sent a note: 'it would be as well if Mr Ponsonby was cautioned not to be so funny'.

Laughter was certainly in short supply at court and melancholy hung heavy. The Queen, of course, remained in full mourning, as did the attending lady-in-waiting, though the maids-of-honour, as a concession to their youth, were permitted half-mourning colours after the requisite year of court mourning was over – grey, white and mauves (in 1897 an edict was issued, for no apparent reason, for 'deeper mourning', forbidding mauve 'in its fashionable pink tints' to the maids-of-honour). Not until 1865 did the band once again play after dinner. There were no balls, no entertaining of foreign Royalties – apart from close relations – and no theatre outings. Victoria did not wish to hold drawing rooms, or to drive about London and expose herself to crowds and noise and soupy yellow fogs. She certainly did not feel up to opening Parliament, or attending Privy Council meetings; for the latter a compromise was reached whereby she sat in an adjoining room, with the door ajar, relaying replies through a third party. She preferred to see as little as possible of her household and to dine with just her ladies. The 'path of duty', as Her Majesty saw it, led to retreat and withdrawal from public life, to private communion with grief.

By the late 1860s, the Queen was consenting to occasional public appearances, but only under duress, and only, so it seemed, when she needed money. In 1866 she agreed to open Parliament in order to obtain a dowry for Princess Helena, who was to marry Prince Christian of Schleswig-Holstein, and an annuity for Prince Alfred. It prompted, however, an anguished protest. Who, she wondered, could possibly want 'to witness the spectacle of a poor, broken-hearted widow, nervous and shrinking, dragged in deep mourning, alone in State as a Show, where she used to be supported by her husband'?

This reluctance to perform public duties led to clashes with Charles Grey, her private secretary. Unofficial private secretaries had existed since the reign of George III, but until 1861 Victoria had managed perfectly well without: initially she had had Baroness Lehzen and Lord Melbourne, and then there had been Albert, assisted by *his* secretaries, Anson, Phipps and, finally, Grey. Only after Albert's death did the full extent of the Queen's reliance on him become apparent and the need for a private secretary became pressing. When Charles Phipps died in 1866, the household underwent a reshuffle, with Colonel Thomas Biddulph, hitherto master of the household, replacing Phipps as keeper of the privy purse, Major John Cowell (formerly governor to Princes Alfred and Leopold) stepping into Biddulph's shoes and Charles Grey becoming Her Majesty's first official private secretary, with an understanding that Henry Ponsonby would take over on Grey's retirement. It was decided that the private secretary and the keeper of the privy purse would work in tandem, with the former concentrating on public and political matters, the latter on private and financial.

While Grey had greatly admired Albert, he found serving Victoria a frustrating and dispiriting business. The workload was great, the rewards were small and the battles to persuade Her Majesty to appear in public constant. He took a hard line: 'All she says of "the weight of work", "weakened health", shattered nerves etc. – has simply no effect whatever on me. Neither health nor strength are wanting, were inclination what it should be.' The 'Royal Malingerer', who on her part found Grey increasingly irritable and 'impatient of any difference of opinion', proved stubbornly resistant.

Grey also felt that he did not enjoy the Queen's confidence and that she excluded him from her dealings with William Gladstone, who became prime minister in 1868 (all complaints that would be echoed by Henry Ponsonby). He badly wished to retire, but was persuaded, for the Queen's sake, to carry on. In 1869, he wrote gloomily to his wife, of whom he saw all too little, 'if confidence is withheld it takes from one even the feeling of being useful which alone reconciles me to going on with my slavery . . . I have promised you to endure this wretched life as long as I can, for your sake. Thank God I have kept clear of all the miseries of the Palace. I know, for Lady Ely told me so, that the quarrels in certain quarters are of daily occurrence.'

A good many of the palace 'quarrels' were occasioned by John Brown, the Queen's Highland servant, whom, like most of the household, Grey loathed. Brown, the second of nine sons, had started out as one of the Prince Consort's gillies at Balmoral in 1851, before being swiftly promoted to the Queen's 'special servant', with pony-leading duties. He was tall, powerfully built, firm-jawed and blue-eyed. His 'strong arm' made the Queen feel safe; his devotion made her feel loved. Used as she was to her household tiptoeing nervously around her, Brown's brusque manners, his disregard for etiquette, his fearlessness, combined, as she knew, with absolute loyalty, acted as a bracing tonic.

In the dark years after the Prince Consort's death, Brown emerged as one of the very few who could lift Victoria's spirits. Noting this, Dr Jenner and Charles Phipps had him brought down to Osborne for the winter of 1864. A year later he became 'The Queen's Highland

Servant', with indoor as well as outdoor duties, his own cottage at Balmoral and a salary, paid from the privy purse, of £120 (by 1872 this had risen to £400, equal to that of a page of the backstairs, who personally waited on Her Majesty). The Queen found him entirely satisfactory: he came to her room every day after breakfast and luncheon for 'orders – and everything is always right'. 'I only wish higher people had his sense and discretion,' she added meaningfully. But Brown was no ordinary servant, possessing as he did 'feelings and qualities which the highest Prince might be proud of – viz: unflinching straightforwardness and honesty; great moral courage; unselfishness and rare discretion and devotion. This quite independently of his excellence as a good, handy, thoughtful servant.'

The Queen's satisfaction was not shared – indeed, was much resented – by her household and children, who were not only denied the kind of access and confidence accorded to her Highland servant, but were subjected to Brown's high-handedness and disdain. When Lady Churchill asked for a special steamer to bring her to Osborne, the answer came back from Brown, 'certainly not . . . it was one of Lady Churchill's dodges'. Lady Churchill came on the public boat. At Balmoral, Brown controlled the shooting and made sure that he, not the Princes or royal guests, had the best of it. He would barge into rooms unannounced, barking peremptory orders. He was quite frequently drunk. He argued regularly with Herr Sahl, Dr Robertson (the factor at Balmoral) and the Duke of Edinburgh (Prince Alfred).

Only through Brown could the equerries communicate with the Queen, and their needs took second place to his. When he complained to the Queen that he was overworked, she wrote to Lady Biddulph (presumably chary of appealing directly to the Colonel, who particularly disliked Brown), 'my poor Brown . . . it wd be a great relief if the Equerries cd receive a hint not to be *constantly* sending for him *at all hours* for trifling messages; he is often *so tired* from being so constantly on his legs that he goes to bed with swollen feet and can't sleep from fatigue'. When he objected to the royal smokers keeping him up, Lord Charles Fitzroy, an equerry, received a note: 'Lord Charles would perhaps simply mention to Prince Christian *without* giving it as a *direct* order that the Queen felt it necessary for the sake of the *servants* . . . that the smoking room should be closed . . . by 12 o'clock, not later!'

Inevitably such partiality bred gossip. The sculptor Edgar Boehm (known to Brown as 'Mr Bum'), a wiry, dashingly rumpled Hungarian, who was kept more or less permanently on the royal payroll with commissions for busts and statues of family, dogs and servants (in 1882 he became the Queen's sculptor in ordinary), claimed that whilst working on a bust of Brown 'it was the talk of all the household that he was "the Queen's stallion".' Rumours spread beyond the palace, encouraged, it was said, by Landseer, whose portrait of the Queen at Osborne, sitting on a pony held by Brown, caused a great deal of sniggering when it was shown at the Royal Academy in 1867: the Queen and Brown were lovers; they'd married; they'd had a child together. A pamphlet circulated titled 'Mrs John Brown'. *Punch* published a spoof of the Court Circular: 'Mr John Brown walked on the Slopes. He subsequently partook of haggis. In the evening Mr John Brown was pleased to listen to a bag-pipe.'

Henry Ponsonby dismissed the marriage rumours. The 'child of nature', as he liked to call Brown, was 'certainly a favourite', but he was 'only a servant and nothing more'. What had begun as a joke had been 'perverted into a libel'. And indeed even a rudimentary acquaintance with the Queen's character makes any relationship beyond a romantic friendship – though many found even that bewildering and unseemly enough – highly improbable. Apart from the fact that she deeply disapproved of widows remarrying, she was too guileless for sexual intrigue. It was precisely because of the essential innocence of her relations with Brown that she could send him artlessly effusive lace-edged greetings cards inscribed, 'To my best friend J.B. From his best friend VRi.'

'When one's beloved husband is gone and one's children married one feels that a friend, near your own age, who can devote him or herself entirely to you is the one thing you do require to help you on – and to sympathise entirely with you.' So wrote the widowed Queen. Friendship was hard to come by – the Queen did not make friends amongst her household – but in Brown she found someone approaching the devoted 'friend' she longed for, someone 'whose whole object I am'. 'I am alas not old,' she told Vicky, a year after the Prince's death, 'and my feelings are strong and warm; my love is ardent.' If Victoria found Brown attractive, as she most probably did, since she was both susceptible to a handsome face and passionate by nature, then that just added a certain piquancy.

In Brown's wake, other Highlanders followed. Three of his brothers, Hugh, Donald and Archie, also entered royal service – Hugh became keeper of Her Majesty's kennels at Windsor, Donald keeper of the Queen's Lodge at Osborne and Archie valet to Prince Leopold. When Walter Stirling, Leopold's governor, complained about Archie, who, like all the Highlanders, was often drunk and allegedly abusive towards Leopold, he was promptly dismissed. Archie subsequently became a page of the royal presence.

The Highland servants, it seemed, were beyond criticism, possessing, the Queen felt, 'a higher sense of what is gentlemanlike than the most over polished and cringing Englishman' – on second thoughts, she amended 'man' to 'servant'. She found it immensely 'soothing and refreshing . . . to be able to talk freely with those below you and to find such open independence, such sense and such affection'. Blithely disregarding minor failings, such as the predilection for alcohol, she found much to admire amongst the 'lower classes' – straightforwardness, loyalty, honesty, good sense. The aristocracy, on the other hand, and particularly the Prince of Wales's raffish friends, were, in the main, a 'frivolous, pleasure-seeking, heartless, selfish and immoral' lot.

Mary Ponsonby was right in claiming that the Queen was on 'more natural terms' with her servants than her household. In many ways she felt more comfortable with Brown, or her wardrobe maids, than with her master of the household or her ladies – less constrained, less shy, more herself. 'Civility and consideration for the servants is another thing the Queen is *very* particular about,' she wrote. This was only true up to a point – the Queen was also 'very particular' about her servants' duties and the correct performance of those duties. Here both her love of regulation and her passion for minutiae came into play. So the duties of the wardrobe maids, many of which overlapped those of the dressers, were set out in minute, and sometimes mystifying, detail. The maids were to be 'fully acquainted with all the things in Her Majesty's sitting room . . . books, drawings, music etc.'; they were to notify the dressers when new stockings, shoes, boots or slippers were needed; they were never to go out without telling the dressers and they were expected to be 'neat and tidy but not smart in their dress', smartness amongst maids being deeply suspect.

There were instructions about when to enter the Queen's rooms with seltzer water, when to leave, when to 'rub the knees with the soap liniment', when to fetch a handkerchief, and in what order to hand the Queen items of clothing and jewels. In the mornings, having opened Her Majesty's bedroom shutters at 7.30, both maids were expected to be on hand in the Queen's dressing room, the 'one on duty' having arrived first to get the 'basons, sponges, tooth brushes and combs ready'. The 'on duty' maid was then to sit in the wardrobe (a work room rather than a clothes store, just off the Corridor at Windsor, near the Queen's sitting room) all day so as to be able to answer Her Majesty's bell; between three and four she could go to dinner, during which time the 'off duty' maid would take her place; she might go out for a walk on alternate days. Meanwhile the 'one off duty' was to clean and iron Her Majesty's dresses and do any mending.

When the Queen returned from riding or driving in the afternoon, her stockings had to be changed for silk ones and silk shoes. Then the dressing room had to be prepared for her pre-dinner toilette – the candles lit, the bath and washing things set out, the 'large basin' for the hands and face filled with water scented with elderflower, another with camomile tea for bathing the eyes, 'the little round sponge' sprinkled with eau de cologne, the bidet, slippers, chairs and tables correctly positioned, and the sitting room checked for any letters to be sent. The whole rigmarole was repeated before 'the undressing'. Last thing at night the doors to the Queen's rooms had to be locked. One maid always slept, on alternate nights, within call (and in later years the calls were frequent), on a sofa outside Her Majesty's bedroom, or, at Osborne, on a put-up bed in the wardrobe room, next door.

It was hardly surprising, given the long hours, the broken nights and their royal mistress's exacting nature, that the health of several dressers and wardrobe maids broke down. Frieda Arnold was suffering from poor health before she left the Queen's service in 1859; Jane Shackle, a wardrobe maid, had to retire owing to ill health; Selina Tuck and Lizzie Stewart, dressers in the 1880s and 90s, both succumbed to nervous breakdowns.

If Victoria was scarcely more concerned with her servants' conditions of service than those of her household – sodden drives in open carriages, rough crossings to Osborne, hours of standing, none gave a moment's pause – then she was solicitous of their *feelings*. Servants, as she wrote bossily to the Prince of Wales, 'ought to be comfortably lodged, but not luxuriously, but I think and so do *all* right minded *people* that the chief thing is treating them kindly . . . making them feel that *they belong* to the family and are *cared* for and *not* to treat them like other kinds of beings who have *no* feelings – and who may be abused and spoken to harshly and rudely'. Perceived rudeness to servants – of which some of her children stood guilty – brought immediate reprisals. Consideration for the feelings of the 'Personal Attendants' – Löhlein, John Brown (and later the Munshi) – was paramount, with the Queen quick to detect slights and fiercely protective of their rights. It was customary for visiting Royalties to leave a sum of money to be distributed between the servants. Leopold, King of the Belgians, left a stingy £100 after a visit to Windsor, while the King of Prussia left £500 in 1842, and Tsar Nicholas a lavish £1,000 in 1896 (the Queen had left the same sum after staying with Louis Philippe at the Chateau d'Eu). In the Prince Consort's lifetime, his German servants were excluded from such tips, which the Queen put down to 'ill will'. But now his servants had become hers. Moreover, since Löhlein and Brown worked 'far harder' than any of the other servants, it was 'not right that they should be treated differently . . . the money is *nothing* . . . but the *exclusion* is *felt*'.

She also became greatly exercised as to where her personal

attendants ate their meals, even the position they occupied at table. They were to be treated, she insisted, as upper servants, and as such should eat in the steward's room along with the clerk of the kitchen, the assistant clerks, the housekeeper, the Queen's dressers and maids, the gentlemen and yeomen of the wine cellar, the yeoman confectioner, the pastry cook, the first and second table deckers, the pages and the Queen's messengers. Futhermore, in 1868, her master of the household was told that 'the Queen wishes that *all new* Pages of the Backstairs . . . *should not sit above* her 2 *personal* and confidential servants Lohlein and Brown at meals, but either – in the first place, on the *opposite side* – or *below* them on the same side'. It was not right for new pages, 'who had only lately been footmen', to be placed above 'those *confidential* servants who are constantly in *personal* attendance on the sovereign and in far more *responsible* positions than any of the Pages'. Naturally such privileges were deeply resented by the other servants.

The servants' meals themselves were a cause of concern. The Queen worried that those consumed in the servants' hall were overly monotonous and meat-heavy, which was only confirmed by a list of weekly dinners, sent by Thomas Biddulph, with the optimistic claim that 'the food is plain but is varied almost as much as plain food can be'. Beef (roast or boiled) and mutton, accompanied by potatoes and vegetables, were served seven days a week, with plum pudding on Sundays. Quantities of meat were also consumed by the upper servants in the steward's room but here at least it was more imaginatively cooked – beef sirloin, haunch of venison, haricot of mutton, calf's head, veal cutlets, meat pies – and varied to include dishes such as soup, fish and suet puddings. The Queen suggested adding soup to the servants' hall dinners, but in the end it was decided it would be easier to provide puddings three times a week.

As Lytton Strachey wrote, a large part of the Queen's charm resided in her 'absorbing passion for the comfortable commonplaces, the small crises, the recurrent sentimentalities of domestic life'. Just as she had shown a genuine interest in the health of Charlotte Canning's father, or the heights of Sarah Lyttelton's grandchildren, so she entered into the lives (and deaths) of her servants with enthusiasm, filling her journal with their names and histories, most of which were excised by Princess Beatrice after her mother's death. Through the 1860s, when she claimed to be crushed beneath the weight of work and duty, somehow there was always opportunity to fire off notes and memos to her master of the household on the hiring of a new linen room woman, or a confectioner (good confectioners were hard to come by – John Cowell had heard of a promising candidate from Gunters), or the pension due to a retiring housemaid, or the proposed dismissal of a man who waited in the steward's room and had been caught stealing (the Queen felt that given his age and length of service, some provision should be made). If she had bestowed at least some of the time and energy that she expended on her servants' welfare on her public duties, her private secretary's job, for one, would have been made a great deal easier.

CHAPTER 15

Henry Ponsonby: Private Secretary

Whether due to the Brown effect or simply the passage of time, by the late 1860s the worst of the Queen's grief had passed. In 1867 she admitted to Lady Waterpark, who had written to her on 10 February, her wedding anniversary: 'the violent grief is past – I almost grieve for that, for there is a sweetness even in that'. The 'constant blank and the constant cloud' were always present, and she mourned the 'total saltlessness' of her life, but she no longer wished for death. Lord Clarendon, visiting Osborne two years later, took a robust view, declaring that 'Eliza is roaring well and can do everything she likes and nothing she doesn't.'

She could even indulge in a little merriment. In 1868, Henry Ponsonby, in attendance as equerry, accompanied the Queen on a trip to Switzerland. At dinner one evening, Dr Jenner (his pouchy face reminded Lucy Lyttelton of Voltaire, though the Queen, on first meeting, thought him not so 'frightful' as she'd been led to believe, despite his 'large, long teeth like poor Mr Combe') recounted an expedition that he and Miss Bauer (the princesses' German governess, and also no beauty – 'a dear, clever, sensible little person . . . extremely short', said Her Majesty) had made up the Rigi mountain. Henry asked him 'what the tourists thought of their relationship. He replied "Oh of course they thought she was Madame", which created some laughter. Then he added "The guide was very decided and made us give up the horse we rode up and come down in a chair". "What?" I asked. "Both in one chair?" Well, there is nothing odd in this – but everyone laughed. I turned to Mary Bids [Lady Biddulph]. She was purple. On the other side I tried to speak to Princess Louise. She was choking. I looked across to Jenner. He was convulsed. Of course this was too much. I gave way; and we all had a *fou rire* till the tears ran down my cheeks which set off the Queen. I never saw her laugh so much. She said afterwards it was my face. At last we got a pause when Jane [Lady Churchill] to set things straight again began with "Did you find it comfortable?" which started us off again.' Victoria was far too literal-minded to appreciate subtleties of humour, such as irony or self-mockery, but she had a sense of fun and was prone to uncontrollable fits of laughter.

The following year, Sarah Lyttelton, now eighty-one but still in fairly good health, visited the Queen and thought her in good spirits. She 'found H.M. very fat and rather red but by no means disagreeable to look at, and quite as charming as ever in manner and kindness. We had a long, long talk, not notable of course, but about everybody she could think of belonging to me . . . I asked her if it was true that a man had tumbled down before her at the levee? She said "Oh several have done it, but one man, the last time, fell full length and *rolled* away having seized and kept hold of *my* hand to pull himself up!" I said "did he drag Y.M. *along with him?*" "He did", she said, most positively, "but only for a little way", and she laughed immoderately.'

This was to be the last time the two would meet, and laugh together, for in 1870 Sarah died, at Hagley, with her children around her – George Lyttelton and Caroline each holding a hand, her son Billy, the vicar at Hagley, reading the prayers – exactly the kind of 'good death' she would have wished for. Afterwards Vicky wrote to Caroline of 'our dear kind Laddle', whom she remembered 'with affection and gratitude – recalling the days of my early childhood when she was so kind to me and I such a troublesome child'. A few months later, another figure from the Queen's youth also died: Baroness Lehzen, aged eighty-five. Lehzen had lived alone, in Germany, since 1842, keeping in touch with her old pupil by letter, once receiving a visit, and, when she became very infirm, the present of a 'wheeled chair'. 'I owed her much and she adored me! Even when she was quite wandering she spoke of me,' wrote the Queen complacently.

The old guard was vanishing fast. Not just Sarah Lyttelton and Baroness Lehzen, but, in the same year, Sir James Clark, who had stood with the Queen 'in those two chambers of death and woe in '61', and Charles Grey. Grey was only sixty-six and probably suffered a stroke, brought on by strain and overwork; Her Majesty, viewing the 'dear General's' body, reported him 'looking younger and so peaceful and like himself'. After Grey's death, Sir Thomas Biddulph, keeper of the privy purse, wrote to Henry Ponsonby to inform him that he was to be offered the private secretaryship.

Both court and Queen had grown steadily more Conservative over the last thirty years. With the death of Grey, and the departure of his sister, Lady Caroline Barrington, Henry was one of the very few Liberals amongst the household, and his appointment met with some opposition – the Prince of Wales warned that Henry's opinions were of the 'advanced Liberal kind'. The Queen, however, overruled such objections. Colonel Ponsonby represented a link to Albert and her former life; Baron Stockmar had thought highly of him; he came with warm recommendations from Dean Wellesley, Biddulph and Grey himself; unlike the rest of her household, he was well disposed towards John Brown; she knew him to be a 'very decided Liberal', but he never 'mixed in politics'; he was patient, fair, discreet and unflappable (all useful attributes in a private secretary). Henry was the man she wanted.

Henry rather took exception to cavils about his politics. As private secretary, he would have to liaise between Her Majesty and her ministers, and, he assured Biddulph, he would always be scrupulous in *not* allowing his own political views to compromise his dealings with those ministers: 'I will carefully attend to the Queen's wishes with respect to reading all the despatches in the boxes sent to me and will take care that when abstracts are required they should be made and sent to Her Majesty. I will keep a careful watch on public matters and with your assistance shall soon, I trust, learn what points the Queen's attention should be called to . . . I perfectly understand the value of discretion and though I am not aware that I have ever manifested any strong views on political matters, I will be careful not to express myself on these or kindred matters in such a manner as to lead others to consider me an extreme partizan.' Benjamin Disraeli, whose politics Henry did not share and whom he distrusted as an individual, considered himself 'the gainer' by Henry's 'Whiggishness as it makes him more scrupulously on his guard to be always absolutely fair and lucid'.

Like his wife Mary, Henry was born, in 1825, into the Whig aristocracy, and like most of the gentlemen in the royal household, his background was military. His father, Sir Frederick Ponsonby, a younger son of the Earl of Bessborough and a brother of Caroline Lamb, commanded the British garrison in Corfu, but a year after Henry's birth the family moved to Malta, where Sir Frederick had been made governor. When Henry was eleven, his father died suddenly, leaving his mother with six children and short of funds, though she managed, as the wife of a senior officer, to secure a grace-and-favour apartment at Hampton Court.

It was always understood that Henry was destined for the army, and at fourteen he started at Sandhurst. In 1844, the Duke of Wellington, under whom his father had fought at Waterloo (and nearly died from a pike thrust through his chest), offered him a commission in the Grenadier Guards, and two years later, when he was twenty-one, his uncle, Lord Bessborough, the new lord lieutenant of Ireland, invited him to join his staff as an aide-de-camp. After serving successive lord lieutenants during the worst years of the Irish famine, he became equerry to the Prince Consort in 1857. The loss of his father at an early age fostered a sense of responsibility; a military training established habits of duty and service.

At six foot two inches, Henry was unusually tall and slightly stooped; judging from photographs, he carried himself with a certain debonair detachment. His clothes – frock coat and elastic-sided boots – were habitually shabby and his expression was mild and slightly quizzical. A. C. Benson, who as an Eton master came to know the Ponsonbys well, considered Henry 'the most perfectly and beautifully courteous man' he'd ever known. While Mary, as maid-of-honour, struggled to subjugate self, Henry had no such battles; his lack of ego lent itself easily to a life of service. Irony and modesty were his keynotes. A story told by his son Fritz gives something of his flavour: 'The Duke of York [the Queen's grandson] told me that when his brother the

Duke of Clarence died, the Queen asked him to change his name to Albert. He consulted my father Henry Ponsonby, who replied that he would gladly lay down his life for the Queen, but if she asked him to call himself Thomas he would certainly refuse.'

As private secretary Henry was now earning £1,500 a year, paid from the privy purse, and was in constant attendance on the Queen, whether at Windsor, Balmoral or Osborne, apart from six weeks' leave. At Windsor he had an office on the ground floor of the Augusta Tower, on the south side of the castle, close to the offices of Thomas Biddulph and Herr Sahl. He also had a new home. He and Mary and their five children left the Cloisters, in the lower ward of Windsor Castle, and moved into the Norman Tower, in the upper ward, from where they looked out towards Eton Chapel and in towards the quadrangle, housing the Queen's private apartments and the state rooms.

Finding herself at the very heart of the Windsor establishment was hardly something Mary can have welcomed, but at least in the Norman Tower, partly straddling a gateway, with its jumble of staircases and oddly shaped rooms, she had a romantic and unconventional home that delighted her. She especially relished the discovery of some fourteenth-century graffiti beneath the plaster of two rooms above the gateway, former prisons, which became her sitting rooms. Facilities for her 'occupations' were set up all over the house – an easel in her bedroom window, a painting table in the sitting room, a table for silver repoussé work in a corner. She set about making a garden on the slopes beneath, and in the dry moat around the Round Tower, and put up a shed, as a workroom, with her blowtorch, lathe and chisels. But her hopes of knocking a door through from the Norman Tower into the adjacent royal library, where the Queen rarely ventured, were dashed; permission was refused.

In later years Mary would become subject to royal suspicion – was her radicalism unduly influencing her husband? And Her Majesty did not always find her perfectly accommodating. When she wished Henry to change his holiday, Mary failed to fall into line: 'intimations were given to her that she was expected to express regret for her behaviour, which as she had nothing to regret, she declined to do'. This resulted in a severing of the lines of communication, until 'the Queen at last said with admirable humour that it was no use punishing MP when she did not seem to even know that she was being punished'. But in the main, the Queen and Mary continued to regard each other with mutual respect and affection, and Mary became adept at circumnavigating the constraints of palace life without forfeiting Her Majesty's good opinion. On occasion, she stepped in to act as lady-in-waiting to a visiting princess.

The late 1860s had seen Mary less committed to her spiritual life, but still maintaining an emotional life outside of her marriage. In 1867, after her mother's death, Agnes Courtenay came to live with her uncle, the Rev. Charles Courtenay (the Queen's chaplain, the same who had married Charlotte Canning's cousin Car Cocks). On Good Friday 1868, in her diary, Mary reviewed the past year thus: 'the gradual weakening of religious habits and ties . . . My friendship with Agnes Courtenay is a new phase in my life. Since my disappointment about Lily, I have always shrunk from fresh friends, but Agnes came here last year and in her grief for her mother and desire for help and sympathy day by day and hour by hour became very dear. I feel I might be of use to her, for with her gifts of deep feeling, strong imagination, quick intellect and enthusiasm she is impulsive . . . the danger will be of allowing ourselves to be too much engrossed, of giving an exaggerated and morbid turn to a love which may prove the blessing of our lives.'

A year later, things had indeed taken a 'morbid turn'. Agnes was engaged, and Mary was forced to recognise that she had allowed her feelings for her to assume an importance and intensity that only became apparent when she faced losing her to a husband. 'The first disillusionment with her was that as we became better known to each other so it seemed that sympathy upon the highest subjects, intellectual or religious, seemed to diminish and a more *personal* feeling to take its place. That was held fast through all, steadily and deeply, yet I felt as was natural that an impulsive eager wilful nature like hers must possess some one for good and all if she was to be happy . . . it cost me much pain to think these pleasant hours devoted to each other must cease – I did wish that someone would come and not until he did come could I have realised how very much *too much* engrossed with her I have been. I won't dwell upon it – she is happy, they are both together and I begin again.' To the twenty-first-century reader, this sounds like the language of romantic love. Perhaps it was. But we should be wary of over-interpretation: highly wrought, emotionally charged language between women friends, a form of release as much as a measure of feeling, was not so uncommon in the nineteenth century. Mary's relationship with Agnes had followed a similar trajectory to that with Lily: religious and intellectual sympathy giving way to 'more personal feeling'. The latter probably encompassed an element of sexual attraction of which Mary may have been unaware, and certainly would not have admitted to.

Though Mary continued to form close female friendships, and herself became the object of the *engougements* of others, Agnes was be the last of her own serious crushes. In 1871, she wrote to Henry: 'I get no talk of any sort. Do you think we shall get into a fatuous state of thinking nobody else's conversation suits us but each other's?' There were certainly points of difference – Henry could not share his wife's intellectual or spiritual interests – but there was much to unite them: a love of conversation (and argument); their children; an acceptance of the obligations and duties of service; humour. Mary's intensity complemented Henry's studied levity; her tendency to introspection and self-analysis balanced his pragmatism. If Henry was the adorer, Mary was happy to be adored.

'Both Sir Thomas and Col. Ponsonby should *keep watch* on what goes on in and out of Parliament and draw the Queen's attention to *any* questions which affect the prerogative, or the Army, Navy – or in short anything, so that should the Queen *not* have been informed or asked, she can ask for explanation or remonstrate. *This* is of the *utmost* importance for the Queen has not the *time* to watch everything and is sadly overworked and is so often unwell now as to require much help.' So read a memo written by the Queen in April 1870, shortly after Henry's appointment. Overwork, poor health, shattered nerves: a refrain that the household had come to know all too well. In fact the Queen's health was generally good, and her workload, thanks to the assistance of such as Henry and Biddulph, light.

If the Queen expected her private secretary to be her eyes, ears and shield, not so much a conduit between herself and her ministers as a buffer, this was never more so than when it came to her dealings with her prime minister, William Gladstone. Sovereign and prime minister had been circling each other warily ever since Gladstone had taken office in 1868, when Gerald Wellesley, Dean of Windsor, and a friend of Gladstone's from Eton, had offered some wise advice: 'Everything depends upon your manner of approaching the Queen . . . You cannot show too much regard, gentleness, I might say even tenderness towards Her. Where you differ it might be best not at first to try and reason her over to your side but to pass the matter lightly over with an expression of respectful regret . . . Put off, till she has become accustomed to you, all discussions which are not absolutely necessary for the day.' Unfortunately this was advice Gladstone was congenitally incapable of taking. Lightness of touch was not part of his make-up; dictation his modus operandi. And there was nothing the Queen liked less than being dictated to. 'Arrogant, tyrannical and obstinate . . . a very dangerous and unsatisfactory Premier', so she judged Gladstone. The fact that he was a 'fanatic in religion', with extreme High Church views bordering on the 'ritualistic and sacerdotal' (John Brown told Henry that he considered Gladstone a 'Roman'), was just another mark against him.

Henry, however, greatly liked and admired Gladstone, both politically and personally. How, he marvelled, did he find time, aside from government business and speechifying and letter-writing and tree-felling and Hawarden, to write poetry, in *Italian*? He was aware, though, that many women besides the Queen, including Mary, found him impossibly preachy. Even Henry admitted that 'he always addresses one as a sort of chairman'. Restraining the Sovereign's antipathy towards her prime minister, without becoming caught between 'two iron-clads colliding', became one of the least enviable of Henry's tasks.

His job was made all the more difficult by the Queen's seclusion. In 1870, she once again declined to open Parliament, declaring it 'a very unwholesome year'. By now her subjects were growing restive and the press hostile. All respect and honour had been shown to the Prince Consort's memory, but after nine years, was it not time for the Queen to do her duty by her people? It seemed not. To expect her to make public appearances was to show inhuman cruelty. Up to five months a year at Balmoral was essential for her health. And she was scarcely more visible to her household than to her subjects. Attended by a fluttering phalanx of ladies, she might not emerge from her rooms – other than to venture out for an afternoon drive – for days on end. Henry hoped for a daily audience, but was frequently reduced to communicating through a lady-in-waiting, a governess, or Brown. Lady Ely in particular was a favoured 'messenger', delivering her communications from the Queen in a 'mysterious whispering', usually quite incomprehensible to Henry.

Yet for all her invisibility, the Queen retained an uncanny ability to monitor and regulate the activities of her household. Royal orders were often issued in a quite arbitrary fashion, a small jerk of the reins: at Osborne, one baking July, the edict came that all windows were to be kept shut, an instruction Henry ignored, unlike one equerry, whom he found 'stifled and loyal' in the equerries' room. Transgressions were noted, and retribution, in the form of 'stingers' or 'stinkers', was swift. So at Osborne, Henry received a 'blowing up' for being out at the same time as his assistant: 'The Queen *must* ask that both Sir Henry and Major Edwards shd *not* be out on Sunday morning or any other *at the same time*. Not 5 minutes after the service in the Chapel was over she sent to say she wished to see Sir Henry in a quarter of an hour but was told he was gone to church. She then sent for Major Edwards and was then told he was out too. This is extremely inconvenient . . .'

'Blowings up' were invariably delivered via letter or a third party. For alongside, and sometimes conflicting with, the Queen's compulsion to control the lives of those around her came an entrenched distaste for confrontation – a letter was preferred to an interview, and when a reprimand was deemed necessary, Her Majesty preferred to pass the buck. On noticing an overly made-up lady-in-waiting, she had announced, 'Dear General Grey will tell her.' 'Dear General Grey will do nothing of the kind,' murmured Grey, on receiving Her Majesty's message. When it came to the Queen's ears that Lord Dunmore, a lord-in-waiting, had apparently complained to the lord steward that the Queen's dinner had been served cold, Horatia Stopford, a maid-of-honour since 1857, was sent to deliver a sharp rap on the knuckles. '*Interference* of *that kind*', relayed Horatia, was something Her Majesty 'would never tolerate in *anyone*'. Lord Dunmore, clearly flustered, denied everything: 'I hope the Queen does not think it was *me* for I never *should think* of doing anything *so impertinent*, also I never *thought* of Her Majesty's dinner being cold, such a thing never *entered my head* even, and if it had done so I certainly never should have taken it upon myself to complain, to anyone much less the Lord Steward.' Then, said Horatia, it '*must* have been someone else as undoubtedly a complaint was made and the Queen was extremely displeased'. Henry came to dread delivering some unpleasant 'hint' to one of the Queen's children, or another member of the household.

Officially, Henry's province was public and political affairs, but thanks to his reputation as a good listener, as well as for fairness and good sense, he frequently found himself embroiled in domestic matters. He could just as easily be employed in the dismissal of a drunken piper at Balmoral, as the wording of a letter to the prime minister, and household or family disputes were frequently laid at his door. Thus Henry was called in when an equerry, Sir Charles Fitzroy, accused Dr Marshall, resident medical attendant, of dining with the household: doctors, apart from the physician-in-ordinary, were expected to eat in their rooms. The Queen said that he hadn't done so. Fitzroy insisted, rightly, that he had, several times. Three messages came via Lady Ely, reiterating that he hadn't. Fitzroy took offence, appealed to his brother, the Duke of Grafton, and wrote to Lady Ely listing the dates on which Marshall had dined. The Queen wrote demanding to know who was responsible for inviting him. Henry, brought in as intermediary, merely succeeded in offending Fitzroy further. The row rumbled on for six months, ending with Henry's memo – 'Row concluded. Biddulph advised me to shake hands. I did so. May 1873. Ended.'

Henry – like Mary – tended to scorn fawning courtiers, such as Jane Ely or Charles Phipps, who appeared enthralled by the spell of royalty. And Henry had admired his predecessor Charles Grey for his forthrightness – 'he always boldly wrote what he thought and tho' it irritated her it sunk in and did good'. According to Mary's friend Ethel Smyth, the Queen once asked Mary to 'tell Sir Henry kindly' (she didn't like to tell him herself, she said, for fear of hurting his feelings) that when she made a remark he really must not say 'that is absurd'. Yet Henry came in for criticism for failing to stand up to the Queen, who once complained herself: 'he has no backbone . . . He has no courage but agrees with me, and then is talked over by others and agrees with them. He agrees with everybody.' In fact he shied away from direct opposition not from lack of backbone but from a conviction that such opposition was futile.

While engaged in the service of the Queen, it was crucial to understand, in the words of Henry's son Arthur, that she 'did not belong to any conceivable category of monarchs or women'. It was something Henry never lost sight of. While acknowledging her 'fundamentally sound judgement' and good sense, he understood the importance of working with and around, rather than against, her complex and contradictory character. As he explained: 'People constantly say "why don't you advise the Queen" – one can do so once, but she takes care you shan't press unwelcome advice upon her by preserving strict silence on the subject.' Realising she did not respond well to unwelcome advice, let alone direct contradiction, Henry preferred more circuitous methods, to proceed 'gingerly', as he put it; he learned how to direct with an unseen hand and thus showed himself the consummate royal servant.

Adopting a kind of autosuggestion, he would draft a letter for the Queen stating her own views with his own lightly crossed out. Or he would plant the seed of an idea and simply leave it to bear fruit. In 1873, for an expedition from Balmoral to Loch Maree, the Queen proposed taking just one housemaid. The servants protested and asked

Henry to intervene. He sent a note: 'Of course quite right that only one housemaid should go for the smaller work. I would send to hire a girl from the Hotel. Stray girls were not always very honest. So I hoped the Queen would not leave things about to tempt her. I got an answer that another housemaid should go from here.' In June 1880, he described to Mary how the Queen had asked him who could represent her at the funeral of the Empress of Russia: 'I said the Duke of Edinburgh. The Queen said "No, of course he couldn't". I said "Of course he couldn't". But as I did not know why, I got back to him in the course of the conversation and said it was a pity he couldn't. So she telegraphed him if he could and he said he would.'

In widowhood, routine, to which the Queen had always been partial, became a source of reassurance and comfort, and by 1870 her annual migrations were set in stone. She spent Christmas and the first two months of the year at Osborne, before returning to Windsor, now regarded as a dreary 'prison', forever associated with Albert's death, for the spring, with perhaps a brief Continental holiday. May saw a visit to Balmoral, then back to Windsor for a few weeks, and Osborne again in July. In August she decamped to Balmoral for a long sojourn, through till November, with the last few weeks of the year, up until Christmas, at Windsor. Only with the greatest reluctance did she spend a night in Buckingham Palace, such was her distaste for the crowds and noise of London. And where the Queen went, her private secretary followed. The autumn of 1870 saw Henry's first long incarceration at Balmoral.

CHAPTER 16

Balmorality

The Queen arrived at Balmoral in mid-August. For Henry Ponsonby this meant that, apart from a couple of weeks' leave, he would not see Mary or the children until November. At Osborne he had the use of Osborne Cottage – actually a substantial, rambling house – which meant he could at least bring his family with him, but at Balmoral this was impossible. Hopes that Mary might stay nearby, in the manse at Abergeldie, the Prince of Wales's Scottish home, were dashed; the Queen wanted Henry close at hand, not spending time with his wife.

Transporting Her Majesty, her family, household and servants the 600 miles from London to Scotland was no easy matter, though at least by 1870 it was possible to make the journey by train, travelling overnight to Perth and then on to Ballater, arriving at around three in the afternoon. The London and North Western Company provided a royal saloon for the Queen (the sleeping saloon was shared with Princess Beatrice, with the dressers and personal attendants next door), further saloons for the royal family and the gentlemen and ladies of the suite, three first-class carriages for the servants, two carriage trucks, two brake vans and a special engine decorated with the royal insignia. In hot weather, when the train became stifling, a large cooling footbath of ice sat in the Queen's saloon. The journey was accompanied by some serious eating – a 'sumptuous breakfast' (trout, salmon, scones, strawberries and peaches) at the Station Hotel in Perth on the outward journey and a six-course dinner (soup, turbot in lobster sauce, fried smelts, foie gras, mutton cutlets, roast beef and turkey, pheasants, Sefton pudding, Madeira jelly and apple compote) on the return, not to mention a 'hearty tea' at Aberdeen. As back-up, hampers were supplied by the royal kitchens crammed with cold meat, stuffed rolls, grouse, cakes, biscuits, tea, cream, claret, champagne, sherry and seltzer water.

The new Balmoral, completed in 1855, was a turreted castle of white granite, a hybrid of Scottish baronial and German schloss. It had been designed by the architect William Smith, but Albert's hand was everywhere. In the farm. In the lending library, established 'with the view of encouraging Reading and for the social and moral improvement of the People of the District' (the library books – Walter Scott, *Robinson Crusoe*, Livingstone's travels and Washington Irvine being particularly popular – were kept in the servants' hall; single men could borrow one volume at a time, families two, and books could be kept for four weeks). In the busy, highly coloured interiors of the castle – carpets and upholstery a sea of tartan, maple and birch joinery and furniture, a mass of hunting trophies and

Balmoral Castle, photographed by Roger Fenton in 1856

'loads of curiously devised and tasteful, as well as elaborately executed articles', like the candelabra of stag horn, gilt and cairn-gorms designed by Albert, all amounting, as even the loyal Augusta Stanley had acknowledged, to 'a certain want of harmony of the whole'. Lord Rosebery thought the drawing room at Osborne the ugliest room in the world until he saw that at Balmoral. In Victoria's eyes, though, it was perfection.

And perfection it would remain. On the Queen's insistence, not a picture hung, or a mounted stag's head, shot by the Prince's hand was to be moved an inch (and there were certainly no new pictures; royal patronage of the arts died with Albert). A few changes *were* permitted. In 1866, as a concession to Princess Helena's husband, Prince Christian of Schleswig-Holstein, a dedicated smoker, a smoking room was added, reached by crossing the kitchen courtyard. And two years later the Queen ordered the construction of a new retreat, the Glassalt Shiel. As she explained to Dr Robertson, the factor at Balmoral, she felt 'the great want of some *little* spot to go to *occasionally* for a night or 2, to have 2 or 3 days of *quiet* and seclusion to *rest* from the never ceasing interruptions and work which she has to endure every day of her sad and desolate life'. The Glassalt stood at the other end of Loch Muich from Allt-na-Guibhsaich, which, as the scene of so many happy stays with Albert, now held too many memories. The Queen would disappear there for days on end, with the minimum of attendants (one of her ladies, perhaps a princess, John Brown, a few servants), rendering herself quite unreachable and invariably returning in high spirits.

She had proclaimed her adoration for all things Scottish with the publication of *Leaves from the Journal of Our Life in the Highlands* in 1868, an artlessly banal record of damp picnics, faithful Highlanders and visits to elderly crofters. To her immense satisfaction, it proved a great success ('rather amusing the literary line the Queen has taken since her book was published', said Mary Ponsonby), selling 100,000 copies in three months. It was however deplored by the royal children and the household, past and present. Augusta Stanley thought it disarming: the 'faithful record of the luncheons show . . . that the text has not been tampered with', but she could not but fear derision from 'the more educated classes', when it came to the footnotes detailing the histories of footmen. It might, she felt, do 'great harm to our dear One'. Sarah Lyttelton, having been sent an inscribed copy by the Queen, couldn't understand how it could have been published – 'it should have been printed for herself and the children and nobody else'.

The Queen's enthusiasm for Balmoral was not shared by her household or visiting ministers (there was always a minister in attendance), who, safely out of earshot, complained bitterly about the cheerlessness, the discomfort and the paucity of amusements. Winter or summer, the castle was invariably horribly cold. A heating system, and occasional, grudgingly allowed fires, made little differ-ence; Henry Ponsonby, playing billiards, found the cushion of the billiard table quite frozen. While the Queen positively thrived on cold – it made her feel 'brisk' – her household and guests did not; Lord Salisbury, as prime minister in the 1890s, had his secretary write to insist that his room be kept at a minimum of 60 degrees, as 'a cold room is really dangerous to him'. The new Balmoral, though larger than the old, remained cramped: ministers wrote their dispatches perched on the ends of their beds; the ladies dodged cues in the billiard room that doubled as their sitting room; four laundry maids shared a bed. Henry thought that any house he'd ever known seemed comfortable 'after the severe dreariness of our palatial rooms' at Balmoral, though Mary, on a rare visit, declared herself delighted with a 'capital solid bench' in her 'cosy' sitting room, ideal for carving.

One minister in attendance, William Harcourt (Mary Ponsonby's erstwhile suitor, now expanded to elephantine proportions and with a reputation as a foul-tempered bully to match), referred to his room as a 'hole'. Another, Henry Campbell-Bannerman, likened Balmoral to a convent: 'We meet at meals, breakfast 9.45, lunch 2, dinner 9, and when we have finished each is off to his cell.' In fact, life at Balmoral resem-bled nothing so much as a second-rate boarding school – indifferent food, nagging cold, unpopular compulsory activities, numerous petty rules and regulations – with the Queen its beady-eyed headmistress. Her household and children were subjected to orders as to when they were to arrive and leave, who was to dine, who might fish, or shoot, or ride and which ponies – themselves divided into five categories – were to be ridden. Even when the Queen left Balmoral, to go to the Glassalt, for instance, she exerted a kind of remote control – the household were not free to pass the time as they pleased, and any expeditions had to be made secretly. When the Duchess of Atholl settled down to do some sketching near the house of one of the Brown brothers and afterwards went in for some tea – imagining the Queen would approve, since she'd told the Duchess that she should pay more visits to the local people – she was informed 'that the household has no right to force themselves into people's houses and take possession of their rooms for tea'.

Due to lack of space, the Queen took a reduced household to Balmoral (no master of the household or lord-in-waiting). In the autumn of 1870, Henry found himself with Lady Ely, the Hon. Emily Cathcart and Lady Florence Seymour (the maids-of-honour), an equerry, Dr Jenner, who had become physician-in-ordinary on the death of Sir James Clark, Herr Sahl, the German secretary and librarian, Miss Bauer and Mlle Norèle, Princess Beatrice's German and French govern- esses, together with Princesses Louise and Beatrice. The maids-of- honour, 'Flo' and 'Catch', Henry thought plain and tedious; Lady Ely, in a permanent state of abject terror of the Queen, was so 'confidential' as to be virtually inaudible; the terminally gloomy and touchy Herr Sahl spent much of his time in his room nursing imagined slights.

With ladies' dinners most evenings, Henry, left with the men, amused himself by picking quarrels with Dr Jenner, an arch-Tory. Sometimes Dr Robertson came to dine, a welcome addition, since he was 'full of point and chaff' and, like Jenner, enjoyed a good-humoured argument. And it was a great boon when 'Bids' (Thomas Biddulph) arrived – owing to lack of space, the Biddulphs were billeted at Abergeldie – to 'enliven the dullness'. Bids, a keen-eyed, bewhiskered ex-soldier, was a firm ally and friend of Henry's, despite their political differences. Henry suspected that the more reactionary members of the Queen's family saw the Tory Bids 'as a bulwark against the radicalism I might instil into the Queen's mind'. At Windsor the Biddulphs lived in the Henry III Tower, as neighbours of the Ponsonbys.

On the occasions when Henry was invited to dine with the Queen, lively debate was out of the question, since controversial topics, like politics, were strictly off limits. If the Queen detected signs of controversy, she headed them off by calling out the name of one of the many dogs under the table. Dogs were a topic guaranteed to excite interest, though not one without its own hazards. Biddulph found himself put on the spot when the Queen drew his attention to a new dog: 'Oh Ma'am, I thought that was the old dog.' 'Which old dog Sir Thomas?' enquired Her Majesty, a question that 'stumped up Bids', who, like Henry, could 'never remember the names of the dogs'.

At one royal dinner, with Lady Ely, Prince Leopold and Harriet Phipps (a maid-of-honour) 'we tried one or two subjects which were either too political or too immoral and after long pauses we always got back to the dullest platitudes'. However, Leopold, who alone amongst the Queen's children was prepared to defy her and, in protest at having his every movement regulated (his haemophilia made his mother more than usually anxious), sometimes flatly refused to come to Balmoral, held his own. The Queen: 'I heard your music box playing most clearly this afternoon even as far off as your room.' 'Impossible for my musical box never plays.' 'But I know it was your musical box – there was that drum in it I recognised.' 'That shows it wasn't my musical box, as there is no drum in it.' Occasionally, when she was in good spirits, all kinds of generally 'forbidden' topics could be 'plunged into', but far more often dinners were silent, gloomy affairs. At least, since the Queen ate at speed and liked dinner to last no more than half an hour, they were mercifully short.

But the greatest deprivation Henry suffered at Balmoral was separation from Mary. As a poor substitute for talking to her, he wrote daily and longed for the sight (infrequent enough) of the brown envelopes bringing a letter from her. Mary suffered rather less. She had distractions aplenty: the children, dinners at the Deanery, her 'occupations', concerts, balls, the races, visits to her new acquaintance George Eliot to discuss French plays, Girton committee meetings. In some respects Henry's absences suited her, allowing her the independence and freedom to pursue those interests and friendships that she couldn't share with him. While she was off gallivanting or entertaining her highbrow friends for dinner, Henry had to contend with the low spirits and dullness, 'pounds of it', that came with Balmoral. When, in 1874, the Greville memoirs were published (devoured by the household, dismissed as 'disgraceful' and 'lying' by the Queen), Henry was much struck by the parallels between then and now – the fondness of Victoria's Hanoverian prede-cessors for their servants and their suspicion of intellectualism, George IV's ingenuity at 'turning conversation' from subjects he didn't like and the dreadful boredom of court. 'What would he have thought of our life here?' he wondered.

'There seems a curious charm to our beloved Sovereign in doing the same thing on the same day year after year,' commented one of her ladies. In Scotland, routine lay heavily, and by October Henry had endured a number of Balmoral milestones: a gillies' ball, with the usual chaotic scenes of inebriated Highlanders stumbling and tripping up Royalties; the Highland Games at Braemar; the 'melancholy anni-versary' of the Prince's birthday, when, in drenching rain, the house-hold gathered around a commemorative statue, on the road to Crathie, to drink to his memory (whisky, and on the part of the gillies, a great deal of it). There had too been one of the frequent rows. This time Dr Robertson, offended by some insulting behaviour of John Brown's, had written to the Queen offering his resignation. The Queen had persuaded Brown to apologise, whereupon, reported Henry, 'all is love'.

Rows blew up and through Balmoral like squalls at sea. A small number of people in a confined space, not necessarily sympathetic to each other, with little in the way of occupation or amusement, meant, as Henry put it, that 'the veriest trifles become important and rows are almost watched for'. It was all too easy to lose a sense of propor-tion. Even Dr Jenner admitted that it was 'bad mentally and physically' to spend too long at Balmoral, that 'he found himself excited about small things which when he got away he didn't care a damn for'. The Queen quarrelled with her children, via a third party – Lady Ely or Henry. Rivalries and jealousies simmered amongst the maids-of-honour. Brown quarrelled with his fellow Highlanders. Everyone took umbrage at Brown.

Henry actually liked Brown and rather admired the Queen for resisting calls for his dismissal. Brown, he felt, was a known quantity, and had his uses, keeping the servants at Balmoral, who were afraid of him, in order for one. Cheering the Queen for another. A maid-of-honour seeing him preparing to drive out with Her Majesty asked whether she was going to have tea. No, he replied, 'she don't much like tea, we tak out biscuits and sperrits'. If required, Henry was prepared to cover up for Brown. When he failed to appear one afternoon to drive the Queen, Henry went in search and found him dead drunk on his bed, whereupon he quietly locked the door and climbed on to the box of the Queen's carriage himself.

At least Henry, unlike the ladies ('we just exist from meal to meal'), didn't lack for occupation. Mornings were spent studying the papers, from the Foreign Office, the Home Office and the lord chamberlain, that arrived daily at 6.30 with the messenger, having left London the previous afternoon. Any papers or letters that needed to be returned were sent back with the messenger at 12.30. Henry hoped to see the Queen once a day to discuss any government business, but that could only be arranged via notes sent through Brown, or a footman or one of the ladies, and sometimes he wouldn't see her for days on end. After household lunch at two, he would wait until four or five, when the Queen rode or drove out, rain or shine – and rain more often than not. Only then were the household free to leave the castle, for a walking or riding expedition, or a visit to Mrs Symons' shop, where one could be weighed on a weighing machine. Henry himself liked a long walk, perhaps with Bids or the minister in attendance.

New diversions were seized upon. When the Queen discovered that her dressers had taken to visiting an enormously fat woman in a cottage near Balmoral, she ordered that her carriage be driven in the

general direction of the cottage, whereupon, wrote Henry, 'in consequence of the Queen having been to see the Fat Woman, all the
household have now been and Spor the packer, who is our fattest
individual, has exchanged photographs with her'.

Partly to amuse Mary, partly himself, Henry played up the comedy
of Balmoral. So, a June visit in 1874 saw 'Eliza' on the warpath: Henry,
sitting next to the unmarried Princess Beatrice at dinner and mentioning
a broken engagement, had 'received a communiqué' from Lady Ely
that he 'was not to talk of marriages to Beatrice'. Lord Bridport, a
genial retired general, now an equerry and a friend of Henry's, had
been ticked off for sending questions about carriages through the
pages instead of John Brown. Miss Macgregor's legs (Miss Murray
Macgregor was a Scotswoman of literary bent, who had helped the
Queen with *Leaves*) had been deemed 'too large for the carriage and
the Q is incommoded by them'. Lady Erroll, the lady-in-waiting, had
blurted out at dinner 'some observation that was beyond the weather'
– a reference to politics – and had subsequently been told not to allude
to such subjects. One afternoon Henry, the Hon. Mary Pitt (a maid-
of-honour), Lord Bridport and Lady Ely went to call on Dr Robertson,
where they had tea, served with a tea cosy. On the drive back to
Balmoral, Miss Pitt observed that the tea cosy given to the Queen for
her birthday by the Princess of Wales was a 'very odd present', whereupon Lady Ely, scenting a whiff of disrespect, swiftly countered with,
'A very nice thing dear.' This was exactly the kind of detail that Henry
knew Mary would appreciate.

'I am very nearly a Dissenter – or rather more a Presbyterian in my
feelings, so very Catholic do I feel we are,' the Queen confessed to
Vicky. Presbyterianism was just a further mark of the superiority of
the Highland race. In 1870, Her Majesty attended the communion
service at Crathie for the first time and looked forward to the day
when she might take communion there herself. It came three years
later. In November 1873, Henry reported to Mary that there was great
excitement about the Queen taking the sacrament at Crathie the
following Sunday, persuaded, according to 'Bids', by John Brown and
Lady Erroll. The latter had become a lady of the bedchamber in 1873,

on the recommendation of Lady Churchill, who, knowing what Her Majesty looked for in her ladies, informed her that Lady Erroll had 'nice eyes' but was 'not good looking otherwise', that she was 'sympathetic', a good musician and not a 'fine lady'. The Queen found her 'wonderfully unselfish and devoted', but the household were driven mad by her passion for evangelising, handing out tracts on temperance and the end of the world, and holding prayer meetings.

There was to be no mention of the Queen's attendance at Crathie in the Court Circular. Henry received several letters from the Dean of Windsor, who, though not entirely happy at the Queen's decision, felt she was free to act as an individual. The household were encouraged, but not forced, to join her in taking the Scottish sacrament. When asked by Lady Erroll whether he would do so, Henry, who had no very strong views one way or the other, but couldn't help feeling that Presbyterianism was 'not a religion for a gentleman', refused. Lady Erroll, as a Presbyterian herself, was naturally happy to take it. Flora Macdonald, the maid-of-honour ('very little conversation and chiefly persiflage', thought Henry), felt she couldn't refuse, though Mary Pitt, her fellow maid, was not asked, as 'too staunch a church woman'. The Biddulphs 'abstained from church' and Lord Bridport declined.

Some, Mary for one, thought it quite wrong, indeed scandalous, for the Queen to have taken communion at Crathie, and that Henry should have told her so. Accused by his wife of having no opinions, Henry defended himself, explaining that it was a question of not forcing one's opinions on the Queen: she 'says 2 and 2 make 5. I humbly point out that no doubt she has some good reason for thinking so, but that I cannot help thinking they make 4. She replies that there may be some truth in what I say but she knows they make 5. Thereupon I drop the discussion. It is of no consequence and I leave it there knowing the fact. Bids however goes on with it . . . no one can stand admitting they are wrong . . . and the Q can't abide it.'

'Bids', like Mary, strongly disapproved. But Henry felt he was mistaken in taking so 'serious a view of some of the Queen's sayings and doings'. 'What she does is not prompted by deep designs but is usually the effect of some strong desire or passing whim.' Though the Queen certainly regarded ritualism – an offshoot of the Oxford Movement – with horror, and ritualistic practices such as facing east at the communion table, incense, candles and coloured stoles as 'mere aping of Catholic forms', Henry didn't believe that her taking of the Scottish sacrament was intended as a blow against ritualists, but rather because 'she really does like the Kirk and its Scotch entourage and that she felt a comfort in taking the communion at Crathie simply for its own sake, increased possibly by a dislike to Ritualism'. Whereas Bids looked for some 'hidden meaning' behind the Queen's actions, Henry was inclined to take her at face value.

The event of the autumn of 1870 was Princess Louise's engagement to the Marquis of Lorne, something of a departure from the usual royal matches, since Lorne was neither royal nor German. Louise was much the most attractive of the Queen's daughters (not in itself saying a great deal) – less stolidly Hanoverian. Men found her 'fascinating'; women mistrusted her. Even Henry, who only had eyes for Mary, thought her lively and attractive. A sculptor, of moderate talent, she studied with Edgar Boehm at the National Art Training School and had a studio in the grounds of Kensington Palace, designed by Edward Godwin.

'Eliza', Henry thought, was pleased about the match, having decided that Lorne was actually preferable to a 'poor, small German Prince', and Henry was kept busy trying to resolve various thorny questions of precedence. There was a celebratory bonfire and the inevitable ball, where Henry danced with Princess Beatrice, the Balmoral housekeeper and one of the Queen's dressers. And then, at the beginning of November, just when the household could finally allow themselves to look forward to leaving Scotland, Louise developed a bad knee, a seemingly minor setback, which escalated, as things tended to at Balmoral, into a full-blown drama. The Queen and Louise quarrelled over doctors, leaving Lady Ely quite worn out from acting as go-between, and Her Majesty, to universal dismay, seized upon the knee as an excuse to delay her return to Windsor. Finally Henry heard, from John Brown, that the train south had been ordered for 23 November.

*   *   *

By 1871, the Queen's continued seclusion and refusal to perform public duties was causing general discontent, not to mention providing ammunition for a small but vocal republican movement. In February she opened Parliament, but only, claimed her critics, because she needed an annuity for Prince Arthur and a dowry for Louise. She was said to be hoarding; her ill-health was a fiction; the court was nothing but a 'pack of Germans' ('better sacrifice Sahl and Bauer', suggested Henry). That August Her Majesty refused to delay her departure for Balmoral in order to prorogue Parliament, despite, or to spite, Gladstone's pleas. Vicky composed (but in the end did not send) a letter, signed by all the children, warning their mother of the danger in which she was placing the monarchy. The Queen remained unmoved, insisting that the fragile state of her health did not allow her to put off her Scottish journey, which she was quite well enough to make.

In fact, that August, she became genuinely ill, with multiple ailments: a painful abscess under her arm, gout in her ankle, a sore throat and earache. Jenner placed an anonymous paragraph in *The Lancet* announcing that Her Majesty could not be expected to go to London and that it was quite impossible for her to do any more than she did at present. When Henry saw her in mid-September, for the first time since he'd arrived at Balmoral, sitting in a tent in the garden, he was struck by how pale and thin she looked – she'd lost a stone in two months – though his concern was somewhat tempered by the knowledge that ill-health had not prevented her from throwing herself into the 'Brown v. Alfred' row that had been simmering for the past few weeks. Henry suspected that the Queen suffered from boredom at Balmoral; 'rows' provided a form of excitement. 'Brown v. Alfred' had all the classic ingredients of a Balmoral row: long-standing resentments and jealousies, a number of parties both directly and indirectly involved and maximum offence extracted from minimal provocation.

As usual, Henry was called in to mediate between Prince Alfred, the Duke of Edinburgh, and John Brown, as he relayed over a series of letters to Mary. Henry disliked Alfred: his feeble jokes, tediously nautical conversation (the Duke had gone into the navy) and 'execrable' fiddle playing after dinner. He was notoriously rude to servants, as the Queen was quick to note, immensely boring (Henry's avoidance of the smoking room was partly due to dread of being buttonholed by Alfred) and devoid of charm. The Duke, arriving at Balmoral, refused to shake hands with Brown, who complained to the Queen, who instructed Henry to speak to 'Affie'. Hostilities had commenced, it emerged, back in May at the gillies' ball when, according to the Duke, Brown had spoken rudely to him on being ordered to stop the music. Lady Churchill, currently in waiting at Balmoral, advised the Queen not to interfere and said Brown had been 'impertinent'. The Queen, who had every intention of interfering, said he hadn't.

It was decided that Henry should see each of the aggrieved parties separately and then attempt to bring them together. Brown 'positively denied having used the language imputed to him viz. "I'll not stand this from you or any man"' but admitted he was angry and 'some words may have slipped from him which were not respectful'. He blamed Grant, another Highlander with whom he was often at logger-heads, for telling tales about him to the Duke. The latter, though initially extremely reluctant to see Brown, finally agreed as long as Henry remained present as referee. The meeting took place in the smoking room. Alfred expressed surprise at the 'extraordinary language' used by Brown at the ball, and Brown said that he could 'scarcely conceive it possible' that he had used any 'nasty words', but if he had, he asked forgiveness – it pained him to think that any of the Queen's children were angry with him. Henry, feeling that there was little more to be said, 'observed I think YRH seems satisfied and closed the meeting. Unfortunately Brown said "I am quite satisfied too" which gave a decided air of equality but I got him out and hope the matter is concluded. My private belief is that neither are satisfied.'

During an afternoon drive, Henry and 'Bids' 'bemoaned the present state of things'. The Queen, they felt, was growing ever fonder of her isolation and of 'governing the country by means of messages through footmen to us!' Henry and Dr Jenner had a 'hot argument', in which Henry deplored the Queen's refusal to wait for the prorogation, and

Jenner insisted that 'not a woman in the kingdom' worked as hard as Her Majesty, and that to claim that her crown depended 'on her waiting for a day or two at Osborne or driving about in London was an insult to common sense'. 'Well,' replied Henry, 'you will see by and by when she asks for money for her next son, there will be a considerable difficulty, the middle and lower classes believe she is hoarding it and will vote no more.'

William Jenner was a competent doctor and a man of good sense, but when it came to dealing with Her Majesty he had simply decided to adopt the line of least resistance. In Jenner Victoria had an ally willing to back up her protestations of overwork and fragile nerves. Henry felt sceptical about the Queen's nerves, 'a species of madness', and believed that contrary to Jenner's insistence that she worked tirelessly at her dispatch boxes, she actually did very little. Nor did he think her greatly interested in public affairs, apart from those few matters that personally touched her, such as ritualism, cruelty to animals, or the Deceased Wife's Sister Bill. What she *was* currently interested in was creating a new order, a Faithful Service Medal, to be awarded to those servants who had rendered her invaluable service. Henry foresaw trouble: she might get away with giving it to Brown and Löhlein, but beyond that it would simply create all manner of jealousies. In the event, Brown was the only recipient.

In September a pamphlet appeared entitled *What does she do with it?*. Its author, G. O. Trevelyan, a Liberal MP and a nephew of Macaulay, claimed the Queen was squirrelling away £200,000 a year. This alarmed Henry, since it seemed 'very dangerous to allow the false impression to take root and grow that the Queen is saving money and living in seclusion because as *The Universe* [a Catholic penny paper supporting Liberal causes] said she cd not afford a new bonnet to drive about in London'. He tackled Jenner: surely it would be better to tell the ministers the truth about the Queen's health? 'How can he and is it not far better to say the Q can't do so and so because of her health – which is to a certain extent true – than to say she won't. Very well that may be necessary but why not tell all this to the Ministers . . . he says they won't believe him.' In Jenner's view it made no difference to the government whether the Queen went to London or not. Henry conceded there might be some truth in this, that having the Queen 600 miles away allowed her ministers a free hand.

Lord Halifax, an uncle of Mary Ponsonby, who had come to Balmoral as minister in attendance, and who called the Queen's obstinacy and nerves 'small evidences of insanity', lamented that the Queen didn't have a 'good woman about her' – an old nurse, a governess, one of her ladies – to proffer some sensible advice. Henry entirely agreed, feeling the Queen lacked a proper friend: 'She won't have her children round her, she has no lady who she really likes and it seems to me she is terribly alone.' Since 1861, the Queen had come to rely on her ladies as go-betweens, to help her through social ordeals such as large dinners and drawing rooms and to offer a sympathetic and uncritical ear. She had absolutely no wish for advice, not that there was any lady either capable or prepared to give such.

Victoria derived little satisfaction from her adult children, who showed themselves ungrateful, more interested in their own lives and families than their mother and resistant to maternal guidance. Really, she told Vicky, children brought 'more anxiety and sorrow than pleasure'. Princess Alice had arrived at Balmoral, offering to stay for the winter, to which 'the Queen sniffed but did not reply'. Alice, who had been such a comfort and support during the Prince Consort's last illness, had, since her marriage, become combative and critical. She told Henry that when the children offered to come and stay, the Queen rebuffed them, claiming that Sir John Cowell considered the expense too great, and that none of them could get anywhere with their mother, while Brown could talk to her 'on all things'. Lady Ely confided to Henry 'perfectly inaudible secrets . . . about struggles going on with Alice and Louise and others. The general tenor of which seems to be they want to do what they like not what the Q likes and want her to pay for doing what they like, while she is ready to pay if they will do what she likes. The first thing she likes is that Alice shd. go back to Darmstadt. And Alice won't.'

The rain poured, the household resorted to badminton and battledore in the ballroom and Henry told Mary, 'I get into states of utter vacuity here sometimes, at breakfast and dinner, and cannot think what to say.' Lady Ely and Jenner were 'continually in deep confab' and when Benjamin Disraeli, leader of the Conservatives, made a speech in the Commons claiming that the Queen was 'physically and morally incapable' of performing public duties, Henry suspected that they had been feeding him lines. Was that the case? he asked Lady Ely. She 'got very red and incoherent' but denied everything.

He looked forward to the arrival of William Gladstone, who was coming for just over a week's stay (Gladstone did not relish a visit to Balmoral; this time he was made to wait several days before the Queen saw him and then to feel the full force of her 'repellent power'). Over long walks they discussed the question of the Queen's seclusion, with Gladstone – as virtuoso a talker as he was a walker – dominating the conversation. During the eleven miles from the Glassalt Shiel to Balmoral, 'Gladdy' told Henry that the Queen had 'laid up in early years an immense fund of loyalty but she is now living on her capital'. In fact, he was more worried about the damaging effect of scandalous stories circulating about the Prince of Wales.

In November, Sir Charles Dilke, a radical MP, made a speech at Newcastle attacking the Queen and calling for a republic. This did rouse Her Majesty. During the gillies' ball she told Henry that if Dilke was to go round telling 'lies' – that she didn't pay income tax, for example – then something should be said. Would Henry write a letter, to be sent to Gladstone? Henry did so, as did Thomas Biddulph, who, from Windsor, wrote a rather 'stronger' letter, urging the Queen to demand that Gladstone should denounce Dilke (something Henry thought impossible – how could Gladstone speak for the Queen?). The Queen chose Biddulph's letter, incorporating some of Henry's. 'I quite see that it was better to make it strong but if you do you must be prepared to follow it up, which I don't think we are,' Henry told Mary. He had heard, from Lady Ely, that the Queen was very low, 'crying and regularly unhappy'. About Dilke? he asked. 'Well no, that may have something to do with it, but it is about Alice coming to Windsor for so long.'

Then, at the end of November, came alarming news – the Prince of Wales had typhoid. The Queen, accompanied by Henry, hurried from Balmoral to Sandringham, the Waleses' Norfolk home, where she promptly took charge as to which of the family were permitted to stay and which were to leave. Henry, going out into the garden, was 'suddenly carried away by a stampede of Royalties, headed by the Duke of Cambridge and brought up by Prince Leopold, going as fast as they could. We thought it was a mad bull. But they cried out "The Queen, the Queen" and we all dashed into the house again and waited behind the door till the road was clear.'

As the Queen sat at her son's bedside, memories of the Prince Consort's last days must have been painfully present. Over the past ten years Victoria had softened towards her son: she might deplore his 'small empty brain', his friends and his endless 'gadding about', but she could not deny that he was unfailingly amiable, courteous and affectionate. The crisis came on 13 December, and for one terrible moment it looked as though Bertie might die on the anniversary of his father's death (as Princess Alice would do in 1878). And then he turned a corner. In February 1872, a thanksgiving service was held in St Paul's, an occasion regarded by the Queen as an unnecessary ordeal, but in the event 'a day of triumph – really most marvellous! Such touching affection and loyalty cannot be seen anywhere I think.' Republicanism was dead.

CHAPTER 17

Eastern Questions and Domestic Affairs

When the Conservatives, under Benjamin Disraeli, came to power in the 1874 elections, the Queen could barely conceal her delight. She had enjoyed a brief taste of Disraeli as prime minister back in 1868, when he had taken over the leadership of the Conservatives on the resignation of Lord Derby. Disraeli, she told Vicky, was certainly very 'peculiar', 'thoroughly Jewish looking' with his 'livid complexion' and black ringlets, but he was 'full of poetry, romance and chivalry'. Moreover, he declared his acquaintance with the Prince Consort, who had distrusted *him*, to have been 'one of the most satisfactory incidents of his life'. The Queen had seen him go, soundly defeated by Gladstone's Liberals, after less than a year in office, with regret. She had endured Gladstone for six years, but now Disraeli was returned to her and in him she had a very different kind of premier, one who never lectured, but consulted and confided, who wrote her long, gossipy letters, who offered devotion as well as respect. 'He told the Queen everything . . . and said "I wish you to know everything so you may be able to judge",' she wrote happily to Henry Ponsonby.

Thomas Biddulph, who disliked Disraeli, thought him a humbug and a 'perfect slave' to the Queen. Henry was inclined to be more charitable: 'he really does believe much of what Bids thinks he is humbugging. And his flowery sentiments are part of his style.' He thought him 'cleverer than Gladstone with his terrible earnestness', but how anyone could 'put faith in Dizzy' he couldn't understand. Beneath the courtly deference and fulsome flattery with which Disraeli lavished 'the Faery', Henry detected more than a hint of the 'burlesque'. He really had 'an admiration for splendour, for Duchesses with ropes of pearls, for richness and gorgeousness, mixed also I think with a cynical sneer and a burlesque thought about them' (Henry himself of course was no stranger to the 'burlesque thought' when it came to royalty). Henry also recoiled – as the Queen did not – from Dizzy's Jewishness – he was 'not one of us . . . an alien without root . . . not English in blood or heart or relationship'.

However, he understood that Disraeli had 'got the length of her foot exactly', that, like the Emperor Napoleon, he'd recognised the importance of sympathy, of the personal touch, of treating Victoria as a woman as much as a queen (and she responded in kind, sending bunches of primroses and Valentine cards). How could she resist Dizzy's murmured 'we authors, Ma'am'? Then too he succeeded in forcing through two unpopular pieces of legislation, the Royal Titles Bill and the Public Worship Bill, both dear to the Queen's heart (and heartily disapproved of by the Ponsonbys). 'I am an Empress and in common conversation am sometimes called Empress of India,' she had written to Henry. 'Why have I never officially assumed this title? I feel I ought to do so and wish to have preliminary enquiries made.' Thanks to Disraeli's efforts, the title became hers, while the Public Worship Bill set out to quash those ritualist practices she so abhorred. Disraeli was now firmly secured in the Queen's favour. In his early years as private secretary, Henry had struggled to persuade Her Majesty to communicate with her ministers; now she appeared to be actively leaning on the government, to be acting in cahoots with her prime minister and independently of her private secretary.

Ironically it was not Disraeli, but Gladstone, so Henry believed, who genuinely revered the monarchy, but to such a degree that his very respect became a constraint and handicap. He had 'so high an opinion of the Queen that he entered too deeply and painfully into questions which bored her. He went too much into detail to which she did not listen and then cut short his argument which she didn't understand by a direct refusal.' He told her both too much and too little and all of it without a trace of humour.

Henry frequently modified the language of reprimands intended for Gladstone. Some years later, in 1884, with Gladstone back in office and touring Scotland to drum up support for the Franchise Bill, which extended the franchise from the towns to the countryside, effectively a third Reform Bill, the Queen became incensed. Henry was asked to write 'strongly' and to 'take opportunity of remarking on his "stump oratory" and the bad taste of his progress under her very nose'. The Queen was more than a little jealous of 'the people's William', and to have to read what she called a 'Court Circular' in the Scottish papers reporting his 'triumphal progress' as he stopped to speak at every station was really too much. 'The Q told me to tell him that his speeches out of the window at each platform were rather absurd which I did, though not exactly in that language.' In fact Henry wrote wishing Gladstone a good rest after his 'most successful visit to the North'.

However, in 1876, the Queen believed Gladstone to have safely retired from politics. In August, at Balmoral, she and the household pored over the horrifying details in the *Daily News* of a massacre of 12,000 Bulgarian Christians by the Turks, an atrocity the British government did not initially appear to take very seriously. Liberal opinion, though (including clerics and men of letters – Carlyle, Froude, Ruskin), was outraged. As was the Queen, who told Henry Ponsonby that the government must speak out, condemning the Turks. Their failure to do so immediately she blamed not on Disraeli, but his ministers.

The massacre of the Bulgarian Christians was the spark that ignited, or rather reignited, the 'Eastern Question', which would dominate politics – and Henry's time – through the late 1870s, polarising the Queen's feelings about the two party leaders and consequently requiring considerable tact and patience on the part of her private secretary. The Eastern Question was played out in the same territories in which the Crimean War had been fought, the Balkans, where Turkey's territories bordered Russia, and where Christians and Muslims uneasily coexisted, thus creating a tinderbox of ethnic and religious hatreds. Here too the larger countries jostled for power, anxious to secure their own positions and a slice of the vast and disintegrating

Turkish Empire. In 1875 and 1876 there were revolts, and Muslim massacres, on the part of the Christians, in Bosnia, Herzegovina, Serbia and Bulgaria, ruthlessly suppressed by the Turks.

On 6 September, Gladstone, who had consistently opposed Disraeli's pro-Turkish policy in the East (in 1875, in a provocative gesture of support for the Turks, Disraeli had sent the British fleet to Besika Bay), suddenly burst forth with a rousing and highly emotive pamphlet, *The Bulgarian Horrors and the Question of the East*. This called on Britain to protect the Balkan Christians, to join 'Holy' Russia and drive the Turks out of those provinces they 'had desolated and profaned'. Thousands bought it and thousands gathered at a rally in Blackheath to listen to its author, righteous, fiery-eyed and unstoppable. The Queen was nonplussed: here was Gladstone, that old 'mischief-maker and firebrand', who she had sincerely hoped to have heard the last of, apparently stealing the moral high ground from under Dizzy's nose.

As Henry pointed out, the Queen, before she was bamboozled by Disraeli, had believed that the Turks 'should be made to understand we were not supporting them', advice which unfortunately 'was not followed'. She had actually gone further than Gladstone, in suggesting that 'giving as much independence as possible to the Turkish princi-palities' would create a 'barrier against Russian aggression' – a good idea, thought Henry. But such arguments fell by the wayside in her wholehearted support of Disraeli; she would not desert him; as a gesture of support, she even opened Parliament in February 1877. The Turkish atrocities were deplorable, but it was the Russians, she decided, who were at the root of it all.

Henry did his best to temper the Queen's Russophobia, though he accepted that the Russians were essentially motivated by self-interest – with a covetous eye on Constantinople – and that they were every bit as guilty of atrocities as the Turks. While supporting Gladstone in his condemnation of the Turks, he neither shared his militancy, nor championed Russia. He admitted that he could 'see Dizzy's point': 'sweeping the Turks out of Europe' was simply not possible, and anyway, the Turks were crucial as a bulwark against Russia. Here he disagreed with Mary, who, like Gladstone, was virulently anti-Turk.

'I am with you as against Turkey I am against you when you are pro Russia,' he told her. 'Between you and the Queen I find great difficulty in repelling arguments. You on one side and she on the other. My line is anti-Turk, anti-Russian. Do not let us give up on one barbarian so as to throw ourselves blindly into the arms of another.'

The Queen threw herself into the Eastern Question; she was, reported Henry, 'deeply interested in the East. Sends orders and tele-grams incessantly.' In large part this was due to Disraeli, who became Lord Beaconsfield in August 1876, and to his habit of including and consulting her – or at least appearing to. Above all things, she dreaded a repetition of the Crimea, a subject on which she felt particularly well informed, since she had just finished the second volume of Theodore Martin's *Life of the Prince Consort*. Here too all her loathing and distrust of Russia came into play. While she had no desire to fight for Turkey, she believed, like her prime minister, in supporting the Turks as a means of containing Russia. 'Oh if the Queen were a man she would like to go and give those horrid Russians, whose word one cannot trust, such a beating,' she told Disraeli.

For Henry, the Queen's sudden enthusiasm for foreign affairs proved a very mixed blessing. Whereas hitherto he had battled to engage her interest and attention, now the very strength of her interest meant he found himself sidelined. There was no room, it seemed, for a private secretary who voiced dissent. For daring to criticise govern-ment policy Henry found himself cast out in the cold. He received a 'hint' from Dean Wellesley that the Queen was 'pained at my taking Gladstone's part and . . . that it was desirable I should be silent'.

As Henry recorded, Lily Wellesley told Mary, whilst walking on the Slopes at Windsor, 'that the Q objected to our "advanced views" and later Lady Ely told her that the Q was distressed at my taking the part of the Liberals on the controversy and feared that she (my wife) urged me on. Mrs P replied with some indignation that she did not influence me and that she was sure I never acted agst the Gov. tho' I told the Q sometimes what I thought. Lady E apologised. Later Lord Beaconsfield said to me "I know you don't agree with me, but I know you convey my messages accurately".'

By 1876, Jane Ely, not for the first time, was at the end of her tether. She had made a bid for freedom in 1872, when, her health buckling under the strain of being in almost constant attendance on the Queen and longing to spend more time with her only son, she had absented herself from court. Dr Jenner had been brought in to apply pressure.

He explained that while Her Majesty was sorry she was not well, she should know 'how absolutely essential it is that the Queen should have some *one* Lady about Her in whom Her Majesty can repose perfect confidence, to whom she may speak on *all* family matters and other matters . . . You, I know, feel as strongly as possible that the Ladies of the Court, partly from the necessarily short time each is in waiting and partly from individual peculiarities and family exigencies could not one after the other succeed to this important post. It must be filled by one and the same Lady. The worry, anxiety and work which must devolve on the Queen from the want of such a Lady would I am sure soon tell on Her Majesty's health.' No one, insisted Jenner, could 'render Her Majesty this special service' but Lady Ely. In return, the Queen was willing to make concessions: Lady Ely might absent herself from drawing rooms and dinner; she was to be excused from walking or driving; her rooms at Windsor – in the Victoria Tower, the same as once occupied by Sarah Lyttelton – could be moved to a lower floor; her son could visit whenever he wished. Jenner laid it on thick – if she left her post, and once her son married, her life would be 'lonely and purposeless', while at court she might have 'society or rest and quiet as it might please . . . and a real and important object in life'. The message was loud and clear: Lady Ely's health and well-being were of little consequence beside those of the Queen. There could be no doubt as to where her duty lay.

The following year, Lady Ely, who was recovering from an operation for an abscess, was unable to accompany the Queen to Balmoral for her autumn visit. This time Her Majesty herself waded in. She had no intention of losing Lady Ely, who was both familiar – and Victoria clung to the familiar – and endlessly biddable. Lady Ely's 'long absence' had added to her 'anxiety and worry of late'; she had said she would be happy to devote herself to Her Majesty and that two or three months' leave a year would be sufficient; 'now illness [has] intervened and upset all this'. No other lady could replace her; Lady Churchill's family obligations prevented her from spending long periods at court; Horatia Stopford's health was delicate. 'It is almost a public duty to try and *help me* and to have one so gentle, and attached and kind as you are, knowing me so long is an immense help.' In 1873, Lady Ely obeyed the call of duty and crumpled, agreeing to remain at court, with four months' annual leave. But by 1876 little had changed and she appealed to Thomas Biddulph for advice, claiming that she couldn't go on as it was 'killing her', that six weeks' waiting at a time was as much as she could do, and that the Queen was refusing to allow her son to visit.

'Eastern questions' did not entirely eclipse 'domestic affairs', and Henry weathered the usual Balmoral rows and 'bothers' through the autumn of 1876. Leys, one of the pipers, had to be dismissed after waiting at table drunk on several occasions, then frightening Princess Beatrice by looming up (drunkenly) in front of her in a passage, which even the Queen agreed was not acceptable. Lady Ely came to Henry with a 'hint' from Her Majesty, that the ponies were being over-ridden. Herr Sahl refused to appear at the gillies' ball, informing Lady Ely enigmatically that 'the causes which prompted the issuing of the ordinance of September 1869 were similar to those which prevented his appearance at the Ball'. This referred back to the great 'pony row' of 1869, when the Queen had decided that the Rev. Robinson Duckworth, governor and tutor to Prince Leopold, Edgar Boehm and Herr Sahl were to be banned from riding her ponies on account of their poor horsemanship, an order that she deputed to Henry, thus causing maximum resentment amongst the banned riders. In fact, as Henry pointed out, Sahl had danced several times since 1869. Henry himself, disappearing from the ball for a couple of hours of ciphering on Eastern business, met with 'some asperity' on his return, culminating in his dancing a Hooligan with the Queen.

Then the Queen became greatly exercised about the treatment of her new factor, Dr Profeit, who had replaced Dr Robertson. Profeit, while a 'good, honest sort of rough man', was not the gentleman Robertson had been, but the Queen, who was remarkably free from the snobbery of her household and family, was anxious that he should be treated as such. She wanted the Prince of Wales to ask Profeit to dinner at Abergeldie. The Prince refused, on the grounds that as the Queen didn't ask him, why should he? The Queen, enraged, said that she intended to, and that anyway Profeit was 'more respectable than some of the Prince's friends' – and so Henry was to tell the Prince. Subsequently Horatia Stopford brought Henry a memo 'on the social position' of Robertson and Profeit, 'the father of one being a boot-maker and of the other a farmer – as if that had anything to do with the matter'. He hoped it would all 'blow over'. But it merely blew up again when the Queen ordered the Prince of Wales to ask Profeit to shoot and he refused. Henry crisply summed up the denouement: 'At last the Q sd. she wd. see him herself. I sd. by all means much the best way. She did. He was frightened as they all are when they see her and succumbed to everything she wanted. I say then it would be much better to see him than send messages to which she rather agrees. I hope therefore there will be fewer of the unpleasant hints I have to send.'

Meanwhile, Eastern affairs rumbled on. In April 1877, Russia declared war on Turkey, thus confirming all the Queen's worst fears. Her ladies were put to work making bandages for Turkish soldiers, and the maids-of-honour were asked for subscriptions (Miss Stopford and Miss Lascelles told Henry they'd rather support Russia; 'Say you have already devoted all your spare cash to your fellow subjects in India,' Henry advised). Henry was branded pro-Gladstone and pro-Russian and thus unpatriotic, unfairly he felt, since while he had no wish to fight for the Turks (as Disraeli advocated), he certainly did not support the Russians. Once again Dean Wellesley was brought in, as a kind of guided missile, to inform Henry that the Queen was unhappy with his 'Russian proclivities', his 'support for Gladstone' and especially his 'want of sympathy for her'. Henry smarted. Where had such accusations come from? Disraeli? Prince Leopold, who had been helping the

Queen with correspondence that should have been the preserve of her private secretary? The source, it turned out, was the Prince of Wales.

At Balmoral, unable to say what he thought, or to voice any criticism of Disraeli, or even 'hint that it is possible there can be another side to the views held by the Government', without being accused of 'want of sympathy', Henry felt effectively muzzled. And not just muzzled, but kept in the dark. He and Biddulph only heard of the resignation – in protest at Disraeli's militancy – of Lord Derby (the foreign secretary) from Mlle Norèle, the French governess. At household dinner there seemed 'no use talking about Gladstone when one mustn't say a word for him and Jenner dashes forth with his howlings of personal abuse against him – so I am silent'. How he pined to have 'a good strong argument' with Mary.

There was the inevitable visit from Lady Ely, dispatched 'to say that the Queen wanted me to like Beaconsfield. I replied that I thought he was one of the most amusing people I knew. Lady Ely said no – that is not it – she wants you to like him. "Say then that I will love him". "No, no dear Gen. Ponsonby, that won't do – she wants you to like him politically". "Well if he disagrees with the Q am I to like her politically or to like him?" Lady Ely said she could get no answer from me.' A further letter from the Dean warned him 'to be careful in my correspondence . . . that my letters should smack of nothing but an insipid neutrality'. As Henry told Mary, Beaconsfield had made the Queen a 'strong Turk. Therefore the slightest utterance here must be hushed. He has hushed me and made me silent . . . it is hard that the Q should not know there is another side to the question and that those who do not agree with B do so because they think he is leading the country astray.'

In March 1878, Turkey was forced to accept the Treaty of San Stephano, whereby Russia made considerable and, as far as the Queen and a good many of her subjects were concerned, quite unacceptable gains, regaining all those territories lost after the Crimean. Three months later the Congress of Berlin forced Russia to revise the treaty. Through all this Henry often found himself bypassed altogether. The

Queen preferred to use Prince Leopold or Lady Ely to communicate with her ministers. How could he do his job properly when he wasn't in full possession of the facts? When he was barred from access to ministers? In a moment of frustration, he protested to Lady Ely: sometimes he got 'the Queen's orders and sometimes I did not. Sometimes I heard what was being done and sometimes not, sometimes I received information from Miss Norèle, and sometimes from Sahl . . . whatever advice I give is an opinion formed on half information or none at all.'

Formerly, when he had 'talked freely with ministers', Henry had enjoyed the private secretaryship, despite its occasional frustrations. No longer. A rare beautiful day at Balmoral left him quite unmoved; he merely longed to be off on a 'bracing lark' with Mary. Disraeli, returning triumphantly from the Congress of Berlin, having won Cyprus for Britain, reported that Bismarck (gargantuan in every sense he said) had told him that it was a good thing to marry an ugly woman and that his wife was 'so ugly that every day she became prettier, now if you marry a pretty woman every day she goes off'. 'So says Bismark; wrote Henry, 'but I have my reasons for disagreeing.'

Separation from Mary, an ever-present regret, was particularly so now: 'you are my eyes which see the outer world and know what is going on and who I consult on everything and whose advice is worth more than any one's and who I love and care for more than I can ever say. And to be separated from you is the unhappiness of my life and makes me very often long to give up everything if only I could be with you'. Such regrets were not entirely one-sided: 'I do miss you dreadfully. It is tantalising to have a bit and then always be saying goodbye,' wrote Mary, in a rare surviving letter, after one of Henry's brief leaves.

In September 1878, Sir Thomas Biddulph, keeper of the privy purse, died quite suddenly, a great sadness for Henry, since for all their differences of opinion, 'Bids' had been a real ally. It was perhaps a sign of how far Henry had fallen from favour that the Queen, urged on by the Prince of Wales, considered moving him to the privy purse and offering the private secretaryship to Disraeli's own secretary, Montagu Corry (later Lord Rowton). Unsurprisingly, Henry intimated that he would resign rather than accept such an arrangement. And the Queen, however irritated she might be by him, was quite shrewd enough to know that she didn't want to lose him. Besides, she suspected Corry of being 'a man of pleasure'.

Through Dr Jenner, Henry heard that he was to be offered the privy purse, in addition to private secretary, with two assistants. This was a promotion, but not one he coveted. Indeed, Henry had little interest in promotion for its own sake, or honour attendant on royal service (he accepted a knighthood, in 1879, with great reluctance). He merely foresaw more work, just when, aged fifty-three, he was longing to spend more time with his family, and in 'the outer world', and work of a nature that didn't greatly interest him. He would now be responsible for financial matters as well as political affairs, for servants' wages and pensions, for the Queen's estates and the privy purse revenues. Refusal, however, was not an option; the dictates of duty and service demanded otherwise. Henry accepted and became joint keeper of the privy purse and private secretary with an extra £200 a year, taking his salary to £1,700, and the use of a London pied-à-terre in St James's Palace (presided over by the Biddulphs' old housekeeper), which Mary benefited from rather more than her husband, since the Queen so rarely visited London.

When it came to choosing his assistants, Henry was not allowed a free hand. One equerry he suggested was dismissed by the Queen as 'so rough'; Elphinstone (controller of Prince Arthur's household) was 'so tutorial and always pushing himself forward'; Cowell (master of the household) she didn't like. Eventually Fleetwood Edwards and Arthur Pickard (equerries to Princes Arthur and Leopold respectively) were appointed. When Pickard, whose health was delicate, died a couple of years later, he was replaced by Arthur Bigge.

Henry's first month in his new job passed uneventfully enough, though as he told Mary, he missed having Bids to talk to, and felt very much alone. In his new role his duties ranged 'from tackling the prime minister to discussing a scullery maid's wages', and while he enjoyed the former, he did not relish the latter. At least with Lady Ely temporarily absent from court, he and his assistants were able to communicate directly with the Queen: 'when Lady Ely returns and gives incomprehensible messages and when the system begins of divide et impera as was tried on with me and Bids . . . then of course we shall have bothers'.

Congenial colleagues made the trials of Henry's job easier to bear. Amongst the household these were few enough. Not just politically, but temperamentally, he felt out on a limb. Lady Churchill he liked, though he could never remember a word she said, and Lord Bridport was 'a great standby', but there was scarcely anyone to whom he could talk frankly. With such as Sir John Cowell, Henry had absolutely nothing in common. Cowell was another ex-soldier, a neat, upright figure, bristling with correctness. He was excessively devout, quite humourless and took his duties immensely seriously, even such minor matters as the case of the disappearing dusters: in 1881, twenty-four dozen mysteriously vanished from Windsor.

When Henry told Cowell that the Windsor chaplain Charles Courtenay wished to be referred to, quite properly, as the 'Rev. and Hon.' in the Court Circular, for which the master of the household was responsible, Cowell became greatly exercised. 'He smelt the hoof [sic] of popery in it and told me he would not call him so unless I gave an order – I said I had nothing to do with it, it was a mere prefix.' Cowell brooded on this, then wrote a long letter to the Queen about the question of Courtenay's title. It came back with a note: 'it is a matter of perfect indifference to the Q. what he is called'. According to Princess Louise, Cowell had been a marked man ever since John Brown complained to Her Majesty that he'd been trying to limit the servants' drinking.

In 1881, Henry found some compensation for the loss of Bids in a new recruit to the household – Dr James Reid. Here was someone with a shared sensibility – an independent turn of mind, an absence of royal culte, and an ability to laugh at the absurdities of both court and Queen.

CHAPTER 18

James Reid: Resident Medical Attendant

April 1881 saw the Queen at Osborne, anxiously awaiting reports of Disraeli, whose always fragile health had finally given way, and ordering chicken consommé from the Osborne kitchens to be parcelled up and sent to him at Hughenden. Disraeli's death came as a 'terrible' blow. 'Never had I *so* kind and devoted a Minister and very few such devoted friends. His affectionate sympathy, his wise counsel – *all* were so invaluable even out of office . . . my poor faithful Brown was quite overcome when he had to tell me,' she wrote to Lord Rowton. According to Lady Ely, she had been 'inconsolable at not having had that *"last look"* which she has had of so many, high and low' and was now suffering from depression and insomnia.

While Her Majesty mourned Disraeli, James Reid, a thirty-one-year-old doctor in Ellon, Aberdeenshire, heard some news that would change his life: a vacancy had arisen in the royal household for a resident medical attendant. Dr Marshall, the previous incumbent at Balmoral, had resigned and Dr Profeit had been ordered to find a replacement. The Queen wished her new doctor to be a Scotsman, and preferably a Scotsman who spoke German, which was useful for attending visiting Royalties. James Reid was perfectly qualified.

In 1881, Reid had been living in the family home in Ellon and working as the local doctor, as his father had before him, for the last four years. He had been a star pupil at his local grammar school and a high-flying student at the Aberdeen Infirmary, where he began his medical training. This was continued in Vienna, *the* place to study medicine in the 1870s (Freud attended the School of Medicine there in 1876), with a preparatory stint as a tutor in Austria in order to learn the necessary German. In 1877, his studies completed, he returned to Ellon to take up his father's practice. But, however attached to Ellon, Reid had ambitions beyond it – he was highly qualified, bright, personable and, he must have felt, destined for higher things than a mere country practice. When he heard, through his uncle, an acquaintance of Dr Profeit, of a position in the Queen's household, he saw his chance.

In June 1881, the Queen recorded in her journal: 'Saw Dr Reid from Ellon, who has the very highest testimonials, having taken very high honours at Aberdeen and studied for two years in Vienna . . . He is willing to come for a time or permanently in Dr Marshall's place.' After a further interview with Sir William Jenner, senior physician-in-ordinary, Reid was appointed. He was to be in constant attendance on the Queen, as well as on those of her family in residence at court, the ladies and gentlemen of the household, the Queen's personal attendants, the Highland servants and any other servants who required him. He was to report on all medical matters to Dr Jenner.

The Queen's medical staff were organised on a tier system. On the top rung sat the physicians and surgeons-in-ordinary (usually three of each), who acted as consultants, and occasionally as general practitioners. Under them came the physicians and surgeons extraordinary, who could generally expect to be promoted to 'in-ordinary'. Lastly there were the apothecaries, known as surgeon apothecaries, both for the household (excluding the Queen and her family) and for the Person, who actually practised as general practitioners. Serving alongside Reid were Dr James Ellison, surgeon apothecary to the Queen at Windsor, and Dr William Hoffmeister, surgeon apothecary to the Queen at Osborne. At Balmoral, rather than a surgeon apothecary, there was a resident medical attendant. Reid's position was something of an anomaly – he was the first doctor to be in permanent attendance on the Queen, not just at Balmoral, but travelling with her between her palaces and abroad. Even after he became physician extraordinary in 1887 and then physician-in-ordinary in 1889, he remained at her side.

Dr Reid took up his duties in July 1881, on a three-month trial, with a salary of £400, six weeks' leave and, at Windsor, 'very comfortable quarters' on the first floor of the York Tower, looking down the Long Walk. He was permitted to eat breakfast and luncheon with the rest of the household, but in the early days he was debarred from dinner – doctors being considered 'below the salt'. Not in the least put out, he began holding merry dinner parties in his room, a fact the Queen soon got wind of – 'I hear Dr Reid has dinner parties!' Henceforth he was invited to join the household dinners, and in 1885, he was even granted permission to wear the Windsor uniform, with scarlet collar and cuffs, as opposed to the household uniform of tail coat with gold buttons and braid and square tails.

The new resident medical attendant was compact and small of stature, blue-eyed, luxuriantly moustached and with a soft Aberdonian accent that he kept all his life. The Queen found in him the Scottish virtues of straightforwardness and plain-speaking; Reid, unlike Jenner, was prepared to do battle with Her Majesty when occasion demanded. She also, crucially, found him sympathetic, as indeed did women in general. Easy-going, amusing and gregarious, he soon made himself popular with his colleagues. A lady-in-waiting found him refreshingly 'open', a rare enough quality amongst the household. Fritz Ponsonby, Henry's son, summed up his appeal thus: 'he was always so pointful and his sense of humour made him such a delightful companion . . . I think she was guided more by him than by anyone else . . . his absence of Royal Culte and a delightful way of stripping the leaves from the trees and putting things in a blunt way was always a pleasure to me.'

'Throw Physic to the dogs and come and see Barnum. I have got a box and a place for you in it,' reads a note from Henry Ponsonby, who forged a warm friendship with Reid, though some twenty years older. There are few bonds so uniting as humour, and with Reid, Henry could share jokes. Reid was occasionally invited to stay at Slains Castle, near Ellon, with the Errolls. Lady Erroll was the Queen's evangelising lady-in-waiting and Lord Erroll, in Reid's view, was 'a decided lunatic', who apparently nursed some form of pathological and entirely irrational jealousy of Henry Ponsonby, a man he'd never met. Returning from a visit to Slains, Reid told Henry that he'd been woken at six in the morning by Erroll, who had taken him to his gymnasium, 'where he practised on the crossbar and turned head over heels on it 20 times. Then perspiring freely he came breathless to the ground and said "there Ponsonby could not do that!" R had never mentioned my name. In the evening he said to Reid "I have 5 children – my first is 25 years older than my last – Ponsonby could not do that!"' 'It seems to be a formula,' commented Henry drily.

'Let Dr Reid go out from quarter to 11 to one, *unless* the Queen *sends before* to see him and from 5 till *near 8*. If he wishes on any particular occasion to go out sooner he shd ask. These are the regular hours. But I may send *before* to say he is *not* to go out before I have seen him shd I not feel well or want anything. This every Doctor in attendance has done and must be prepared to do.' So read Reid's first hand-written note – a barely legible sequence of dashes and underlinings – from the Queen, at Balmoral in August 1881. Particular, contradictory and emphatic, it set the tone.

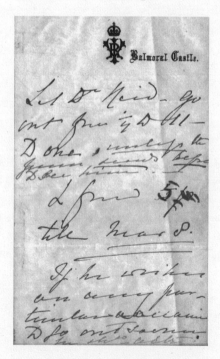

James Reid's first note from the Queen

Reid's primary responsibility was the health and care of Her Majesty. He attended her several times a day, every day (his last visit at 10.30 at night), yet he never used a stethoscope (to which the Queen had an aversion) and the first time he saw her in bed was when she lay dying. In fact Reid was only really required to treat minor ailments, since the Queen, who was sixty-two when she first came under his care, generally enjoyed good health. She suffered from rheumatism, exacerbated by cold, damp drives in open carriages, for which Charlotte Nautet, known as 'the Rubber', was summoned regularly from Aix-les-Bains to give massages (Reid found her ill-tempered and obstreperous). And her digestion was poor, but that was hardly surprising given her vast meals and the speed at which she consumed them. For her occasional bouts of insomnia Reid prescribed Dover's Powder, sparingly, 'for fear of establishing a habit' (it contained opium), or a draught of Ammonium Bromide and Tincture of Henbane. He thought she would sleep much better if she didn't go to bed so late – it was often 1.30, with another hour taken up by 'the undressing'. Whenever she woke during the night she rang for a wardrobe maid, which meant sleepless nights for the maids, who then succumbed to 'nervous exhaustion', for which they consulted Dr Reid. On the whole he believed most of Her Majesty's ailments could be cured by eating less and going to bed earlier.

The Queen quickly became reliant on her doctor, not so much for his medical expertise – she preferred to ignore his advice – but as a reassuring presence and confidant. During his brief periods of leave, Reid liked to return to Ellon, where he helped his mother by working in the garden, hanging pictures and supervising home improvements, and where he would invariably be pursued by notes: the Queen's voice was a little 'husky'; she was sleeping badly; her walking was not of the best; her finger was swollen; her digestion was poor with an 'inclination to griping'; she had a little catarrh; her eyes were itchy and she had no one to put in her drops; she was feeling a little 'nervous'.

Frequently his leaves were cut short by a summons back to

Balmoral, as in September 1885, when the Queen complained of 'huskiness' and a pain between her shoulders. This time Reid found her quite well, but, as he told Jenner – always a source of sound advice and moral support – 'feeling very nervous' and fancying she had heart trouble, of which he could see no sign. Unwilling to alarm her by using a stethoscope, he suggested a 'soda, sal volatile and ginger draught twice or thrice daily after meals and an occasional dose of salt in the morning'. Jenner suspected that the trouble was 'merely flatulence from indigestion' and remembered 'an attack of indigestion from Cranberry tart and cream when Sir James Clark's only remark to Her Majesty was "Don't eat it again", whereat Her Majesty was very much annoyed'. Back at Ellon, further notes arrived detailing headaches, eye strain and hip pain. But as Reid came to realise, the Queen's upsets tended to be emotional rather than physical, brought on by 'family squabbles and misunderstandings' or domestic troubles. For such she needed calming and counselling rather than medical treatment. Like Henry Ponsonby, Reid understood that the Queen was not to 'be measured by the same standard as ordinary people'.

Besides Her Majesty, Reid had to attend to her family: the confinements of Princess Beatrice, after her marriage, in 1885, to Prince Henry of Battenberg; the illnesses of the Battenberg children; the 'imaginary ailments' of Princess Christian (Helena), 'a great bore', who became addicted to opium and laudanum; and the alcoholism of the Duke of Coburg (formerly the Duke of Edinburgh). There were occasional dramas, as at Christmas 1891, when Prince Christian was shot in the eye by the Duke of Connaught, requiring the removal of the eye by George Lawson, the Queen's eye specialist, aided by Reid. The Queen only consented to the operation with extreme reluctance, and afterwards her wardrobe maid Annie Macdonald told Reid that she 'is now quite reconciled to what we have done, and she is glad all is over, but that Mr Lawson is not to feel hurt if she does not see him and I am not to speak of the operation when I see her!'

His services were also demanded by the household and servants.

An insane housemaid, a hysterical dresser, a depressed chaplain all required the ministrations of Dr Reid. But the great majority of the cases Reid saw amongst the servants were drink-related: Rankin, the Queen's footman, 'the fat Highlander' as one of the ladies called him, had to be removed from Osborne after becoming 'violently maniacal' from drink (he was reinstated, but relapsed three years later), while Mrs Chapman, who was in charge of the linen room at Windsor, was habitually so drunk as to have 'virtual delirium tremens' at night. Alcoholism, endemic in all the Queen's palaces, was particularly so at Balmoral, where the pipers, the footmen, the lamplighters and the Brown brothers were all habitually drunk. Smith the messenger was sometimes so inebriated as to be unable to travel, and Dr Profeit became so hopelessly and embarrassingly alcoholic that Reid persuaded him to resign. The Queen's dinner was routinely accompanied by the sound of crashing china and the sight of wine poured liberally around rather than into glasses. To all of this Her Majesty affected perfect indifference. Highlanders were never 'drunk', merely 'confused' or 'bashful'. She leapt to the defence of a lamplighter accused of drunkenness – both the lamplighters at Balmoral were 'perfectly sobre men', it was simply the police telling tales. When Hugh Brown died from alcoholic poisoning, Reid was 'commanded' not to tell the household.

Reid was amazed at the Queen's tolerance. 'It is quite astonishing how lenient the Queen is to drunkenness among her servants. When any of the constantly recurring cases comes to her knowledge she always tells me I am on no account to breathe a hint of it to anyone "especially the Gentlemen and Sir H. Ponsonby and Sir J. Cowell", and she often fancies no one knows anything of it, while in reality there is hardly a soul in the house who does not know. Any other offence is never overlooked.' While in many respects an extremely selfish and exacting mistress – thinking nothing of ringing for a dresser or wardrobe maid at any hour of the night, or curtailing Reid's precious holiday on the flimsiest of pretexts – the Queen showed herself curiously indulgent towards misdemeanours, be it drinking, stealing or gambling, on the part of her servants. There was a good deal here of championing the underdog; petty crimes committed by her children or the household never went unchecked.

Dr Reid's remit was a broad one, reaching far beyond the medical. He could find himself, as in March 1885, asking Dr Jenner to write to Henry Ponsonby – a letter which could be shown to the ministers – explaining that it was necessary for the Queen's 'health that she should go abroad now . . . she thinks you might say (in order that they do not think she is going simply for her amusement) that unless she goes where she can have some rest, she might break down'. Victoria made shameless use of the poor health card when it suited her; this time she had her way, travelling to Aix-les-Bains. Reid could be asked to cipher the Crown Princess of Prussia, on the subject of her husband's health (Fritz, suffering from throat cancer, briefly became Emperor of Germany in 1888, but died just ninety-eight days later), or to advise her that Her Majesty would be bringing her own mattress when she visited and was most insistent that no stoves should be lit in her rooms. But he could just as easily be ordered to buy gloves for the Indian servants who arrived at court in 1887, or to minister to the Queen's dogs. When her beloved collie Noble died at Balmoral, aged sixteen, Reid sat up late with the weeping Queen, finally leaving her at 12.45 with a stronger than usual sleeping draught, and taking away with him her instructions for Noble's burial. The procedure was to be similar to that followed on the death of the Prince Consort's grey-hound Eos forty-three years earlier: 'I wish the grave to be bricked. The dear dog is to be wrapped up in the box lined with lead and charcoal, placed in it, as well as some coins. I feel as if I could not bring myself to go and choose the spot. Dr Profeit would perhaps suggest it.'

In the absence of Henry Ponsonby, Reid was pressed into service as the deliverer of unpleasant messages. At Balmoral in 1885, while Henry was taking the waters at Aix with Mary, Reid told him that he was 'well away from Balmoral at present as the atmosphere is highly charged with electricity and there are frequent discharges all around and in all directions'. The Queen had ordered him to tell Herr Muther – Herr Sahl's replacement and seemingly equally touchy – who wished to go stalking, that he was not to do so. Muther threatened to resign, refused to go to luncheon, and was only mollified by being invited to the royal dinner.

At other times Reid had to adjudicate between two warring ladies-in-waiting, or settle the grievances of a servant, which was strictly speaking the province of the master of the household. It was to Reid that Donald Brown – one of the many Brown brothers and a known troublemaker – gave a petition, addressed to the Queen, asking to be moved from Osborne 'on account of the evil doings of his neighbour the gardener'. His request was granted and he was given a position at Windsor, as a porter at the main gate, where he continued to be uncooperative and recalcitrant. The Queen, highly displeased, wrote to Reid: Brown's duties were very light, yet he did nothing but complain; he had been given the place 'out of regard' for his eldest brother and had been 'more indulged' than anyone else in his position, yet he was 'never satisfied', which set 'a very bad example to the other servants in a similar position'; he had to be 'told plainly and decidedly' that if he did not obey the orders of the master of the household, she would have to 'pension him off', which, for the sake of his brother, she would regret. Donald wrote to Reid resigning: 'I will resine on Friday . . . all unpleasantness I hop will end when I am gon' – and booked a passage to Australia.

Responsibility for the Indian servants became one of the most time-consuming and tiresome of Reid's duties. Amongst the very great number of Royalties who congregated in London to celebrate the Queen's Golden Jubilee in 1887 were a delegation of Indian princes who arrived, uninvited, to pay their respects to their Queen and Empress. Amongst their entourage were two Indian servants who elected to remain in England and enter the service of Her Majesty: tall, slim, good-looking Abdul Karim and plump, good-natured Mahomet Buksh. The Queen was intrigued by her new servants, regarding them rather as exotic pets; she enjoyed the sight of them waiting at table in their scarlet and gold costumes and white turbans; she encouraged them to cook up curries for her guests in the royal kitchens; she fussed over their diet, their clothes and their timetables; she engaged tutors to teach them English, while she herself began Hindustani lessons with Abdul. In September she told Henry, who had been given a 'Hindu vocabulary to study', what a 'comfort' she found them: Abdul was 'most handy in helping when she signs by drying the signatures' and Mahomet was 'wonderfully quick and intelligent'.

The Indians – others followed Abdul and Mahomet, and wives and extended families were brought over – were installed in cottages at Windsor, Balmoral and Osborne and put in the charge of Major-General Dennehy, an extra groom-in-waiting, who had served in India. However, Dennehy proved unequal to the task and Reid, much against his will, found himself increasingly preoccupied by 'Indian questions'.

In August 1887, shortly before the departure for Balmoral, he received a lengthy memo from the Queen, typically precise yet incoherent, titled 'Rules for Scotland': the Indians were to wait at breakfast, whether indoors or out, wearing 'their new dark blue dress', with a turban and sash; they were to have an English lesson between 11 and 11.30; they were to attend at luncheon, tea and dinner, wearing, for the latter, 'the red dress and gold and white turban and sash'. If the Queen went out for tea in the carriage then they should do 'some extra waiting instead either *before* I go out or when I come in. Better before I go out – stopping half an hour longer & should wait *upstairs* to answer a hand bell – they should come in and out & bring boxes, letters etc. *instead* of the *maids.*' She worried how the Indians would adapt to the cold: 'They should not put on the thickest underclothes at once, but gradually'; 'warm Tweed dress and trousers . . . made in the Indian fashion', together with woollen stockings, socks, gloves and walking shoes were to be bought for them at Balmoral to wear off duty; turbans were to be worn at all times. They were to speak slowly to the Queen in Hindustani, so as to help her learn their language. Reid, rewriting the memo before giving it to Dennehy, omitted this last instruction.

Further notes followed as to exactly what the Indians were to do after meals: 'It seems to me that they need not hurry away after meals to their rooms and may stay either in the corridor below or above, or with anyone if they like.' And the Queen was anxious to establish their status within the household. With regard to the train journey north, Reid was told: 'Pray take care that my good Indian people get one of the *Upper Servants places* which Hyam knows is their proper position and they are not put far from our saloons, also that they have every comfort so that they are warm at night.' She did not wish Francis Clark (her chief Highland attendant) to have any 'hand in the arrangement' because she knew him to be 'very prejudiced' and 'not inclined to be kind'.

All this took its toll. Overworked and overburdened with incessant demands, Reid's own health suffered, not helped by long hours in the smoking room, and he periodically succumbed to exhaustion and strain manifested in painful boils. One January at Osborne he raced between Prince Christian (recovering from his eye operation and demanding constant attention), a bedridden Duke of Connaught, Princess Louise suffering from a sprained wrist, a maid-of-honour with a stiff neck, a groom-in-waiting with a bad cold, one of the Indian servants with ophthalmia, other Indians with influenza, an ailing Lady Biddulph, and a number of sick children. In just one day of bedside visits he clocked up nine miles on his pedometer. And somehow in between he had to make time for rehearsals for the *tableaux vivants*: he was appearing in *The Duel of the Corsican Brothers*. The tableaux were a great bore, but had one benefit, in that they kept 'people from thinking of at least their imaginary ailments'.

It was under the auspices of Prince Henry of Battenberg that *tableaux vivants* – once performed by the royal children, and supervised by Sarah Lyttelton – were revived. Prince Henry and Princess Beatrice met in 1884, in Darmstadt, at the wedding of Princess Victoria of Hesse (daughter of Princess Alice, who had died in 1878, of diphtheria) and her cousin Prince Louis of Battenberg. Beatrice and Henry's announcement of their wish to marry met with stony silence on the part of the Queen. The marriage of anyone close to her, family or household, now felt like desertion, and the prospect of losing Beatrice, her constant companion, was insupportable. For six months communication was reduced to notes passed across the dining room table, until finally Her Majesty relented, on condition that Beatrice and Henry made their home with her, at court. In fact she grew extremely fond of her genial son-in-law, 'Liko', whom she considered the handsomest of the handsome Battenberg brothers.

In 1888, on Twelfth Night, the *tableaux vivants* kicked off with *The Queen of Sheba*, starring Beatrice as the Queen and Henry Ponsonby as Solomon, followed by *Carmen* with Prince Henry alongside Arthur Bigge, Marie Adeane, and Harriet Phipps (maids-of-honour) and Minnie Cochrane (lady-in-waiting to Princess Beatrice), *Queen Elizabeth and Raleigh* (played by Beatrice and Prince Henry), *The Winter's Tale* and *Homage*. Each tableau had two poses and each pose was shown twice, by means of raising and dropping a curtain. Costumes and sets were elaborate, intervals lengthy and the whole performance stretched well over two hours.

As well as tableaux there were theatricals – short comic plays, sometimes accompanied by songs. Participation in the tableaux and theatricals was non-negotiable and something of an occupational hazard for the household, though the Queen entered into them with childlike enthusiasm, attending rehearsals, supervising sets and costumes, and occasionally censoring, when language was deemed too strong, or doctoring scripts, in order to beef up a part for one of the princesses. Alick Yorke, a groom-in-waiting, acted as stage manager and master of revels. Yorke was something of an anomaly amongst the gentlemen at court, a short, rotund, decidedly camp figure, extravagantly perfumed and bejewelled, sporting piped suits, a finely waxed and curled moustache and a large Malmaison carnation in his button hole. He had formerly been an equerry to Prince Leopold, and according to Henry Ponsonby, his 'chief recommendation' in the eyes of the Queen had been his complete lack of interest in all forms of 'manly' activities.

Reid resigned himself to appearing in theatricals. In 1889 he had his first speaking part as Fennel, a lawyer, in *Used Up*, an adaptation of the comedy *L'Homme Blasé*, performed in the ballroom at Balmoral, before local gentry, cottagers and servants. The scenery, lent by the Aberdeen Theatre, represented views around the castle, Princess Beatrice played Lady Clutterbuck and Arthur Bigge a blacksmith. Reid, his hair and whiskers whitened, 'got through' it better than expected. He got off lightly as prompter in *Little Toddlekins*, in which the Queen thought Beatrice and Louise (who rowed bitterly over the theatricals) 'excellent', though Henry Ponsonby was reproved for failing to learn his lines. Footmen were strategically placed at the back of the room and ordered to applaud in this event. Occasionally Mary Ponsonby was roped in as stage manager, and the Ponsonby children as actors. For Reid and Henry, overworked as they were, a week spent learning lines (tableaux at least were silent) and rehearsing for a theatrical was the very last thing they needed. Fritz Ponsonby thought the only person who truly enjoyed the theatricals, apart from Her Majesty, was Clarkson, the wig maker.

But for much of the time, when he wasn't feeling 'besieged', and certainly in his bachelor days, court life suited Reid 'to a T'. He enjoyed the perks: his comfortable quarters at Windsor, a luxurious hotel room, fine food, a 'good haul' of Christmas presents. In 1889, when he had Christmas dinner with the Queen for the first time, he netted a solid silver salver from Her Majesty, a silver inkstand from Louise, a silver cigarette case from Beatrice and a gold watch chain and pencil case from Lady Ely. He was able to keep his mother supplied with grapes, gooseberries and strawberries from the kitchen gardens at Windsor, and venison and salmon from Balmoral. He enjoyed travelling with the Queen, in the absence of crises and dramas. Snobbery played a part – familiarity with Royalties, rubbing shoulders with the great and the good, holidaying with Lord Bridport at the latter's family home, Cricket St Thomas, with its eighteen gardeners – all gave satisfaction.

*   *   *

Reid's first real crisis at court came in March 1883. On the 17th the Queen sprained her knee falling on the stairs at Windsor, leaving her unable to walk. On the same day a certain Lady Florence Dixie claimed that while walking in the plantation close to her home, The Fishery, near Windsor, she'd been attacked by two knife-wielding men dressed as women (said to be Fenians) and that her life had only been saved by the timely appearance of her faithful St Bernard, Hubert. Hubert was duly photographed, and a copy sent to the Queen. There was a good deal of scepticism about this tale – 'most of the Gentlemen here think the story is an invention of her own . . . She is rather a queer customer,' Reid noted. But Henry Ponsonby was sent to enquire after Lady Florence's health and John Brown too drove to The Fishery, in an open dog cart, in a biting wind, to ask after her and to examine both the scene of the crime and Hubert.

Brown subsequently caught a chill, which left him weakened and vulnerable when he contracted erysipelas, which he'd suffered from before, in his face. Visiting him in his room in the Clarence Tower on the 26th, Reid found him worse and suffering 'from delirium tremens' (alcoholism exacerbated erysipelas). The Queen, confined to her room by her knee, and unaware of the severity of Brown's condition, insisted on regular reports but was unable to visit the patient herself. On the 27th, Reid received a telegram announcing the death of his father at Ellon; that same evening, John Brown died. It was left to Prince Leopold to break the news to his mother the following day. For six days Brown lay in state in the Clarence Tower, after which the Queen managed to hobble up the stairs to his room for the funeral service. On the coffin she placed a wreath of white flowers and myrtle, bearing the message, 'From his best and most faithful friend, Victoria R.I.' The body was taken to Crathie for burial.

In her grief and shock, the Queen could not spare Reid immediately, and he didn't leave for Ellon until the 29th. But her own misery did not entirely blind her to his. On 2 April a telegram arrived – 'Anxious to know how you and your mother are, thought much of you yesterday, am very miserable and stunned.' A few months later he received a little portrait of his father, painted on enamel, in a silver frame, with the inscription, 'The Queen hopes Dr Reid will accept the accompanying recollection of a day so terribly sad to him and her, the remembrance of which will ever be one of the most painful ones in her life.'

This was no exaggeration. For the Queen, the loss of her 'dearest best friend' was a bitter blow, and one for which she could expect scant sympathy from her family or household. A few days after Brown's death, she wrote to Henry Ponsonby: she was 'utterly crushed . . . every moment the loss of the strong arm and wise advice, warm heart and cheery original way of saying things and the sympathy in any large and small circumstances – is most cruelly missed . . . The Queen can't walk the least and the shock she has sustained has made her very weak – so that she can't stand.' Edgar Boehm was put to work on a life-size bronze statue of Brown, with an inscription by Tennyson on the plinth. This was installed in the garden at Balmoral, where it loomed over Her Majesty as she sat working on her dispatch boxes; under Edward VII it was removed and hidden in trees behind the house the Queen had built for Brown.

Henry Ponsonby, unlike the rest of the household, was generous in his estimate of Brown and understood something of the Queen's loss. Brown, he noted, 'was the only person who could fight and make the Q do what she did not wish. He did not always succeed nor was his advice always the best – but I believe he was honest and with all his want of education, his roughness, his prejudices and other faults he was undoubtedly a most excellent servant to her.' He pointed out that at least in Brown 'we knew what we had', and since he had 'confined his interference chiefly to the stables, shooting and the servants', he hadn't been able to do a great deal of harm.

At Osborne, in April, the Queen was still dining alone, Lord Rowton and Tennyson came to 'condole' and a new face officiated at the Sunday service: Randall Davidson, chaplain to Archbishop

Benson. As there was no private chapel at Osborne, the service was held in the dining room, with the Queen, who didn't feel equal to appearing before her household, in the next room, listening through a half-opened door. Davidson was being mooted as the new Dean of Windsor, and Henry approved: 'We incline here to Davidson as the new Dean, tho he is very young.'

In May, the Queen, taking James Reid and Henry Ponsonby with her, left for Scotland. Henry, writing to Mary on the train, his handwriting shaky, remarked on how depressed everyone seemed at breakfast – lack of sleep on the train perhaps, or the prospect of Balmoral. Once there, low spirits continued. Dinners were silent, though the news that a dog, Bones, belonging to a friend of the Prince of Wales had been shot by the keeper at Windsor, according to an order from Prince Christian, the park ranger, that all wandering dogs were to be destroyed, briefly roused the Queen from her melancholy. Mistreatment of dogs never failed to excite.

Her knee was a little better, but she was still only able to walk short distances and resorted to a pony chair for expeditions (for the ladies, 'trotting' up mountains behind her chair was no joke). Charlotte Nautet, the masseuse, arrived from Aix-les-Bains and Henry predicted a 'tug of war'. 'The Rubber' stipulated no going out, no sitting on wet grass, no late dinners and no cold rooms, and Reid, having dismissed her as a 'charlatan', began to think she might have her uses. A couple of days later, Her Majesty had 'defeated the Rubber on all points and has her way completely'. Seeing the Queen driving out in an open carriage on a particularly cold day, 'the Rubber was a little surprised . . . but makes up her mind that these are the ways of the country and rubs on'.

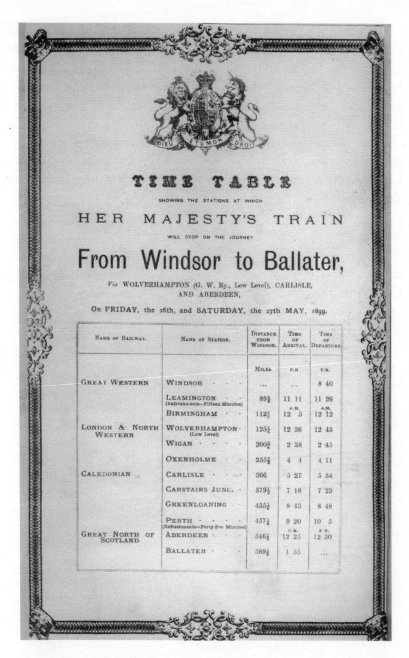

Timetable for Her Majesty's train, travelling from Windsor to Ballater

Henry thought it hardly surprising that the Queen was depressed, given that she had nothing to do but drive out in the afternoon and reorganise the servants. Brown's duties had been jointly taken on by his brother Hugh and Francis Clark; Henry was told to inform John Cowell that Brown and Clark were *not* to have their meals in the servants' hall at Windsor, but were to dine in a room of their own, with the same allowance of wine as the men in the steward's room. At Balmoral, the Highlanders, no longer 'kept in order' by Brown, were soon trying to take their orders directly from the Queen and causing trouble. It was just as Henry had predicted.

CHAPTER 19

Randall Davidson: Dean of Windsor

Gerald Wellesley, Dean of Windsor and domestic chaplain to the Queen for nearly thirty years, died in September 1882. For Victoria this meant 'the last of that group of old devoted friends gone', while for Lily Wellesley it meant the loss of a father, son and husband in the space of a year. Charles Phipps, Charles Grey, James Clark, Augusta Stanley (Augusta had died in 1876, thus severing the 'last link' with the Duchess of Kent), Caroline Barrington, Thomas Biddulph, all of whom had served the Queen as a wife as well as a widow, all were no more. On Prince Leopold's suggestion, George Connor was appointed as the new Dean, but Connor's health was poor and in May 1883, just weeks after the death of John Brown, and six months into his appointment, he too died. 'Windsor is indeed a tomb to me!' lamented the Queen.

However, she knew who she wanted to succeed Connor – Randall Davidson, chaplain to the Archbishop of Canterbury, Edward White Benson. The position of Dean of Windsor and domestic chaplain required a very particular kind of individual, as the Queen explained to Henry Ponsonby: 'What the Queen wants is a tolerant, liberal minded, broad church clergyman who at the same time is pleasant socially and is popular with all members and classes of her Household – who also understands her feelings not only in ecclesiastical matters but also in social matters.' He needed to be the right kind of clergyman – not overly clerical, not too long-winded, certainly not High Church – but also the right kind of man. Though he would not, officially, be part of the household, he would be in close contact with its members, not to mention the Queen's family. He would have to dine with Her Majesty and meet visiting Royalties and statesmen. He would have to preach before them. All this required a certain worldliness and social confidence. Davidson had plenty of both.

But it was just as important that the Dean be sympathetic, someone in whom the Queen could confide. She wrote to Archbishop Benson, unusually in the first person, 'as I can better express myself and wish to consult you on a subject *of very great importance* to myself'. 'I have now lost almost all of those who were associated in any way with my altered and saddened life since December 61,' she told him, 'and I must look around for other helps. It is therefore *most* important, nay *imperative* that I should *find someone* who possesses a kindly sympathetic nature – who could be a comfort to me, now, that I get older and have been sorely stricken as Mr Davidson can tell you!'

If the Archbishop could spare him, she felt Davidson would make an excellent dean, for 'his great knowledge of society and of the Clergy generally, and his great charm of manner'. His youth might tell against him, but she did not think this an 'insurmountable obstacle'. 'Think of my sadly lonely position,' she begged Benson, 'and of the great need I have of loving and sympathetic help and of someone to lean on.' She reminded him that she did not wish her domestic chaplain to 'interfere with the Servants (who are of a superior class) unless they seek his advice and assistance', and she finished by saying that she thought Edith Davidson would do well at Windsor, 'which is a place of rather a gossiping nature'.

Benson assured her that he was ready to give up Davidson and that he considered him a man of sound judgement, as well as 'of a deeply sympathetic and loyal nature'. His youth had 'all the advantage of spring and freshness . . . besides it is a shortcoming of which he is daily being cured as Your Majesty says, and it will be cured all too soon'. His reply came as 'a great relief' to the Queen. In a further letter, she confessed that the first time she had met Randall Davidson she had felt 'drawn towards' him in much the same way that, on first sighting, she had been 'irresistibly drawn towards' John Brown.

Davidson, she felt, would be just the person she needed during her 'declining years which have been so over shadowed'.

Like James Reid, Randall Davidson was a Scotsman, from a professional, middle-class background ('so cool and Scotch and right and always to the point', wrote his biographer, and much the same could have been said of Reid). The eldest of four children, he was born in 1848 in Edinburgh. His father was a prosperous wood merchant in Leith and both he and his wife were devout – subscribing to the Presbyterian and Episcopalian faiths – without being in the least dour. Family life was affectionate and boisterous.

Randall was sent to Harrow, where he flourished. In his final year he suffered a near-fatal accident (his second – he had narrowly escaped drowning a few years earlier) when, during a rabbit-shooting expedition, a cousin shot him in the back at close range, leaving a hole 'big enough to hold an average orange', and, as was discovered later, 164 pieces of shot. Miraculously, after being laid up for many months and on crutches for many more, he recovered, though the accident shadowed his years as an undergraduate at Oxford and its after-effects lingered on in the shape of lumbago and a hernia. Davidson suffered bouts of ill health throughout his life, but as with many semi-invalids, his proved a long one.

After Oxford, he combined training for Holy Orders with a health-improving programme of Scottish air and foreign travel. In 1874 he was ordained as deacon and three years later he became resident chaplain to Archbishop Tait at Lambeth Palace, stepping into the shoes of the Archbishop's son Craufurd – a friend from Oxford – who was leaving Lambeth to get married. Besides Craufurd, the Taits had three daughters, Lucy, Edith and Agnes (five elder daughters had died, in the space of a month, from scarlet fever). In 1878, in Trollopian fashion, Randall proposed to and was accepted by the middle daughter, nineteen-year-old Edith, who promptly set about 'improving' herself, by reading French and German and the Old Testament. Six months before the wedding, the Taits lost another child, their only son Craufurd, a blow from which Mrs Tait never fully recovered, dying herself in December, on the birthday of the newly married Edith. The Archbishop had lost and gained a son. By the age of thirty, Randall, the merry boy, had known much of pain and grief; here perhaps resided the capacity for sympathy that drew the Queen.

For the next four years Randall and Edith made their home with the Archbishop at Lambeth, not what every newly married couple might wish for, though each flagged up the selflessness of the other. 'I positively *dread* her unselfishness after our marriage,' Randall had written of Edith, while she confessed, wistfully, 'I can't help a little wishing in the bottom of what I am pleased to call my heart that you and Father weren't quite so "devoted and excellent". But of course you will say that is very wicked and it is all for the good of the Church and I don't know what. Well then I submit, as there's nothing else to do.' Both knew their duty and submitted.

By December 1882, Archbishop Tait was reaching the end of his life. As he lay dying at Lambeth (Lady Ely visited bearing flowers and a message of sympathy from the Queen), his son-in-law received a few affectionate parting words: 'My dear Randall. Dear, dear boy. You have been a true son to me ever since Craufurd died. Take care of them all.' It was a request that Davidson would not forget. Shortly after the Archbishop's death, one of Edgar Boehm's men arrived, on the order of Her Majesty, to take a cast for the requisite commemorative bust (Boehm had his hands full through 1883, working on Tait's bust, John Brown's statue and a portrait of Noble, the Queen's collie).

The Queen knew of the promising young chaplain at Lambeth, but her first direct contact with Davidson was the satisfyingly detailed account he sent her of the Archbishop's last days. She wrote thanking him, requesting a lock of Tait's hair and asking him to come and see her at Windsor. There they talked for an hour and discussed the question of the Archbishop's successor; Tait, Davidson told the Queen, had hoped for either the Bishop of Winchester or the Bishop of Truro. Their meeting was gratifying to both. The Queen found Davidson 'singularly pleasing both in appearance and manner, very sympathetic and evidently very intelligent'. Davidson was struck 'by the openness of her confidence and by her genuine anxiety to hear all that I had to say'.

The Queen and Gladstone, who, to Her Majesty's dismay, had returned to office in 1880, disagreed about church appointments as about most things, with the Queen favouring Broad Churchmen with 'large-minded ideas' and Gladstone preferring High, believing them harder workers. But when it came to the new archbishop, they differed merely over age: the Queen thought the Bishop of Truro too young (and a bad preacher, 'prosy and long'); Gladstone thought the Bishop of Winchester too old. The Queen asked Randall Davidson if he could tactfully ascertain, from his wife, the true state of health of the Bishop of Winchester. Gladstone, indefatigable, sent a list of the ages of archbishops, at the time of their appointments, over the last 220 years. In this instance Gladstone had his way and the archbishopric went to the Bishop of Truro, Edward White Benson.

So taken had the Queen been with Davidson that in January 1883 she invited him to come to Osborne to officiate as chaplain, a curious and somewhat unnerving experience, as he described to his father. After settling into his comfortable 'but in no way luxurious' rooms, he was taken to the Queen at 7.30 and received in the Prince Consort's dressing room, where Victoria liked to conduct private interviews. Nothing had changed. In a corner sat the Prince's harmonium. On the blue walls hung his beloved early Renaissance pictures. There stood at the ready, as always, a wash-stand, towels and a kettle of steaming water. Davidson saw the Queen's insistence on keeping Albert's rooms untouched, on hot water being brought in daily, as a harmless foible, the consequence of 'having nobody on the appropriate terms with her for friendly remonstrance or even raillery of a kindly sort'.

The Queen stood throughout their interview and talked of the new Bishop of Truro, who she found 'too sacerdotal'. On the following day, a Sunday, 'after being initiated by Sir John Cowell in the mysteries of the strange service', he preached in the drawing room, delivering his sermon from a desk. The Queen (with a copy of the sermon on a little table in front of her), her family and the household sat to the left, the upper servants to the right, and a posse of footmen stood out in the corridor. There was no music. 'You may imagine the chilling effect of this sort of service,' Davidson told his father. The 'trying ordeal' over by 11.30, he fled for a walk with Arthur Bigge. That night he had another interview with the Queen (this time she sat), who told him she'd been delighted with his sermon. Later came 'a long sit' with the household, as Lady Ely told ghost stories. If this was a test, Davidson passed with flying colours.

The new Archbishop urged Davidson to continue as his chaplain, but Randall had other ideas: it was time to leave Lambeth, to make a life for himself and Edith. The possibility of St Peter's, Eaton Square, was mooted but came to nothing. And then in April, just as a letter arrived from Gladstone offering St Mary's, Bryanston Square, came the news that Dean Connor was dying at Windsor. As Davidson prevaricated as to how to reply to Gladstone, he received another request to preach at Osborne. He went, knowing that the Windsor appointment was as good as his.

'Oh God give me grace . . . yet the call comes so unexpectedly, so solemnly, that there is no alternative left as to acceptance' comes the entry in his diary on 7 May. Two days later he received a letter from Gladstone, formally offering him the deanery (ecclesiastical appointments were the gift of the prime minister, something the Queen preferred to forget, but the Windsor post was de facto her nomination). Davidson professed, perhaps disingenuously, to being 'overwhelmed' by the prospect, but the call of duty chimed comfortably with personal ambition and he accepted without hesitation.

Gladstone had worried about Davidson's youth and inexperience, as he told Henry Ponsonby: 'I should have submitted my scruple on the score of age to Her Majesty had I not been stopped by the heavy artillery she was pleased to bring into the field which reduced my little point to dust and ashes.' Still, he believed, rightly, that Randall Davidson would make an 'excellent Dean'. Others also objected to his youth. *Truth*, the often libellous weekly journal edited by Henry Labouchère, Liberal MP and radical, declared that it was 'not right that at thirty-five he should be promoted to the luxurious indulgence of Windsor'.

A congratulatory note arrived from Henry Ponsonby: 'I am very glad of the appointment for my own sake as well as yours.' A sympathetic colleague was always most welcome and at Windsor, after morning prayers, the two men liked to pace up and down the castle walks, discussing the business of the day. Arthur Bigge, Henry's assistant and Davidson's contemporary, became another firm friend and regular companion during rides in Windsor Great Park.

The Davidsons moved into the Deanery in June. Edith, at just twenty-five, was now mistress of 'a delicious quaint old house', adjoining St George's Chapel. She had a sitting room with lovely views of Eton, a study with a little window on to the Cloister, and plenty of room for her sisters, Agnes – until she married the Rev. Ellison in 1888 – and Lucy, who both spent the greater part of their time at the Deanery. There was a butler (who absconded, to be replaced by John Cowell's former butler, altogether more satisfactory and capable of receiving Royalties with aplomb), a footman, three housemaids and a housekeeper. A cook had still to be found.

As Edith ironed out domestic difficulties, her husband embarked on his new duties. Every morning at nine he took prayers in the private chapel. On Sundays, after attending early communion in St George's, he frequently took two services, at 10.45 and 12, in the private chapel, for the benefit of the Queen and the household, preaching at one if not both. The Queen liked to be given a copy of the sermon and Davidson had to get used to frequent last-minute requests to allude to a recent death or illness of a member of the royal family or household. Sundays drew to a close with a five o'clock service at St George's, where he delighted in listening to the chapel's organist, Walter Parratt.

He was also expected to conduct the ever-multiplying memorial services, by which the Queen set great store and which required no small measure of tact and diplomacy. Davidson's first memorial service, on 14 December in the mausoleum, caused much anxiety. In addition to the obvious references to the Prince Consort and Princess Alice, he was 'directed to prepare prayer . . . and to introduce reference to the Duke of Connaught in India, successive deaths of Wellesley and Connor and above all J.B., a very difficult task'. Having given Horatia Stopford (after twenty years as maid-of-honour, Horatia had become a woman of the bedchamber) a draft of a prayer, he was told that she thought it lacked 'enough definite reference to J.B.'. Davidson agonised in his diary: 'What shall I write next? The whole subject is fraught with difficulties which Miss S told me of but wh I dare not commit to paper even here. Miss S has a difficult task – may God give her grace and wisdom for the burden she has to bear.' In the event, the memorial service left Her Majesty perfectly 'satisfied'.

As domestic chaplain, Davidson, leaving Edith behind, was some-times required to accompany the Queen on her spring jaunts to the Continent, or to spend Christmas at Osborne. And he had to be on hand to offer advice, or consolation, or simply a sympathetic ear to one of the Royalties, or a member of the household, or a servant. However, with the Queen's horror of interfering clerics, and her fear of 'such confidences as might lead, as she used to say to "the very border of Confession", he was strongly discouraged from visiting the servants, even those who were sick. Above all he was expected to act as counsellor and confidant to the Queen herself.

When Davidson arrived at the Deanery in 1883, he found Victoria acutely vulnerable and lonely. This was not the terrible devastation of '61, but nevertheless the loss of John Brown, on whom she'd come to depend, who indeed she'd loved, was a very real grief. And this time one not easily shared. Since the Queen's family and most of her household had heartily disliked Brown and regarded her attachment to him with disbelief if not derision, sympathy for his loss was in short supply. Like most of the household, the subject of Brown filled Davidson with alarm (quite harmless references in his diary are couched in Greek), but he listened while the Queen 'poured forth'. He allowed her to talk. In May 1883 he recorded, 'Interview with the Queen. Most touching, solemn and interesting but terribly difficult. Oh God give me guidance and grace if I am to be called on thus to counsel and strengthen in spiritual things.' He had a further 'most important talk with Miss Stopford' about Brown, which filled him 'with deep thankfulness and anxious fear'.

Then there were Davidson's responsibilities to his weekly Windsor Ladies' Bible Class, attended by an enthusiastic group of 'devout and old-fashioned ladies', to church affairs in general – ecclesiastical appointments perhaps, or the question of Sunday opening of museums, which he favoured, or some point of ritualist controversy – and finally, to his 'pen', as he was writing a life of his late father-in-law, Archbishop Tait. The combined weight of such duties at times oppressed him. 'The burden squeezes me down and prevents me (and you too) from having the time for the refreshing and beautiful side of life which you so rightly feel the lack of for us both,' he wrote wearily to Edith in 1885. Edith was busy enough herself – working on a history of Windsor, taking Sunday school, riding in the Home Park, presiding over a Shakespeare circle which met at the Deanery, taking bicycling lessons, starting a Society for the Care of Friendless Girls at Windsor, and entertaining the stream of visitors – family, friends, Eton masters and their wives, Windsor canons, Royalties, Eton boys – who passed through the Deanery, invariably greeted by 'Go away' from the parrot in the hall.

On rare evenings at home, when Randall was not dining with the Queen or otherwise engaged, the Davidsons read aloud to each other, *Paradise Lost*, or a life of Bishop Wilberforce. One senses that an atmosphere of conscientious duty hung over the Deanery, which might have been lightened by the presence of children; the Davidsons, however, had none. The Dean's sense of duty was probably no greater than that of Sarah Lyttelton, or Henry Ponsonby, but it had a harder, more self-immolating edge. Davidson typified a new breed at Victoria's court, which, by the 1880s, had undergone something of a sea-change, becoming both more middle class and more Conservative. He, like James Reid, or John Cowell, or Arthur Bigge, understood the opportunities that court offered for social and professional advancement. These were High Victorians: resourceful, conscientious, driven and morally serious, far removed from those easy-going, aristocratic,

Whiggish courtiers of old, far removed even from the relative levity and cynicism of such as Charles Grey or Henry Ponsonby.

Randall Davidson's face was dominated, beneath a high, domed forehead, by a pair of dark, deep-set eyes, their gaze earnest and intense. A friend described his expression as sometimes wearing 'the appearance of discomposure and almost intellectual distress. He saw, no one saw more clearly, the dislocation of things.' He made rigorous and exhaustive demands of himself, examining questions, large and small, with immense thoroughness, from every angle, frequently resulting in an agony of indecision. He dashed off forty letters in a single train journey between London and Edinburgh. He berated himself for the lapses in his journal-keeping. Like Ponsonby and Reid, he took on too much, pushed himself too hard and suffered for it. 'Indigestion and pain' comes the regular entry in his diary, and during the 1890s he suffered three serious gastric haemorrhages.

He had a passion for information and an extraordinary memory, and could recall, verbatim, lengthy conversations, though discretion prevented him from recording his more 'private and personal' exchanges with the Queen, 'for fear of mischief making'. Here perhaps was a tendency to self-aggrandisement – he certainly took satisfaction in enjoying Her Majesty's confidence and being privy to royal secrets, and he sometimes exaggerated the importance of such secrets. Like James Reid, he took a snobbish pride in his friendships with such as Gladstone and Lord Rosebery, in their invitations to Hawarden or Dalmeny, in his dinners at the Literary Society and his membership of the Athenaeum, where he could hobnob with 'episcopal and other'.

An astute judge of character, Davidson was perceptive about the Queen, identifying her 'irresistible charm' as 'the combination of absolute truthfulness and simplicity with what had become an instinctive realisation of her position and what belonged to it'. He noted her dislike of 'conversational controversies' and direct criticism, and her preference for employing a third party, sometimes Davidson himself, to do her dirty work for her. He felt that her lack of 'stately or splendid appearance . . . combined with the reality of her dignity in word and movement' constituted 'a sort of charm because of the very way in which it took people by surprise'. 'As a woman she was both shy and humble . . . but as Queen she was neither shy nor humble and asserted her position unhesitatingly.'

Her Majesty's 'religious position' he tactfully described as 'rather unusual'. Suspicion of Sarah Lyttelton's High Church ways had hardened into an abhorrence of ritualism and an inclination towards the austerity of Presbyterianism. In the private chapel at Windsor she insisted on black gowns and Mercer's hymn book – 'a most dreary compilation', thought Davidson, who eventually succeeded in introducing *Hymns Ancient and Modern*. She could not abide religious mawkishness, dismissing many of the condolence letters she'd received on the death of the Prince Consort as 'twaddling religious nonsense', and she intensely disliked what she called 'over-churchiness'. She was a dutiful rather than an enthusiastic church-goer, memorial services being the exception to the rule. The clergy in general, and bishops in particular, were objects of some suspicion (perhaps this went back to her childhood, and lessons with the Rev. Davys, who, as she told Davidson, she had never liked) and she could pay a clergyman no higher compliment than to describe him as 'unclerical'. Of the Rev. Robinson Duckworth, who became governor to Prince Leopold, she wrote: 'the only objection I have to him is that he is a clergyman. However he is enlightened and so free from the usual prejudices of his profession that I feel I must get over my dislike to that. Mr Duckworth is an excellent preacher and good-looking besides.' Much could be overlooked for the sake of a handsome face.

When it came to sermons, the Queen held decided views: not too long; not too loud; not in any way improper. Against a list of preachers submitted by Dean Wellesley to Henry Ponsonby in 1879, she made trenchant comments: 'The Dean of Westminster – too long. The Dean of Christchurch – sermons are like lectures. Dr Bradley – excellent man but tiresome preacher.' Others merely received an 'X' and the comment 'those crossed are most disagreeable Preachers and the Queen wonders the Dean cd mention them'. The Rev. Campbell, who preached at Crathie (and who was treated for depression by James Reid), was admonished on one occasion, via Lady Ely, for spouting 'improprieties' from the *Song of Solomon*, and on another for the volume of his delivery. 'The Queen wishes me to ask,' wrote Harriet Phipps to Henry Ponsonby, 'that somebody should remind Rev. Campbell that the chapel is small and his voice powerful.' In 1886, at Osborne, the Queen was complaining about Prothero, the rector at Whippingham (the same who had caused offence for drawing attention to the alcoholism of the Osborne tenants, and for overzealous, i.e. interfering, visiting of the sick). Henry wrote to Davidson, passing on a message from Her Majesty: 'Prothero preached a long and most tedious and rambling discourse. He lost his place, repeated himself and H.M. thought it would never end. She cannot let him preach again.' Davidson's own sermons however generally met with warm approval, so much so indeed that the Queen repeatedly urged him to publish a selection, a suggestion he vigorously resisted.

At the heart of the Queen's faith – and this at odds, Davidson thought, with her general common-sense, anti-twaddle approach to religion – lay a belief in the afterlife and the immortality of the soul (that went for dogs too), though just occasionally she was assailed by doubts. In 1889, in a reversal of roles, the Queen commiserated with the Dean on the death of his sister-in-law Agnes after the birth of her first child; this was a terrible sadness – 'no sorrow' in Davidson's life compared 'with the death of dear Agnes' – and thereafter her small son became a regular visitor to the Deanery. The Queen asked Davidson whether he was ever overcome, as she was, by 'waves or flashes of doubtfulness, whether, after all, it might be all untrue. "And yet", she added, "these feelings never last, for it is simply impossible to believe that lives that have been cut short in the full swing of activity (e.g. Prince Consort, Emperor Frederick and others she had named) can really have come then to an utter end or that we shall not see them and know them hereafter".'

Sympathy was the quality the Queen had recognised in Davidson, and he did not disappoint. She continued to feel the loss of Brown most acutely: 'the load of sorrow and the ever growing sense of the absence of he who cheered and helped her in an increasingly difficult and trying life never leaves her for a moment', she confessed after returning from Balmoral in June 1884. The Dean made a point of writing to her on the anniversaries of such deaths as the Prince Consort, the Duchess of Kent and John Brown, and his letters were gratefully acknowledged. On the second anniversary of Brown's death, she told him that she had been much 'touched' by his letter: 'What the Queen lost on this night 2 years ago no one who does not live constantly with her can understand. *All* she can say is that she *feels* it *more* and *more* as time goes on and the right hand is gone who was a help and comfort and security in endless ways, not to speak of the sympathy in all past sorrows, in anxieties great and small and the serious loss in the house from his vigilance, justice and unflinching straightforwardness.' A year later, having received Davidson's letter on the anniversary of her mother's death, came the sad admission, 'she has lost *all* who really cared *more* for her than for any one else'. This went right to the heart of the matter: there was now nobody for whom the Queen came first.

Davidson may have prided himself in commanding the Queen's trust, but there was nothing in him of the toady. That very trust sometimes brought him 'into rather sharp conflict with her' when he 'wanted to press some point of which she disapproved or still more to object to something which she wished'. In 1884, a year into his appointment, such an occasion arose.

In January 1884, as New Year's gifts, the Queen presented James Reid and Henry Ponsonby with advance copies of her latest literary work, *More Leaves from a Journal of a Life in the Highlands*. Flushed with the success of the first *Leaves*, she had produced a second volume, dedicated to 'the memory of her devoted personal attendant and faithful friend John Brown', a dedication that had given rise to some anxiety amongst the household. It was published in February. To Vicky, who had been insufficiently enthusiastic about *More Leaves*, the Queen wrote reprovingly, 'I . . . know perfectly well what my people like and appreciate and that is "home life" and simplicity.' Which was exactly what she had given them. She had, however, a further publication in mind.

Back in July 1883, four months after John Brown's death, the Queen had told Henry Ponsonby that she wished to publish a memoir of Brown, and to this end she had enlisted the help of Miss Macgregor. Sir Theodore Martin, who had worked with Her Majesty on *More Leaves*, a not altogether harmonious collaboration, had declined to take on the Brown book, supposedly on the grounds of his wife's health. Miss Macgregor was summoned to Balmoral to start work. There was, Henry told Mary, 'always point in old Macgregor who is not so ugly in her old age'.

The memoir was not mentioned again until February 1884, when the Queen sent a manuscript to Henry, accompanied by a letter: she wanted him to have a look at the manuscript since she didn't agree with some of Miss Macgregor's corrections; she wished to show that Brown had been a 'gt deal more' than a devoted servant; and she proposed that Brown's private diary should be printed. Henry, secretly appalled by what he'd read, prevaricated, saying that he thought it a good idea for Her Majesty to seek advice from Dr Cameron Lees, the Queen's chaplain in Scotland and regarded as something of a literary authority. A note came back from the Queen – 'Sir Henry has not said if he liked the extracts'. Henry wrote again – showing his letter to Randall Davidson – expressing doubt 'whether this record of Your Majesty's innermost and most sacred feelings should be made public to the world'. The Queen replied that the memoir was intended for private circulation only and asked for the manuscript back to show Lord Rowton, formerly Disraeli's secretary, a 'boot-licker' according to a lady-in-waiting, who had successfully ingratiated himself with the Queen. Rowton, so he told Henry, 'suggested delay in any form'.

He took a rather different line with Her Majesty, assuring her that he could see nothing against a private publication, but, perhaps conscious of niggling doubts about the project, she sought further affirmation. Having failed to get the support she hoped for from Henry – though she took his advice and engaged Dr Lees to edit the memoir – she tried a different tack. At the beginning of March she presented Randall Davidson with a volume of *More Leaves* and told him of the proposed memoir. Dr Lees had already shown Davidson some of the Brown material, including extracts from diaries, quite enough to make him feel that publication was 'absolutely out of the question'. The 'terms' used to describe Brown were 'painfully almost ludicrously inappropriate' and 'unsuitable in any case for the Queen to use about one of her servants'.

As further ammunition, Davidson had obtained a satirical pamphlet, *John Brown's Legs*, published in New York, at twenty cents. There was no need to read further than the title page, 'To the memory of those extraordinary Legs – poor bruised and scratched darlings – the writer dedicates this volume.' This, felt Davidson, was simply a 'foretaste of the far worse things which would certainly be said'. Lees quite agreed, but didn't dare say so to the Queen. He explained to the Dean that he had been 'pressed . . . as a Scotsman and a Highlander' to take on the memoir and that he had only done so to avoid the task falling into worse hands, specifically those of Dr Profeit, whom the Queen had also consulted. [4] Since, said Lees, the Queen was determined on publication, an exercise in damage limitation was as much as could be hoped for.

Davidson, bolstered by his belief that the Queen 'liked and trusted best those who occasionally incurred her wrath provided that she had reason to think their motives good', was not prepared to give up. Now he composed a 'careful' letter. He told the Queen that he thought there was much in *More Leaves* to 'do real and permanent good', that 'in the main [they had] been received and read among the humbler classes of Your Majesty's subjects in the very spirit in which Your Majesty has given them to the world', but that there were some 'who do not show themselves worthy of these confidences'. This, he felt, must be said in view of the 'further publication'.

His letter caused a scene, as he learned from Horatia Stopford in a 'startling' interview. Horatia, who, like Lady Ely, was much used as a messenger and go-between, told Davidson that Her Majesty had been greatly taken aback by his letter and wished him to reconsider

---

[4] When Profeit died in 1897, his sons threatened to use as blackmail supposedly compromising letters that Victoria had written to him about Brown; these were eventually retrieved, and destroyed, by James Reid.

his remarks. The Dean was willing to risk head-on collision when he could see no alternative. This was a case in point. He composed a stronger letter – 'I told her I thought it my duty to speak quite plainly.' He believed that publication would be 'so inappropriate' that he felt 'bound to take every means of persuading her to desist'.

This brought Ponsonby to the Deanery. Davidson's letter, Henry told him, had caused the Queen 'great pain and illness'; she had sent for Sir William Jenner 'to give her medical advice'; she would rather not see him 'at present' and he 'was not to dine with her that night as had been arranged because it would upset her' to meet him. Late that night Dr Jenner appeared and assured Davidson that there was absolutely nothing wrong with Her Majesty 'except that she was in a tantrum of wrath and excitement'. Then came Horatia Stopford, in a state of some agitation, bearing a message from the Queen: would the Dean withdraw his comments, and apologise 'for the pain' he 'had given her'.

Davidson duly apologised for the said pain, but stuck to his guns, reiterating his position and offering to resign. For two weeks silence ensued. Another preacher took his place in the pulpit. Then the Queen sent for him, 'was more friendly than ever' and never mentioned the Brown memoir again. He was right in believing that Her Majesty appreciated honesty in certain circumstances – James Reid, Davidson himself, even Henry Ponsonby (who the Dean thought 'lacked courage', though theirs was really a difference of approach) stood as testimony. But he was also right in considering her 'in many respects like a spoiled child, a nice child, but one who had not been properly handled or subjected to due restraint and there is a good deal more difficulty in dealing with a spoilt child at the age of 60 or 70 than with a spoilt child of 6 or 7'. Wilful, impulsive, stubborn, excitable – there was much of the child in the Queen, yet such qualities were under-pinned by a bedrock of good sense. 'In the long run,' wrote Davidson, 'her sound common sense judgement always prevailed.'

On 15 March 1884, the day before the twenty-third anniversary of her mother's death, the Queen told Davidson that from that point on 'the clouds' had become 'heavier and heavier and have never . . . really lifted'. March and December were the 'saddest' months for her. Less than two weeks later came a further sorrow. On the 28th, Prince Leopold, the Duke of Albany, the Queen's youngest son, died in Cannes, on the anniversary of the day on which he had broken the news to her of John Brown's death – 'an extraordinary and awful coincidence', noted the Queen, on whom morbid coincidences, however tenuous, were never wasted. Victoria seldom passed up an opportunity for extravagant expressions of grief, but she bore Leopold's death with relative equanimity. It was, after all, remarkable that he had lived to adulthood, let alone married – the Queen thoroughly approved of the Duchess of Albany – and had children.

Davidson, now fully restored to royal favour, conducted the funeral, sitting up till four a.m. writing his sermon. The Queen expressed her gratitude: 'Let me however express to you *now* from the *bottom of my* poor bleeding heart, which has been so cruelly torn of late – for all your great and tender kindness and thought on this most solemn and overwhelming occasion! You have been such a help to us, and we feel it more as you had not the long acquaintance with us and experience of our dear old friend Dean Wellesley!' In the days after the funeral a steady procession of Royalties passed through the Deanery. Beyond, Windsor Great Park, awash with blackthorn blossom, had never looked more beautiful.

CHAPTER 20

Spring Holidays

Since Dean Wellesley had been perfectly content to remain at Windsor until his death, the Queen simply assumed the same would be the case with Randall Davidson. He suited her so well; he had made himself so indispensable; he was such a part of Windsor life. It did not occur to her that he might have ambitions beyond the castle walls.

The possibility of making Davidson a bishop was first raised by Lord Salisbury, Conservative prime minister of the past three years, in December 1889, only to be scotched by the Queen, who said that she couldn't possibly spare Davidson and wrote to tell him so. She was surprised to find his reply somewhat equivocal: while he sincerely wished to serve her in whatever way he could, he hinted that he might be prepared to leave Windsor if called upon. This disconcerted Her Majesty: 'she owns that the Dean's answer is not *quite what* she expected', she told Henry Ponsonby, 'the Queen wonders if the Dean is at all an ambitious man'. Henry was instructed to tell him that 'he really must not expect to be made a bishop for some time to come' and that furthermore 'his present position was one in many ways of far more importance than the one of bishop who in the Queen's opinion do not do much good!' Having spoken to Davidson, Ponsonby reported that he was happy at Windsor, but he was not insensible of his wider duties to the Church, nor to the fact that 'useful men' were needed in the House of Lords.

The Queen digested this, and by the beginning of 1890 had adjusted her position, admitting to Archbishop Benson that while

The photograph that the Munshi succeeded in having published in the Jubilee edition of the *Daily Graphic* in 1897, showing the Queen 'receiving a lesson in Hindustani from the Munshi Hafiz Abdul Karim C.I.E.'

John Brown, a former gillie, who became 'The Queen's Highland Servant' in 1865, with the Queen's dogs. Brown was loathed by the household almost as much as the Munshi

James Reid, physician-in-ordinary,
and Susan Baring, maid-of-honour,
shortly after they became engaged during
a bicycle ride at Osborne in July 1899.
'Jolly ride home together – so happy',
wrote Reid

Randall Davidson, appointed Dean of Windsor and domestic chaplain to the Queen in 1883. The Queen found him 'singularly pleasing both in appearance and manner, very sympathetic and evidently very intelligent'

The Queen of Sheba, a *tableau vivant* performed on Twelfth Night, 1888. Henry Ponsonby plays Solomon and Princess Beatrice the Queen. The Munshi stands behind Henry

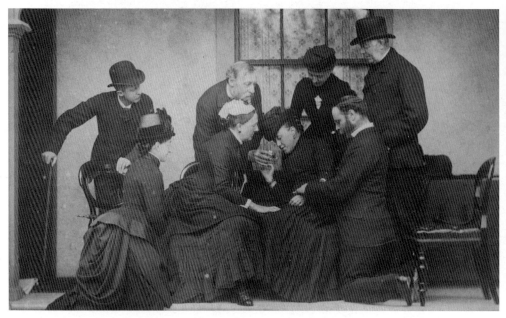

A household mime, 1885. James Reid takes Horatia Stopford's pulse as Henry Ponsonby, Lord Bridport *(standing, right)* and Mlle Norèle *(kneeling, left)* hover anxiously

The Queen in the garden at Osborne, 1898, with children, grandchildren and great grandchildren. The future George V, in a white suit, stands with his hands on the shoulders of the future George VI

Royal dressers and servants. Selina Tuck stands fourth from the left, and Annie Macdonald sits in the centre

The Queen and her youngest daughter, Princess Beatrice. A stolid pair. The Queen gave this photograph to James Reid on her sixty-third birthday in 1882

she remained reluctant to give up her dean, she would not stand in his way. As the Archbishop pointed out, men of Davidson's calibre were rare, and he would make a fine bishop. There then began several months of uncertainty for Davidson, as bishoprics were dangled and withdrawn and his future hung in the balance. Writing to his friend Arthur Bigge, he insisted that he was 'perfectly well satisfied' to stay where he was, and that to leave Windsor would be a 'severe wrench . . . greatly due to the strong links of affection and regard' he had formed with 'many in the Household'. Privately he was less sanguine and looked to the support of Edith, who remained 'characteristically splendidly helpful and strengthening and uplifting'.

In June he took the funeral of one former member of the household, Lady Ely, who had finally resigned the previous year, after the death of her son. This came as something of a relief to the Queen, since Lady Ely had become so enfeebled that she could no longer wield her knife and fork at table and had to have her food cut up for her, which caused comment amongst the household and prompted the Queen to wonder whether she was 'fit' to come to court. She had written to James Reid: would he get Dr Jenner to see Lady Ely and persuade her 'on medical grounds' to have dinner early in her rooms, and thus out of sight? For the Queen, Lady Ely's death meant the severing of yet another link with the past: now only Lady Churchill remained from those pre-1861 years. Jane Ely, wrote Her Majesty in her journal, had been 'absolutely devoted to me . . . she understood all my feelings and likings perhaps more than anyone else'. Since she was at Balmoral, she did not attend the funeral, though she subsequently visited Kensal Green cemetery to lay a wreath.

At Osborne that August, Davidson had a long talk with the Queen, in her tent in the shrubbery. She talked of the Oxford Movement and its leaders, Newman and Pusey, and then moved on to possible candidates for the soon-to-be-vacant bishopric of Winchester, forbearing to mention that she had Davidson in mind for this very position. A month later, when the Davidsons dined with the Ponsonbys in the Norman Tower, Henry revealed that the Queen did indeed wish him for Winchester. However the nomination was not her gift, but her prime minister's, and Lord Salisbury had other ideas.

While admitting Davidson to be extremely able, Salisbury felt he lacked the necessary experience and gravitas, that appointing him to Winchester would look like favouritism and that he was better suited to Rochester. The Queen insisted that she was not motivated by 'personal regard', but rather that she would feel consoled for Davidson's loss if he went to a 'post of real usefulness'. He would be wasted on Rochester, she thought, and besides, she worried that his delicate health would suffer in the foul air of south London. As further ammunition she enlisted the support of Archbishop Benson – would Benson write to Salisbury 'without mentioning' her? But Salisbury had his way and the Queen, despite feeling that her 'personal wishes and convenience' had been disregarded, could only acquiesce.

October saw both the Queen and Davidson in Scotland, the former at Balmoral, where she danced a quadrille with her grandson Prince Albert Victor ('Eddy'), the eldest son of the Prince of Wales, and the latter visiting cousins. On the 13th, as Davidson was about to go out partridge shooting, a letter arrived from Salisbury, offering him the choice of the bishopric of Rochester or Worcester. He accepted Rochester. It was a relief to have his future settled, in the short term at least.

The Queen had a poor opinion of bishops ('I do not like bishops,' she once announced to a lady-in-waiting. 'Oh, but your dear Majesty likes some bishops . . .' 'Yes,' replied Her Majesty, 'I like the man but *not* the bishop!'). 'The Queen must honestly confess,' she told Davidson, 'that She has . . . never found people promoted to the Episcopate remain what they were before. She hopes and thinks this will not be the case with the Dean. Many who preached so well before did no longer as bishops.' Davidson assured her that he would be on his 'guard against any such danger as your Majesty's experience suggests'. Then the Queen insisted that his leaving was subject to conditions: he was to return to preach in the mausoleum at Frogmore once in the summer and again on 14 December, as well as twice a year at Osborne, and, perhaps more importantly, he was to continue to act as a confidant. 'It is a very solemn thing', wrote Davidson with some satisfaction, 'to feel that she is thus dependant on my counsel even after I have gone.'

On 15 March 1891, Davidson preached his last sermon as Dean, and that evening he and Edith dined at the castle. Afterwards the Queen wrote a note 'to say that she had not felt equal to bidding' him 'a regular goodbye' – it would have been 'too painful'. In her eyes Davidson was irreplaceable, and she worried that his successor, Canon Eliot, was a 'v. low Churchman' and a 'terribly dull preacher', to boot, but Eliot was at least 'behind the scenes as to Castle difficulties and complications', as his wife, Mary Pitt, was a former maid-of-honour. Davidson left the Deanery with regret, but it was time to move on. The Queen presented him with a bust of herself, by Edgar Boehm, while from the household he received a 'first rate travelling bag'.

As the Davidsons left for Italy, for a few weeks' holiday before Randall took up his new duties, the Queen set off on her spring jaunt to Grasse, a timely distraction from the loss of her Dean. From the 1880s it had become her habit to take a spring holiday on the Continent, leaving in March and returning some three or four weeks later. She tried Switzerland, Germany and Italy, but her favoured destination became the South of France – Aix-les-Bains, Biarritz and, in later years, Nice. In 1891, for the first and only time, she holidayed in Grasse.

On 23 March, the Queen – travelling as the Countess of Balmoral, a subterfuge that fooled nobody – and her entourage, including Princess Beatrice and Prince Henry, Princess Louise, James Reid, Henry Ponsonby, Arthur Bigge, Lady Churchill, Marie Adeane (maid-of-honour) and a number of servants (Highlanders, Indians, dressers, maids, a French chef and a detective), set off from Windsor in a blizzard. The party numbered thirty-nine in total, on the small side for Her Majesty's Continental holidays, which more usually amounted to around sixty, and sometimes as many as a hundred.

There were a vast number of trunks containing a month's worth of luggage, various articles of furniture from Windsor – the Queen's bed, her desk and armchair – assorted pictures, photographs, mementoes and trinkets, three carriages, a pony chair, a bath chair, ponies, horses and a donkey (the latter had been acquired in Aix-les-Bains and was sometimes used to pull the pony chair). All of which Her Majesty was quite insistent she could not do without. Only the Indians travelled light, their belongings wrapped up and carried in a couple of handkerchiefs. The unloading, on arrival, took a full half-hour. Transporting the Queen, her entourage and baggage, no small undertaking, was managed by E. Dosse, Director of Her Majesty's Continental Journeys.

By the time the royal party reached Portsmouth, where the *Victoria and Albert* awaited, snow had given way to brilliant sunshine and a glassy sea promised a smooth passage to Cherbourg, so smooth in fact that the Queen and her ladies, well wrapped up, sat on deck and Her Majesty had her Hindustani lesson. After a night on the royal yacht, outside Cherbourg, came the next leg of the journey – the train south.

Arrangement of carriages for the royal train

The royal train had been built in Belgium and was kept at the Gare du Nord in Brussels. It consisted of seven coaches, two of which (day and sleeping cars) were the personal property of the Queen. The day car had a small compartment for the Highland servant and a drawing room, a kind of luxurious mobile padded cell, tastefully upholstered in shades of blue and yellow – walls hung with blue and grey silk brocaded in pale yellow, lights set into a padded ceiling, an Indian carpet, a sofa, armchairs and footstools (in the style of Louis XVI) covered in blue silk with yellow fringes and tassels. A short corridor connected to the sleeping car, which was divided into a bedroom, dressing room and a compartment for light luggage, where the maids slept on sofas. The dressing room sported a Japanese motif, with bamboo hung around the walls and a wash-stand covered in dark red morocco leather. In the bedroom were two beds, a larger for the Queen and a smaller for Princess Beatrice, who continued to share her mother's carriage even after her marriage.

The train travelled at 35 m.p.h. during the day and 25 m.p.h. at night and stopped between eight and nine in the morning in order for the Queen to dress. Gentlemen who wanted hot water sent word ahead to the next station. One could dine on Irish stew, from the Windsor kitchens, kept 'tepid' in stone jars wrapped in red flannel, but French meals, at station restaurants, were far better. The journey to Grasse passed without incident, other than one of the Indians accidentally pulling the alarm bell.

In Grasse, the royal party were installed in the Grand Hotel. So as to give the Queen some private space in which to sit and walk, Baroness Alice de Rothschild had made available the grounds of her house, the Villa Victoria. She had gone to some trouble – creating walks, cutting a pony chair road through her woods – and had offered to put up Princess Louise, since there was no room for her in the Grand. Prior to the Queen's arrival there had been some alarm about an outbreak of smallpox in the town, and James Reid vaccinated as many of the royal party as would submit.

As far as Reid was concerned, smallpox was just the beginning. Grasse looked enchanting, with the orange trees in flower and the air scented with violets, but the Queen's stay took on a sickly, not to say funereal, theme. Prince Henry of Battenberg contracted measles, the head chef succumbed to diphtheria, the Queen's housemaid Elizabeth Reynolds became seriously ill with blood poisoning from a needle prick and everyone suffered severe colds. Out of thirty-nine people, twenty-two were ill, and what with nursing Prince Henry day and night, sending the chef off to hospital and performing an operation, aided by a French surgeon, on the housemaid's arm, Reid, with a terrible cold himself, had never been so busy. 'Our party have taken rather a dislike to Grasse in consequence of everyone being ill,' he told his mother, to whom he found time to send flowers. Only the Queen, who was every bit as amused by France as she had been on her very first visit with Charlotte Canning in 1843, remained in high spirits.

While Reid was taken up attending to the sick, Henry Ponsonby – the two of them managed to fit in a trip to Menton – felt similarly harassed. Aside from his usual political correspondence, there was the leaving of cards, the arranging of introductions for those who wished to be presented to the Queen (a few years later, at Cimiez, a 'doubtful Comtesse' gave the Queen an ostrich egg on which she had scrawled her name, 'just as if she had laid it herself', remarked the Queen), and the managing of the foreign press. Complaints and problems, however trivial, all were laid at Henry's door. The sentries and policemen posted around the hotel had nothing better to do than to regale him with lengthy and pointless stories. Alice de Rothschild complained that she didn't like being 'ordered about' by Princess Louise, and Louise complained that Alice wouldn't give her a moment's peace.

Then there were 'ecclesiastical troubles', quarrels between the two canons brought from Windsor, Percy Smith and Erskine Gledge. Furthermore the Queen became 'wrath' when, at the Sunday service in the English church, Smith and Gledge turned to the east, thus facing the altar, while reciting the Creed, rather than standing at its north end. Ponsonby wrote off to Randall Davidson for advice – was this, as the Queen suspected, a dubious piece of ritualism? Davidson wrote back reassuringly, though not entirely accurately – facing eastwards had 'no High Church significance' and was perfectly common.

'Grasse à la Royale is not a toothsome dish,' decided Marie Adeane, the Queen's maid-of-honour. Grasse brought her first taste of royalty abroad, and it was not to her liking. The roses, carnations and mignon-ette that filled her room were certainly lovely, but she worried about catching measles and suffered greatly from boredom and cold. 'The monotony of our lives is awful,' she told Bernard Mallet, her husband-to-be. Even Balmoral seemed preferable.

Marie had become a maid-of-honour in 1887. Intelligent, devout (with a puritanical streak – she was a committed teetotaller and, like Sarah Lyttelton's granddaughter, Lucy, found services at court disap-pointing, paltry affairs) and dutiful, Marie could not entirely stifle rebellious sentiments as she handed Princess Beatrice her paintbrushes, read the *Pall Mall Gazette* to Princess Louise (whom she thought 'ill-natured' and a terrible liar), accompanied Prince Henry as he played on the cello, visited and entertained the myriad Royalties who had descended on the Riviera, and, swathed in furs against the bitter cold and the swirling mistral, drove out with the Queen, returning coated in dust and 'white as a miller'. 'Trotting demurely' behind the pony chair was no better. How she longed to go off for a walk on her own. How she dreaded the task of writing up, for the Queen's memorandum book, descriptions of expeditions, including one to a perfumery, and daily drives – 'absolutely wanting in interest and inci-dent and yet I am expected to supply both in my descriptions and messages arrive from the Q "Why do you not mention the old woman on a mule or the brown goat with a tuft on its head" and I rack my poor brains in vain and feel desperate'.

At the beginning of the year Marie had become engaged to Bernard Mallet, a development the Queen had initially taken well on the understanding that the marriage was not to take place for some time. In Grasse she discovered, from Princess Beatrice, that Marie was actu-ally planning to marry in July, just three months away. This 'raised a storm'. Marie was told that Her Majesty was most 'disappointed' to lose her so soon (four years after her appointment); indeed, 'less reconciled than ever to the prospect'. Much soothing was required from Lady Churchill to bring her round. 'Really', decided Marie, the

Queen was 'very reasonable when you can get at her but the odious practice of doing everything through a third person makes endless difficulties and misunderstandings'.

One afternoon Marie drove with Her Majesty to the cemetery at Cannes to visit and lay wreaths on the tombs of friends. On another she sat and watched the procession for a military funeral (Marie got off lightly – Arthur Bigge was forced to don a uniform and attend a three-hour ceremony). Far from dampening Her Majesty's spirits, 'these melancholy entertainments' had quite the opposite effect; as she told James Reid, she 'never was depressed at a funeral'. Then Elizabeth Reynolds, the housemaid who had been suffering from blood poisoning, died. The Queen had followed the patient's progress closely, making five bedside visits. Now she busied herself with the grave, the inscription and the service.

Victoria was quite as punctilious when it came to the etiquette surrounding the deaths of her servants as those of family. She liked to have a 'last look' at the bodies of those who died in her service, and she held firm views about how those bodies should be treated. When, in 1869, Hall, one of the royal messengers, had died while carrying out his duties in London and been taken to a hospital and examined without the permission of his family, the Queen had written an emotional letter to Thomas Biddulph: the way Hall had been treated had 'produced a very painful impression amongst *all her* servants' and she was 'determined to protect them' from such a '*very unfeeling* practice'. 'The Queen looks on her servants as belonging to her family and as *such* their remains should be treated!'

The circumstances of Hall's death resulted in a memo. If one of the royal servants died in a 'public place', the body was to be taken to the palace, not to a hospital or a workhouse, while if a servant died in the palace the body was not to be moved except for sanitary reasons or at the request of relatives. Always unwilling to pass up the opportunity of a funeral, she assiduously attended those of servants, even ex-servants. One morning at Balmoral, Henry Ponsonby came across a couple of ladies 'dodging' in the woods 'for fear of being

caught by the Royal party who were bent on their mournful mission'
– an ex-housemaid's funeral.

'There are few things the Queen likes better than the arranging of
a funeral,' observed Henry. She was quite determined to do her best
by Elizabeth Reynolds. Having driven past the Grasse public cemetery,
she told James Reid, 'I *cannot bear* the thought that my poor Elizabeth
should be put for two whole *nights* in that *dreary* place out by herself
all alone, so far away.' Rather she wished her to be taken to the English
church nearby, 'but I cannot let her be taken there *tonight*. No, my
whole soul and body revolt against it.' So Elizabeth's coffin remained
in the Grand and a service was performed at ten that evening in the
hotel dining room, attended by the Queen, the suite and the servants
– 'the coffin in our midst not even screwed down, everyone in evening
dress, the servants sobbing; it was too dreadful and got upon my
nerves to such an extent that I never slept all night', wrote Marie
Adeane. At 1.30 in the morning the coffin was taken to the English
church. 'This afternoon we had to visit it again,' complained Marie,
'the final funeral is tomorrow and after that we may hope for a little
peace. Of course I admire the Queen for taking such a lively interest
in her servants, but it is overdone in this sort of way and it is very
trying for the Household.'

There was general rejoicing as the day of departure loomed. For
Henry Ponsonby, the choosing and distribution of presents, and the
giving of orders at the end of the Queen's Continental holidays
presented one final 'bother'. A trunk of gifts – watches and chains,
pins, bracelets, rings, framed photographs, pens and inkstands – was
brought from Windsor, to be handed out to station masters and
porters and hotel staff (details of presents given were recorded in a
'gift book'). Then presents had to be chosen for the entourage. Henry
invariably received 'confits and perfumes', neither of which he liked.
At the end of April the royal party left Grasse. Back at Windsor,
Marie made her farewells, which reduced her to tears – 'the kinder
the Queen was the more I cried'. She left to begin married life with
a cheque for £1,000, a diamond brooch, an Indian shawl and several
royal photographs.

*   *   *

Randall Davidson's holiday in Italy had also been marred by ill health – the usual pains and indigestion. On returning, in April, he was consecrated as Bishop of Rochester and moved into his new Kennington home. A month later, by now extremely ill, he managed to get through his Sunday sermon with the aid of some brandy, but on his way back home in a hansom cab he fainted and was violently sick, not realising, in the dark, that he had vomited blood. When Edith learned, from the servants, that the cabman had discovered blood in his hansom, she secretly hurried off to consult James Reid, who urged Davidson to see a colleague, Dr Thomas Barlow, as soon as possible. Barlow diagnosed a serious duodenal ulcer and prescribed three months in bed and a diet of tripe, Dutch rusks, Benger's Food and milk, supplemented by grapes and peaches sent by the Queen.

Once well enough to be moved from Kennington, Davidson went to stay with the Ponsonbys in the Norman Tower, then to Osborne Cottage, lent by the Queen, and finally to Scotland. The months in bed were not wasted. He was allowed to write letters, flat on his back, and he read voraciously, sometimes taking notes. There was nothing lightweight about his reading material, listed carefully in his diary: biographies of Robert Browning, Laurence Oliphant, Thomas Macaulay and Warren Hastings, Walter Scott's *Journal*, Carlyle's *Past and Present*, Charles Booth's *Life and Labour of the People in London*, Dean Church's *The Oxford Movement*, a history of the American War of Independence, Macaulay's *Essays*, some Plato and Aristotle, Pascal's *Letters*, the Bible, Ibsen's plays and a selection of novels (mainly read aloud by Edith), Hawthorne's *Archibald Malmaison*, *The Last of the Mohicans* and several Walter Scotts. By 14 December, he was fully recovered and taking the memorial service in the mausoleum at Frogmore.

Even after leaving Windsor, Randall Davidson's close relationship with court and Queen remained essentially unchanged. He destroyed 'at her request, though to my chagrin', many 'deeper and more sacred communications' from Her Majesty, though given his tendency to inflate the confidential nature of their relationship, these may have been of rather less import than is implied. He continued to listen and advise as she 'poured forth' on political matters (the impossibility of Gladstone and her disappointment with his successor Lord Rosebery) and 'domestic trials' – quarrelling princesses, her grandchildren's marriages, her grandson, Kaiser Wilhelm II. Her grandson was a particular bugbear. Wilhelm had succeeded his father as German emperor in 1888 and promptly proceeded to incense the Queen by his ill-treatment of his mother, Vicky, his insulting behaviour towards his uncle the Prince of Wales and his rampant Anglophobia. But however grandiose, self-deluding and unstable, Wilhelm had real charisma and charm. Randall Davidson succumbed to the full force of both. He met the Kaiser at Cowes, where he brought his great gleaming yacht, the *Hohenzollern*, every year, and found him 'most agreeable and genial – very odd and opinionative, full of himself and his doings, full of the glory of the German army and navy'.

In 1895, Wilhelm added another offence to his list of crimes with the 'Kruger telegram', sent after the Jameson Raid. Led by Dr Jameson, Administrator of Rhodesia, with the knowledge and support of Cecil Rhodes, prime minister in the Cape, and Joseph Chamberlain, Britain's colonial secretary, this was a shameless attempt (a prelude to the Boer War) to incite revolt against President Kruger's Boer government in the Transvaal. After the raiders were ignominiously defeated by the Boers, the Kaiser sent a telegram to Kruger congratulating him on preserving his 'independence'. As far as Her Majesty was concerned, this was a quite unwarranted act of anti-British aggression. Wilhelm was no longer welcome at Cowes. Nevertheless she retained a soft spot for her first grandson, while he remained quite devoted to 'Grandmama'.

As well as preaching on agreed dates, Davidson returned to officiate at important services. In January 1892 he conducted the funeral of Prince Albert Victor, Duke of Clarence, who had died suddenly of pneumonia (both Davidson and Henry Ponsonby had privately considered 'Eddy', known as 'Collars and Cuffs', a feeble-minded and listless youth). A year later he took part in the marriage ceremony of Eddy's brother the Duke of York (much more suitable king material, thought Davidson) to Albert Victor's former fiancée May of Teck (of whom he also approved as a steady, sensible sort). In 1896 he officiated at the funeral of Prince Henry Battenberg (a very rare occasion when he disappointed the Queen – his sermon too long, his allusions to Prince Henry's death too vague). Acting as chaplain, he sometimes accompanied the Queen on her Continental spring holiday. He made frequent visits to Windsor ('very enjoyable'), advised on household appointments and was consulted, by James Reid and Henry Ponsonby in particular, about household 'bothers'.

CHAPTER 21

Household Bothers

Henry Ponsonby, after many years of overwork, felt more than usually beleaguered during 1894, both personally and professionally. The year began with an appeal from James Reid. In January, on the retirement of Sir William Jenner, Reid officially became senior physician-in-ordinary, though he had effectively been acting as such ever since Jenner's health had broken down in 1889. Reid felt the loss of Jenner's moral support more than anything: 'Your wise counsel and your lofty standard of character . . . have been always in my mind and have helped me through many difficulties and perplexities.' He felt too that his salary, a modest £800, was hardly commensurate with the extent and weight of his responsibilities. Knowing he would get nothing unless he asked, he wrote a long letter to Henry: not only had he had 'the sole care of the Queen's health' for several years, but he was 'daily besieged by people in trouble', not to mention the many 'miscellaneous duties and questions' which fell to his lot; he had 'devoted' and was 'still devoting' the 'best years' of his life to the Queen when he 'should otherwise have been building up a practice for the future'. In the light of which, it seemed entirely reasonable to ask for a rise.

Henry sympathised and took his letter to the Queen, who showed herself amenable. Reid's salary was more than doubled, to £1,700, and, in theory at least, he was 'relieved from . . . the constant applications of the servants' – excepting Her Majesty's personal attendants – who, the Queen agreed, could perfectly well make do with the surgeon apothecaries. 'This is capital,' Reid wrote to his mother, 'and I consider I am now well paid. I hope to be able in future to save at least £1,000 a year; so now you must on no account deny yourself any luxury or any travelling about that you feel you would like, as I can well afford you anything!' Reid was content, but political troubles loomed.

In February, the resignation of Gladstone, who had once again returned to office in 1892, and the appointment of his successor, the enigmatic, neurotic, melancholy Lord Rosebery, meant much delicate and time-consuming negotiation for Henry. At eighty-five, Gladstone was finally showing signs of flagging. His sight and hearing were failing, his behaviour appeared increasingly eccentric and he was losing the support of his colleagues: the Lords had definitively thrown out the Home Rule Bill, upon which Gladstone had staked so much, in 1893. His conversational powers, though, were still formidable. Randall Davidson, encountering him at dinner with the Asquiths, could only listen in amazement as he 'poured forth . . . in unceasing flow' for over two hours on subjects ranging from the opening of the Kiel canal, which he'd witnessed, to Alsace-Lorraine, the new cult of Joan of Arc, Zola, Afghanistan, Cromwell ('overrated'), Charles II ('denounced violently'), reminiscences of his youth, his regret at not having known Melbourne and Walter Scott, and an encounter with Wordsworth (a 'noble specimen of simple peasant-like man' and entirely humourless). On all topics he 'was brilliant, vehement and terrifically in earnest', and he was much amused by the news that the Duke of York's one-year-old baby weighed three stone.

Somewhat bizarrely, Gladstone asked Henry to tell the Queen of his intention to resign provided that she told no one else, a request that, unsurprisingly, was refused. On 27 February, he wrote to Her Majesty formally offering his resignation, and on the following day he went to Buckingham Palace for his last official audience as prime minister. The Queen dwelled at some length on the fog and rain and her forthcoming trip to Italy but could not bring herself to express any regret for the departure of a man who had served as prime minister four times over the last twenty-five years. Gladstone, with uncharacteristic irony, reported her as 'at the highest point of cheerfulness'.

Henry worried about the Queen's refusal to consult Gladstone as to his successor, but since Her Majesty had set her heart on Lord

Rosebery, hitherto Gladstone's foreign secretary, she saw no need for consultation. Rosebery himself, as he explained to Henry, had no designs on the premiership – he was happy where he was, he considered himself unfit for office and he thought it inappropriate for a prime minister to sit in the Lords. The Queen, however, was determined that all should be quickly settled in order that she might set off for her spring holiday in Florence. Her doctors, she claimed, were insisting that she go south, and James Reid was ordered to write to Rosebery to 'urge him to take office as Prime Minister on the grounds of saving the Queen's health'. Reid duly wrote: 'She tells me that you are the *only* man of your party she likes and trusts and that if you do not help in the present crisis, she does not know what she can do as it would worry her beyond measure to have to fall back on anyone else.' Such an appeal was hard to resist.

The day after sending his letter, Reid heard that 'Lord Rosebery accepted office as P.M., being in great measure influenced thereto, as he told Ponsonby, who informed the Queen, by my letter to him yesterday.' But Rosebery, a reluctant politician let alone prime minister, had accepted with a sick heart. In April he wrote wearily to Randall Davidson, who had been due to accompany the Queen to Florence but was once again prostrated after a gastric haemorrhage: 'I am sick to death of the eternal babble and bustle of parliament – such endless parade of work with so little done, of the whole system of politics which amounts to no little more than the outs become the ins. So strong is this feeling that I doubt my being long a minister or even a politician.' After just a year as premier he resigned.

On leaving office, Gladstone paid Henry Ponsonby generous and sincere tribute: 'forgive me for saying you are "to the manner born" and such a combination of tact and temper with Loyalty, intelligence and truth I cannot expect to see again'. This pleased Henry greatly, but smoothing the path of Gladstone's departure had taken its toll and he was further shaken by the unexpected deaths of his younger brother Fred and of Sir John Cowell, master of the household.

Cowell died in his sleep at Osborne in April. Henry had never found him particularly sympathetic, but he felt his loss (so, he thought, did the Queen, though she wasn't admitting it). Cowell had done a difficult job well and Henry was all too aware of the difficulties of replacing him. No one coveted the position of master of the household. Not only did it involve a great deal of time-consuming and tiresome work (arranging accommodation for the Queen's guests, devising *placement* for dinner, writing the Court Circular, tracking down missing dusters), but, crucially, it meant managing the servants, who were determined not to be managed. By the 1890s, the Prince Consort's system had quite broken down; the servants, knowing they could generally count on the support of Her Majesty, had come to regard themselves as autonomous and beyond the authority of the master of the household. Princess Louise told Henry that Cowell, after attempting to make some changes in the kitchens, had been informed by the Queen that he 'had no business to interfere'.

Looking around his colleagues, none seemed suitable to Henry: Alick Yorke was 'not good in shape for Master of the Household', besides being too 'painted' and preoccupied with theatricals; Colonel Carington (an equerry) was married and it was no job for a married man; Colonel Byng (also an equerry) was too 'fussy' and Henry thought he'd row with the servants; Lord Edward Pelham Clinton (groom-in-waiting) was possible but not ideal. It needed to be someone of a certain age, given what 'a lot of patapouffes' dominated the household, as well as someone who wouldn't be frustrated by having to communicate with the Queen through her ladies. When the Queen decamped to Balmoral for the autumn, the post remained vacant.

While Henry worried over household 'bothers', Mary was absorbed by her new friendship with Ethel Smyth, some twenty-five years younger than herself, a composer and future suffragette, and a passionate pursuer of women; Virginia Woolf, another of Ethel's passions, likened her attentions to 'being caught by a giant crab'. Mary had first met Ethel when Edith Davidson (Ethel's sister was married to Randall Davidson's brother, and Ethel was a regular guest at the Deanery) had brought her to tea at the Norman Tower in 1890, at about the same time Mary acquired another female admirer, the writer Vernon Lee. Ethel, hectoring and histrionic but undeniably forceful, was soon making extravagant declarations of love: 'You want to know what hurts me? Well just that you won't kiss me. Love and longing to see you accumulates in me in these long absences and when I see you . . . I want to say nothing but hold you close to me. This you won't have and I can't resign myself.' Ethel convinced herself that 'fire' lurked beneath Mary's cool exterior, but that may simply have been wishful thinking on her part. At any rate Mary seems to have rebuffed her advances, which is not to say that she didn't enjoy them.

It was irksome for Henry, marooned at Balmoral and hearing of nothing but Ethel. 'It is no use. I can't get on without you at all. I have dozens of things to say, but you are folstering [sic] with Ethel Smyth and I have no one to discuss with.' Who, he wanted to know, was this Miss Smyth? 'A celebrated composer . . . daughter of an artillery General, lately an atheist but now goes to early Communion Service on a tricycle,' according to Princess Louise, who did not apparently think much of Ethel – she 'advertises herself and thinks more of her talents than others do', Henry reported with some satisfaction. Ethel suspected, probably correctly, that Henry did not relish her frequent presence at the Norman Tower; he kept her at bay with extreme courtesy.

As the autumn wore on, Henry's humour, his sense of the ridiculous, always his standby, seemed to desert him, and his letters to Mary, now written with a noticeable quaver, grew uncharacteristically repetitive and querulous. The new master of the household had still to be found. Clinton appeared the most suitable candidate, or rather the least unsuitable, but, when offered the position in September, he declined. Henry fretted. Could Clinton be persuaded to change his mind? He had been recently widowed, but James Reid thought that a demanding job might provide exactly the distraction he needed. Henry suspected that he dreaded being ruled by the servants. Finally, urged by Randall Davidson amongst others, Clinton accepted. For Henry this came as a great relief, but when all he longed for was peace at the Norman Tower, he found himself waiting for Clinton to come to Balmoral, as the Queen was insisting that Henry convey to him in person her lengthy list of instructions. He had to endure tedious drives with Her Majesty and three nights in a row of sitting next to the pretty but 'dreadfully dull' Duchess of York. And he was grappling with the logistics of transporting Max Beerbohm Tree's company to Balmoral, since Her Majesty had taken a fancy for some theatricals.

Weary and frustrated, yearning for home, he scribbled a note: 'After the terrible events of this year of Fred and Cowell, I should always be prepared to go, but my grief and pain would be to leave my dear dear wife and my children. Bless and protect my dear dear wife and my children and may they be happy. And my dear Magdalen how [happy] I have always been with you all. But I hope a long time before I go away yet. God bless you all. Henry F. Ponsonby.' This he placed in an envelope, with the instruction that it was only to be opened after his death.

Henry was at Osborne Cottage with Mary and his daughter Maggie when he collapsed on 7 January 1895. Mary sent immediately for James Reid, who confirmed that Henry, at sixty-nine, had suffered a massive stroke. He regained consciousness, but was left semi-paralysed and incoherent, a sad 'wreck' of a fine man, thought Reid, who visited three times a day and was, according to Fritz Ponsonby, quite 'supreme'. Fritz, who had recently been made an equerry, was in waiting at Osborne and the unmarried Maggie lived at home, but the other children – Betty, Johnny and Arthur – were summoned, only to leave again when it became clear that their father might remain in his present state for some time.

To Henry's colleagues his stroke did not come altogether as a surprise – James Reid and Arthur Bigge had both noted signs of something amiss. The Queen too had noticed a deterioration in Henry's handwriting and had thought him not quite himself, uncharacteristically forgetful and confused. According to a possibly apocryphal story, at their last interview Henry observed, 'what a funny little old woman you are'. 'Sir Henry,' replied Her Majesty, 'you cannot be well', and rang the bell. Now the Queen kept away, thinking it 'too painful' to see her private secretary of twenty-five years brought low, though she occasionally drove to Osborne Cottage with Beatrice, and waited for Mary or Maggie to come out and report on the patient.

In February, Fritz told his brother Arthur that Henry became excited when he saw him and he felt that he wanted 'to send some message to the Queen' but couldn't 'quite get it out'.

Henry's stroke was not just a calamity for Mary and the children but for the Queen and the household. Clearly Henry, who had done so much, who had occupied such a pivotal position within the household, who had brought such patience, intelligence, tact and humour to that position, was not going to be able to resume his duties, but nor was he easily replaced. At the Queen's request, Randall Davidson came to Osborne, where he and James Reid held long discussions about Henry's condition and who might take over from him. After some 'delicate' consultations, it was decided to make Arthur Bigge and Fleetwood Edwards, formerly Henry's assistants, acting private secretary and keeper of the privy purse respectively. Bigge was soon complaining to Reid that his job was virtually impossible, since the Queen refused to see him and would only communicate via notes and memos, which simply wasted time. Reid succeeded in persuading her to at least see her private secretary regularly.

Later in the year Reid had reason to consult Davidson on another, equally delicate matter: the alleged 'relations' between Arthur Bigge and Princess Louise, which he had first heard of from Princess Beatrice. 'It was a scandal and something must be done,' she told him. 'Lady Bigge was in despair; she [Louise] had ruined the happiness of others and would his. Prince Henry had seen Bigge drinking Princess Louise's health at the Queen's dinner. She had him in her toils. If the Queen knew all she would not keep Bigge.'

Louise's marriage to the Marquis of Lorne had proved unhappy and childless; the Marquis preferred guardsmen to his wife, and Louise took lovers of her own, including, it was said, Edgar Boehm; she was with him in his studio when he died suddenly in 1890. She was bored, attractive, troublemaking and inclined to flirt. She probably flirted with Arthur Bigge. It may have been no more than that. Bigge came from a middle-class (his father was a Northumbrian parson) and military background. At Woolwich and then in the Royal Artillery he had befriended Louis Napoleon, the Prince Imperial, son of Napoleon III and Eugénie. Together they had served in the Zulu War, and it was Bigge who brought the Prince's body back from Zululand to England after he was speared to death, thus coming to the attention of the Queen, who subsequently appointed him equerry. Bigge possessed intelligence, a fine singing voice much admired by the Queen and (also admired) the refined good looks of a sixteenth-century miniature. Such was his reputation for discretion that he was known as 'Better Not' amongst the household, though in the case of Princess Louise discretion temporarily deserted him.

Randall Davidson, in consultation with the Queen, was dispatched to have a discreet word with Bigge, while Reid administered soothing draughts, over daily teatime visits, to a hysterical Lady Bigge. He also found himself the unwilling confidant of Louise, who enlisted his support, or at least sympathy, in what she saw as a smear campaign, led by Beatrice – she and Princess Christian 'had laid their heads together to ruin her position here and had succeeded'. References to 'long talks' with Louise 'as to all her real and imaginary grievances' crop up in Reid's diary with wearisome regularity. The Bigge scandal receded; hostilities between the princesses did not.

Jealousy lay at their root. Beatrice's allegations about Louise and Bigge were fuelled by her suspicions about Louise and her own husband, Prince Henry. Beatrice, the once charming 'Baby', had solidified into a stolid hausfrau, little loved amongst the household, who variously found her impossibly stiff, impossibly shy, or, less charitably, petty and mean-spirited. Louise and Lorne, with the Queen's tacit agreement, led largely separate lives, and Louise spent much of her time at court. Trapped at court himself and utterly lacking in occupation or amusement, it would hardly have been surprising if Prince Henry had cast admiring looks in the direction of his lively, still youthful-looking sister-in-law.

In December 1895, desperate to escape the confines of court, longing for independence and action, Prince Henry insisted on joining a military expedition to Ashanti on Africa's Gold Coast. This was meant to bring Prempeh, Ashanti's native ruler, who was resisting imperial will, to heel. Just a month later Henry was dead from malaria, a great sorrow for the Queen, who had grown much attached to her genial son-in-law, and a 'very busy and trying time' for James Reid, with 'H.M. crying and sobbing much'. It did not help that Louise promptly announced that '*she* was Liko's confidante and Beatrice nothing to him'. Louise continued to complain to Reid of Beatrice's 'cruel treatment', not to mention the 'unkindness' of Princess Christian, the Queen and some of the ladies, in particular Minnie Cochrane, Beatrice's lady-in-waiting, Harriet Phipps, now a woman of the bedchamber, and Lady Bigge. In 1898, Louise told Reid of 'Prince Henry's attempted relations with her, which she had declined'. Thereafter the 'long talks' ceased.

Henry Ponsonby remained at Osborne. His cognitive powers were unimpaired, he recognised family and friends, and he occasionally spoke, but he was mostly confined to his bed, often restless and sometimes violent. The Queen, who had stopped paying his £1,700 salary as soon as he became ill, reducing it to a £1,000 pension, was happy for the Ponsonbys to remain in Osborne Cottage for as long as Henry lingered on, but wanted to give the Norman Tower to Fleetwood Edwards. She wished too to confirm both Edwards and Arthur Bigge in their posts. This was not unreasonable – nobody expected Henry to recover – but for Mary, who had the painful daily reality of nursing him, it must have been a bitter moment nevertheless. She still had the apartment in St James's Palace, but she was losing her home. In May, she sadly wrote a letter of resignation on her husband's behalf, while Maggie was dispatched to Windsor to pack up the Norman Tower. It would be a 'great pang', Mary confessed to James Reid, to leave after twenty-five happy years.

Mary and Maggie lived in a strange kind of limbo at Osborne. They were greatly cheered, and Henry soothed, by visits from Reid, who, in June, was able to proudly report that he had received a knighthood, a KCB (the Queen, on seeing the top of her doctor's head for the first time, remarked on his baldness), though his obligations to the Queen took him elsewhere. And Fritz, when in waiting at Osborne, was a comforting presence and a link to court.

On his appointment as junior equerry in 1894, Fritz had been struck by how the household had aged with the Queen, not just his own father, but Lord Bridport and General Gardiner (an equerry), both coming up for eighty, Lady Churchill and Lady Erroll, nearing seventy, and the maids-of-honour distinctly long in the tooth. He soon discovered that his duties were pretty much 'nil'. Sometimes he rode alongside the Queen's carriage. Occasionally he deciphered a telegram. The order for a carriage brought a small flurry of activity – the writing of the order in a book, the giving of the book to a footman, the donning of a frock coat and top hat in order to see off whichever Royalty was leaving. But for much of the time he sat in the equerries' room twiddling his thumbs and reading the papers.

Golf and bicycling provided some amusement. Fritz, a keen golfer, played most afternoons on the course at Osborne, to the Queen's bemusement. Did he really like golf? she wondered. Fritz replied in the affirmative. 'It always seems to me such a stupid game,' mused Her Majesty. Whereupon Beatrice chimed in, 'that Mama is because you have never played it'. 'Perhaps that is the reason!' replied her mother. Like his father, Fritz was alive to the absurdity of court life. When the Queen went out in her pony chair at noon, the household

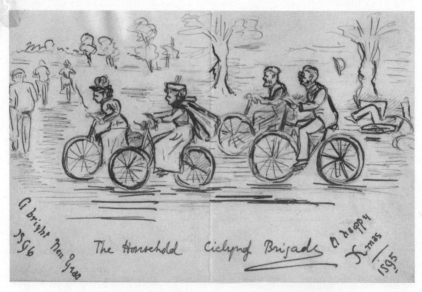

Drawing of the household bicycling, given to James Reid
by a fellow novice cyclist, Christmas 1895

hurried out for their walk, 'but it was like a lunatic asylum as everybody went alone in different directions'. And then it was a 'great crime' to meet the Queen – if she came into view you dived for the bushes.

Fritz was one of the first members of the household to acquire a bicycle, a new 'safety bicycle', vastly improved by a lighter frame, pneumatic tyres, a chain and front gears. By 1895, 'biking' mania had really taken hold and black-clad figures could be seen sallying forth from the Queen's palaces with varying degrees of confidence and steadiness. Bicycling brought freedom of a kind, especially for the ladies. Marie Mallet, formerly Marie Adeane, now back at court as an extra woman of the bedchamber, practised determinedly every day on the Slopes at Windsor, as did Lady Antrim (Louisa Antrim, Charles Grey's daughter, had become a lady of the bedchamber in 1890). Princess Louise cycled, badly. Even Princess Christian took to a tricycle. At Balmoral that autumn, Fritz and Arthur Bigge gave James Reid lessons and all three, together with Louise, set off on ambitious expeditions.

On 25 November 1895, Henry Ponsonby died. During the previous months of nursing the husband who had loved her so selflessly, Mary had sometimes berated herself for failing to match his devotion. Now she sent a brief note to Ethel Smyth: 'The blank of being no longer wanted, the missing of a beautiful smile always greeting me . . . !' James Reid, along with many of the household and servants, took a special train from Windsor to Osborne for the funeral at Whippingham church, conducted by Randall Davidson, who had finally become Bishop of Winchester a few months earlier. Afterwards Reid made a 'painful' visit to Osborne Cottage to see Mary and Maggie, and back at Windsor he relayed all the 'particulars' to the Queen, who had been represented by her son, the Duke of Connaught.

Both household and Queen missed Henry keenly. Arthur Bigge paid tribute to 'the entire effacement of self; the absolute non-existence of conceit, side or pose; the charming courtesy to strangers old, young, high, low, rich, poor. His extraordinary wit and sense of the ridiculous, his enormous powers of work – too much – it killed him.' 'I feel the actual fact of his being really gone very deeply,' the Queen told Vicky (and she could not help remarking on the sad coincidence of Henry dying on Vicky's birthday). And to Mary she wrote: 'He was always so kind and so fair and just that I miss him terribly.' Mary was granted a pension of £800, kept her St James's Palace apartment and became an extra woman of the bedchamber, thus perpetuating her connection to court.

James Reid received a letter from Maggie Ponsonby, full of gratitude for all his kindness and care and giving him her father's pair of scissors, given in turn to him by Lady Churchill. 'He never had many things of his own,' she wrote. 'I never remember his buying a thing for himself and if somebody gave him something nice he generally passed it on to one of us.'

CHAPTER 22

The Year of the Munshi

By 1897, the year of the Diamond Jubilee, Her Majesty's Indian servants, gliding silently about the palaces, had been a fixture at court for ten years. The Queen delighted in eating her breakfast egg – sitting outside, under canvas, weather permitting – served in a gold egg cup, with a brace of Indians, clad in dark blue coats, sashes and white turbans, standing attentively behind her. She took reassurance in having an Indian permanently on hand, proffering an arm to lean on. But with the Indians came Indian dramas. These seemed to positively energise the Queen, as Lord Salisbury shrewdly observed: 'she really likes the emotional excitement as being the only form of excitement she can have'. Not so the household, especially James Reid, who reluctantly found himself sucked into such dramas.

In June 1889, at Balmoral, one of the Queen's brooches disappeared. Rankin, her footman, said he suspected Abdul Karim's brother-in-law, Hourmet Ali, but nobody dared tell the Queen, who blamed her dresser for losing it. In July, Mahomet Buksh told Annie Macdonald and Mrs Tuck (wardrobe maid and dresser respectively) that Hourmet Ali had sold the brooch to Wagland, the Windsor jeweller, for six shillings. In reply to a letter from Mrs Tuck, Wagland returned the brooch, confirming that he had indeed bought it from Hourmet. Mrs Tuck immediately took both brooch and letter to the Queen, who, as Reid recorded, 'at first was much surprised, but immediately became furious with Mrs T and Wagland for insinuating that Hourmet had done or could do anything wrong'. Accusing the Indians of dishonesty was no more acceptable than accusing the servants of drunkenness. '"That is what you English call justice" she shouted, and was dreadfully angry. After a conference with Abdul she told Mrs T that "not a word of it was to be mentioned to Rankin or Miss Dittweiler [her former dresser, now the house-keeper at Balmoral], or a single soul; but that Hourmet was a model of honesty and uprightness and would never dream of stealing anything, that Abdul said that he had picked it up, and that it was an Indian custom to keep anything one found and say nothing about it and that he was only acting up to the customs of his country!!" . . . So the theft, though proved absolutely, was ignored and even made a virtue of for the sake no doubt of Abdul about whom the Queen seems off her head.'

Among his fellow Indians Abdul Karim had quickly risen to prominence. Soon after he first came to court in 1887, as a handsome twenty-four-year-old, the Queen had decided that he was of an alto-gether different class – his father, so she believed, was an army doctor, and Abdul himself had been a clerk (a *munshi*) in India. It was therefore most unsuitable that he should be waiting at table. In 1889, Abdul became the Munshi Hafiz Abdul Karim, with secretarial duties – looking after the Queen's dispatch boxes and looking over petitions from India. On Her Majesty's order, all photographs of him waiting at table were destroyed.

The Queen worked diligently at her daily Hindustani lessons with Abdul (the Munshi's phrase book – 'The tea is always bad at Osborne', 'The egg is not boiled enough', 'You will miss the Munshi very much' – revealing much of both master and pupil). She signed herself, in notes to him, 'Your loving mother'. On learning that his wife was having difficulties in conceiving, she offered advice: she should pay attention to her bowels and 'be careful at the *particular time* every month not to tire herself or to go on rough roads'. James Reid was instructed to find her a lady doctor. Believing that her Indians were especially vulnerable and in need of her protection, the Queen took a maternal interest in their welfare. In 1890, Vicky was regaled with a series of misfortunes: Yussuf Bey had fallen off a tricycle and broken his arm; Karim al Ali had had to return to India as he could not bear the English climate; and the 'good excellent Abdul' had a boil on his neck. 'Poor things, one must feel so much for them, away from all their belongings and dearest and nearest, and they are so touchingly gentle and patient that it is a pleasure to try and do anything for them.' She visited Abdul, bedridden with his boil, several times a day, examining his neck, smoothing his pillows and stroking his hand.

Inevitably, Abdul's promotion led to resentment among the other Indians. When the Queen asked James Reid to find out why Ahmed Hussain was depressed, Ahmed explained that he had become so because of his treatment at the hands of the Munshi. Reid reported as much to the Queen, only to be told that he should have gone straight away to the Munshi with Ahmed's 'complaints and insinuations', that both the Munshi and the Queen were 'deeply hurt' and that the Queen was 'much annoyed' that Reid seemed so ready to believe Ahmed. 'The Queen wishes to repeat in the strongest terms her desire that Dr Reid should *never* allow Ahmed Hussain to complain and speak against the Munshi Hafiz Abdul Karim, who is the *first* . . . He looks after the accounts of all the Indians, orders them clothes and is *the* person, who besides looks after the Queen's boxes, letters, papers. And it has been the Queen's object to wish that the others should look to him for advice and help in every way. Abdul has shown them every reason of pride in his promotion and has always wished to do what the others like and has objected to nothing. But he disapproves with right of any extravagance and likes the Queen's written orders to be strictly *adhered to*. He knows Ahmed Hussain thoroughly and his wish to be the 1st or at least equal in every thing will *not* do . . .'

The resentment of the Munshi's compatriots was as nothing compared to the disgust with which the household regarded his elevation. The Queen's ladies were ordered to call on the Munshi's wife. The gentlemen were told that Her Majesty wished them to dine with him – a proposal they vigorously resisted. While the Queen herself was remarkably free from 'race prejudice' and snobbery, her family and household were not. Indeed, the household, and in particular its more middle-class members, were united against the Munshi, whom they regarded, with some justification, as both morally and socially beyond the pale.

However, the advance of the Munshi seemed inexorable. In 1889, Reid's old room at Osborne (on the second floor of the Main Wing), together with a large adjoining sitting room, which the Queen had 'declined' to give Reid until the previous year and then only 'under conditions and restrictions', was freely given to the Munshi, who already had the use of Arthur Cottage. This, thought Reid, merely proved 'the relative estimation in which Abdul and I are held!' As the Munshi's status rose, so girth and self-importance expanded correspondingly. The Queen, as Henry Ponsonby, with his usual good sense, had observed, had made Abdul a 'gentleman', and as a gentleman he wished to be treated. No one of course was more sensitive as to the Munshi's status than the Munshi himself. His *amour propre* was carefully tended and easily wounded; slights were promptly detected and offence quickly taken. At the theatricals, in which the Indians made regular appearances, in August 1889 at Balmoral (the Queen stayed at the Glassalt Shiel for the first time since John Brown's death, taking Abdul with her), Reid reported how Abdul, now 'a bigger man than ever . . . left the theatre because he was told he could not sit in the same row of chairs with H.M.'s invited guests!'

While at court Henry Ponsonby had not quite been able to summon up the outrage of the rest of the household at the ubiquitous presence of the Munshi. He took, rather, a position of tolerant detachment – Abdul was a tiresome nuisance, but essentially harmless, while Her Majesty's championship was an absurdity, but no more. The Queen, however, had done her best to make him an ally, writing in August 1894: 'Might the Queen ask Sir Henry kindly not to ask Dr Reid anything abt the Munshi's affairs & people . . . as he has not always been very nice, though he has abt illness.' And on Henry's death she wrote to Maggie Ponsonby: 'There is one person who feels your beloved Father's loss more than anyone . . . and that is my good Munshi Abdul Karim. Your dear father was kinder to him than anyone, always befriending him and the loss to him is, as he says, that of "a *second* Father". He could not well go to the funeral tomorrow to his regret, but sends a wreath, and I enclose what he wrote on it as I fear in the multitude of similar wreaths this tribute of gratitude might be overlooked.' Maggie asked James Reid for advice: should she write to 'the Moonshi'? Definitely not, came the answer. 'The wreath,' Reid added tartly, 'was made in the Gardens by H.M.'s special command and she dictated to the Munshi what he was to write on it.'

In early 1894, Reid and Arthur Bigge led a protest, sending a report to the Queen that suggested that the Munshi was fraudulent and not, as he claimed, a doctor's son at all. The Queen was indignant: 'to make out that the poor good Munshi is *low* is really *outrageous* & in a country like England quite out of place . . . She has known 2 Archbishops who were sons respectively of a Butcher & a Grocer . . . Abdul's father saw good & honourable service as a Dr & he [Abdul] feels cut to the heart at being thus spoken of.' To dispel any doubts about the Munshi's origins, she asked Fritz Ponsonby, who, though soon to become an equerry, was still in India on the staff of the viceroy, to visit his father. Fritz's report was damning: the *soi-disant* 'doctor' was actually an apothecary in a jail. This was not what the Queen wanted to hear; she put it down to 'race prejudice' and Fritz was not invited to dinner for a year.

During the Queen's 1894 spring holiday in Florence, Reid drew up a list of offences committed by the Munshi: complaining about the position of his railway carriage; refusing to let his fellow Indians cross the threshold of his carriage; appropriating the bathroom and lavatory intended for Her Majesty's maids; proposing that he drive with the gentlemen; visiting Rome and spending £22; and complaining to Dosse, the courier, that the newspapers took too little notice of him. Hearing of the latter, the Queen dispatched Annie MacDonald to see Dosse and tell him that he was to make sure that the papers mentioned the Munshi more often.

Increasingly Reid found himself embroiled in 'Indian questions', pulled between the Munshi's demands, complaints of 'tyranny' from his fellow Indians, protests from the household, and accusations of injustice from the Queen. Naturally he attended to the Munshi's health, but he did not wish to associate with him on an equal footing, he did not believe him worthy of the trust the Queen placed in him and he was not mollified by the Munshi's attempts to ingratiate himself ('I send two mangoes today in a small parcel for you, which is best fruit in India'). When asked by Abdul to send a vast quantity of drugs to his father in India, Reid demurred: 'I came to the conclusion that I could not take the dangerous responsibility of ordering in my name poisons (which I have calculated are amply sufficient to kill 12,000 or 15,000 full grown men or an enormously larger number of children) for a man I don't know.' The Queen, told of this, merely said that Abdul was not to be annoyed.

In 1897, matters came to a head. By now the Munshi was a regular feature of the Court Circular and his 'exalted position' had become the subject of comment in the press – he travelled, it was said, in a 'semi-regal state', accompanied by a Highland servant, a cat and a canary. The Queen had succeeded in awarding him an honour – the CIE (Companion of the Order of the Indian Empire) – and had been persuaded to take an interest in his friend, Rafiuddin Ahmed, a dubious lawyer associated with the Muslim Patriotic League and suspected (wrongly) of leaking, via the Munshi, the contents of the Queen's dispatch boxes. The Queen had proposed to Lord Salisbury that Rafiuddin Ahmed be given a place in the embassy at Constantinople, since it would be useful to have a 'Moslem', a rather enlightened suggestion firmly scotched by her prime minister. The household, who regarded the Munshi as wholly undeserving of the honours conferred on him, seethed.

In January, Randall Davidson, who took the view that the Queen was quite 'off her head' when it came to Abdul, came to Windsor to discuss (one of many such discussions) the 'Munshi problem' with James Reid. Reid was now treating Abdul for gonorrhoea, as he informed the Queen, who, though shocked, was chiefly concerned that it should not become general knowledge. It in no way altered her determination to take the Munshi to Cimiez, which, by the late 1890s, had become the favoured destination for her spring holiday. This meant he would have to dine with the household, to which the gentlemen greatly objected. They appealed to Harriet Phipps, who was deputed to tell Her Majesty that she must make a choice: either the Munshi was left behind or the gentlemen resigned. This merely resulted in the Queen flying into a rage and sweeping the clutter on her desk – the inkstand and blotting book, the pens and pen wipers and paperweights, the scent bottles and photographs and statuettes and trinkets – on to the floor.

On 11 March, the royal party, including the Battenbergs, the Queen's granddaughter Princess Victoria of Schleswig-Holstein ('Thora'), Lady Antrim (lady of the bedchamber), Arthur Bigge, James Reid, Harriet Phipps, Colonel Carington (equerry) and Arthur Davidson (groom-in-waiting), set out for Cimiez, attended as usual by M. Dosse. After sailing to Cherbourg, they boarded the morning train to Cimiez, arriving at four the following day. Reid, sharing a saloon with Colonel Carington, had a 'capital time'. The Munshi too travelled in comfort in his own saloon. The Queen had had her way, but the household were mutinous. Battle lines had been drawn.

At Cimiez, just above Nice, they were installed in the vast, shining white Hotel Excelsior Regina, with over 300 rooms, all fitted out with electric lighting and lifts (an eight-week stay – the Queen was staying for six – cost 80,000 francs). Having opened just three weeks earlier, it still smelled strongly of paint. The Queen and her entourage occupied eighty rooms (including a private chapel) in the hotel's west wing. Her Majesty's boudoir, reported the English papers, was 'hung with pale blue tapestry with a carpet of saffron hue', while her drawing room, 'rich in maroon hints', displayed a selection of (bad) pictures lent by M. Gambart, an art dealer in Nice. Her private rooms, partly furnished as usual with pieces brought from Windsor, opened out on to a balcony and a conservatory, where she could breakfast, and, for sitting and working on her dispatch boxes in the mornings, she had the use of the garden of the neighbouring Villa Liserb, owned by Victor Cazalet.

But for James Reid, though more than satisfied with his 'excellent quarters' – a bedroom and 'magnificent' sitting room with views across Nice, towards the sea – Cimiez was dominated by Munshi dramas.

No sooner had they arrived than he was summoned by the Prince of Wales, also holidaying on the Riviera along with the Empress Eugénie and the Salisburys, to discuss 'the Munshi and the crisis which the Queen's treatment of, and relations with him is bringing on'. The Prince promised his support 'in any action' the gentlemen decided to take. They had already been put on their mettle by the sudden arrival, uninvited, in Cimiez, of Raffiudin Ahmed. Arthur Bigge had sent him packing.

On 27 March, Prince Louis of Battenberg, Prince Henry's elder brother, who had been roped in as mediator between the Queen and her household (he too thought the Queen quite 'mad' when it came to the Munshi), told Arthur Davidson that Her Majesty wished the gentlemen to 'associate more' with the Munshi. Reid, Arthur Bigge, Arthur Davidson and Colonel Carington, a gang of four, held a conference at which all agreed 'to stand together and to resign if H.M. presses the matter further'. The next day there were further conferences and a talk with Prince Louis, who had been dispatched by the Queen to find out the exact nature of the gentlemen's objections. James Reid, as the only gentleman with regular access to the Queen, as well as the only one prepared to confront her, became the household's designated spokesman. That evening, at 11.30, he went to the Queen and spent an hour telling her everything he knew about the Munshi – that her favoured personal attendant was dishonest, self-seeking and riddled with gonorrhoea.

Some of this sank in. On the 30th, the Queen sent for Reid several times, 'admitting she had been foolish in according to his constant requests for advancement but yet trying to shield him'. Reid told her that he'd been 'questioned as to her sanity'. The 31st brought 'another killing day', with the Queen claiming that her doctor, along with everyone else, 'was in league against the Munshi', and anxious that Reid should tell Prince Louis all he had told her, but that not a word should be breathed to Princess Beatrice or Harriet Phipps. As a mark of his sincerity Reid offered to resign.

By now the Queen, in the face of overwhelming evidence, and feeling herself backed into a corner, was prepared to back down, to an extent, though she still insisted resolutely on the Munshi's essential honesty and the injustice of much that was said against him. On 2 April, 'another stirring day', she 'broke down', admitted 'she had played the fool about the Munshi' and cried. Two days later, at yet another interview, Reid did not mince his words: 'It seems to me that Your Majesty is only thinking of the Munshi's feelings: but that is of infini-tesimal importance compared with the gravity of the situation as regards Your Majesty. As I said to Your Majesty before, there are people in high places, who know Your Majesty well, who say to me that the only charitable explanation that can be given is that Your Majesty is not sane, and that the time will come when to save Your Majesty's memory and reputation it will be necessary for me to come forward and say so.' Overhearing some of this, Annie Macdonald couldn't resist chipping in – 'Your Majesty sits there and hears nothing of what is being said. No one tells you the truth about this.' The Munshi was no more popular amongst the servants, who were subjected to his arrogance and rudeness, than the household.

Then Reid tackled the Munshi himself: 'To be called "Secretary" is perfectly ridiculous; you could not write either an English or an Indian letter that would not disgrace the name of Secretary. You have a double face, one which you show to the Queen and another when you leave her room. The Queen says she finds you humble and "honest" and kind to everybody! What is the reality? The Queen says the other Indians like and respect you. What do they tell me? . . . No one of the Queen's Gentlemen can recognise you in any way whatever . . . The Queen says you tell her you are in great distress and can't sleep or eat and Her Majesty in her great kindness is sorry to hear it. But if you do this again, and try to humbug the Queen, the Q will be told everything about you, and then her pity will be turned to anger when she finds out how you have deceived her and you will only hasten your ruin.' If the Munshi was cowed by this dressing-down, it was not for long.

When not engaged in Munshi battles, Reid was busy attending the Duke of Coburg (formerly the Duke of Edinburgh), who was staying near Cimiez and whose health was steadily failing, thanks to excessive smoking and drinking. As respite he managed the occasional excursion: a walk into Nice; a drive to Monte Carlo with Bigge and Carington for some gambling in the casino, followed by hot chocolate and cream at Rumplemeyer's; a donkey ride up to a deserted village.

As the Cimiez visit drew to an end the Queen sent a memorandum to the gentlemen, both answering and repelling complaints: they were 'not to go on talking about this painful subject either among themselves or with outsiders and not combine with the Household against' the Munshi; while they might not consider him an equal they were to 'treat him with common civility'; Raffiudin Ahmed was not to 'come to the Castle unless specially asked by the Queen'; and since 'the much and absurdly talked of carriage' used by Abdul was exactly the same as that used by the dressers (a hired one) there was to be no further talk.

It was with enormous relief that Reid left Cimiez on the 28th (subsequently the Queen told him, 'I took a dislike to my room at Cimiez from the scenes I had there [with Reid] and from the pain I suffered but I got over it' – there was no acknowledgement of Reid's own sufferings). Back at Windsor, he held talks with Major Dennehy, who was nominally in charge of the Indians, about what privileges were to be stripped from the Munshi. Her Majesty, he thought, seemed generally 'more reasonable but much mortified', though she became 'greatly exercised' about Abdul travelling to London in an ordinary, rather than the royal, train.

Temporarily, however, the Munshi was sidelined by the Diamond Jubilee. The Queen regarded the Jubilee with a good deal of nervousness and some dread. In June 1897 she wrote to Reid, from Balmoral: 'I am feeling tired and somewhat depressed and not as well as usual here in the spring. I don't sleep badly, but I have so much to do, so many questions to answer, that I know no rest.' She hoped that Reid would hurry back from Ellon, as she wanted him to see Annie Macdonald, her wardrobe maid for the past forty-one years, who was unwell. Annie, she complained, was 'in a strange selfish state. She *never* asks after me or if I am well' and she was being most unhelpful towards the dresser, Lizzie Stewart. Her Majesty's much-vaunted consideration for servants operated only so long as she was in no way inconvenienced herself. On the 16th, the Queen travelled south, leaving Annie behind (she died in July).

Given that the Queen was now seventy-eight, the Jubilee programme was somewhat lighter than that of the Golden Jubilee, but nevertheless involved a round of services, receptions, garden parties, banquets, military reviews and parading public schoolboys. At the suggestion of Joseph Chamberlain (the colonial minister), it was decided that the occasion should be a celebration of Imperial Britain – prime ministers and representatives from the Empire were to be invited rather than European Royalties. This pleased Her Majesty, as it meant she did not have to fill her palaces with endless relations and their suites, and she had a perfect excuse not to invite, to his rage and frustration, her grandson the Kaiser.

Randall Davidson was caught up in plans for the Jubilee service, to be held on 22 June at St Paul's, two days after a private thanksgiving service, for the family and household, in St George's. This was complicated by the fact that the Queen was too lame to get out of her carriage, so the service had to be held outside the cathedral, at the west door. In addition Her Majesty, as she told Davidson, had decided views as to what kind of service it should be – 'well under twenty minutes', with the *Te Deum*, to be composed by Sir George Martin, 'simple with no additions or flourishes'. Davidson duly passed this on.

The day of the Jubilee dawned cloudy and grey, but shortly after eleven, as the Queen, in a black silk dress rendered marginally less sombre by panels of grey satin and a bonnet trimmed with white flowers and white aigrette, set out from Buckingham Palace in an open landau, the sun broke through: the proverbial 'Queen's weather'. 'The crowds were quite indescribable,' she recorded in her journal, 'and their enthusiasm really marvellous and deeply touching.' As the procession slowly wound its way towards St Paul's, tears occasionally rolled down the Queen's pendulous cheeks, whereupon the Princess of Wales, sitting opposite her and the most affectionate of her daughters-in-law (more so than her own daughters), leant across to pat her hand.

James Reid, in order to keep a watchful eye on Her Majesty, also rode in the Jubilee procession, in the sixth carriage. He had had his fair share of celebrations, attending the St George's thanksgiving service, a great banquet and a garden party. To his great pleasure and pride, he also received a Jubilee honour: a baronetcy. But Munshi dramas soon resumed.

Abdul had started bullying the Queen, with requests for money and honours. From one of the dressers Reid heard that he'd shouted at her during a 'violent row'. And according to Ahmed Hussain, he'd managed to extract 100,000 rupees from her. Ahmed himself expressed matters succinctly: 'Munshi always wants more and every day ask Queen plenty thing. Queen give him too much and plenty present and too much money. India Rajah very angry Munshi get C.I.E. when Rajah and big Indian man not get, and Munshi very little man like Queen footman and some Queen footman better man. He tell me all Englishmen cross, but he say I fight all and Queen always help me. I tell Munshi much better you quiet. You only 10 year servant, very little man in India, and your father very little doctor, and brother and sister husband very little servant and policemans . . . You better quiet and not always ask Queen and want be big officer.'

When Fritz Ponsonby was promoted to assistant private secretary in July, Reid was sent off with a message – the Queen hoped that Fritz would be 'kind to the poor Munshi . . . would not join the set against him' and would remember that his father, Henry, had always been a friend to him, which simply meant, as Fritz perfectly understood, that he was 'to be a tool for her and the Munshi'. In reply Fritz composed a letter: his views on the Munshi had not changed in the slightest; he would be civil, but it would be impossible 'to associate with him or treat him on any but the most distant terms'. Reid read this to the Queen 'with great emphasis'. She was, he reported, disappointed, but seemed 'resigned . . . as if she had half expected it'. In his new job Fritz was occasionally asked to write up accounts of state occasions, as material for the Queen's journal. After she had reviewed the Colonial troops, in 1897, he wrote, as had been reported in the newspapers, that she had spoken in Hindustani to the Indian regiments. Not true, said the Queen, on being read this by Mrs Grant, one of her ladies – she had spoken in English. Should it be erased? wondered Mrs Grant. 'No,' replied Her Majesty, 'you can leave it, for I could have done so had I wished.'

Resigned she may have been, but defeated she wasn't. 'She evidently knows what he really is but is resolved to stick to him,' wrote Reid after a long talk. A week later he received a sixteen-page letter: the fact that Bagley the footman had not been promoted was absolutely *nothing* to do with the Munshi; it was most 'offensive to me that I sh. always be supposed to be *made* to do things – it is like Miss Cadogan who always thought the other ladies *ruled* me – I will not have that said'. (Ethel Cadogan was a woman of the bedchamber with a reputation as a troublemaker; 'gushing but has points' had been Henry Ponsonby's generous verdict). In a 'stormy interview' Reid begged to differ, informing her that it was generally believed that she was 'entirely under the Munshi's influence'.

At Balmoral that autumn, the Queen continued to worry about 'the shamefully persecuted Munshi'. 'It is *wicked* to listen to idle stories which are distorted and exaggerated,' she wrote to Reid. 'You *must* not allow such stories to be told to you. The poor M. is most deeply hurt at the accusations. It is injurious and ungenerous to a man who is totally different to us and whose life is a very dreary one thanks to the treatment of those whom I will *not* mention but who must be suppressed. I *do* feel indignant.' Reid dismissed her worries – 'judging from his robust appearance and undiminished stoutness I do not think that, although no doubt his feelings may be considerably hurt, he can be worrying so much as YM fears'.

In October a further storm blew up with the publication of a photograph in the *Daily Graphic* showing the Queen sitting at a table, a dog at her feet and the Munshi, looking corpulent and self-important, at her side, handing her papers. It bore the caption, 'The Queen's Life in the Highlands, Her Majesty receiving a lesson in Hindustani from the Munshi Hafiz Abdul Karim C.I.E.'. Reid immediately bicycled off to Ballater to see the photographer, and discovered that the photograph had appeared in the Jubilee number of the *Graphic* on the order of the Munshi. He reported as much to the Queen, who became flustered and upset: Abdul had taken exception to Reid's questioning of the photographer; 'it may produce very painful consequences for me as the Munshi looks on you as his bitter enemy'.

There followed a fourteen-page outpouring: the Queen was 'terribly annoyed and upset' and blamed herself for allowing the publication of the picture: 'I don't know what to do. You don't see this and don't put yourself into that cruel position of doubting a person against whom I personally cannot after 10 years service say to him I disbelieve you and believe others. I feel continually aggrieved at my Gentlemen wishing to spy upon and interfere with one of my people whom I have no personal reason or proof of doubting . . . I am feeling dreadfully nervous. I thought you stood between me and the others and now I feel you also chime in with the rest.' By now the Queen was feeling isolated and embattled, bullied by the Munshi, whose demands she'd come to fear, and browbeaten by her gentlemen. She knew she'd made mistakes, that she should not have allowed the publication of the photograph, but as Abdul's self-appointed champion and defender, she stubbornly refused to abandon him. She advised Reid, though, not to see him, as he was 'so furious against you all'.

Reid worried that he would pay for having made an enemy of Abdul. He was a man of generally equable temperament, but the strain of months of rows, of being buffeted between Queen, Munshi and household, had quite worn him down – he was suffering from painful boils on his neck and a carbuncle on his thigh. After a sleepless night of pain and worry, he got up at five and composed a letter of resignation. In the event this wasn't sent, because the Queen suddenly became 'very gracious and nice'. Rather than resigning, he went to Ellon to recover, leaving Dr Thomas Barlow to take over his duties. At Ellon a letter arrived from Arthur Bigge: 'you have simply become poisoned with Munshiania'. Then another, from Her Majesty, greatly 'distressed' at his becoming ill 'from the worry I caused you the last few months and especially the last week which might all have been prevented but for my senselessness and want of thought'. The Queen, however selfish, demanding and stubborn, could still disarm with a sudden display of humility.

On Reid's return to court, health restored, Munshiania had not entirely abated. One evening in December was taken up with a 'private talk' with Randall Davidson about the Munshi problem, followed by a summons from Princess Louise, who proceeded to air her grievances until midnight. Just before Christmas, he had to tell the Queen how serious was the Munshi's gonorrhoea: 'H.M. was greatly taken aback.' Christmas Day brought a 'stormy' talk before dinner, with the Queen 'quite mad with rage', but Reid stood his 'ground firmly'.

The following year saw further eruptions. In the spring, Lord Salisbury stepped in to prevent the Queen taking Raffiudin Ahmed to Cimiez (the French press, he suggested, might poke fun), though the Munshi, having been left behind himself, much to the satisfaction of the household, turned up anyway. But after 1898, the Munshi largely disappears from James Reid's diary (during 1900 he would literally disappear, spending a year in India, to general relief). Perhaps he learned to keep a low profile; perhaps the household simply resigned themselves to his presence; perhaps the Queen no longer had the energy to fight his battles.

CHAPTER 23

Accommodating Bipps

By the late 1890s, James Reid attended the Queen at least four, and sometimes as many as eight times a day, though his visits were largely to reassure rather than treat, since her health remained essentially robust. Now nearly eighty, she was suffering of course from the inevitable depredations of age: sleepiness, a rheumatic knee (never fully recovered from her fall in 1883), failing eyesight and indigestion. The latter in no way curtailed her appetite. After consuming a substantial tea of two scones, two pieces of toast and a good many biscuits, she regretfully admitted to Lady Lytton (Edith Lytton, a widow, became a lady of the bedchamber in 1895), 'I am afraid I must not have any more.' Tea featured largely in the Queen's day. The order, sent four times a week from the confectionary at Windsor to Balmoral, gives some measure of Her Majesty's penchant for all things sweet: one box of biscuits, one box of drop tablets, one box of pralines, sixteen chocolate sponges, twelve plain sponges, sixteen fondant biscuits, one box of wafers, one and a half dozen flat finger biscuits, one sponge cake, one Princess cake and one rice cake.

The Queen's increasing blindness *was* a problem, making for endless trouble with spectacles, rendering her handwriting – hard to read at the best of times – virtually illegible and preventing her from reading papers and correspondence. This made Fritz Ponsonby's job difficult. As assistant private secretary Fritz spent much of his time ciphering and deciphering and then writing out copies for the Queen, who complained she couldn't read his writing. Using a schoolgirls' copybook, he practised a large, clear hand. He bought special 'boot black' ink and Arthur Bigge invented an ingenious ink-drying device – a copper tray, the size of a letter, which could be heated from beneath by a spirit lamp. This worked for a time, but then came a request to write bigger and blacker. Fritz did so. The Queen objected that the ink came through the paper. He wrote on just one side. This was 'very inconvenient'. He bought thicker paper, which took up too much room. A typewriter might have helped, but Her Majesty disliked typewriters. There was no solution, and increasingly the Queen relied on Beatrice, or her ladies, to read her telegrams, memos and dispatches.

'The result,' as Fritz told his mother in 1898, 'is that the most absurd mistakes occur & the Queen is not even *au courant* with the ordinary topics of the present day. Imagine B [Beatrice] trying to explain the vaccination question or our policy in the east. Bigge or I may write out a long précis of these things but they are often not read to HM as B is in a hurry to develop a photograph or wants to paint a flower for a bazaar.' For the gentlemen of the household, with the exception of James Reid, it was a source of continual frustration that they had no access to the Queen save through her ladies. Marie Mallet reported 'Biggy' as annoyed 'because the Queen had made me read some War Office box to her and he thinks it absurd that military messages should go through the Ladies!'

Marie had returned to court, as an extra woman of the bedchamber, in 1895. This meant leaving her small son Victor for a month at a time, though the Queen, with whom Victor, her godson, was something of a favourite, made a point of inviting him to court. Marie's first waiting, in her new position, took place at Balmoral. Her promotion meant superior quarters: a cramped but comfortable sitting room (sofa, armchair, writing table and the ubiquitous dwarf palm) in addition to her bedroom. But she was struck by how little had changed: 'everything is so exactly the same as when I left five years ago . . . the same plum cake, even the number of biscuits on the plate and their variety, absolutely identical, the same things said and the same done, only some of the old faces gone and a selection of new dogs follow the pony chair'.

Unchanged too was the daily routine: breakfast at 9.45 was followed by desultory chat until 11, when Marie returned to her room to write letters for the messenger. At 12, when the Queen went out, she was free to go for a walk. At 1 she sometimes played duets with or read to Princess Beatrice, or took messages for Her Majesty. She lunched with the household at 2, and afterwards sat in the billiard room drinking coffee and waiting for 'driving orders'. At 4 she drove out, usually with the Queen (manoeuvring Her Majesty into her carriage and supplying the requisite shawls and cloaks and wraps and rugs – 'the white knight's paraphernalia', as the ladies termed it – was no easy matter). After 5 o'clock tea, Marie went back to her room or paid visits to her colleagues. The Queen's dinner was at 9. At 11 Her Majesty left the drawing room and shortly afterwards Marie was summoned to read to her, or take orders, or simply talk, until at least 12.30, when she fled to her bed. There were occasional diversions – bicycling expeditions, a scone-making lesson from the head keeper's wife, a game of 'willing'. But in general, wrote Marie, the 'routine never varies by a hair's breadth, as soon a revolution as to drive in the morning and walk after lunch, and boiled beef on Thursday and "mehlspeise mit ananas" on Friday recur with unfailing regularity'.

Marie's responsibilities were essentially those of a lady-in-waiting, with the addition of secretarial duties – reading the contents of the Queen's dispatch boxes and drafting replies – which she shared with Mrs Grant, also an extra woman of the bedchamber, and secretary-in-chief Harriet Phipps. Harriet occupied a permanent position (with just three weeks' holiday) at court, where her approach was heralded by the rattle of innumerable bracelets hung, with lockets containing the hair of loved ones, a source of occasional irritation to Her Majesty. She was the daughter of Sir Charles Phipps, one-time keeper of the privy purse, and had inherited something of his reverence for royalty. Like her father, too, she was kindly and discreet to a fault.

Harriet had been brought up at Windsor, becoming a maid-of-honour, aged twenty-one, in 1862, and a woman of the bedchamber in 1889. Since she had never married, her existence was entirely bound up with court. Lacking a sense of perspective, she made it her business to encourage and perpetuate the essentially spurious sense of mystery and awe which enveloped the doings of Her Majesty and which frustrated such as Marie, who grumbled that 'mere nothings are shrouded in deep mystery and one never knows what is going to happen till a few minutes before it comes off'. When it came to royal service, Harriet invariably adopted a tone of hushed solemnity. After Marie reported another contretemps with Arthur Bigge – the usual annoyance at only getting messages from Her Majesty through her ladies – Harriet composed a soothing letter. It was of course 'more difficult for men to accept messages and directions from one of us', but Marie should not get 'discouraged but remember you have first to stand on your feet and carry out to the best of your ability the Queen's orders – we are sheets of paper on which H.M. writes words as less trouble than using her pens and we have to convey her words as *a letter* would do – what you would feel free to do with a letter you are free to do with her words – no more'.

Apart from acting as secretary, Harriet was responsible for arranging the ladies' waitings, a position of some power which led to a good deal of bargaining and wrangling. Marie, who, like everyone, was keen to avoid Balmoral, sometimes found herself at loggerheads with Harriet (requiring James Reid's arbitration) over the question of her waitings. So did Ethel Cadogan, though Ethel was known for feuding.

By 1899, Sir James Reid was fifty and bearing the hallmarks of middle age: a receding hairline, a burgeoning paunch, pince-nez glasses. That he'd been able to make his life at court had been greatly eased by bachelorhood; without wife and children he could devote himself entirely to the Queen. Reid was pragmatic and unemotional, a man who kept his feelings in check, which served him well as a doctor, but he was also warm-hearted and companionable, and if he had not actively sought marriage, he was certainly not averse to it. Now, with a baronetcy and a handsome salary, and knowing too that the Queen must be nearing the end of her life, he felt able to take a wife.

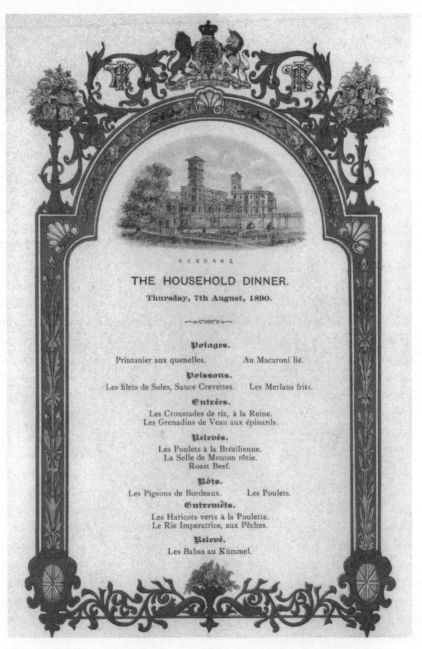

OSBORNE

THE HOUSEHOLD DINNER.

Thursday, 7th August, 1890.

Potages.

Printanier aux quenelles. Au Macaroni lié.

Poissons.

Les filets de Soles, Sauce Crevettes. Les Merlans frits.

Entrées.

Les Croustades de riz, à la Reine.
Les Grenadins de Veau aux épinards.

Relevés.

Les Poulets à la Brézilienne.
La Selle de Mouton rôtie.
Roast Beef.

Rôts.

Les Pigeons de Bordeaux. Les Poulets.

Entremêts.

Les Haricots verts à la Poulette.
Le Riz Imperatrice, aux Pêches.

Relevé.

Les Babas au Kümmel.

Menu for household dinner at Osborne

The first mention in Reid's diary of Susan Baring, a maid-of-honour, who had taken up her appointment in August 1898, comes on 9 December – 'went to tea in Miss Bulteel's room to meet Misses Baring, Ponsonby and Biddulph' (Elizabeth Bulteel was a cousin of Susan's and lady-in-waiting to Beatrice). As the daughter of Lord Revelstoke (also a niece of Mary Ponsonby, and the sister of the writer Maurice Baring), Susan was well connected – indeed, Reid's social superior – and whatever she lacked in the way of beauty and fortune she made up for in intelligence, accomplishments and good humour. When she received a letter from the mistress of the robes, the Duchess of Buccleuch, inviting her to join the royal household, she was studying piano and singing at the Royal College of Music. At twenty-nine, she was the youngest of the far-from-youthful maids-of-honour, and her marriage prospects looked uncertain. Reid's diary charts the progression of their courtship.

Susan was in waiting over Christmas at Osborne. On Christmas Eve the household gathered in the Durbar Room to admire the trees and receive their presents. The Durbar Room, used for receptions and banquets, had been designed by Lockwood Kipling (father of Rudyard), in collaboration with Ram Singh, to resemble the throne room of an Indian raja, and had been completed in 1893 after a good deal of interference from and bickering between Princess Louise and the Queen, who each had their own views about decoration. On Christmas Day, Reid and Susan joined Her Majesty for a Christmas feast in the Council Room: consommé, oysters, sole fillets, fried smelts, lamb cutlets, chine of pork, roast beef, plum pudding, asparagus with hollandaise sauce, mince pies and chocolate eclairs, with baron of beef, boar's head, game pie, woodcock pie and brawn on the side table. After dinner, huge satin boxes of bonbons were handed out and everyone descended on the tree to despoil it of sugar plums and decorations. On 3 January, Susan was in the Durbar Room while the band was practising and Reid asked the bassoon and the cornet to play into his new phonograph (he was the first amongst the household to acquire a phonograph, an early form of gramophone that recorded as well as played sound, and it was an object of some fascination to his colleagues).

In February, Reid called on Miss Baring for tea at her home in West

Halkin Street. Further teatime visits followed, ostensibly for the purpose of treating Susan's maid, who was suffering from phlebitis. In May, Miss Baring came to Reid's room to be weighed. On 22 July, at Osborne, Reid had tea with the ladies – Lady Erroll, Marie Mallet, Misses Lambert, Bauer and Baring – under the spreading cedar tree on the lawn outside the house. The next day he had a 'nice talk' with Miss B in the ladies' drawing room before dinner. On the 24th, he and Miss B went for a bicycle ride. 'Halted to rest by the tree at the foot of the Swiss Cottage and asked her to be my wife which she consented to – jolly ride home together – so happy.' A photograph shows the pair of them, with bicycles and boaters, looking self-conscious and pleased. A day later 'Miss B' had become 'Susan'.

Reid wrote to his mother: 'She is not very pretty, nor has she much money; but she is clever, accomplished and sensible to a degree, and she likes *me* which is the chief point! She does not care for riches or gaiety, and is just the woman to be a real companion to me. We are not to tell anyone here until she goes out of waiting a week or two hence.' Old Mrs Reid was delighted that her only son had finally found himself a wife, as were Susan's family, who did not in the least object to Reid's inferior social status.

Reid could not quite stop himself from telling *anyone* at court. He confided in Randall Davidson, who happened to be visiting Osborne – 'you have no idea how good she is, quite apart from all her cleverness and accomplishments'. The Bishop showed gratifying interest and sympathy and agreed to marry them. And Reid asked his friend Arthur Davidson to be best man. 'Dear old chap,' wrote Arthur, 'you deserve the very best and nicest of wives and I think you have secured one who answers the description!'

How the Queen, or 'Bipps',[5] as Reid and Susan privately referred to her, would react was quite another matter. On 5 August, Reid confided in Harriet Phipps and enlisted her support. Three days later, Harriet broke the news to Her Majesty, by reading out a letter composed by

---

[5] The origin of 'Bipps' is unclear. It was probably coined by Susan, who had the Baring family fondness for neologisms, and possibly derived from 'Vic'.

Reid. When he made his usual evening visit, she was 'gracious' but said nothing at all. She continued to say nothing at all. Reid relied on Harriet to relay developments, which he in turn reported to Susan, who had now gone out of waiting: 'H.M. was very much astonished, and of course she does not quite like it, as she always very much dislikes any of her Gentlemen about her getting married! But she is much less ferocious about it than we expected: and I am quite sure she will be quite reconciled in a day or two. She has told the Princesses today, but no one else knows it yet; and she wishes us to abstain from announcing it, or from telling any of the Household here, for a few days longer, until she has quite digested it, and thought it all out!' Susan longed for the news to be made public. She herself 'was feeling a little more bird [Baring slang for 'happy'] if possible every day'.

While counting her own marriage as the great blessing of her life, Victoria had come to regard a desire to marry on the part of members of her household as a personal affront and betrayal. Spouses, she feared, might extract confidences or make inopportune demands, or simply act as a distraction. This applied to maids-of-honour, who, as Marie Mallet had discovered, received a grudging blessing, but particularly so to the gentlemen: the Queen had no desire to play second fiddle to another woman. When she learned that Fritz Ponsonby wished to marry, she 'at first roared with laughter as if it were a huge joke but afterwards said that she thought it very unnecessary and that she disliked the idea of her Gentlemen marrying, that they were never the same afterwards and that she wd therefore do what she cd to stop it'. Fritz was made to wait for three years, until finally, in 1899, the Queen, after some tactful prompting from Harriet Phipps, granted her permission, though Fritz was firmly told that he was not to have a house. James Reid, whom the Queen regarded as essential to her health and well-being, was a very different case. Having enjoyed the undivided attention of her doctor for nearly twenty years, she was highly disconcerted, indeed outraged, that he should feel the need to seek a wife.

The Queen clung to such control as she could – if she could not actually forbid Reid from marrying, she could at least dictate the terms. She continued to insist that nothing be said of the engagement. Through Harriet Phipps, Reid learned that Susan was to come to Balmoral in September, for her last waiting, when Reid was away on leave, and that they were to marry in November. Harriet counselled patience and Reid initially took the Queen's high-handedness in good part, but became increasingly frustrated. 'Domestique [Harriet Phipps] was defeated last night by Bipps, who said that she and Princess Christian thought it would be soon enough to announce when we left here!! This is quite monstrous, and I told Domestique that I am getting dangerously near "breaking out".'

He appealed to Princess Christian, explaining how he and Susan longed to announce their engagement, and she promised to speak to the Queen. 'It is *ridiculous* to have to submit to be treated as if we were children about all these things which are only *our own* business. So ridiculous indeed that it rather *amuses* as well as *irritates* me!! . . . it is a farce like most things here!' he wrote to Susan in exasperation. And he couldn't resist telling Arthur Bigge, who was delighted and said he'd seen it coming. Lord Rowton, in whom the Queen had confided, and who could be relied upon to do her bidding, came to see Reid and impress upon him the importance, indeed the necessity, for the sake of Her Majesty's health, of not leaving his post. Reid had no intention of leaving; he merely wished to share his happiness and to marry on his own terms.

On 21 August, with the Queen's injunction still in force, the Duchess of York wrote to her husband how Grandmama had told her 'in profound secret' of the engagement – 'she does not approve and did not wish it to be announced . . . Oddly enough when I was driving with Gdmama one day we met these two bicycling and she asked who they were and I told her and she said "Dear me, how odd".' Vicky had been told too, with the Queen betraying typical selfishness, but untypical snobbery: 'I must tell you of a marriage (wh. annoys me vy. much) . . . Sir J Reid!!! And my late M of H Susan Baring! It is incredible. How she cd accept him I cannot understand!' Susan, she went on, accepted that Reid must continue to live at court, 'But it is too tiresome and I can't conceal my annoyance. I have never said a word to her yet. It is a gt. mésalliance for her, but he has money of his own.'

'Domestique quite nice, but full of fuss!' Reid reported to Susan. 'She says Bipps is writing me a paper, laying down all the conditions we have to observe when we are married!' Before leaving for Balmoral, the Queen dictated her 'conditions' to Harriet Phipps: Reid was to continue to live at court, except when on leave; he was to come and see her after breakfast, before luncheon, and before he went out in the afternoon; if he wished to dine out he was to ask permission and be sure to be back by eleven or half past; Susan was not to come to his room at Osborne or Balmoral, though she might occasionally do so at Windsor; 'it is absolutely necessary that they should be fully aware of these conditions so that they cannot complain afterwards'. Susan, fortunately, 'was very much amused by the Dossier', though it ensured that she would scarcely see her husband.

'I wish the shackles that restrain you from telling your friends at Osborne were removed,' wrote Randall Davidson on 22 August. 'I am sure you are wise in not letting H.M. know that I was in the secret. It is far better that she should think that she was the first to know. There is a pathos as well as a comicality in what you tell me as to the conditions she lays down for you!' Finally, on the 24th, nearly three weeks after she had learned of it herself, the Queen consented to the announcement of Reid's engagement. Amongst the household it was greeted with surprise and a good deal of 'jokes and chaff', but universal pleasure. 'I was surrounded and mobbed by everybody and my hand nearly shaken off,' Reid wrote to Susan happily, 'even Miss Bauer is now satisfied! I told her that I had heard that she was shocked at our ongoings, and that we had taken it so much to heart that we felt we must get married, to put it all right! I have to promise to go to the ladies' tea under the cedar tree.'

Congratulations poured in. Mary Ponsonby, Susan's aunt, declared herself delighted: 'of all the golden, supreme characters I know, Susan takes quite the first place'. So did Lord Rosebery: 'I never thought of you as a marrying man but you were too wise not, sooner or later, to embrace the prospect of happiness.' Princess Louise wrote warmly, 'it's the most cheering piece of news I have had for a long time' – and sympathised with Reid's frustration at the Queen's behaviour. Only Arthur Bigge's young daughter Daisy sounded a note of disappointment: 'no doubt it is a blow to me, because although I couldn't marry you I did think that you would still stay single. All the same of course we must try and like Miss Baring.'

The Queen made her first allusion to the marriage on 31 August, as she was about to leave for Balmoral, writing a friendly but stiff congratulatory letter: 'Before leaving Osborne the Queen is anxious to express to Sir James Reid her sincere good wishes for his happiness in his intended marriage with Miss Susan Baring. The Queen cannot deny that she thinks their position will present many difficulties, but she feels sure that they will both do their utmost to lessen as much as possible the unavoidable inconvenience to the Queen and that Sir James will still faithfully devote himself to his duties as in the past.' Reid gave her all possible assurances.

At Balmoral he was kept busy attending Mrs Tuck, the Queen's dresser, who had suffered a nervous breakdown (her second). Earlier in the year Lizzie Stewart had also collapsed with 'nervous exhaustion'; the strain of serving the Queen, and especially being summoned throughout the night, was taking its toll on the dressers. On leave, at Ellon, he was reunited with Susan, who met his family for the first time and acquitted herself 'beautifully'.

Leaving her husband-to-be at Ellon, Susan began her last waiting at Balmoral, with 'fearful curling toes', unsure of the kind of reception she would receive from Her Majesty. In the event her apprehensions proved groundless. Whilst out driving with 'Bipps' and Harriet Phipps, in a closed carriage for once, she read aloud from the newspapers – with some difficulty given the lack of light and the jolting of the carriage – until the Queen, waking from a nap, became positively jocular: 'The Queen laughed when I told her Maggie [Ponsonby] was most amused about my engagement! She said "we were all very much amused! We didn't know he was so dangerous!" That broke the ice and really she was more than nice.' To Susan's cousin Elizabeth Bulteel Her Majesty was rather more explicit: 'I'm afraid I was more than astonished. I was rather *angry*. I did not expect to have my Maid-of-Honour snapped up before my very nose!'

As a wedding present the Queen gave Reid a fine set of silver cutlery and Susan a diamond brooch, an Indian shawl and a signed photograph. On 28 November, a day of warm winter sunshine, James Reid and Susan Baring were married by the Bishop of Winchester in St Paul's, Knightsbridge, in the presence of Princesses Louise, Beatrice and Helena, and many of the household and servants, so many indeed, that the Queen, who remained at Windsor, was heard to ask plaintively, 'And who shall bring me my tea?'

Sir James and Lady Reid spent the first few days of their honeymoon at Taplow Court, the Grenfell family home near Maidenhead, where almost immediately a letter arrived from Her Majesty: she was suffering from indigestion and flatulence; her shoulder was aching; her appetite was poor; and the Boer War, which had begun in October, was making her anxious. In addition, her footman Rankin, returned from Harrogate where he had been dispatched to dry out ('I am getting better but will take a little while yet to get rid of the troublesome affliction a great many has come here yesterday to take the waters please to thank the Queen from me,' he had written to Reid), was drinking again and being 'quarrelsome' and she needed advice. Just as Reid was about to set out for Windsor, a further letter arrived: Rankin was 'really trying to behave himself'; she didn't need him after all.

Returning from his honeymoon, Reid found the Queen much preoc-cupied by the ever-worsening news from South Africa. The Boer War, a wholly inglorious, ugly conflict, was ostensibly provoked by the Boers' refusal to grant basic rights to British 'Uitlanders' (immigrants) in the Transvaal, but had far more to do with British imperialism and greed for gold. The Boers proved unexpectedly fierce and effective adversaries, and by the end of the month, British troops were under siege at Ladysmith, Kimberley and Mafeking, and the casualty lists were steadily mounting. 'Black Week', in December, saw three humili-ating British defeats, and the Queen vilified in the foreign press, the war being as unpopular abroad as it was popular at home. At Windsor, enveloped in fogs so dense that candles were lit at breakfast and carriages were guided down the Long Walk by footmen, conditions outside reflected the mood within.

Reid, expecting to spend Christmas at Osborne, had taken a modest semi-detached house for Susan in East Cowes. But such was the Queen's anxiety about the war that for once she abandoned her usual routine and decided to remain at Windsor, and throw herself into morale-boosting hospital visits, troop reviewing and the sending of tins of chocolate to the men in South Africa. Victoria's world had narrowed through the 1890s; Princess Louise's intrigues, Indian dramas, alcoholic footmen, household theatricals – such absorbed her, not affairs of state. She was quite content to leave the business of government in the safe hands of her smoothly patrician prime minister Lord Salisbury, who never allowed his essential respect for his sovereign (especially as a reliable barometer of middle-class opinion) to stand in his way. However, the Boer War – a wholly righteous war, so she believed, along with most of her subjects – roused her. Her people needed her and she was not going to let them down. Hastily Reid installed Susan in the White Hart Hotel, where he visited her whenever he could and from where she could at least visit him. The Reids spent Christmas Eve with the Bigge family and dined together on Christmas Day at the White Hart, with Reid returning to the castle at eleven p.m. in time to make his final visit of the day to the Queen.

CHAPTER 24

'A last look'

Sir James and Lady Reid saw in the new century at Osborne, with Susan ensconced in the little house in East Cowes and Sir James doing his best to bicycle over to see her twice a day. Occasionally Susan was invited to dine with the Queen, and whenever opportunity arose, she walked to meet Reid at their 'engagement tree', but essentially she was living alone, apart from her new husband. To amuse herself she held tea parties. Later in the year the Reids were given the use of May Cottage, within easy reach of the house, which made life at Osborne a great deal easier.

When Marie Mallet came back into waiting in February, she found thick snow, the house, cold at the best of times, bitterly so, and the Queen 'much older and feebler'. She fell soundly asleep on Marie's shoulder during their afternoon drives; she fell asleep again as Marie read to her in her room after dinner, though she insisted on being woken, by shaking if necessary, which Marie couldn't bring herself to do, resorting instead to paper rustling and fan dropping.

The household shivered and endured a 'gloomy little funereal service' to mark Prince Henry of Battenberg's burial day. Since his burial had taken place a full three years earlier, this seemed to Marie to be honouring the memory of the dead to an excessive degree. But the Queen, if no one else, appeared to enjoy it. She was still capable of enjoyment, and not just of memorial services. Fritz Ponsonby gave her 'a memorandum in which her approval was asked for the Royal Irish Fusiliers to wear a green hackle in their busbies. Instead of "busbies" she read "breeches" and wondered on what portion of these garments a hackle could be worn.' She laughed so much he 'was afraid she would have a fit'. Fritz, who had finally been allowed to marry the previous year, went to see his actress wife performing in a tableau in Cowes, appearing firstly as the Pacific Islands and then as the Virgin Mary. '"Most extraordinary" was the Queen's only remark.'

The talk at Osborne was all of war and the siege of Ladysmith, with the household bemoaning amongst themselves the incompetence of the commander-in-chief Sir Redvers (otherwise known as Reverse) Buller, the war office and the government. The Queen, thought Marie, hid her private misgivings beneath an outward show of confidence. She had the ladies making caps, cholera belts, socks and waistcoats for the troops, while she herself turned out 'khaki comforters as if her bread depended on it'. She wept at the lists of casualties and began to compile an album of photographs of dead officers, until it all became too sad. During one of their late-night tête-à-têtes, Marie aired her moral and religious objections to war, while the Queen insisted that it could be a force for good, a spur to selflessness. Surely, she thought, it could do no harm 'for all those smart idle young men to miss a Season and rough it with the troops'.

In March, back at Windsor, came the news that Ladysmith had been relieved, which left the Queen 'beaming with joy'. She presented Marie's small son Victor, who had been invited for a week's stay, with a splendid box of toy soldiers. For fear of looking unpatriotic, and with the French press full of attacks on Britain, the Queen's spring holiday was abandoned. Instead, with James Reid in attendance, she went to Ireland. This was only the second visit of her reign and partly intended as a mark of gratitude to the bravery of the Irish soldiers in South Africa.

Good news such as the relief of Ladysmith may have brought a smile to the Queen's face, but the Boer War cast a long shadow across 1900: by December, 11,000 British soldiers were dead. 'A horrible year, nothing but sadness and horrors' came the entry in her journal. Her health was letting her down – she was now so lame as to be dependent on a 'wheeling chair' (a man wrote helpfully suggesting that a balloon be attached to Her Majesty, to take the weight off her knees), and her indigestion was worse than ever (hardly surprising, felt Marie, watching the Queen devour a huge chocolate ice cream, followed by several apricots all washed down with iced water). James Reid thought she was simply eating more than she could digest and told her as much, provoking 'a lively discussion . . . as she disagrees in toto with my views!' He had at least persuaded her to try Benger's Food – a powder mixed with milk, something like Complan – but the Queen insisted on treating it as a supplement rather than a substitute, a kind of garnish to be added to her usual hearty helpings of 'roast beef and ices'.

Then in July came the news that the Duke of Coburg had died from throat cancer. To Reid, who had long been treating the Duke for alcoholism, this came as no surprise, but the Queen, who had been quite ignorant of his condition (none of the Duke's family was aware that he had been fed through a tube for two months), was greatly shocked and upset. Reid was in almost constant attendance and Marie struggled to find topics of conversation at ladies' dinners, gratefully alighting on 'the merits of different kinds of tea', at which 'the Queen quite brightened up'. 'Affie' was the third of her children to predecease her and she, if no one else, felt his loss. She knew too that she faced losing a fourth – Vicky had cancer of the spine and at her home, Friedrichshof, was suffering bouts of agonising pain, which she struggled to hide.

At Balmoral, in October, Marie thought the Queen had grown thinner, and noted a 'look of pain and weariness on her face'. She was suffering from insomnia and loss of appetite and her memory, hitherto so sure, was faltering. To add to the roll call of sorrows came the death of her grandson Prince Christian Victor of Schleswig-Holstein (son of Princess Christian), at Pretoria from enteric fever, the first royal casualty of the war. Reid worried – the Queen appeared 'most depressed and cried much'. He worried too about Susan, who was pregnant, having suffered a miscarriage earlier in the year, and was staying at Ellon. 'We remain in the same melancholy state here,' wrote Marie, 'Ladies' Dinner every night, gloomy evenings, silence only broken by the receipt of consoling telegrams in divers tongues and by the replies sent to them.'

For all the dreariness of Balmoral – the silent dinners, the drives in open carriages buffeted and flayed by wind and rain, the mournful expeditions to lay wreaths on the tombs of various Browns – Marie's devotion to the Queen remained undimmed. Late one night in her room, Her Majesty confided how much she loved her Jubilee hymn, saying 'it was all so simple and true', and Marie told her she could never sing it without tears in her eyes, to which the Queen replied, 'I always cry too.' 'This is the most touching thing in the world,' wrote Marie, 'these little Sunday evening talks with the greatest of Queens, who before God is the humblest of women, and it is the greatest privilege to serve her be it ever so feebly.' It was such instances of humility, or vulnerability, or sudden, unexpected acts of consideration – inviting little Victor Mallet to stay at Windsor perhaps – that endeared her to Marie.

She felt quite disgusted with the servants at Balmoral: the Queen's dinner was 'like a badly arranged picnic'; the cooks were a 'disgrace'; and the footmen stank of whisky. Things were no better at Windsor, where Her Majesty returned in early November – the single dish of 'noodles' that she ordered for her dinner was forgotten (the clerk of the kitchen, thought Marie, deserved to be strung up). After dinner, once Her Majesty and the household had retired, the servants and the band routinely descended on the table, to polish off any remaining wine or port. Sensing a loosening of the reins, the servants were growing ever more cavalier.

Lord Edward Pelham Clinton had taken up his post five years earlier fired up for reform, determined to be master of the household in more than name, and to reduce the below-stairs drinking, pilfering and gambling (though he feared, rightly, that the police were 'too well in with the servants to be of any real use'). At the time, Henry Ponsonby had warned him not to try and attempt too much – it would only 'make people cross and appeal to the Queen'. It did. Clinton's hands were tied; it was quite impossible 'to check abuses' unless Her Majesty gave 'him full powers', which she had absolutely no intention of doing; attempts to exert his authority as master of the household were regarded as unwarranted interference; complaints about drunkenness or dishonesty positively resented.

After a week's holiday at Ellon, James Reid returned to Windsor on 10 November. At least he and Susan now had a home of sorts at Windsor, since, prompted by Princess Louise, the Queen had given them the Small Tower (indeed 'very small, but will do' was Reid's verdict), next to Lady Biddulph. And Her Majesty had received the news of Susan's pregnancy with equanimity. But Reid wasn't happy about her: she was 'looking and feeling far from well. Foul tongue, no appetite, digestion very bad, much emaciated, bad night etc'. He spent several nights up with her, administering Dover's powder. 'HM nervous and depressed' comes the regular entry in his diary.

By the end of November she seemed rather better, well enough to review the Canadian contingent from South Africa in the Quadrangle, and to lunch with the officers afterwards, but nevertheless Reid decided to send a report to the Prince of Wales, who, in common with the rest of the Queen's family, seemed unaware of, or unwilling to recognise, her failing health. Her Majesty, wrote Reid, was eating and sleeping better, but both he and his colleague Sir Thomas Barlow, physician extraordinary, believed her to be deteriorating, and they did not think it advisable that she should attempt a holiday abroad the following spring. The Prince of Wales replied, seemingly confident that his mother's 'extraordinary vitality and pluck' would pull her through and suggesting that she see his own doctor, Sir Francis Laking, who Reid did not think highly of.

He found a more receptive listener in Randall Davidson, who came to Windsor for a long talk about the Queen's condition. Davidson had now been Bishop of Winchester for five years, although it had looked, for a moment, as though he might be destined for higher things. In 1896 Archbishop Benson had suddenly dropped dead in Gladstone's pew during morning prayer at Hawarden Church (the very death Gladstone had wished for himself). The Queen had wanted Davidson for the archbishopric, but once again Salisbury objected – such an appointment would be attributed to Her Majesty's partiality, and besides, Davidson was too young and not physically strong enough. Salisbury urged Temple, the Bishop of London, and Salisbury won. But if Davidson had been disappointed (temporarily as it turned out), his health had greatly benefited from living in Farnham Castle with its great park on the edge of Winchester, and drinking in plenty of clean, pure Hampshire air.

On 18 December, Reid accompanied the Queen to Osborne, a journey that left her greatly tired, and with 'a long fit of nerve restlessness and depression'. She still insisted on driving out daily, but she no longer came down to the dining room and remained in her rooms eating invalid meals – egg flip in the mornings before she got up, then broth, warm milk and Benger's Food. On Christmas Eve she managed to get to the Durbar Room for the present-giving, but seemed weak and low, her eyes so bad that she complained of the dimness of the candles and could scarcely see her presents.

Early on Christmas morning Reid was called to Lady Churchill's room, where he found her dead, from heart failure. She had been in the Durbar Room the previous evening, had retired at eleven intending to go to the morning service, had drunk her usual glass of brandy and water in the small hours and had died by the time her maid came to wake her. Reid broke the news to the Queen, who was much upset – Lady Churchill had served as lady of the bedchamber since 1854 – but remained relatively calm. The last forty years had seen a steady crescendo of loss. This was only one further. 'This Christmas has been one of the saddest I ever remember, excepting '61,' she wrote (or rather dictated to Beatrice) on the 27th to Vicky.

'Another year begun and I am feeling so weak and unwell that I enter upon it sadly,' read the Queen's New Year's Day entry in her journal. On 5 January, Sir Francis Laking, the Prince of Wales's doctor, arrived at Osborne to relieve Reid for a week, in theory at least, although since the Queen flatly refused to see Laking and could hardly bear Sir James so much as going home for dinner, Laking's presence provided little in the way of relief. On the 12th, Reid dealt with a drunken piper and noted that Her Majesty seemed 'rather forgetful and childish', though two days later, in what would be her last official duty, she was able to receive Lord Roberts, recently returned from South Africa, where, as commander-in-chief, he and Lord Kitchener had pursued the war with rather more success than Sir Redvers Buller.

On 16 January, Reid saw the Queen in her large, canopied bed for the first time. He was much struck by how tiny and diminished she appeared, and he felt increasingly anxious: the Queen was 'very confused, aphasic and drowsy' and showed definite signs of 'cerebral degeneration'. She stayed in bed until the evening and was then dressed and wheeled into her sitting room. Reid persuaded her to see Laking, who, merely confirming Reid's opinion of his incompetence and Her Majesty's ability to rise to the occasion, judged her 'all right' and quite herself. Having already written privately to Sir Douglas Powell (physician-in-ordinary) telling him to ready himself to come at short notice, Reid asked permission from Princess Beatrice and Princess Christian – the only two of the Queen's children at Osborne – to summon him at once.

In 1898 the Queen had given Reid two memoranda, written in 1875 and so somewhat out of date, with instructions in the event of her serious illness or death: she wished to be attended by none but her own doctors and to be nursed by her 'own *four female* attendants' (the dressers and maids); John Brown, 'whose strength, care, handiness and gentleness make him invaluable at *all* times and most *peculiarly* so in illness', was to be close at hand and was to place her body in its coffin. Brown, of course, was long dead, but in other respects Reid stuck to the letter of Her Majesty's wishes.

On the evening of the 17th, Mrs Tuck telephoned him at May Cottage: the Queen was anxious that he might 'break down' and felt that he must have help, since he was 'the only one' who understood her. Help would have been welcome – Reid rarely managed to spend an evening at May Cottage, or to see Susan, by now several months pregnant, at all – but in actuality the Queen did not want any other doctor. He was grateful, and surprised, when Princess Beatrice 'volunteered' that Susan should come to Osborne as much as she wished, and use the room next to the Council Room, though in fact Susan preferred to keep out of the way. She managed an occasional snatched rendezvous with her husband at the 'bicycle house'.

Reid felt that the time had come to publish something about Her

Majesty's condition in the Court Circular, and he and Bigge jointly drafted a statement. But this did not meet with the approval of the Prince of Wales, who, along with his sisters, and even Harriet Phipps, persisted in believing that the Queen would rally, though all agreed that her spring holiday should be cancelled. When Dr Powell arrived at Osborne, it was decided that in order not to alarm Her Majesty, she should be told that he had principally come to see Reid rather than herself. For the first time on seeing a stranger, she 'did not pull herself together', and Powell agreed with Reid that she had certainly suffered 'cerebral degeneration and that her condition was precarious if not hopeless'.

On the 18th, Reid decided, of his own volition and knowing the Princesses would not approve, to send a telegram to the Kaiser: 'Disquieting symptoms have developed which cause considerable anxiety. This is private. Reid.' Like Randall Davidson, he had become acquainted with the Kaiser during the latter's visits to Cowes, on the *Hohenzollern*, and, also like Davidson, had been dazzled and charmed. He had promised to keep him abreast of 'Grandmama's' health.

Not the least difficult part of Reid's job during these dark January days was negotiating family tensions. Princess Louise, on arriving at Osborne, was immediately 'much down on her sisters'; all three Princesses quarrelled amongst themselves; Helena and Beatrice wanted to discourage the Prince and Princess of Wales from coming to Osborne, unlike Louise, who was close to the Waleses. All the children were united in wishing to keep the Kaiser away; and none of them seemed willing to face the fact that the Queen was dying.

But Reid's primary duty of care, as he never forgot, was to Her Majesty. On the 19th, with the Queen now 'very weak, wandering and incoherent', and directly contradicting reports from Laking and the blindly 'sanguine' Princess Christian, Reid sent a message to the Prince of Wales advising him not to go to Sandringham, but rather to ready himself to come to Osborne at a moment's notice. He arrived that afternoon and agreed to Reid and Powell issuing their first public bulletin: 'The Queen is suffering from great physical prostration accompanied by symptoms that cause anxiety.' Much to the indignation of the Princesses, the Kaiser too was on his way, accompanied by the Duke of Connaught, who had been in Germany. It was too late to stop him.

By the evening the Queen seemed better, clearer and more coherent. She told Reid she thought the Prince of Wales should be made aware of how ill she had been, not realising that he was already in the house. Later she told Mrs Tuck that she wanted everyone to leave the room 'except Sir James', and then, looking him in the face, said '"I should like to live a little longer, as I have still a few things to settle. I have arranged most things but there are still some left and I want to live a little longer". She appealed to me in this pathetic way with great trust as if she thought I could make her live.' The Prince of Wales, clearly thinking he'd been summoned unnecessarily, decided to go back to London to 'intercept' the Kaiser and prevent him from coming to Osborne.

Reid had been sending the Bishop of Winchester reports on the Queen ('very grave but not hopeless'), so Davidson was quite prepared when, on the evening of the 19th, while at Fulham Palace visiting the widow of Mandell Creighton, the Bishop of London, he received a telegram from Arthur Bigge confirming the severity of the Queen's condition. Davidson interpreted this as a summons and promptly set off for Osborne, just managing to catch the last boat to Cowes, along with a great many journalists and telegraph clerks, and a large crowd of 'rather boisterous' footballers. After a rowdy and stormy crossing he got to Cowes at eleven p.m., spent the night in the rectory of St Mary's and the next morning went to Osborne, where he learned that the Queen was a little better. The gentlemen, he thought, seemed greatly 'fagged out' from constant telephoning and telegraphing, and Clinton was grappling with the logistics of accommodating and feeding the numerous Royalties – children, grandchildren and their attendants – who had descended, or were about to descend, on Osborne. The Bishop arranged to stay with the Rev. Clement Smith at Whippingham rectory.

Childlike in her dying, the Queen had become quite dependent on the presence of Sir James. He sat up with her through the nights, administering oxygen to ease her breathing. 'She often smiles when she hears my voice and says she will do "anything I like". The whole thing is most pathetic and rather gives me a lump in the throat,' he wrote to Susan. To make nursing easier – she was quite lost in her great bed – it was decided to move her to a smaller. With Her Majesty shielded from view by a screen, Mr Woodford, the head of works at Osborne, and a couple of his men erected a day bed on wheels, on to which Reid and the maids manoeuvred the Queen. By that evening, the 20th, she was barely conscious; Reid told the Princesses they might see her without causing alarm. She failed to recognise them.

Reid telegraphed Dr Barlow, asking him to come to Osborne the next morning, and advised the Prince of Wales, who was back in London, to return as soon as possible, bringing the Kaiser with him. But he then grew anxious that the Queen might not last the night. At midnight a conference took place in Arthur Bigge's room – Reid, Powell, Bigge, Edwards, Clinton, Ponsonby and Randall Davidson, who had been summoned from Whippingham. Should the Prince of Wales come immediately? They agreed, in the end, that the next morning would be soon enough.

Davidson found a bed and began a letter to Edith from 'one of the most solemn houses I am ever likely to spend time in'. In actuality he was at rather a loose end, with no specific role and not as yet needed by the Queen, but as he hovered about the house, there were plenty of opportunities for conversation. He talked at some length to Princess Thora, who relayed her grandmother's thoughts on illness and death. 'My dear,' the Queen had told her, 'do you know I sometimes feel that when I die I shall be a little, just a little, nervous about meeting Grandpapa for I have taken to doing a good many things that he wd not quite approve of.' The Bishop felt he had been right to come: 'I should never have forgiven myself if when they wanted me at the close I had been far away and I do think my talks this afternoon were of some good.' Having always prided himself on the position of trust he occupied at court, he was not going to miss out on 'the close'.

But by the next morning the Queen had rallied, and was able to speak and to swallow more easily. Dr Barlow arrived and saw her, with Reid and Powell. She suddenly asked for her little dog Turi (a white Spitz from Florence), who happened to be out for a walk, but was subsequently brought to her and put on her bed, where she patted him. In the afternoon the Prince of Wales, the Kaiser, the Duke of Connaught and the Duke of York arrived and Reid took each of them into her room, to gaze at her small white sleeping form from the foot of the bed (the Queen's eyes were now so bad that even if awake she would not have recognised them). He promised the Kaiser that he would do his best to arrange for him to see the Queen alone, as he longed to. In the evening the Prince of Wales saw, and this time spoke to, his mother again.

After dinner, the Bishop, the Kaiser and the Duke of Connaught discussed what would happen in the eventuality of the Queen surviving 'with just a bare modicum of life' (Davidson couldn't but feel that in such circumstances it would be better if she didn't survive). The Kaiser – 'a striking fellow, let people say what they will' – loved to talk and the Bishop loved to listen. For all the bombast and bluster, Wilhelm could be disarmingly direct and genial. He was 'full of the terribleness of a life that is no real life' and 'poured forth (really rather eloquently though too much *ex cathedra*) his views as to what a splendid life hers had been'.

Writing to Edith before he went to bed, Davidson reported that the Kaiser was being 'as nice on this occasion as anybody could be . . . reiterating to the whole family that he is here as the Queen's grandson and not as Emperor and will do just what they would like him to do'. To general surprise the Kaiser was indeed conducting himself with wholly uncharacteristic restraint and sensitivity, hoping to see his grandmother before she died but (loudly) reiterating his desire to be as unobtrusive as possible and not to press his claims. So close to death, Davidson's thoughts turned to love: 'I love you very much and in the 23rd year of its reign it glows even hotter than it did in the first,' he told Edith.

That night the Bishop stayed close by, at Kent House, and Arthur

Bigge and Fritz Ponsonby decided that one of them should sit up, keeping vigil. Ponsonby took the first watch, and as he sat in his armchair in the deep chill and silence of the night, with only himself and 'a few policemen' awake, and Reid and the nurse tending Her Majesty as she struggled for breath, he 'thought of all the people crowded into Osborne House and what the Queen's death would mean to them'. At six a.m. he was relieved by Bigge.

At eight, on the morning of the 22nd, Davidson was summoned from Kent House. It looked as though the Queen was dying. In her room the family, some half-dressed, stood around her bed, calling out their names (pointedly omitting that of the Kaiser), while Reid administered oxygen and the Bishop said prayers. Then, to the amazement of the doctors, she rallied once more, and Reid sent the family away. For a few hours she was left alone, mostly sleeping, watched by the nurse and the maids, with Reid checking her regularly, and some of the gentlemen stealing in for a look. At noon, with the permission of the Prince of Wales, Reid took the Kaiser to see his grandmother, and left them alone for five minutes. 'The Emperor is very kind,' she murmured afterwards.

At three o'clock, as the Queen began to fade, Reid called the family back (the Duchess of York, the Connaught children, the Duke of Argyll and Prince and Princess Louis of Battenberg had arrived earlier in the day). They passed in and out of the Queen's room, while Randall Davidson and Clement Smith, who had been summoned from their late lunch, intoned prayers and hymns, until Reid, finding this oppressive and 'painful', asked the Prince of Wales if the prayers could be stopped until the Queen was actually dying. Davidson and Smith withdrew and waited in the Prince Consort's dressing room, where the Bishop chatted to the Kaiser, who was, as usual, 'full of touching loyalty to Grandmama', repeatedly insisting, 'My proper place now is here; I could not be away.'

The final bulletin went out at four: 'The Queen is slowly sinking.' For the last hour Reid and the Kaiser knelt on either side of the bed, supporting the Queen, while her children and grandchildren stood or knelt about the room. She frequently looked at her doctor, murmuring,

'Sir James' and 'I'm very ill.' 'Your Majesty will soon be better,' he replied each time. At six, Reid saw the end was near and the family crowded into the room, taking it in turns to step forward and say farewell. At 6.25, Powell called in Davidson and he began to pray. At 6.30, the Queen died in the arms of Reid and the Kaiser. Davidson discreetly withdrew and hurried off to the equerries' room to break the news, while members of the family shook hands with Reid – a silent squeeze from the Kaiser – and thanked him.

After dinner Reid helped the maids and the nurse arrange the Queen's body and lift it back on to her usual bed. Only now, when he examined her body for the first time in the twenty years he'd attended her as doctor, did he realise she had a prolapsed uterus and a ventral hernia. That night, at 10.15, Davidson conducted a service in the Queen's bedroom, where she lay covered in white lace, the bed strewn with flowers, the little silver crucifix that had hung over her bed in her hand. For the Bishop it had been 'an overwhelmingly interesting and pathetic day'.

The next day Susan Reid went to see the Queen's body. She found 'her face like a lovely marble statue, no sign of illness or age and she still looked "the Queen", her wedding veil over her face and a few loose flowers on her bed – all so simple and grand. I shall never forget it!' 'I feel a shattered woman and here the blank and emptiness are impossible to realise,' she wrote to Mary Ponsonby, now living in her new home near Ascot. She added that according to her husband, 'of all the family the two that showed real true human feeling were the Kaiser and the Princess of Wales'. In the afternoon the servants and the Osborne tenants were allowed to pass through the Queen's room.

Just as her family had struggled to accept that she was dying, so, for her subjects, life without Victoria, that 'sustaining symbol' as Henry James called her, seemed scarcely imaginable. Amid a rapidly changing world the Queen had stood fixed, immutable and dependable. Mary Ponsonby told Ethel Smyth that 'Apart from the grief, which is one of the greatest sorrows of my life, everything being changed makes me at times doubt my own individuality.' Coming from Mary, whose sense of self was so sure, that says a great deal about the Queen's capacity to determine and define the lives of others. At Osborne, Reid was too busy to think much of the future, but many among the household felt disorientated and uncertain. They were formally received by the new King, Edward VII, and kissed his hand (Alexandra refused to be acknowledged as Queen, or to allow her hand to be kissed, until after the funeral), and, for the moment, were told to carry on with their duties as usual. But none knew what their futures held: the King would appoint his own household; some would retain their positions; many would not.

There was confusion and uncertainty about practicalities too. So long had it been since the death of a monarch that no one could remember what the official protocol was. Fritz Ponsonby, who had been put in charge of funeral arrangements by the King, frantically looked up records of the procedure followed on the deaths of George IV and William IV. The coffin at least was in hand: Reid had been asked to write to Lord Clarendon, the lord chamberlain, to order the wooden 'shell' from Banting's undertakers in London and have it brought to Osborne within thirty-six hours.

On the 24th, the man from Banting's arrived without the shell, explaining that this was merely a preliminary visit, to measure up the body. Reid consulted the Kaiser: they couldn't wait for Banting's; the coffin would have to be made locally, in Cowes. With the Kaiser firmly quashing the objections of the Banting's man, he and Reid went to the Queen's room to take the necessary measurements, where they were joined, somewhat to Reid's irritation (and greatly to the Kaiser's – 'If I were dead and my pastor came in the room like that he would be hauled out by the neck and shot in the Courtyard!'), by Randall Davidson, who 'seemed to think he ought to be there and who made himself prominent in giving directions'. That afternoon the Bishop held a communion service in the Queen's room, in the presence of many Royalties, Reid, Harriet Phipps and the dressers. Later Reid helped Mrs Tuck and the nurse to dress the Queen in a white satin dressing gown and the Order of the Garter, and to cut off some of her hair.

Given the Queen's enthusiasm for arranging funerals, it was no surprise to discover that she had left precise instructions as to her own (military, no lying in state, and purple and white rather than black). There were instructions too as to what objects she wished to accompany her into her coffin, 'some of which none of the family were to see'. On the 25th, with the shell arrived from Mr Marvin, the Cowes undertaker, and after seeing the Duke of York, who was suffering from fever (which developed into measles), Reid, together with Mrs Tuck and Miss Stewart, performed his last service for Her Majesty.

From an envelope labelled 'Instructions for my Dressers to be opened directly after my death and to be always taken about and kept by the one who may be travelling with me', dated 9 December 1897, Mrs Tuck produced a list written out, legibly, by Harriet Phipps. It included a number of rings, to be placed on the Queen's fingers – her wedding ring, gifts from Albert and the children and the plain gold wedding ring that had belonged to John Brown's mother and that she had worn since his death; various lockets, containing the hair of Albert, of Stockmar, of Augusta Stanley; photographs of Albert and the children and one of Brown, together with some of his hair; a cast of 'my beloved Husband's hand'; a cloak belonging to Albert, embroidered by Princess Alice; one of Albert's handkerchiefs; one of Brown's and 'some souvenir of my faithful wardrobe maid Annie MacDonald' (Annie had died shortly before these instructions were written and was clearly on the Queen's mind). The clutter that crowded the Queen's rooms was to surround her in death, but not just any clutter; these were all objects very 'dear' to her, mementoes of the dead, talismans of those she had loved, of those who had served her.

Over the layer of charcoal on the floor of the Queen's coffin, Reid carefully placed the cloak, handkerchiefs, plaster cast, photographs, lockets, bracelets and a sprig of heather from Balmoral. On top of these, hiding them from view, he laid a quilted cushion. Then the King, the Kaiser, the Duke of Connaught and Prince Arthur of Connaught came in, with Woodford and his men, and, together with Reid and the dressers, placed straps under the Queen's body and lifted her (Reid and Mrs Tuck holding her head) into the coffin. When the Royalties had left, Reid and the dressers rearranged the Queen's dressing gown, veil and lace, Reid packed the sides of the coffin with bags of charcoal, and finally, just as the Queen had wished, but respecting the feelings of her family, he put the photograph of John Brown and a lock of his hair, inside a small case worked in silk by Annie MacDonald, in Her Majesty's left hand, discreetly wrapping them in tissue paper and covering them with Queen Alexandra's flowers. 'And my duties were over with the Queen after twenty years' service!'

Before the coffin was closed, the royal ladies came in for a 'last look', followed by Harriet Phipps and some of the gentlemen – Clinton, Edwards, Bigge, Carington and Ponsonby. Lastly, knowing the Queen would have wished it, the King sent for the Munshi. When all had left, in the presence of the King, the Kaiser, the Duke of Connaught, Prince Arthur, the Duke of Coburg and Reid, Woodford and his men screwed down the lid of the coffin. Covered in a white satin pall, it was carried downstairs by a party of Bluejackets from the royal yacht to the dining room, which had been converted into a temporary chapel.

This had given rise to some disagreement: Randall Davidson had felt that the dining room was insufficiently religious and that the family portraits should be removed; the Princesses had objected. As a compromise, part of the room was curtained off and the walls, and offending portraits, were covered with crimson drapes, rushed down from London. On these were hung religious paintings from elsewhere in the house and, at the suggestion of the Kaiser (who later claimed it as a memento), a great Union Jack. And there lay the coffin, no bigger than a child's, covered with the coronation robes, and with the Queen's small diamond crown sitting on a cushion above her head, guarded day and night by four Grenadiers, the air heavy with the scent of tuberoses and gardenias.

Lady Lytton had been due to come back into waiting the day the Queen died, but, since there was not a bed to be had in the house, had held off until the 30th, when she received a summons from Harriet Phipps. She was, wrote Harriet, to 'have the very great privilege of attending our most beloved Queen on her last journey'. As far as dress went, 'orders' were 'difficult to obtain', but Harriet had provided herself with a dress of black cashmere with a 'deep band of crape on the skirt and deep crape on the bodice, white lawn collars and cuffs, a crape bonnet with a long crape veil at the back nearly to the ground and of course a deep veil over the face'. 'I write all this just from *me* to *you*, dearest,' Harriet finished, at her most solemn and confidential.

The Queen made her 'last journey' on 1 February, a fine, still day after days of storms and darkness. At 1.30 a gun carriage bearing the coffin passed slowly down the hill from Osborne to Trinity Pier, followed by Davidson, Reid (in full court dress) and the rest of the household. The coffin was placed on the deck of the *Alberta*, the smallest of the royal yachts, accompanied by Edith Lytton and Harriet Phipps, while the rest of the household and the Royalties followed in the *Victoria and Albert*, with the Kaiser in the *Hohenzollern*. The sight of the yachts steaming across the glassy sea to Portsmouth was one the Bishop would never forget: 'a quite calm sea, the very slow motion of the vessels, which made them seem to glide without visible propelling power, the little Alberta going first (with the coffin on deck) through the broad avenue of towering battle-ships booming out their salutes on either side, the enormous mass of perfectly silent black-clothed crowds covering Southsea Common and the beach; and then the Alberta gliding silently out of sight into Clarence Yard just as the sun set and the gloom of evening fell. I do not envy the man who could pass through such a scene dry-eyed . . .' James Reid for one found his eyes dimming.

The following morning the coffin was carried by train from Portsmouth to Victoria station – Edith Lytton, peering out from behind the blinds, saw people kneeling all along the tracks – and then, on a gun carriage pulled by eight white horses, to Paddington. Reid walked – a slow two hours – alongside the carriage, past vast, silent crowds, through streets festooned in purple cashmere, and white satin bows and laurel wreaths, hanging from lampposts, soundless save for the rumble of wheels, the hollow clip of hooves and the jingle of swords. At Windsor station a small hiccup occurred when one of the horses took fright and broke its traces, and at the suggestion of Fritz Ponsonby, a party of Bluejackets stepped in and dragged the carriage on its last leg to St George's. It rolled down the Long Walk to the sound of cannon firing a salute of eighty-one guns, one for each year of the Queen's life. During the funeral service Reid stood beside the coffin (an honour conferred on no previous doctor). 'My last journey with Bipps is over,' he told Susan, 'and I feel rather sad.'

It was not quite over. On 4 February, Reid took part in 'the last act of the drama', when the Queen was finally reunited with the Prince Consort. Her coffin, with Royalties and household following on foot, processed from the Albert Memorial Chapel to the mausoleum at Frogmore. The burial service, remembered Randall Davidson, was 'touching beyond words'. After the blessing, it had been arranged that the royal family would pass across a platform, looking down into the grave with its two coffins lying side by side. 'The King came first alone, but, instead of simply walking by, he knelt down by the grave. Then the Queen followed, leading the little Prince Edward [the future Edward VIII] by the hand. She knelt down, but the little boy was frightened and the King took him gently and made him kneel beside him, and the three, in perfect silence, were there together – a sight not to be forgotten. Then they passed on, and the Emperor came and knelt likewise, and so in turn all the rest of the Royal Family, in a continuous string. Then the Household . . .' As the mourners emerged from the mausoleum, fine sleet was falling. By the time the Bishop reached Bagshot, to catch his train to Farnham, snow lay thick on the ground.

Postscript: After Victoria

A new reign brought a new regime, and court under Edward VII was a very different place, both tightened up, in terms of efficiency, and relaxed, with free-range smoking and a general brightening, lightening and decluttering. Some amongst the old Queen's household retained their positions. Arthur Bigge (created Lord Stamfordham in 1911) and Fritz Ponsonby saw a further two reigns come and go, with Bigge becoming private secretary to the Duke of York, the Queen's grandson, serving him both as Prince of Wales and as King George V, and Ponsonby remaining assistant private secretary and assistant keeper of the privy purse to both Edward VII and George V. Lady Lytton and Lady Antrim became ladies-in-waiting to Queen Alexandra, Harriet Phipps left court, and Marie Mallet returned to her family, but occasionally acted as a temporary lady-in-waiting to Princesses Christian or Beatrice. On the orders of Edward VII, all the Queen's letters to the Munshi were burned; the Munshi himself and his compatriots were packed off back to India.

The Queen's death left James Reid feeling adrift, his connection to court much diminished, though by no means lost. Edward VII had no resident physician and retained Francis Laking as his personal doctor, but Reid was kept on as a physician-in-ordinary, with a consulting role, and was granted an annual pension of £1,000. He still needed a home – he was about to become a father – and an income. In April 1901, Susan gave birth to a son, the first of three children, to whom the King offered himself as godfather. The Reids set up home in Grosvenor Street and

Reid began to build up a practice, beginning with Susan's numerous relations, though money remained short. In 1903, when Osborne was turned into a convalescent home, he became a consultant. Occasionally he was invited to Balmoral, in his capacity as doctor, or accompanied the King on his spring visits to Biarritz. He attended the dying Edward in 1910 and was appointed physician-in-ordinary to George V. Sir James Reid died in 1923, aged seventy-three, from heart failure.

Shortly after the Queen's death, Edmund Gosse approached Mary Ponsonby on behalf of John Murray, the publisher of *The Quarterly Review* – would she write a piece about Victoria? Mary demurred, but agreed to a collaboration: Gosse was to write the article using Mary's notes. 'The Character of Queen Victoria' was published anonymously in April 1901 and met with a good deal of indignation for falling short of out-and-out hagiography. In fact the criticisms are mild enough: the Queen was stubborn, shy, a poor judge of art and tyrannical in minor matters such as time-keeping and domestic arrangements; 'her originality lay in her very lack of originality, in the absence of salient eccentricity'; she disliked extremes especially when it came to religion. And they are more than balanced by tributes to such qualities as 'shrewdness, simplicity and sympathy'. The King, however, was greatly put out and asked Mary, through Fritz, if she was the author, which she denied, as was technically true. One suspects that she rather enjoyed the subterfuge and speculation. Mary continued to divide her time between her home near Ascot and her apartment in St James's. She was occasionally troubled by money worries but retained all her spirit. She died in 1916.

In 1901, Randall Davidson was urged, by Lord Salisbury and Archbishop Temple amongst others, to accept the bishopric of London – Mandell Creighton had died just a week before the Queen – but his doctor, Sir Thomas Barlow, was adamant that his health would suffer and Davidson remained at Winchester. In 1903, however, on the death of Temple, all Davidson's ambitions were realised and he became Archbishop of Canterbury. He resigned, reluctantly, in 1928, aged eighty, but did not take easily to retirement and died two years later. The last time he left his Cheyne Walk house was for dinner with Arthur Bigge.

Notes

Notes on sources:

Much of this book is based on letters and diaries in the following private archives: the Lyttelton papers at Hagley Hall (HH), the Canning papers at Harewood House (Harewood), the Ponsonby papers at Shulbrede Priory (SP), and the Reid papers at Lanton Tower (LT). Henry Ponsonby's letters to his wife Mary, as well as correspondence between Queen Victoria and her household, are held at the Royal Archives, Windsor (RA) and Randall Davidson's papers are at Lambeth Palace Library (LPL). I have also consulted material in the British Library (BL).

Introduction

1   'You must accustom': Georgiana Baroness Bloomfield, *Reminiscences of Court and Diplomatic Life*, 1883, p.22.
6   'the swaddling bandages': Anthony Trollope, *The Prime Minister*, 1876, p.58.

Chapter 1: Windsor 1838

Unless stated otherwise, all quotations from Sarah Lyttelton's letters are taken from *Correspondence of Sarah Spencer Lady Lyttelton 1787–1870*, Hon. Mrs Hugh Wyndham (ed.), 1912.

9 'long winding staircase': Sarah Lyttelton, quoted in Betty Askwith, *The Lytteltons*, 1975, p.64.

10 'She is at an age': Thomas Carlyle, quoted in Giles St Aubyn, *Queen Victoria*, 1991, p.63.

11 walked along the Corridor: Description of the Corridor at Windsor taken from *The Private Life of the Queen, by One of Her Majesty's Servants*, 1898.

11 'a very nice girl': Queen Victoria, quoted in Vera Watson, *A Queen at Home*, 1952, p.17.

14 The Queen's dinner: RA MRH/MRHF/MENUS/WC/1838: Oct.

14 'the great difficulty': Lytton Strachey and Roger Fulford (eds.), *The Greville Memoirs*, 1938, vol. 4, p.383.

15 'nothing but another meal': ibid., p.108.

15 'Have you been riding': ibid., p.41.

15 comfort of her room: Description of the furnishings in a lady-in-waiting's bedroom taken from the Windsor Inventory, 1866, Windsor Castle.

16 'it is a kind of duty': Sarah Lyttelton to Caroline Lyttelton, July 1843, Lyttelton Papers, Hagley Hall.

16 'I know very well': SL, quoted in Askwith, p.80.

17 'I know she likes': quoted in Wyndham, p.xiii.

17 'What happiness': SL, quoted in Askwith, p.17.

17 'one munching a hunch': Mrs Pole-Carew, quoted in Askwith, p.17.

18 'the very question': SL to Lord Spencer, 27 July 1837, HH.

19 'this new planet': SL to George Lyttelton, 8 October 1838, HH.

19 'the thick walls': SL, quoted in Askwith, p.64.

20 Besides the kitchen: For descriptions of the Windsor kitchens see William Strange, *Sketches of Her Majesty's Household*, 1848, also *The Private Life of the Queen*.

21 'willing to cease': Horace Walpole, quoted in Dulcie Ashdown, *Ladies-in-Waiting*, 1976, p.144.

21 'preserve the dignity and morality': Queen Victoria, quoted in K. D. Reynolds, *Aristocratic Women and Political Society in Victorian Britain*, 1998, p.196.

21 'weekly shoal of guests': SL to Lavinia Glynne, no date, HH.

22 'amiable person': Queen Victoria, quoted in Askwith, p.66.

NOTES 367

22   'formerly nobody': Christopher Hibbert (ed.), *Queen Victoria in her Letters and Journals*, 1984, p.39.

23   'Everything is new': Charles Greville, in Strachey and Fulford, vol. 3, p.395.

Chapter 2: A Scandal and a Crisis

25   'The whole town': Charles Greville, in Strachey and Fulford, vol. 4, p.132.

26   'kindness and softness': SL to George Lyttelton, 13 September 1842, HH.

27   indiscretion of a maid-of-honour: Baroness Lehzen to Queen Victoria, Royal Archives, VIC/MAIN/Z/159/1.

27   five drops: ibid., RA VIC/MAIN/Z/159/16.

27   'during your Majesty's': ibid., RA VIC/MAIN/Z/159/14.

27   'perpendicularly': ibid., RA VIC/MAIN/Z/159/24.

28   'protect their purity': Charles Greville, in Strachey and Fulford, vol. 4, p.146.

28   'is – to use plain': Queen Victoria, quoted in Elizabeth Longford, *Queen Victoria*, 1964, p.97.

28   'suspicions that Lady Flora': Lady Portman, RA VIC/MAIN/Z/486/23.

28   'Well I don't think so': Lady Flora's statement, *Morning Post*, 14 September 1839.

29   'Sir James Clark having expressed': Lady Portman, RA VIC/MAIN/Z/486/2.

29   'there are no grounds': Sir James Clark, RA VIC/MAIN/Z/486/1.

30   'I blush to send you': Lady Flora to Hamilton Fitzgerald, *Morning Post*. Also see Sir James Clark's statement in *The Times*, 9 October 1839.

30   'atrocious calumnies': Lady Hastings to Queen Victoria, RA VIC/MAIN/Z/486/12.

31   'poor, poor Lady Flora': Elizabeth Barrett Browning, in Philip Kelley and Ronald Hudson (eds.) *The Brownings' Correspondence*, 1986, vol. 4, p.171.

31   'behaved like a hapless': Thomas Carlyle in Charles Richard Sanders (ed.), *The Collected Letters of Thomas and Jane Welsh Carlyle*, 1995, vol. 11, p.86.

31   'more folly than malice': Lady Holland, in Earl of Ilchester (ed.), *Elizabeth, Lady Holland to her Son*, 1946, p.172.

32   'like him as a friend':, Queen Victoria, A. C. Benson and Viscount Esher (eds.), *The Letters of Queen Victoria 1837–61*, 1907, vol. 1, p.224.

32   'All ALL my happiness': Queen Victoria, in Hibbert, *Queen Victoria in her Letters and Journals*, p.45.

32   'How different': Queen Victoria, in Benson and Esher, vol. 1, p.200.

33   'If Sir Robert Peel presses': ibid., p.204.

33   '*pretended* that I had': ibid., p.208.

34   'insisted on my giving up': ibid., p.205.

34   'the Queen having considered': ibid., p.210.

34   'a clever, but rather thoughtless': Charles Greville, in Strachey and Fulford, vol. 4, p.169.

34   'there was mismanagement': Henry Ponsonby to his mother, February 1874, Shulbrede Priory.

35   'I found poor Ly. Flora': Queen Victoria, quoted in Monica Charlot, *Victoria*, 1991, p.137.

36   'just like the White Lady': SL, quoted in Askwith, p.59.

36   'The books you mention': SL to George Lyttelton, 4 January 1840, HH.

36   'What do you mean': SL to GL, 6 October 1839, HH.

37   'I have not seen': SL to GL, 14 October 1839, HH.

37   'physically and mentally': Henry Ponsonby to Mary Ponsonby, RA VIC/ADDA36 12.11.85.

37   'Your Majesty would owe it': *The Dangers of Evil Counsel*, Conroy Papers 2C, Balliol, Oxford.

38   'I have a general': SL to George Lyttelton, 31 October 1839, HH.

38   'experience of proper': SL to Rev. Gurdlestone, 17 December 1842, HH.

39   'So excessively handsome': Queen Victoria, quoted in Charlot, p.164.

Chapter 3: 'Love rules the court'

40   'the Queen – impertinent': SL to George Lyttelton, 25 October 1839, HH.

41   'Think of my position': Prince Albert, quoted in Cecil Woodham-Smith, *Queen Victoria*, 1972, p.200.

42   'the happiest happiest': Queen Victoria to King Leopold, Benson and Esher, vol. 1, p.274.

42   'handsome enough': SL to George Lyttelton, October 1839, HH.

43   'only the husband': Prince Albert, quoted in Charlot, p.189.

44   'Dandies and Roués': Prince Albert, quoted in St Aubyn, p.288.

46   'those odious things': SL to Lady Grant, British Library, EUR E308/38.

46   Under the lord chamberlain: For the composition of the Queen's household, see Public Record Office LC3/23, William Strange, *Sketches of Her Majesty's Household*, and Vera Watson, *A Queen at Home*.

47   'properly speaking': quoted in Christopher Hibbert, *Queen Victoria: A Personal History*, 2000, p.139.

49   'In the present lamentably': William Strange.

50   'I must confess': Queen Victoria to SL, 21 December 1840, HH.

51   'totally unfit': Queen Victoria to Lord Melbourne, RA VIC/MAIN/M/12/16.

51   'Dr Clark has mismanaged': Prince Albert, quoted in Charlot, p.211.

51   'an influence over': Prince Albert, quoted in Robert Rhodes James, *Albert, Prince Consort*, 1983, p.126.

52   'a quiet home': Queen Victoria to Baron Stockmar, in Hibbert, *Queen Victoria in her Letters and Journals*, p.94.

52   'a channel for intrigue': George Anson, quoted in Charlot, p.209.

52   'the two years': Queen Victoria to Stockmar, quoted in Woodham-Smith, p.231.

Chapter 4: Sarah Lyttelton: Superintendent of the Nursery

53   'No bird can return': Mrs Southey to Prince Albert, RA VIC/MAIN/M/12/9.

53   'good and intelligent': Stockmar memo, RA VIC/MAIN/M/12/14.

54   'the Queen should heartily': SL, quoted in Askwith, p.72.

54   'none was so fit': Queen Victoria, quoted in Askwith, p.73.

54   'should not be considered': SL memo, RA VIC/MAIN/M/12/24.

54   'to ask questions': ibid., RA VIC/MAIN/M/12/24.

55   'devote as much time': Stockmar memo, RA VIC/MAIN/M/12/29.

55   luncheons – soup or fish: Menus for meals eaten at Windsor, by royalty, household and servants, are in the Royal Archives, MRH/MRHF/MENUS/WC.

55   'into the views': SL to Stockmar, RA VIC/MAIN/M/12/19.

56   'to judge by': SL to Caroline Estcourt, 3 August 1842, HH.

56   'Ly L. so agreeable': Queen Victoria, quoted in Askwith, p.78.

56   'Yesterday I was playing': SL, quoted in Askwith, p.82.

56   'My dear Mama': Princess Royal to Queen Victoria, RA VIC/
      MAIN/M/13/55.

58   'She sends up': SL to Lavinia Glynne, 14 January 1845, HH.

58   'comfortable perch': ibid.

58   'It will be too horrid': SL to LG, 20 October 1844, HH.

58   'it will be a great separation': Lavinia Glynne to Mary Lyttelton, 6
      October 1843, HH.

59   'not the man': SL to Caroline Estcourt, 28 August 1845, HH.

59   'I have a sort of': Caroline Lyttelton, quoted in Askwith, p.75.

59   'takes her share': SL to Caroline Estcourt, 14 January 1843, HH.

60   'The children should': Queen Victoria, quoted in Charlot, p.293.

60   'an account of': SL to Mary Lyttelton, 3 January 1850, HH.

61   'as if I ought': SL to George Lyttelton, September 1842, HH.

61   Sarah reported on: For Sarah Lyttelton's reports to Queen Victoria
      during August/September 1842, see RA VIC/MAIN/M/13/21–37.

62   'I have advised': Baroness Lehzen, RA VIC/MAIN/Z/159/30.

62   'most eager in her': Charles Phipps to Queen Victoria, RA VIC/
      ADD/Q/1/17.

62   'quite a superior person': Queen Victoria, quoted in C. Grey, *The Early
      Years of the Prince Consort*, 1867, p.348.

63   'kept properly': Duties of the Queen's dressers, RA VIC/MAIN/Z/202/62.

63   Dressers were explicitly: For the undesirability of dressers making
      friends, see Charles Grey to the Queen, RA VIC/MAIN/Z/202/17.

63   'a good memory': Marianne Skerrett to Mr Andrews, RA VIC/
      ADDC/4/231.

64   'there is no such thing': Marianne Skerrett to Edwin Landseer, RA VIC/
      ADDC/4/360.

65   'opening the eyes': ibid., RA VIC/ADDC/4/208.

65   'change and bettering': ibid., RA VIC/ADDC/4/207.

65   'weak and feckless': ibid., RA VIC/ADDC/4/230.

65   'in good feather': ibid., RA VIC/ADDC/4/355.

65   'There are things': ibid., RA VIC/ADDC/4/214.

65   'great many pin pricks': Marianne Skerrett to Charles Kean, RA VIC/
      ADD/X1/42.

65   'a great deal of auld': Marianne Skerrett to Mrs Barrett, BL Eg 3705.

66   'I am treated': SL to Caroline Estcourt, 3 August 1842, HH.

66 'I sometimes feel': SL, quoted in Askwith, p.80.

66 'sadly insufficient for': SL to Rev. Gurdlestone, 30 October 1842, HH.

67 'blessings and comforts': SL to Rev. Gurdlestone, 4 December 1842, HH.

67 'Are we on the path': SL to Lady Grant, 16 September 1844, HH.

68 'its usual trials': SL to Caroline Lyttelton, 1 December 1844, HH.

68 'having been for a few': SL to George Lyttelton, 13 July 1849, HH.

68 'in accepting my awful': SL to Rev. Gurdlestone, 17 December 1842, HH.

Chapter 5: Charlotte Canning: Lady of the Bedchamber

Unless stated otherwise all quotations from Charlotte Canning's letters are taken from *Charlotte Canning: Lady-in-Waiting to Queen Victoria and Wife of the First Viceroy of India, 1817–1861*, Virginia Surtees, 1975. All quotations from Eleanor Stanley's letters are taken from *Twenty Years at Court: From the Correspondence of the Hon. Eleanor Stanley, 1842–1862*, Mrs Steuart Erskine (ed.), 1916.

70 'The Queen considers': Queen Victoria, in Benson and Esher, vol. 1, p.345.

71 'The Queen said': George Anson, quoted in Charlot, p.200.

72 From 1841: For further discussion of the appointment of the Queen's ladies see K. D. Reynolds.

72 'choose moderate people': Queen Victoria to Melbourne, in Benson and Esher, vol. 1, p.390.

74 'most amiable and conversible': Augustus Hare (ed.), *The Life and Letters of Frances Baroness Bunsen*, 1879, vol. 2, p.150.

75 'short and stumpy': Lady Clodagh Anson, *Victorian Days*, 1957, p.22.

75 'beautiful sisters': William Holman Hunt, quoted in Virginia Surtees (ed.), *Sublime and Instructive: Letters from John Ruskin to Louisa, Marchioness of Waterford, Anna Blunden and Ellen Heaton*, 1972, p.4.

79 'After luncheon': Queen Victoria, quoted in Surtees, p.71.

79 'the most proper': Duke of Atholl, quoted in Reynolds, p.11.

80 'talking over the absurdities': Mary Ponsonby, quoted in William Kuhn, *Henry and Mary Ponsonby*, 2002, p.69.

80   'would have been really great': Dante Gabriel Rosetti, quoted in
      Surtees (ed.), *Sublime and Instructive*, p.9.
81   'temperate meal': Lady Waterford, quoted in Augustus Hare, *Two
      Noble Lives*, vol. 1, 1893, p.243.
81   'your sister's duties': Queen Victoria, quoted in Surtees, p.185.
81   'Everything else changes': Bloomfield, p.108.
82   'up a steep hill': SL to George Lyttelton, 31 March 1842, HH.
82   'to bring literary': George Anson's memo, Benson and Esher, vol. 1,
      p.322.
83   'so I took to spinning': Bloomfield, p.123.
84   'I have no husband': Lady Jocelyn, quoted in Ethel Smyth, *What
      Happened Next*, 1940, p.140.
84   'stands before me': Mary Ponsonby, quoted in Smyth, ibid.

Chapter 6: 'Gone afloat'

All quotations for Charlotte Canning's expeditions to France and
Belgium are taken from her loose-leaf journals, 1843, Canning Papers,
Harewood House.

87   'sad and dispirited': SL to Caroline Lyttelton, 28 August 1844, HH.
88   'luxuriously fitted up': Charles Greville, in Strachey and Fulford, vol. 5,
      p.128.
88   'Please my Lord': quoted in Bloomfield, p.77.
91   'in a family circle': Queen Victoria, quoted in Longford, p.175.
91   'the old King': Prince Albert, quoted in Woodham-Smith, p.244.
92   'lay in a stock': SL to Queen Victoria, RA VIC/MAIN/M/13/40.
92   'worst crime': ibid., RA VIC/MAIN/M/13/45.
92   'but I fear': ibid., RA VIC/MAIN/M/13/46.
93   'habit of dashing': Surtees (ed.), *Sublime and Instructive*, p.28.
94   'Forty decanters': quoted in Charlot, p.243.
97   'a little stout': Charlotte Brontë, quoted in W. Gérin, *Charlotte Brontë*,
      1967, p.243.

Chapter 7: Osborne

98   'During our morning': Queen Victoria, quoted in Longford, p.175.

98   'a strange, odd': Queen Victoria, quoted in Woodham-Smith, p.150.

98   'It sounds so snug': Queen Victoria to King Leopold, Benson and Esher, vol. 2, p.41.

99   'Here we sit': Prince Albert, quoted in Stanley Weintraub, *Albert: Uncrowned King*, 1997, p.153.

99   'we feel crushed': Queen Victoria to King Leopold, Benson and Esher, vol. 2, p.7.

100   It meant donning: For Victorian mourning dress see Lou Taylor, *Mourning Dress*, 1983 and Judith Flanders, *The Victorian House*, 2003.

100   'Great events': Queen Victoria to King Leopold, Benson and Esher, vol. 2, p.197.

100   'Great care about': CC to Lady Clanricarde, 22 September 1861, BL ADDMSS 47469.

102   'thankful when the trial': SL to Lavinia Glynne, 29 March 1844, HH.

102   'It does my heart': Queen Victoria, quoted in John Matson, *Dear Osborne*, 1978, p.32.

103   In a journal: For Sarah Lyttelton's journal, August 1844, see RA VIC/MAIN/M/13/67–68.

104–5 'The evening of': SL to Queen Victoria, RA VIC/MAIN/M/13/70.

104   'the horrid dirt': SL to Lavinia Glynne, August 1845, HH.

104   'free from levity': SL to Queen Victoria, RA VIC/MAIN/Z/129/53.

105   'much less high': Queen Victoria to King Leopold, Benson and Esher, vol. 2, p.103.

110   'very fine but': Queen Victoria, quoted in Surtees, p.172.

110   'The account of': Queen Victoria, quoted in Surtees, p.171.

110   'I have always': SL to Queen Victoria, RA VIC/MAIN/M/13/78.

111   'a mixture of regret': SL to Caroline Lyttelton, March 1847, HH.

111   'uncommonly dull': Marianne Skerrett to Landseer, RA VIC/ADD/C4/211.

111   'They have made': CC to Lady Stuart, 7 July 1848, Harewood.

112   'noisy, merry': SL to Mary Lyttelton, 12 July 1849, HH.

112   'poor R. Albertanson': Queen Victoria to Sir John Cowell , RA VIC/MAIN/Z/203/21.

113 'this supposed evil': Henry Ponsonby to Rev. Prothero, RA VIC/MAIN/Z/204/104.

113 'must have been misinformed': ibid., RA VIC/MAIN/Z/204/108.

Chapter 8: In the Highlands

Quotations for Charlotte Canning's stay at Blair are taken from her journal, *In the Highlands 1844*, Harewood.

114 'Little cheeks': SL to Queen Victoria, RA VIC/MAIN/M/13/51.

116 'hardly real sport': Queen Victoria, quoted in Charlot, p.237.

120 'blue stick': George Lyttelton to SL, RA VIC/MAIN/C/56/31.

120 'leaving the work': John Gibson to Marianne Skerrett, RA VIC/ADD/C4/125.

121 'There is a nice': Queen Victoria, quoted in David Duff, *Victoria in the Highlands*, 1968, p.97.

121 'she was better lodged': CC to Lady Clanricarde, 22 September 1861, BL ADDMSS 47469.

121 'the Queen in very good': Charles Greville, in Strachey and Fulford, vol. 6, p.186.

122 'the Prince's shooting': CC to Lady Stuart, in Hare, vol. 1, p.360.

123 'like a goat': Johnny Stanley, quoted in Nancy Mitford (ed.), *The Stanleys of Alderley*, 1939, p.221.

123 'the best rainbow': Marianne Skerrett to Landseer, RA VIC/ADD/C4/189.

124 'to hear that': Queen Victoria, quoted in Surtees, p.178.

125 'To the one in which': Queen Victoria, quoted in Duff, p.111.

125 'rather foolish-looking': Thomas Carlyle, Sanders (ed.), vol. 24, p.212.

126 'very happy': CC to Catherine Gladstone, BL ADD 46226.

Chapter 9: 'The object of Education'

127 'The Queen has returned': SL to Catherine Gladstone, 14 October 1848, HH.

127 'The object of Education': Baron Stockmar memo, RA VIC/MAIN/M/12/14.

128 'a lesson given': SL to Queen Victoria, RA VIC/MAIN/M/13/90.

128 'that I had desired': SL to Queen Victoria, RA VIC/MAIN/M/13/68.

128 'had enjoined her': ibid., RA VIC/MAIN/M/13/70.

128 'Our new governess': Queen Victoria, quoted in Askwith, p.82.

129 'I have been overwhelmed': SL to Caroline Lyttelton, 9 October 1847, HH.

129 'I perceive no longer': SL to Queen Victoria, RA VIC/MAIN/M13/89.

130 'after many expressions': SL to Lavinia Glynne, 17 February 1847, HH.

130 'an exaggerated copy': Baron Stockmar, quoted in Robert Rhodes James p.243.

130 'much improved in size': SL to Caroline Lyttelton, 9 October 1847, HH.

130 'great quickness': SL to Queen Victoria, RA VIC/MAIN/M/13/68.

130 'spirits and boyish': ibid., RA VIC/MAIN/M/13/52.

131 'neither studious': SL to Queen Victoria, RA VIC/MAIN/M/13/89.

131 'a virtuous, sturdy': SL to Lavinia Glynne, 24 July 1847, HH.

131 'painting numberless': SL to Kitty Estcourt, 29 March 1849, HH.

131 'essentially a nervous': Baron Stockmar, RA VIC/MAIN/M/12/40.

132 'the brain of': George Combe, RA VIC/MAIN/M/15/2.

132 'The one thing needful': Baron Stockmar, RA VIC/MAIN/M/12/40.

132 Stockmar followed up: Stockmar's memorandum on the education of the Prince of Wales and the Princess Royal, RA VIC/MAIN/M/12/50.

133 A few months: Victoria and Albert's memorandum on the education of their children, RA VIC/MAIN/M/12/55.

133 In 1848: Princess Royal's timetable, RA VIC/MAIN/M/12/66.

133 'be strictly adhered to': Queen Victoria to SL, RA VIC/MAIN/M/12/62.

134 'much too childish': ibid., RA VIC/MAIN/M/12/63.

134 'It quite grieved': Queen Victoria, quoted in Askwith, p.79.

135 'R Catholics at heart': Queen Victoria, quoted in St Aubyn, p.309.

136 'very strict': Lady Holland, in Ilchester, p.201.

136 'on every opportunity': Queen Victoria, quoted in Askwith, p.79.

136 'I dread the *extreme*': Queen Victoria, quoted in Hannah Pakula, *An Uncommon Woman*, 1996, p.40.

136 'making her fully': SL to Mary Lyttelton, 30 November 1850, HH.

137 'He must obey': Henry Birch, quoted in Robert Rhodes James, p. 327.

137 After breakfast: Prince of Wales's timetable, RA VIC/MAIN/M/14/39 and M/15/47.

138 'whatever relaxation': Prince Albert to Henry Birch, RA VIC/MAIN/M/14/15.

138 'almost despaired of': ibid., RA VIC/MAIN/M/15/16.

138 'he was undergoing': Birch to Prince Albert, RA VIC/MAIN/M/15/1.

138 'the organs of Combativeness': George Combe, quoted in Robert Rhodes James, p.238.

139 'quite *en train*': SL to George Lyttelton, 3 May 1849, HH.

139 'Mr Birch consented': SL to Mary Lyttelton, 11 July 1849, HH.

139 ' a brain of sufficient': George Combe, RA VIC/MAIN/M/15/78.

140 'You cannot wonder': Bertie, quoted in Woodham-Smith, p.336.

141 'I have just had': SL to Lavinia Glynne, 1847, HH.

Chapter 10: Departures

142 'extraordinary beauty': SL to Queen Victoria, RA VIC/MAIN/M/13/101.

142 'the excitement of': ibid., RA VIC/MAIN/M/13/100.

143 'accounts, tradesmen's letters': SL to Lavinia Glynne, 4 October 1849, HH.

143 'No words can express': SL to Catherine Gladstone, 10 October 1849, HH.

143 'this doubt and chance': SL to Mary Lyttelton, 13 October 1849, HH.

144 'Here I am established': SL to Lavinia Glynne, 24 December 1849, HH.

145 'my prospect is fast': SL to Lavinia Glynne, 19 October 1849, HH.

145 'she does feel': SL to Mary Lyttelton, 27 November 1850, HH.

146 'I could not remain': SL to George Quin, 5 December 1850, HH.

146 'the Queen and I': SL to Mary Lyttelton, 30 November 1850, HH.

146 'both intimate with': SL to Mary Lyttelton, 23 December 1850, HH.

146 'Poor Lady Lyttelton': Queen Victoria, quoted in Askwith, p.87.

147 'one of the saddest': Lord Elgin, BL MSS EUR D661.

148 'said not to be': F. W. H. Cavendish, *Society, Politics and Diplomacy*, 1913, p.181.

149 'so noble': SL to Queen Victoria, RA VIC/MAIN/F/24/139.

149 'the proudest': Queen Victoria to SL, RA VIC/MAIN/F/24/144.

149 'no enthusiasm for': SL to Caroline Lyttelton, 6 May 1851, HH.

151 'the power and encroachments': Queen Victoria, quoted in Orlando Figes, *Crimea*, 2010, p.160.

152 Some claimed: For contemporary comments on the Cannings' marriage see Charlotte Canning's Memorial Album, BL MSS EUR D661.

152 'It is an immense': CC to Catherine Gladstone, BL ADD 46226.

153 'the Princess Royal': CC to Lady Waterford, in Hare, vol. 2, p.3.

153 'After our breakfast': Queen Victoria, quoted in Surtees, p.194.

Chapter 11: Mary Ponsonby: Maid-of-Honour

Unless stated otherwise, all quotations from Mary Ponsonby's letters and memoir are taken from *Mary Ponsonby: A Memoir, Some Letters and a Journal*, Magdalen Ponsonby (ed.), 1927. Mary's self-examination diary is at Shulbrede Priory.

154 'I have very few': CC to MP, quoted in Magdalen Ponsonby, p.32.

155 'neither too shy': Miss Macgregor to Lady Biddulph, RA VIC/MAIN/C/63/56.

158 'from dining to': MP, in Ethel Smyth, *As Time Went On*, 1936, p.312.

160 'forgiven her earnestness': MP's journal, SP.

160 'If you are violent': Prince Albert, quoted in Woodham-Smith, p.329.

160 'fidgety nature': ibid., p.331.

161 'very ardent': MP's journal, SP.

161 'charmed whenever': Bloomfield, vol. 1, p.29.

163 'pretty, simple stories': Queen Victoria, in Roger Fulford (ed.), *Your Dear Letter*, 1971, p.110.

163 'a woman who': A. C. Benson, *Memories and Friends*, 1924, p.58.

163 'the character and': ibid., p.65.

165 'I think the time': CC to MP, in Magdalen Ponsonby, p.29.

165 'the absolute necessity': MP in Smyth, *What Happened Next*, p.140.

166 'You will be delighted': CC, quoted in 'The Character of Queen Victoria', *The Quarterly Review*, April 1901.

Chapter 12: Glimpses of Abroad

167 'my dear kind': Queen Victoria, quoted in Woodham-Smith, p.355.

168 'the grand-daughter of': Queen Victoria, in Raymond Mortimer (ed.), *Leaves from a Journal*, 1961, p.39.

169 'little iron railings': Frieda Arnold, in Benita Stoney and Heinrich C. Weltzein (eds.), *My Mistress the Queen*, 1994, p.89.

170   'to battle him': Augusta Stanley, in Dean of Windsor and Hector Bolitho (eds.), *Letters of Lady Augusta Stanley*, 1927, p.69.

171   'like water': Frieda Arnold, in Stoney and Weltzein, p.108.

171   'I am delighted': Queen Victoria to King Leopold, in Benson and Esher, vol. 3, p.172.

171   'No royal person': Lord Clarendon, quoted in St Aubyn, p.300.

171   The Queen's wardrobe: For the Queen's outfit on her arrival in Paris, see Stoney and Weltzein, p.17.

172   'Isn't it odd': Queen Victoria, quoted in Longford, p.254.

172   'should not fear': Queen Victoria, quoted in Charlot, p.362.

174   'We have great': Queen Victoria, quoted in Surtees, p.232.

175   'Our poor Victoria': ibid., p.249.

175   'so fine a death': Sarah Lyttelton's account of Mary Lyttelton's death is part of a family memoir of that event, BL ADD 46269.

176   'By the side': Lord Curzon, in *British Government in India*, 1925, vol. 2, p.227.

176   'snubbed her dreadfully': Johnny Stanley, quoted in Mitford, p.223.

176   'Poor thing!': Colonel Stuart, quoted in Charles Allen, *A Glimpse of the Burning Plain*, 1986, p.118.

176   'I cannot imagine': CC to Lady Stuart, 2 May 1859, Harewood.

177   'I have been so': Queen Victoria to CC, quoted in Surtees, p.268.

179   'household marriage': Queen Victoria, in Roger Fulford (ed.), *Dearest Child*, 1964, p.304.

180   'They use old-fashioned': Arthur Ponsonby, SP.

Chapter 13: Three Deaths

Quotations from Augusta Stanley's accounts of the deaths of the Duchess of Kent and the Prince Consort are taken from *Letters of Lady Augusta Stanley*, Dean of Windsor and Hector Bolitho (eds.), 1927.

182   'completely overwhelmed': Queen Victoria, in *Dearest Child*, p.308.

183   'the thought of': Queen Victoria, quoted in Dean of Windsor and Hector Bolitho (eds.), *Later Letters of Lady Augusta Stanley*, 1929, p.25.

184   'I do not want': Queen Victoria, in *Dearest Child*, p.320.

184   'it was a satisfaction': Lord Clarendon, in A. L. Kennedy (ed.), *My Dear Duchess*, 1956, p.141.

184 'to lose a *Mother*': Queen Victoria, quoted in Surtees, p.285.

185 'simple and true': CC to Lady Clanricarde, 1 September 1861, BL ADD MS 47469.

185 'for a few minutes': George Lyttelton to CC, quoted in Askwith, p.149.

186 'Mary Ponsonby': Queen Victoria, in *Dearest Child*, p.361.

189 'low and weak': Henry Ponsonby to his mother, RA VIC/ADDA36/4.

190 Despite the diagnosis: There is some debate as to whether the Prince Consort died from typhoid or some other cause. He may have been suffering from stomach cancer; Helen Rappaport in *Magnificent Obsession* (2011) makes a case for Crohn's disease.

191 'to wear black': Watson, p.145.

191 'The Queen though': Charles Phipps, quoted in Woodham-Smith, p.430.

191 'I did nothing': Queen Victoria, in Roger Fulford (ed.), *Dearest Mama*, 1968, p.23.

191 'It is really': Henry Ponsonby to his mother, RA VIC/ADDA36/6.

192 'It was a terrible': Augusta Stanley, quoted in Rappaport, p.102.

192 'Yesterday evening': Marianne Skerrett, quoted in Erskine, p.389.

193 'We are all so': Catherine Gladstone to Sarah Lyttelton, 17 December 1861, National Library of Wales, LLGC Glynne of Hawarden (1) 4678.

194 'You can scarcely': Lady Waterford to Lady Stuart, in Hare, vol. 3, p.176.

194 'there never was': Charles Canning, quoted in Surtees, p.293.

194 'Lord Canning little': Queen Victoria, quoted in Surtees, p.295.

195 'in his dreary': Bishop of Calcutta, Talbot Papers, U1612, Centre for Kentish Studies.

195 'The grand, pale': Lady Stuart, BL EUR D661.

195 'he is again': Queen Victoria to Lady Clanricarde, BL ADD MSS47469.

196 'Dearest Lady Lyttelton': Queen Victoria to SL, 29 January 1862, Sotheby's catalogue for the sale of Lyttelton Papers, December 1978.

197 'my heart': Queen Victoria to SL, ibid.

Chapter 14: 'Someone to lean on'

199 'You are all so': quoted in Windsor and Bolitho, *Letters of Lady Augusta Stanley*, p.251.

199 'This year I shall': Marianne Skerrett to Landseer, RA ADD/C/4/351.

200 'We are under': Lady Barrington to MP, 1862, SP.

200 'The Ladies might': Augusta Stanley, in Windsor and Bolitho, p.260.

200 'once by accident': Lord Clarendon, in Kennedy, p.189.

201 'my very misery': Queen Victoria, in *Dearest Mama*, p.139.

201 'Yes Ma'am': Lord Clarendon, in Kennedy, p.186.

201 'utter loneliness': Queen Victoria, in *Dearest Mama*, p.263.

201 'I think that we': Queen Victoria to Lady Waterpark, September 1864, in Lady Waterpark's diary, BL ADD 60750.

202 'I have all your': Charles Grey, quoted in Martyn Downer, *The Queen's Knight*, 2007, p.133.

203 'their poor plain': SL to Meriel and Caroline Lyttelton, 12 March 1863, Talbot Papers, U1612, Centre for Kentish Studies.

204 'It is a peculiarity': SL to Lucy Lyttelton, 12 September 1863, HH.

204 'my constant, hard': Queen Victoria, in *Dearest Mama*, p.280.

204 'talking and laughing': Lucy Lyttelton, in John Baily (ed.), *The Diary of Lady Frederick Cavendish*, 1927, vol. 1, p.200.

204 'Dear Lady Augusta': Queen Victoria, quoted in St Aubyn, p.405.

205 'charming . . . the most unclerical': Queen Victoria, in *Dearest Mama*, p.95.

205 'He wd call upon': Katherine Bruce, in Windsor and Bolitho, p.319.

205 'Dear Augusta Stanley': Queen Victoria, in *Dearest Mama*, p.291.

206 'Augusta and the little': ibid., p.304.

206 'it would be as well': Queen Victoria, quoted in St Aubyn, p.383.

206 'in its fashionable': Harriet Phipps to Marie Mallet, in Victor Mallet (ed.), *Life with Queen Victoria*, 1968, p.60.

207 'to witness the spectacle': Queen Victoria, quoted in Hibbert, *Queen Victoria: A Personal History*, p.336.

208 'All she says': Charles Grey, quoted in St Aubyn, p.337.

208 'impatient of any': Queen Victoria, in *Your Dear Letter*, p.272.

208 'if confidence is': Charles Grey, quoted in Downer, p.248.

209 'I only wish': Queen Victoria, in *Your Dear Letter*, p.22.

209 'certainly not': HP to MP, RA VIC/ADDA36/95.

209 'my poor Brown': Queen Victoria, quoted in Longford, p.328.

209 'Lord Charles': ibid., p.330.

210 'it was the talk': Edgar Boehm, quoted in Downer, p.181.

210 'To my best': Queen Victoria, quoted in Longford, p.456.

210 'When one's beloved': Queen Victoria, in *Your Dear Letter*, p.193.

211 'whose whole object': ibid., p.91.

211 'I am alas': Queen Victoria, in *Dearest Mama*, p.106.

211 'a higher sense': Queen Victoria, quoted in Downer, p.183.

211 'soothing and refreshing': Queen Victoria, in *Dearest Child*, p.218.

211 'frivolous, pleasure-seeking': Queen Victoria, in *Your Dear Letter*, p.165.

211 'Civility and consideration': Queen Victoria, RA VIC/MAIN/C/64/77.

212 'fully acquainted': Marianne Skerrett to Mr Andrews, RA ADD C/4/231.

212 'neat and tidy': Duties of wardrobe maids, RA VIC/MAIN/Z/202/55.

213 'ought to be comfortably': Queen Victoria to the Prince of Wales, RA VIC/ADDA3/101.

213 'not right that': Queen Victoria to Sir John Cowell, RA VIC/MAIN/Z/203/46.

214 'the Queen wishes': Queen Victoria to Cowell, RA VIC/MAIN/Z/202/168.

214 The servants' meals: For correspondence about the servants' dinners see RA VIC/MAIN/Z/202/23 and Z/202/44.

Chapter 15: Henry Ponsonby: Private Secretary

Unless stated otherwise, all quotations from Henry Ponsonby's letters are taken from *Henry Ponsonby: Queen Victoria's Private Secretary*, Arthur Ponsonby, 1942.

216 'the violent grief': Queen Victoria to Lady Waterpark, 10 February 1867, BL ADD 60750.

216 'constant blank': Queen Victoria, in *Your Dear Letter*, p.121.

216 'Eliza is': Lord Clarendon, in Kennedy, p.248.

216 'large, long teeth': Queen Victoria, in *Dearest Child*, p.310.

216 'a dear, clever': ibid., p.126.

217 'found H.M.': SL to George Lyttelton, 13 March 1869, HH.

217 'our dear kind': Crown Princess of Prussia to SL, Sotheby's catalogue.

217 'I owed her': Queen Victoria, in *Your Dear Letter*, p.301.

218 'dear General's': ibid., p.273.

218 'I will carefully': HP to Thomas Biddulph, RA C/78/129.

219 'Whiggishness as': Benjamin Disraeli, quoted in Ponsonby, p.247.

219 'the most perfectly': Benson, p.55.

219 'The Duke of York': Sir Frederick Ponsonby, *Recollections of Three Reigns*, 1951, p.45.

220 'intimations were': Benson, p.66.

222 'Both Sir Thomas': Queen Victoria, quoted in Kuhn, p.153.

223 'Everything depends': Gerald Wellesley, quoted in Roy Jenkins, *Gladstone*, 1995, p.336.

223 'Arrogant, tyrannical': Queen Victoria, in Roger Fulford (ed.), *Darling Child*, 1976, p.130.

223 'he always addresses': HP to MP, RA VIC/ADDA36/360.

223–4 'a very unwholesome': Queen Victoria, quoted in Jenkins, p.344.

224 'The Queen *must* ask': Queen Victoria, quoted in Arthur Ponsonby, p.117.

225 'Dear General Grey': Queen Victoria, quoted in Hibbert, *Queen Victoria: A Personal History*, p.350.

225 '*Interference* of that': Horatia Stopford to Queen Victoria, RA VIC/MAIN/Z/206/36.

226 'he always boldly': HP to MP, RA VIC/ADDA36/140.

226 'tell Sir Henry': Smyth, *What Happened Next*, p.103.

226 'he has no backbone': Queen Victoria, quoted in Michaela Reid, *Ask Sir James*, 1987, p.162.

226 'did not belong': Arthur Ponsonby, p.70.

226 'People constantly': HP to MP, RA VIC/ADDA36/1566.

Chapter 16: Balmorality

228 'sumptuous breakfast': Marie Mallet, in Mallet, p.26. Also see dinner menus for Station Hotel, Perth, Reid papers, Lanton Tower.

229 'with the view': RA VIC/ADD/Q/1/24.

230 'loads of curiously': Augusta Stanley, in Windsor and Bolitho (eds.), *Letters of Lady Augusta Stanley*, p.72.

230 'the great want of': Queen Victoria to Dr Robertson, RA VIC/ADD/Q/1/52.

231 'faithful record': Augusta Stanley, in Windsor and Bolitho, *Later Letters*, p.72.

231 'a cold room': Schomberg McDonnell to Arthur Bigge, quoted in Mary Lutyens (ed.), *Lady Lytton's Court Diary*, 1961, p.70.

231 'We meet at meals': Henry Campbell-Bannerman, in John Wilson, *A Life of Sir Henry Campbell-Bannerman*, 1973, p.133.

233 'Oh Ma'am': HP to MP, RA VIC/ADDA36/251.

233 'we tried one or two': ibid., RA VIC/ADDA36/387.

234 'turning conversation': ibid., RA VIC/ADDA36/830.

234 'There seems a': Marie Mallet, in Mallet, p.92.

234 'bad mentally': HP to MP, RA VIC/ADDA36/1537.

235 'she don't much': ibid., RA VIC/ADDA36/332.

235 'we just exist': Marie Mallet, in Mallet, p.37.

236 'in consequence of': HP, quoted in Kuhn, p.104.

236 'received a communiqué': HP to MP, RA VIC/ADDA36/753.

236 'very odd': ibid., RA VIC/ADDA36/1639.

236 'I am very nearly': Queen Victoria, in *Your Dear Letter*, p.161.

237 'nice eyes': Lady Churchill to Queen Victoria, RA VIC/MAIN/C/63/87.

237 'not a religion': HP to MP, RA VIC/ADDA36/681.

237 'says 2 and 2': ibid., RA VIC/ADDA36/693.

238 'she really does': ibid., RA VIC/ADDA36/684.

239 'better sacrifice': HP, quoted in Longford, p.379.

239 'Brown v. Alfred': see RA VIC/ADDA36/342–346.

240 'hot argument': HP to MP, RA VIC/ADDA36/330.

241 'very dangerous': ibid., RA VIC/ADDA36/349.

242 'good woman about': ibid., RA VIC/ADDA36/350.

242 'she won't have': ibid., RA VIC/ADDA36/351.

242 'more anxiety': Queen Victoria, in *Your Dear Letter*, p.193.

242 'perfectly inaudible': HP to MP, RA VIC/ADDA36/386.

242 'I get into states': ibid., RA VIC/ADDA36/355.

242 'continually in deep': ibid., RA VIC/ADDA36/376.

243 'laid up in': ibid., RA VIC/ADDA36/364.

243 'crying and regularly': ibid., RA VIC/ADDA36/389.

244 'a day of triumph': Queen Victoria, in *Darling Child*, p.31.

Chapter 17: Eastern Questions and Domestic Affairs

245 'thoroughly Jewish': Queen Victoria, quoted in Hibbert, p.317.

245 'full of poetry': Queen Victoria, in *Your Dear Letter*, p.208.

245 'He told the Queen': Queen Victoria, quoted in Arthur Ponsonby, p.195.

245 'he really does': HP to MP, RA VIC/ADDA36/1144.

246 'not one of us': ibid., RA VIC/ADDA36/1091.

246 'I am an Empress': Queen Victoria, quoted in Longford, p.404.

246 'so high an': HP to MP, RA VIC/ADDA36/1584.

247 'take opportunity': ibid., RA VIC/ADDA36/22.9.84.

247 'The Q told': ibid., RA VIC/ADDA36/17.9.84.

247 'most successful': HP, quoted in Jenkins, p.495.

248 'had desolated and profaned': Gladstone, quoted in Jenkins, p.403.

248 'sweeping the Turks': HP to MP, RA VIC/ADDA36/1124.

249 'I am with you': ibid., RA VIC/ADDA36/1146.

249 'Between you': ibid., RA VIC/ADDA36/1152.

249 'Oh if the Queen': Queen Victoria, quoted in Hibbert, *Queen Victoria: A Personal History*, p.363.

249 'pained at my': HP, memo September 1875, SP.

250 'how absolutely': Dr Jenner to Lady Ely, RA VIC/MAIN/Z/206/10.

250 'anxiety and worry': Queen Victoria to Lady Ely, RA VIC/MAIN/Z/206/16.

251 'the causes which': HP to MP, RA VIC/ADDA36/1062.

252 'good, honest sort of': ibid., RA VIC/ADDA36/1106.

252 'At last': ibid., RA VIC/ADDA36/1135.

252 'Say you have': HP, quoted in Longford, p.411.

253 'hint that it': HP to MP, RA VIC/ADDA36/1158.

253 'no use talking': ibid., RA VIC/ADDA36/1525.

253 'to say that the Queen': ibid., RA VIC/ADDA36/1163.

253 'to be careful': ibid., RA VIC/ADDA36/1233.

253 'strong Turk': ibid., RA VIC/ADDA36/1234.

254 'the Queen's orders': ibid., RA VIC/ADDA36/1634.

254 'talked freely': ibid., RA VIC/ADDA36/1413.

254 'so ugly': ibid., RA VIC/ADDA36/1503.

254 'you are my eyes': RA VIC/ADDA36/1547.

254 'I do miss': MP to HP, 5 June 1862, SP.

255 'so rough': HP to MP, RA VIC/ADDA36/1538.

255 having Bids: ibid., RA VIC/ADDA36/1568.

255 'from tackling': ibid., RA VIC/ADDA36/1583.

256 'He smelt the hoof': ibid., RA VIC/ADDA36/11.3.83.

Chapter 18: James Reid: Resident Medical Attendant

Unless stated otherwise, all quotations from James Reid's letters and diaries are taken from *Ask Sir James: The Life of Sir James Reid, Personal Physician to Queen Victoria*, Michaela Reid, 1987.

257 'Never had I': Queen Victoria to Lord Rowton, RA VIC/ADDU30/27.

257 'inconsolable at': Lady Ely to Lord Rowton, RA VIC/ADDU30/38.

258 'Saw Dr Reid': Queen Victoria, quoted in Reid, p.31.

259 'I hear Dr Reid': Queen Victoria, quoted in Reid, p.44.

259 'he was always so': Fritz Ponsonby, quoted in Reid, p.255.

259 'Throw Physic': Henry Ponsonby, quoted in Reid, p.120.

260 'where he practised': HP to MP, RA VIC/ADDA36/10.11.84.

260 'Let Dr Reid': Queen Victoria, quoted in Reid, p.46.

262 'merely flatulence': Dr Jenner, quoted in Reid, p.78.

263 'perfectly sobre': Queen Victoria to JR, 8 September 1897, Reid Papers, Lanton Tower.

264 'health that she': Queen Victoria, quoted in Reid, p.75.

264 'I wish the grave': ibid., p.61.

265 'on account of': Donald Brown, to JR, 29 July 1896, LT.

265 'out of regard': Queen Victoria, quoted in Reid, p.162.

265 'I will resine': Donald Brown to JR, 28 December 1896, LT.

266 'most handy': Queen Victoria to HP, Hibbert, *Queen Victoria in her Letters and Journals*, p.308.

266 'Rules for Scotland': Queen Victoria, quoted in Reid, p.129.

269 'chief recommendation': HP, quoted in Charlotte Zeepvat, *Prince Leopold*, 1998, p.104.

269 he netted a solid: For Reid's Christmas presents see diary, December 26 1889, LT.

271 'Anxious to know': Queen Victoria, quoted in Reid, p.54.

271 'utterly crushed': Queen Victoria, quoted in Arthur Ponsonby, p.129.

272 'We incline here': HP to MP, 2 May 1883, SP.

272 'defeated the Rubber': HP to MP, 27 August 1883, SP.

274 Henry was told: For the Queen on Hugh Brown and Francis Clark, see RA VIC/MAIN/Z/204/154.

274 'kept in order': HP to MP, RA VIC/ADDA36/6.6.83.

Chapter 19: Randall Davidson: Dean of Windsor

Unless stated otherwise, all quotations from Randall Davidson's letters and diaries are taken from *Randall Davidson: Archbishop of Canterbury*, G. K. A. Bell, 1938.

275 'Windsor is indeed': Queen Victoria, in Roger Fulford (ed.), *Beloved Mama*, 1981, p.138.

275 'What the Queen': Queen Victoria to HP, Arthur Ponsonby, p.63.

276 'I have now lost': Queen Victoria, quoted in Bell, p.63.

276 'of a deeply': Edward Benson, quoted in Bell, p.65.

276 'drawn towards': Queen Victoria to Edward Benson, 7 May 1883, 4.15, Davidson Papers, Lambeth Palace Library.

278 'I can't help': Edith Davidson, quoted in Bell, p.50.

278 'singularly pleasing': Queen Victoria, quoted in Bell, p.56.

280 'You may imagine': RD to his father, 21 January 1883, 4.1, LPL.

280 'Oh God give me': RD, diary 7 May 1883, 570, LPL.

280 'I should have': William Gladstone, in George Earle Buckle (ed.), *The Letters of Queen Victoria 1862–1885*, 1926 vol. 3, p.421.

280 'not right': Henry Labouchére, quoted in Bell, p.67.

281 'I am very glad': HP to RD, May 1883, 4.17, LPL.

281 'a delicious quaint': Edith Davidson, quoted in Mary Mills, *Edith Davidson of Lambeth*, 1938, p.40.

282 'What shall I write': RD, diary 30 November 1883, 570, LPL.

284 'the appearance of': Sir Michael Sadler, quoted in Bell, p.257.

285 'twaddling religious': RD, Bell Papers, 237, LPL (the Bell Papers contain material used by Bell for his biography, some of which was cut from the published version).

285 'the only objection': Queen Victoria, in *Your Dear Letter*, p.141.

285 'The Dean of Westminster': Queen Victoria, quoted in Arthur Ponsonby, p.46.

286 'The Queen wishes': Harriet Phipps to HP, 1891, LT.

286 'Prothero preached': HP to RD, 3 August 1886, 4.53, LPL.

286 'waves or flashes': Queen Victoria, quoted in Bell, p.82.

286 'the load of': Queen Victoria to RD, 25 June 1884, 25.12, LPL.

287 'What the Queen': ibid., 27 March 1885, 25.23, LPL.

287 'she has lost': ibid., 17 March 1886, 25.43, LPL.

287 'I know perfectly': Queen Victoria, *Beloved Mama*, p.160.

288 'always point in': HP to MP, RA VIC/ADDA36/13.6.83.

288 'Sir Henry has not': HP, quoted in Longford, p.454.

289 'absolutely out of': RD, Bell Papers 237, LPL.

289 *John Brown's Legs*: vol. 19, LPL.

289 'foretaste of the far': RD, Bell Papers 237, LPL.

290 'I told her': RD, Bell Papers 237. LPL.

290 'great pain': ibid.

290 'in many respects': ibid.

290 'heavier and heavier': Queen Victoria to RD, 15 March 1884, vol. 25.1, LPL.

291 'Let me however': Queen Victoria, quoted in Bell, p.81.

Chapter 20: Spring Holidays

All quotations from Marie Mallet's letters are taken from *Life With Queen Victoria: Marie Mallet's Letters from Court 1887–1901*, Victor Mallet (ed.), 1968.

292 'she owns that': Queen Victoria, quoted in Bell, p.185.
292 'he really must': Queen Victoria to HP, 24 December 1889, Bell Papers 227, LPL.
293 'on medical grounds': JR to Dr Jenner, 28 September 1889, LT.
294 'personal regard': Queen Victoria, quoted in Bell, p.188.
294 'I do not like': Queen Victoria, quoted in Lutyens, p.114.
294 'The Queen must': Queen Victoria, quoted in Bell, p.197.
298 'no High Church': RD to HP, 4.106, LPL.
300 'never was depressed': Queen Victoria to JR, 17 January 1892, LT.
300 'produced a very painful': Queen Victoria to Thomas Biddulph, RA MRH/HH/1/75.
300 'for fear of': HP to MP, RA VIC/ADDA36/1061.
301 'There are few': ibid., RA VIC/ADDA36/10.4.91.
301 'I *cannot bear*': Queen Victoria, quoted in Reid, p.160.
302 reading material: See RD's diary, August 1891, 577, LPL.

Chapter 21: Household Bothers

305 'Your wise counsel': JR to Jenner, 25 June 1895, LT.
305 'relieved from': Queen Victoria, quoted in Reid, p.113.
306 'poured forth': RD, diary, 30 June 1895, 579, LPL.
306 'at the highest point': Gladstone, quoted in Jenkins, p.616.
307 'She tells me': JR, quoted in Leo McKinstry, *Rosebery*, 2005, p.293.
307 'I am sick': Rosebery to RD, 5 April 1894, 4.125, LPL.
307 'forgive me saying': Gladstone, quoted in Arthur Ponsonby, p.264.
308 'had no business': HP to MP, RA VIC/ADDA36/8.9.94.
308 'not good in shape': ibid., RA VIC/ADDA36/1.9.94.
309 'You want to know': Ethel Smyth, quoted in Louise Collis, *Impetuous Heart*, 1984, p.68.
309 'It is no use': HP to MP, RA VIC/ADDA36/5.3.94.
309 'A celebrated': ibid., RA VIC/ADDA36/10.11.90.

309　'advertises herself': ibid., RA VIC/ADDA36/12.11.90.

310　'dreadfully dull': ibid., RA VIC/ADDA36/16.9.94.

310　'After the terrible': HP, 19 September 1894, SP.

310　'what a funny': quoted in Kuhn, p.237.

311　'to send some': Fritz Ponsonby to Arthur Ponsonby, February 1895, SP.

313　'she was Liko's': the Duchess of Teck, quoted in Longford, p.544.

314　'It always seems': Fritz Ponsonby to Arthur Ponsonby, 1895, SP.

314　'but it was like': Frederick Ponsonby, p.16.

315　'The blank': MP, quoted in Smyth, *What Happened Next*, p.20.

315　'the entire effacement': Arthur Bigge, quoted in Arthur Ponsonby, p.403.

315　'I feel the actual': Queen Victoria, in Agatha Ramm (ed.), *Beloved and Darling Child*, 1990, p.184.

316　'He was always': Queen Victoria, quoted in Magdalen Ponsonby, p.187.

316　'He never had': Maggie Ponsonby to JR, 4 December 1895, LT.

Chapter 22: The Year of the Munshi

I have drawn on chapter 8 of Michaela Reid's *Ask Sir James* for my account of Munshi dramas.

318　'The tea is always': quoted in Shrabani Basu, *Victoria and Abdul*, 2010, p.83.

318　'be careful at': ibid., p.143.

319　'Poor things': Queen Victoria, in *Beloved and Darling Child*, p.106.

320　'a bigger man': JR to Jenner, 11 October 1889, LT.

320　'Might the Queen': Queen Victoria, quoted in Longford, p.536.

320　'There is one person': Queen Victoria, quoted in Reid, p.142.

322　'I send two': Abdul Karim to JR, 6 June 1895, LT.

323　clutter on her desk: See the Osborne inventory 1900, Osborne House.

325　'Your Majesty sits': Annie Macdonald, quoted by JR, diary, 4 April 1897, LT.

326　'not to go on talking': memo from Queen Victoria, 23 April 1897, LT.

326　'I took a dislike': JR, diary, 4 May 1897, LT.

326　'I am feeling': Queen Victoria, quoted in Reid, p.168.

327　'The crowds were quite': Queen Victoria, quoted in Hibbert, *Queen Victoria: A Personal History*, p.458.

328 'kind to the poor': Fritz Ponsonby to Arthur Ponsonby, 12 August 1897, SP.

329 'you can leave it': Queen Victoria, quoted in Frederick Ponsonby, p.36.

329 'judging from his robust': JR to Queen Victoria, 8 September 1897, LT.

330 'you have simply': Arthur Bigge to JR, 30 October 1897, LT.

Chapter 23: Accommodating Bipps

I have drawn on chapter 10 of *Ask Sir James* for the courtship and marriage of James Reid and Susan Baring.

332 all things sweet: For tea-time treats sent to Balmoral, see *The Private Life of the Queen*, p.117.

333 'very inconvenient': Frederick Ponsonby, p.57.

333 'The result': Fritz Ponsonby, quoted in James Pope-Hennessy, *Queen Mary*, 1959, p.345.

335 'more difficult': Harriet Phipps, quoted in Mallet, p.xxiii.

337 a Christmas feast: Christmas dinner menu, 25 December 1898, LT.

338 'Dear old chap': Arthur Davidson to JR, 7 August 1899, LT.

339 'at first roared': Fritz Ponsonby to Arthur Ponsonby, 12 August 1897, SP.

342 'no doubt it is': Daisy Bigge to JR, 29 August 1899, LT.

343 'I am getting': Rankin to JR, 3 July 1899, LT.

Chapter 24: 'A last look'

I have drawn on chapter 11 of *Ask Sir James* and G. K. A. Bell's *Randall Davidson*, for the Queen's decline and death. Material that Bell did not include in his book can be found in the Bell papers 237, LPL.

345 'a memorandum': Frederick Ponsonby, p.75.

348 'too well in': Fritz Ponsonby to JR, 2 September 1897, LT.

348 'make people cross': HP to MP, RA VIC/ADDA36/27.9.94.

348 'to check abuses': JR, diary, 4 March 1898, LT.

350 'This Christmas': Queen Victoria, in *Beloved and Darling Child*, p.258.

354 'My dear': Queen Victoria, quoted in letter from RD to Edith Davidson, 21 January 1901, 19.101D, LPL.

355   'a striking fellow': RD, Bell Papers, 237, LPL.
355   'as nice on this': RD to Edith Davidson, 21 January 1901, 19.101.D, LPL.
355   'I love you': ibid., 19.101.B., LPL.
356   'thought of all': Frederick Ponsonby, p.81.
357   'her face like': Susan Reid to Mary Ponsonby, 24 January 1901, SP.
357   'Apart from the grief': MP, quoted in Smyth, *What Happened Next*, p.170.
360   'have the very great': Harriet Phipps, quoted in Lutyens, p.152.

Postscript: After Victoria

364   'her originality lay': 'The Character of Queen Victoria', *The Quarterly Review*, April 1901.

Select Bibliography

Allen, Charles, *A Glimpse of the Burning Plain: Leaves from the Journal of Charlotte Canning*, Michael Joseph, 1986

Anon, *The Private Life of the Queen, by One of Her Majesty's Servants*, C. Arthur Pearson, 1898

Anson, Lady Clodagh, *Victorian Days*, Richards P, 1957

Ashdown, Dulcie M., *Ladies-in-Waiting*, Barker, 1976

Askwith, Betty, *The Lytteltons: A Family Chronicle of the Nineteenth Century*, Chatto & Windus, 1975

Bailey, John, (ed.), *The Diary of Lady Frederick Cavendish*, 2 vols., John Murray, 1927

Basu, Shrabani, *Victoria and Abdul: The True Story of the Queen's Closest Confidant*, The History Press, 2010

Bell, G. K. A., *Randall Davidson: Archbishop of Canterbury*, Oxford University Press, 1938

Benson, A. C., *Memories and Friends*, John Murray, 1924

Benson. A. C. and Viscount Esher (eds.), *The Letters of Queen Victoria: A Selection from Her Majesty's Correspondence between the Years 1837 and 1861*, 3 vols., John Murray, 1911

Bloomfield, Baroness Georgiana, *Reminiscences of Court and Diplomatic Life*, Paul K. Trench, 1883

Briggs, Asa, *A Social History of England*, Weidenfeld & Nicolson, 1983

Briggs, Asa, *Victorian Things*, B. T. Batsford, 1988

Cannadine, David, *The Pleasures of the Past*, Collins, 1989

Carter, Miranda, *The Three Emperors: Three Cousins, Three Empires and the Road to World War One*, Fig Tree, 2009

Cavendish, F. W. H., *Society, Politics and Diplomacy*, T. Fisher Unwin, 1913

Charlot, Monica, *Victoria: The Young Queen*, Basil Blackwell, 1991

Collis, Louise, *Impetuous Heart: The Story of Ethel Smyth*, William Kimber, 1984

Cullen, Tom, *The Empress Brown: The Story of a Royal Friendship*, Bodley Head, 1969

Dakers, Caroline, *The Holland Park Circle: Artists and Victorian Society*, Yale, 1999

David, Saul, *The Indian Mutiny*, Viking, 2002

Dennison, Matthew, *The Last Princess: The Devoted Life of Queen Victoria's Youngest Daughter*, Weidenfeld & Nicolson, 2007

Downer, Martyn, *The Queen's Knight: The extraordinary life of Queen Victoria's most trusted confidant*, Bantam Press, 2007

Duff, David, *Victoria in the Highlands*, Frederick Muller, 1968

Duff, David, *Victoria Travels: Journeys of Queen Victoria between 1830 and 1900*, Frederick Muller, 1970

Erskine, Steuart, Mrs (ed.), *Twenty Years at Court: From the Correspondence of the Hon. Eleanor Stanley, 1842–1862*, Nisbet & Co., 1916

Figes, Orlando, *Crimea: The Last Crusade*, Allen Lane, 2010

Flanders, Judith, *The Victorian House: Domestic Life from Childbirth to Deathbed*, HarperCollins, 2003

Fulford, Roger (ed.), *Dearest Child: Letters between Queen Victoria and the Princess Royal, 1858–1861*, Evans Brothers, 1964

Fulford, Roger (ed.), *Dearest Mama: Letters between Queen Victoria and the Crown Princess of Prussia, 1861–1864*, Evans Brothers, 1968

Fulford, Roger (ed.), *Your Dear Letter: Private Correspondence of Queen Victoria and the Crown Princess of Prussia, 1865–1871*, Evans Brothers, 1971

Fulford, Roger (ed.), *Darling Child: Private Correspondence of Queen Victoria and the German Crown Princess, 1871–1878*, Evans Brothers, 1976

Fulford, Roger (ed.), *Beloved Mama: Private Correspondence of Queen Victoria and the German Crown Princess, 1878–1885*, Evans Brothers, 1981

Girouard, Mark, *Windsor: The Most Romantic Castle*, Hodder & Stoughton, 1993

Grey, Hon. Charles, *The Early Years of the Prince Consort*, Smith, Elder & Co., 1867

Hare, Augustus, *The Story of Two Noble Lives*, 3 vols., George Allen, 1893

Hare, Augustus (ed.), *The Life and Letters of Frances Baroness Bunsen*, Smith, Elder & Co., 1882

Helps, Arthur (ed.), *Leaves from the Journal of Our Life in the Highlands, 1848–1861*, 1868

Hemlow, Joyce (ed.), *Fanny Burney: Selected Letters and Journals*, Oxford University Press, 1987

Hibbert, Christopher, *The Court at Windsor: A Domestic History*, Longmans, 1964

Hibbert, Christopher, *Queen Victoria in her Letters and Journals*, John Murray, 1984

Hibbert, Christopher, *Queen Victoria: A Personal History*, HarperCollins, 2000

Hill, Rosemary, *God's Architect: Pugin and the Building of Romantic Britain*, Allen Lane, 2007

Hobhouse, Hermione, *Prince Albert, His Life and Work*, Hamish Hamilton, 1983

Ilchester, Earl of (ed.), *Elizabeth, Lady Holland to her Son 1821–1845*, John Murray, 1946

Jalland, Pat, *Death in the Victorian Family*, Oxford University Press, 1996

James, Robert Rhodes, *Albert, Prince Consort: A Biography*, Hamish Hamilton, 1983

Jenkins, Roy, *Gladstone*, Macmillan, 1995

Jerrold, Clare, *The Married Life of Queen Victoria*, Eveleigh Nash, 1913

Kelley, Philip and Ronald Hudson (eds.), *The Brownings' Correspondence*, Wedgestone Press, 1984–2010

Kennedy, A. L. (ed.), *My Dear Duchess: Social and Political Letters to the Duchess of Manchester, 1858–1869*, John Murray, 1956

Kuhn, William M., *Henry and Mary Ponsonby: Life at the Court of Queen Victoria*, Duckworth, 2002

Lennie, Campbell, *Landseer: The Victorian Paragon*, Hamish Hamilton, 1976

Lindsay, W. A., *The Royal Household*, Kegan Paul & Co., 1898

Longford, Elizabeth, *Queen Victoria RI*, Weidenfeld & Nicolson, 1964

Longford, Elizabeth (ed.), *Louisa, Lady-in-Waiting: The Personal Diaries and Albums of Louisa, Lady-in-Waiting to Queen Victoria and Queen Alexandra*, Jonathan Cape, 1970

Lutyens, Mary (ed.), *Lady Lytton's Court Diary, 1895–1899*, Rupert Hart-Davis, 1961

McKinstry, Leo, *Rosebery: Statesman in Turmoil*, John Murray, 2005

Mallet, Victor (ed.), *Life with Queen Victoria: Marie Mallet's Letters from Court, 1887–1901*, John Murray, 1968

Marie Louise, Princess, *My Memories of Six Reigns*, Evans Brothers, 1956

Matson, John, *Dear Osborne*, Hamish Hamilton, 1978

Millar, Delia, *Queen Victoria's Life in the Scottish Highlands, depicted by her watercolour artists*, P. Wilson Publishers, 1985

Millar, Oliver, *The Victorian Pictures in the Collection of Her Majesty the Queen*, Cambridge University Press, 1992

Mills, Mary, *Edith Davidson of Lambeth*, John Murray, 1938

Mitford, Nancy (ed.), *The Stanleys of Alderley*, Chapman & Hall, 1939

Nevill, Barry St John, *Life at the Court of Queen Victoria: Selections from the Journals of Queen Victoria*, Sutton, 1997

Pakula, Hannah, *An Uncommon Woman: The Empress Frederick, daughter of Queen Victoria*, Weidenfeld & Nicolson, 1996

Ponsonby, Arthur, *Henry Ponsonby: Queen Victoria's Private Secretary*, Macmillan, 1942

Ponsonby, Frederick, *Recollections of Three Reigns*, Eyre & Spottiswoode, 1951

Ponsonby, Magdalen (ed.), *Mary Ponsonby: A Memoir, Some Letters and a Journal*, John Murray, 1927

Pope-Hennessy, James, *Queen Mary, 1867–1953*, Allen & Unwin, 1959

Pope-Hennessy, James, (ed.), *Queen Victoria at Windsor and Balmoral: Letters from her grand-daughter Princess Victoria of Prussia, June 1889*, Allen & Unwin, 1959

Ramm, Agatha (ed.), *Beloved and Darling Child: Last Letters between Queen Victoria and her Eldest Daughter, 1886–1901*, Alan Sutton, 1990

Rappaport, Helen, *Magnificent Obsession: Victoria, Albert and the Death that Changed the Monarchy*, Hutchinson, 2011

Reid, Michaela, *Ask Sir James: The Life of Sir James Reid, Personal Physician to Queen Victoria*, Hodder & Stoughton, 1987

Rennell, Tony, *Last Days of Glory: The Death of Queen Victoria*, Viking, 2000

Reynolds, K. D., *Aristocratic Women and Political Society in Victorian Britain*, Clarendon Press, 1998

Roberts, Jane, *Royal Landscape: The Gardens and Parks of Windsor*, Yale University Press, 1997

St Aubyn, Giles, *Queen Victoria: A Portrait*, Sinclair Stevenson, 1991

Sanders, Charles Richard (ed.), *The Collected Letters of Thomas and Jane Welsh Carlyle*, Duke University Press, 1995

Smyth, Ethel, *As Time Went On*, Longmans, 1936

Smyth, Ethel, *What Happened Next*, Longmans, 1940

Stoney, Benita and, Heinrich C. Weltzein (eds.), *My Mistress the Queen: The Letters of Frieda Arnold, Dresser to Queen Victoria, 1854–59*, trans. Sheila de Bellaigue, Weidenfeld & Nicolson, 1994

Strachey, Lytton, *Queen Victoria*, Chatto & Windus, 1921

Strachey, Lytton and Roger Fulford (eds.), *The Greville Memoirs, 1814–1860*, Macmillan, 1938

Surtees, Virginia *Charlotte Canning: Lady-in-Waiting to Queen Victoria and Wife of the first Viceroy of India, 1817–1861*, John Murray, 1975

Surtees, Virginia (ed.), *Sublime and Instructive: Letters from John Ruskin to Louisa, Marchioness of Waterford, Anna Blunden and Ellen Heaton*, Michael Joseph, 1972

Taylor, Lou, *Mourning Dress: A Costume and Social History*, Allen & Unwin, 1983

Tooley, Sarah A., *The Personal Life of Queen Victoria*, Hodder & Stoughton, 1896

Watson, Vera, *A Queen at Home: An Intimate Account of the Social and Domestic Life of Queen Victoria's Court*, W. H. Allen, 1952

Weintraub, Stanley, *Victoria: Biography of a Queen*, Unwin Hyman, 1987

Weintraub, Stanley, *Albert: Uncrowned King*, John Murray, 1997

Wilson, Andrew, *The Victorians*, Hutchinson, 2002

Wilson, John, *A Life of Sir Henry Campbell-Bannerman*, Constable, 1973

Windsor, Dean of and Hector Bolitho (eds.), *Letters of Lady Augusta Stanley: A Young Lady at Court, 1849–1863*, Gerald Howe, 1927

Windsor, Dean of and Hector Bolitho (eds.), *Later Letters of Lady Augusta Stanley, 1864–1876*, Jonathan Cape, 1929

Woodham-Smith, Cecil, *Queen Victoria: Her Life and Times, 1819–1861*, Hamish Hamilton, 1972

Wyndham, the Hon. Mrs Hugh (ed.), *Correspondence of Sarah Spencer Lady Lyttelton, 1787–1870*, John Murray, 1912

Zeepvat, Charlotte, *Prince Leopold: The Untold Story of Queen Victoria's Youngest Son*, Sutton, 1998

Index